A NINETEENTH CENTURY SCOT IN COLONIAL AUSTRALIA

The adventures, misadventures and enterprises of Robert Muir an entrepreneur and pioneer in the Eastern Australian colonies

Graeme S Cartledge

First Published in Australia in 2023 by Local Research Publishers
Winter Valley Victoria Australia 3358
graemescartledge@iinet.net.au

Copyright © Graeme S Cartledge 2023, all rights reserved

ISBN: 9798394743856

ACKNOWLEDGEMENTS

This biography was, to a large extent, only possible with the resources of the National Library of Australia, especially the digital newspaper archive. I also extend my thanks and appreciation for the assistance given by the facilities and helpful staff in the state libraries of Victoria and South Australia. A special thankyou to the Queensland State library is warranted for their digital photograph collection, the source of the historical photographs in this book. I also extend my thanks and appreciation to the Public Records Offices in Scotland, New South Wales, Victoria and Queensland.

Robert Muir

CONTENTS

Introduction 1
  A Yeoman Activist 1
  The Victorian Goldfields: Where it all Began 5
  A Forgotten Pioneer 6
       PART I 12
TRANSITION TO A COMMERCIAL SOCIETY AT HOME AND ABROAD 12

Chapter 1 13
  Settler Ideology: Stadialism, Old Fogeyism, and liberals 13
       PART II 23
THE SCOTTISH FARMER 23

Chapter 2 24
  Scottish Tenant Farmers: and Scottish Commercialism 24

Chapter 3 31
  Land, Cultural Change and the Challenges of the 1800s 31

Chapter 4 43
  The Wakefield Scheme and Rev John Dunmore Lang 43
    Edward Gibbon Wakefield 43
    Rev John Dunmore Lang 48

Chapter 5 51
  Muir & Paterson Farming Dynasties 51

Chapter 6 66
  Turbulent Teenage Years 66
       PART 111 74
    THE AMERICAS 74

Chapter 7 75
  Emigration: Canada or America? 75

Chapter 8 82
   Trinidad and Useful Lessons for The Victorian Goldfields 82

Chapter 9 89
   Glasgow, Muir Bros and Australia 89

      PART IV 94
      THE VICTORIAN GOLDFIELDS 94

Chapter 10 95
   Trading at Bendigo Amid the Red Ribbon Protests 95

Chapter 11 102
   A New Start at Ballarat 102

Chapter 12 109
   Off the Leash and finding a voice 109

Chapter 13 116
   Capitalizing on the Eureka Chaos 116

Chapter 14 125
   Establishing Law and Order and Local Government 125

Chapter 15 135
   R Muir Municipal Councillor 135

Chapter 16 146
   1857: A Turning Point 146

      PART V 155
      GRAFTON AND BENOWA 155

Chapter 17 156
   A New Beginning on the Clarence River 156

Chapter 18 165
   Business Setback Cotton Queensland and Sugar 165

Chapter 19 175

    Hon Louis Hope MLC and the Travails of Profitable Sugar 175
Chapter 20 183
    CSR and the Yeoman Farmers on the Clarence 183
Chapter 21 196
    Keeping the Yeoman Farmer in the Game 196
Chapter 22 212
    Yeoman Profits with the Sutton Pan Icery-Muir Process 212
    PART VI 218
    POWER AND INFLUENCE 218
Chapter 23 219
    Power Broker in the Electorate of Logan 219
Chapter 24 233
    Land Developer and Return to Local Government 233
Chapter 25 241
    The Polynesian Labour Crisis 241
Chapter 26 251
    Career Twilight – Opposition and Confrontations 251
Chapter 27 268
    The Ending of an Era 268
Chapter 28 285
    An Abrupt Conclusion 285
Epilogue 294
Bibliography 298
    Periodicals & Pamphlets 305
    Theses 309
    Newspapers 310
    Public Records 313

The Author 318
INDEX 319

Introduction

A Yeoman Activist

A Meeting near Grafton on the Clarence River in July 1872 went well into the early morning. The event commenced with a toast to Robert Muir and was followed by congratulatory speeches from leading members of the community. He was being honoured, the MC announced, for his contribution to the local sugar industry and for removing the yoke of the large capitalist from off the shoulders of the local yeomen.[1] The large capitalist was the Colonial Sugar Refinery, the largest sugar producer in the Australian colonies. Its presence, especially for the more entrepreneurial among them, was viewed as a threat from the outset. The prospect of cultivating cane for the CSR mill exclusively, had provoked outrage as they saw any opportunities of deriving extra income from sugar slipping through their fingers. For Robert Muir, this was decisive – his hour had come. He was ready-made for the crisis, with experience in the political cauldron of the goldfields and even more with years of experience in the cultivation of cane and the production of sugar in the Americas. Coupled with a long memory of setbacks due to monopolies of various kinds, he was just who they needed to restore their prospects.

For these fiercely independent farmers, many of whom were Scots, it represented far more than 'just business.' For them it was tantamount to a betrayal by the Government that had encouraged their pioneering efforts in agriculture. It went to the very reason behind their existence on the Clarence River. Many of those present at the dinner, like their guest of honour, had invested everything they had, starting as tent dwellers on their unsurveyed 40-100 acre lots over a decade earlier in anticipation of the passing the Robertson Land Acts. Since then, they had largely enjoyed a

---

[1] Brushgrove, *Clarence and Richmond Examiner and New England Advertiser*, (Grafton) Tuesday 30 July 1872, page 4

Introduction

life of untroubled subsistence farming and surplus cropping of maize and other produce for the colonial market. With a downturn in maize, many had looked upon the fledgeling domestic sugar industry as a lifeline and had invested heavily. Quite a few of them had even created co-operatives and companies, investing large amounts of hard-earned money. Having the large Sydney company uninvited in their midst, had not just inspired competitive opposition, it had rekindled deep-seated cultural animosities. Growing exclusively for a large inter-colonial enterprise under the company's terms reminded them why they had to uproot themselves and their families from their communities and travel to the other side of the globe. For them, just as it was for Robert Muir, it was too disturbingly reminiscent of their economic subjection to landlords and monopolists in Britain. It certainly was not how they envisaged conditions in the colonies would be. It raised the disturbing possibility that it had all been for nothing.

It was a particularly heavy blow, especially after having been heavily exploited by politicians and promoters in the efforts to attract skilled and financially independent British farmers to the colony and to the district. Many had emigrated believing a promotional narrative that they were citizens of the greatest empire on earth and in the vanguard of its 'civilizing' project in the Australian colonies. Heavily utilized by immigration promoters like E G Wakefield and later, Rev. J D Lang, 'a civilized society was settled and agricultural' and above all Christian.[2] Viewed as a collective Christian duty, it was part of a romanticised vision of virtuous hard-working yeomen, the agricultural backbone of British society, replacing the nomadic aborigines that had neglected to make any profitable use of their traditional lands, and Godless transported criminals. Their presence therefore would

---

[2] Stuart Macintyre, *A concise history of Australia (fifth edition)*, Cambridge University Press, Cambridge UK, 2020, p105-196, Richard Waterhouse, the yeoman ideal and Australian experience 1860-1960, *Exploring the British world: Identity, cultural production, institutions* Melbourne: RMIT Publishing 2004, p440-445.

Introduction

prevent the slide of the white pastoral population towards barbarism.³

As yeomen or independent agricultural entrepreneurs, they were also viewed by themselves and increasingly by radical politicians and progressive colonial governments, as essential to 'unlocking the lands' and breaking the squatter monopoly during the 1860s. It was a strong campaign, particularly in the large urban centres and the fertile districts of Victoria, NSW and Queensland for the development of a modern, open, diversified and independent economy.⁴ From the 'gigantic monopoly' of the pastoralists, to the large merchants and financiers who remained linked to the mother countries, all were viewed by radicals as relics of a past life of injustice and obstacles to realizing progress and independence in the Australian colonies.⁵

Thus, another powerful reason why many had chosen to emigrate was that it promised new civic and social opportunities denied them back in Britain by not only economic but also social and political monopolies. There many elements of the pre-modern world persisted, as society made a bumpy transition to an urbanised industrial society. Economic and political reforms in the wake of the 1819 Peterloo massacre, such as the Great Reform Act of 1832 and the 1835 Municipal Reform Act and amendments to the corn laws, were all resisted by those with a vested interest in the old order. Conservative institutions such as the church, the aristocracy and closed corporations that had often owned and run the towns and surrounding countryside with exclusive royal charters, fought to maintain their control as commercialization held out the promise of a more liberal society for all. Likewise, the merchants and the wholesalers and owners of public utilities, maintained their dominance by way of collusion and protracted legal actions amid political unrest and economic instability that

---

³ Richard Waterhouse, the yeoman ideal and Australian experience 1860-1960, *Exploring the British world: Identity, cultural production, institutions* Melbourne: RMIT Publishing 2004, p440-445.
⁴ Stuart Macintyre, *A concise history of Australia, fifth edition*, Cambridge University Press Melbourne 2020, p105-110
⁵ Robin Gollan, *Radical and working-class politics: a study of eastern Australia 1850-1910*, Melbourne University Press, Carlton, 1960, p50-68

Introduction

persisted well beyond the middle of the century.[6] In the colonies, however, all that seemed a world apart as many believed that relocating to the other side of the planet, they had left that kind of baggage far behind. For them, in their chosen land of Australia, they would be running things.

For Scots, particularly, the sense of outrage was informed by a large body of respected and widely circulated work from the 1700s. Much of it was by their own countrymen, offering critiques and roadmaps, as the transition was made from feudalism to a commercialized society. Contemporary Scot, utilitarian and political theorist J S Mill, German theorist Karl Marx and the work of earlier utopians such as Owens, the chartists and free trade activists like Cobden, complemented those of earlier Scottish political economist Adam Smith and modernizers of Scottish agriculture such as Lord Kames. Smith particularly had warned a century earlier about the importance of ethics and regulation in commerce as a necessary and basic principle.[7] Land monopolization, conspiratorial merchants, middlemen and large capitalists hijacking the economic and political system were ruefully identified as pitfalls likely to hinder the operation of a society governed by 'enlightened self-interest'.[8] It all led to the belief in the mid-1800s, that in Britain there was a long way to go with the commercialization of society and its expected liberal outcomes. The colonies, however, was a place where a new beginning could be made.

---

[6] See Derek Fraser, *Power and authority in the Victorian city*, Basil Blackwell Oxford 1979, transition to elected councillors and levying of rates and control of public utilities and spaces often resulted in protracted legal action and social unrest from the 1835 reforms well into the 1850s e.g., Bull Ring riots Birmingham 1839

[7] Ryan Patrick Hanley, Commerce and corruption: Rousseau's diagnosis and Adam Smith's cure, *European Journal of Political Theory*, 2008;7(2):137-158, John Medearis, Labor, democracy, utility and Mill's critique of private property, *American Journal of Political Science, Jan 2005*, Vol 49, No.1 pp135-149

[8] Paul Sagar, The real Adam Smith, *Aeon Newsletter*, 16 January 2018, We should look closely at what Adam Smith actually believed | Aeon Essays accessed 3/6/2018

Introduction

The Victorian Goldfields: Where it all Began.

While the colonies, as many found, were no less immune to the workings of exclusive capitalist interests, there were many young entrepreneurs, now free of British society, who were determined to realize all that a commercial society could offer. Thus, for Robert Muir, a ready-made opportunity was discovered on the Victorian goldfields and its abundant and indiscriminate wealth. Monopolies, in the most part, were gloriously absent and liberal and collegiate ideals flourished among a brotherhood of diggers, small businessmen and agriculturalists. There he discovered a talent for public activism among ex-patriot Chartists, natural rights and anti-transportation campaigners. With Irish and other European separatists adding a revolutionary flavour, they all sought to build a society free of the dominating interests and monopolies they had left behind.

As skilled and independent migrants flooded into the colonies in the wake of the goldrushes, there were increasing numbers like Robert Muir with the aptitude and the money, who thrived on the economic boost from gold and the economic stimulus that it brought. With the old pastoral regime becoming eclipsed by a commercial revolution, a range of new enterprises and industries proliferated using a newfound social and political clout. An 'ideology of economic development' gripped the colonies particularly between 1865 and 1890, where in New South Wales alone, as one study shows, over 1000 companies were formed.[9] With over 250 prominent directors, there was often an overlap between business and politics. In Sydney alone, over 40% were serving as politicians at some level. Similarly in the other colonies, the Chambers of Commerce often created the route into politics.[10] Like Robert Muir, many also became community leaders in the proliferating road districts, utility boards and commissions as well as municipal councils, enthusiastically taking on the project of

---

[9] R W Connell and T H Irving, *Class structure in Australian history: poverty and progress*, Longman Cheshire, Melbourne, first published 1980, p96-97
[10] ibid, see also Terry Irving's 1967 Thesis, *The development of liberal politics in New South Wales 1843-1855*, University of Sydney, 1967

Introduction

laying the civic and infrastructure foundations of a new society.[11] Within fifty years most of eastern Australia was linked with network of railways, roads and telegraph communication, sanitary works, and water supplies.[12] It was all achieved without the massive wealth of monopolies; the aristocracy and the large industrialists, who in Britain, largely funded its modern transformation.[13]

A Forgotten Pioneer

Robert Muir thus came to my attention when completing a thesis on the transition of Ballarat to municipal government after the Eureka Rebellion.[14] Emigrating from Scotland to Australia with three of his brothers in 1853 as a self-funded family group, it was their intention to establish a branch of the eldest brother's Glasgow clothing business. As products of a line of commercial tenant farmers, they were of quintessential yeomen stock, representing a new class of small landless, agricultural capitalist in a rapidly emerging Scottish commercial society. They came, brimming with confidence and possessing a wide array of skills and experience obtained in management, finance, commerce, and farming. As observers noted on the Malabar on the voyage out, they were conspicuous and sure of themselves, certain they would make their mark in Australia now awash with the money generated by the goldrushes.[15]

---

[11] Graeme S Cartledge, *From Goldfield to municipality: the establishment of Ballarat West 1855-1857*, MA Thesis (unpublished) Federation University Ballarat 2018
[12] John Molony, *The penguin history of Australia*, Penguin Books, Ringwood Victoria, 1987, p129-131
[13] Melleuish, Gregory. & Centre for Independent Studies (Australia). *A short history of Australian liberalism*. St Leonards, N.S.W : Centre for Independent Studies, 2000, p1-15, see Derek Fraser ed., *Municipal reform and the industrial city*, Leicester University Press, New York, 1982, Derek Fraser, *Power and authority in the victorian city*, Basil Blackwell, Oxford, 1979, David Spring, English Landowners and Nineteenth Century Industrialism in: *Land and industry: the landed estate and the industrial revolution: a symposium edited by J T Ward and R G Wilson*, David and Charles, Newton Abbot Devon, 1971, pp7-62
[14] Graeme S Cartledge, *From Goldfield to municipality: the establishment of Ballarat West 1855-1857*, MA Thesis (unpublished) Federation University Ballarat 2018.
[15] Law Report, *The Argus* (Melbourne) Wednesday 12 August 1857, page 6.

Introduction

With many of the inherited values of this class, it was clear that their ambition, besides making money, was also to influence colonial society for the benefit of many like themselves by achieving success in their commercial enterprise and securing land ownership which was unattainable at home. On arrival, the company they found themselves associating with in Melbourne and on the goldfields, were mostly in similar circumstances. Mostly British and middle class, they had a shared desire to create a society that maximised their chances of realizing their social and economic potential.

Robert Muir had burst onto the scene in Ballarat seemingly from nowhere. A young local businessman in his twenties with no previous experience in civic leadership, working closely with the well-known Welsh chartist, liberal and free trade advocate J B Humffray. Between them they took on the task of restoring law and order and to establish civil government on the goldfields of Ballarat early in 1855 after the tyranny of the Goldfields Commission. From there he was a constant figure, prominent in the establishment of almost all the local institutions. He then resigned from all his positions and disappeared from the district in 1857. After four years of becoming almost an institution himself, I found this highly intriguing, and embarked on a quest to answer the questions he raised - where did he come from, and where did he go? I was convinced, for someone with such enthusiasm, creativity and a capacity for work, there had to be more to the story.

It did not take long to uncover clues to his subsequent activities. Thus, in her 2002 account of the early pioneers of Labrador Queensland, Dawn Hasemann Rix states that 'the story of Robert Muir is well documented' and is only mentioned in her book in relation to the early development of Labrador.[16] A search for the details of this 'well documented' life of Robert Muir however, revealed widely fragmented sources covering most of the eastern seaboard of Australia from the 1850s to the 1880s. I discovered that apart from his brief sojourn in Ballarat, his name crops up most regularly in the Gold Coast and Northern Rivers district of

---

[16] Dawn Hasemann Rix, *Labrador – the early pioneers*, D H R Publishing, Main Beach Queensland, 2002, p7

NSW. His influence extended in various ways to farming, the sugar industry, the timber industry, local politics, brewing, transport, land development, hotels, tourism, local government, and education. However there have been to date, no attempts to consolidate all this activity and tell the story of this Australian pioneer and his contribution to civic society, industry, and commerce.

Most of the sources available have been obtained from newspaper reports, stories, and advertising. Robert Muir was a busy and active man, often controversial, and often wrote to the editors of many newspapers expressing his opinion on issues of the day. He was also a relentless promoter and expert at utilizing the media in all sorts of ways. Thus, there was no shortage of material available on his activities in the many newspapers now conveniently digitised on Trove, the National Library of Australia. Books on his life, unfortunately, are non-existent and mentions in other historical works are rare. In many cases, his involvement in historical events while important, appear to have been quickly forgotten with the passage of time.

Robert Muir's first association with Australia was on the goldfields of Bendigo and Ballarat which are mainly remembered for the events surrounding Eureka. The key characters often associated with it are easily recalled; the one-armed Peter Lalor, the red-haired Italian revolutionary Raffaello who wrote the only contemporary account, and J B Humffray the 'moral force' moderate. Likewise, the city that arose from the chaos is usually associated with its greatest advocate James Oddie, an original digger and chairman of its first municipal council, as order began to be restored and the elements of civilization established. Robert Muir, well-known to all these characters in the drama, was also a key player. Chairing and sharing many platforms, he also drove and facilitated much of the progress of early Ballarat during and after Eureka. However, much of this appears to have been overlooked in the most prominent historical works on early Ballarat, W B Wither's 1870s *History of Ballarat*, and Weston Bate's more comprehensive 1978 account *Lucky City*.[17]

---

[17] Weston Bate, *Lucky city: the first generation of Ballarat 1851-1901*, Melbourne University Press, Melbourne 1978, W B Withers, *History of Ballarat and some*

Introduction

Reasons for this could be that as his stay in Ballarat was short, it allowed others to capitalize on his hard work. An uncanny knack for involving himself in contentious matters is probably another. Not surprisingly, a move to Grafton in Northern New South Wales at the end of the 1850s, was largely a result of his involvement in highly controversial circumstances. Once again, he made there, an enduring impression with established pioneers such as Thomas Bawden, Mayor in the 1870s and Alexander Meston, an influential farmer and businessman on the Clarence River. He was particularly prominent among many of the local small businessmen and growers in the developing cotton and sugar industries in the 1860s & 1870s.

B W Higman, in a 1968 article argues that this relatively short period of small capitalist dominance, particularly in the Clarence and Grafton district, has been overshadowed by the generally accepted history of Australian sugar which has been predominantly that of the large capitalist enterprises like Colonial Sugar Refineries.[18] Thus, as Higman points out, there is much more to the early history of sugar in northern New South Wales, and southern Queensland. It was, he explains, a short window of time, when the sugar industry was dominated by the yeoman farmer, or man of 'small capital' not a capitalist, developer or landlord, but one who was prepared to accept small profits in return for independent proprietorship and land ownership.[19] In the Northern Rivers district those like Robert Muir seeking such opportunities, fulfilled this ideal, settling in family units and re-establishing themselves through family networks.[20]

Peter Griggs, in a 1997 article, likewise acknowledges the contribution of the yeoman farmer in the establishment of the sugar industry in southern Queensland and Northern New South

---

interesting reminisces, First Published 1870, Published in Ballarat by Ballarat Heritage Services 1999

[18] B W Higman, Sugar plantations and yeoman farming in New South Wales, *Annals of the Association of American Geographers*, Dec. 1968, Vol. 58 No. 4, pp 697-719

[19] Ibid, page 700

[20] Eric Richards, 'Scottish voices and colonial networks in colonial Australia', in Angela McCarthy ed. *A global clan, Scottish migrant networks and identities since the eighteenth century*, I B Taurus & Co, revised edition, 2012, London, pp 165-166

Introduction

Wales. Griggs, like other historians attributes a lot of the success of this class of people, to the questionable utilization of Polynesian workers, at least in the early establishment phase in the decade of 1870 to 1880. I would also add that their success during that small window of time, was also due to fair trade advocates like Robert Muir who, for almost two decades, was particularly effective in fighting monopolists like CSR in the Grafton area and Southern Queensland, by technical innovation, entrepreneurial skill and political advocacy.[21] From Grafton where he began in that phase of his life, his notoriety only grew, becoming even more influential in the Queensland sugar industry and the early development of the Gold Coast.

An early local report on the Queensland south coast regional area states: 'Mr R Muir (of) Benowa with his sugars – and it was from Benowa the real life and zest in the sugar industry took root.' Another story on the sugar industry by the *Sydney Morning Herald* also reports, that 'this gentleman is perhaps the most successful sugar manufacturer in Queensland.[22] But he was much more; for a time, he was a larger-than-life figure whose reach extended into most aspects of early Queensland society for over twenty years from the 1860s to the late 1880s with characteristic flair and showmanship.

Alexander McRobbie, in his history of the 'Real Surfer's Paradise' states that Robert Muir could be fairly described as the original *Mr Surfers Paradise,* beginning a tradition of entrepreneurs and high-fliers who made and lost fortunes in the development of the Gold Coast.[23] McRobbie, who had the privilege of interviewing his granddaughter, states that Robert Muir was 'a remarkable

---

[21] Peter D Griggs, The origins and early development of the small cane farming system in Queensland 1870-1915, *Journal of Historical Geography*, 23, 1 (1997) 46-61, Peter Griggs, *Global industry local innovation: the history of cane sugar production in Australia, 1820-1995*, Peter Lang International Academic Publishers, Bern Switzerland, 2011, Kay Saunders, *Workers in bondage: the origins and basis of unfree labour in Queensland 1824-1916*, University of Queensland Press, St Lucia, Queensland 1982, page 59

[22] Country news, *The Queenslander*, (Brisbane) Saturday 9 September 1882, page 327, Sugar Industry in New South Wales and Queensland, *Sydney Morning Herald*, Monday 26 May 1873, page 5

[23] Alexander McRobbie, *From Seaside village to international resort*, Pan News Pty Ltd, Surfer's paradise, Qld, 1988

Introduction

pioneer' whose energy and resourcefulness had a profound effect on the Gold Coast area. Quoting from an early issue of the *Queensland Geographical Journal*, where it states that 'it is recognized that Southport owes its existence to Robert Muir's industrial and public activities,' he found it puzzling that so little about his life has been recorded.[24]

So how can we account for the actions of this determined and resourceful Scot? What was it that inspired him to take on the task of bringing order and civic government to the Ballarat goldfield? Why would he take on the might of a large monopoly like CSR? Was it his Scottish farming background or was it because of his citizenship of the largest empire on earth and its social and political values? While historians present differing perspectives, the truth however, as it often can be, is connected somehow with them all. Therefore, let us look at some of the factors that shaped this Scotsman before we examine his life as an Australian pioneer

---

[24] Alexander McRobbie, *From Seaside village to international resort,* p31

PART I

TRANSITION TO A COMMERCIAL
SOCIETY AT HOME AND ABROAD

Chapter 1

Settler Ideology: Stadialism, Old Fogeyism, and liberals

Entitled Stadialists

Robert Muir's immediate family and extended family circles, were, as Ayrshire farmers, the products of at least three generations of commercial praxis. Ruthlessly applied by the time he had grown to adulthood, rapid social change in the countryside had almost totally extinguished the old feudal culture. And, from the early 1800s, Scotland was unleashing motivated sons and daughters on the world, believing the British way of life was superior to any other. They came bearing the gospel of a new civic, liberal, and commercial society based on the values of innovation, hard work, and the pursuit of personal success. They were, as was argued by philosophers, politicians and emigration promoters, ambassadors of human civilization developed to its highest level of refinement and civility.[25]

Much of the exodus from the Scottish countryside during the first half of the nineteenth century was accelerated by the arrival of difficult economic conditions. The long boom associated with the European and American wars had run its course. Its ending unfortunately, had exposed the most fundamental of contradictions in Scottish society: that the agricultural industry, despite operating as a commercial enterprise, remained in a semi-feudal state. Land, which in theory, was considered a commodity like everything else, was rarely available for public acquisition. The real-estate, on which so many depended to make a living, continued to remain the property of the descendants of the old feudal overlords. This, along with the increasing rationalization of available farms, as the downturn extended, was contributing to a

---

[25] Christopher Berry, *The idea of commercial society in the Scottish enlightenment*, Edinburgh University Press, Edinburgh, 2015, p199-204, Michael Radzevicius, *Edward Gibbon Wakefield and an Imperial utopian dream*, Ph.D.., University of Adelaide, 2011

profound sense of alienation among farming families. A lifestyle that once existed for most of the population, now only remained within the memories of the rapidly diminishing numbers of older relatives.

Additionally, the ongoing lack of autonomy for those remaining in agriculture, maintained a fundamental sense of insecurity as landlords continued to monopolise farmland by setting the rules and conditions during the hard nineteenth century. Matters were also further aggravated by the lavish lifestyles enjoyed by landlords due to their appropriation of substantial profits. *Their* success, which came at the expense of their tenants, was accordingly displayed by large mansions and the beautification of the surrounding grounds. Additionally, on the estates, the establishment of modern infrastructure such as roads, bridges and railways finally removed what was left of the visible feudal lifestyle. It was all legitimised by laws of entail and primogeniture, securing their holdings within their family lines.

For large numbers of farmers on the estates, therefore, the promises of commercialization remained empty and unfulfilled. For most of them, there was no such security of tenure nor opportunities to succeed or achieve the potential that the commercial capitalist world was offering. And despite many aspects of family and clannish co-operation that endured through private commercial arrangements, the interdependence, security and continuity of the feudal community was gone. Even the church, which was the centre of community life, had changed. After a few short generations, Presbyterian Calvinist sobriety had adapted to commercialization as thrift, hard work and good money management became core Christian values. Thus, as the likelihood of remaining in the vocation of their parents became increasingly remote, many of Robert Muir's generation and station chose to emigrate to maintain their status and way of life. Colonial land, which appeared almost limitless and largely unoccupied, offered a perfect solution.

There was little sympathy therefore, for the indolent which was how indigenous populations in their 'state of nature,' were largely viewed. Thus, commercialization, which had wrought such fundamental change to their own way of life, was imposed and established in the colonies with enthusiasm and urgency by those who, quite ironically, were also its casualties. Just like the landlords back in Britain, the newcomers would set the rules and conditions for the use of the land which would restore their fortunes, maintain their way of life, and provide security for their families.

What made it easy to justify, was Stadialism, a prevailing social development theory emanating from the previous century as the agricultural and industrial revolutions gathered momentum. A basic assumption was that the British Empire and its values represented the highest expression of human progress and social sophistication. It was theorised that humans, from hunter-gatherers to the modern commercial and industrial society, could be conceived as passing through distinct stages of development. With land utilization as a basic measure of progress, it was held that British society was the most complex and sophisticated due to land, unlike in earlier phases, becoming a commodity as well as a source of commercial activity. Along with the proliferation of money, credit, and private property, it was argued, particularly by Scottish intellectuals, that a new type of society had emerged, replacing the old feudal way of life. Defined by the interdependency of widespread commercial relations rather than fealty, the resultant property and social relations thus lead to the emergence of modern civil society with its abstract rules, division of labour, legal equality and claims of liberality.[26]

Incorporating all the existing precepts of philosophy, religion and science, the indigenous lifestyle therefore, was judged by stadial theory, to be simply not developing human potential and living as God intended. It existed, they claimed, at what was deemed to be the lowest level of social development where there were no abstract rules and land was not an exploitable asset for personal gain or a measure of personal wealth and success.[27] Thus, while not denying a common ancestry and 'brotherhood of man,'

---

[26] Christopher Berry, *The idea of commercial society in the Scottish Enlightenment*, Edinburg University Press, Edinburgh, 2013, p45-46, John Gascoigne with Patricia Curthoys, *The enlightenment and the origins of European Australia*, Cambridge University Press, Melbourne, 2002, p54-56

[27] John Gascoigne with Patricia Curthoys, *The enlightenment and the origins of European Australia*, p150-151

aboriginal people were rarely viewed as equals. This facilitated the establishment of large numbers of British pastoralists and farmers in Australia with barely a thought for those they were displacing.

Scots were particularly noted for their commercial values, congregating in locations such as the Western District of Victoria, the Northern Rivers of New South Wales, and Southern Queensland. There they quickly re-established themselves and their reputation for farming, agriculture and business acumen.[28] Ian Donnachie in his 1991 seminar paper reminds us of Anthony Trollope's comment that 'in the colonies those that make money are generally Scotchmen.'[29] However, as Donnachie also reminds us, the study of the history of the Scots in Australia, as it has elsewhere in the world, confirms that 'Scottish capitalism was as ruthless in Australia as it was at home.' It came with memories of a century of enclosure, where large swathes of the countryside were appropriated and turned into profit-making units by the more powerful aristocracy, displacing the feudal social, political and economic systems.[30]

Most believed, therefore, just as it was in their home countries, the more sophisticated and advanced culture would replace the old. Thus, with two populations at opposite extremities of the theorised social development scale, it was expected that it was just a matter of time before the indigenous people and their culture would be extinguished by the Europeans. The 'compassionate' approach towards this uncomfortable problem, would be by way of

---

[28] Margaret Kiddle, *Men of yesterday: a social history of the Western District of Victoria 1834 – 1890*, Melbourne University Press, Parkville, Victoria, 1961, Eric Richards, Scottish voices and networks in colonial Australia, in Angela McCarthy ed., *A global clan, Scottish migrant networks and identities since the nineteenth century*, I B Taurus, London, 2012

[29] Anthony Trollope, Australia, 1873 in: The making of 'Scots on the make': Scottish settlement and enterprise in Australia, 1830-1900, in T M Devine ed., *Scottish emigration and Scottish society, proceedings of the Scottish historical studies seminar*, University of Strathclyde 1990-1991,

[30] See for example, Reynolds, Henry; James Cook University of North Queensland, *The Other Side of the Frontier*, James Cook University, Townsville 1981, Deborah Bird Rose, *Hidden histories: black stories from Victoria River Downs, Humbert River and Wave Hill Stations*, Aboriginal Studies Press Canberra, first Published 1991

assimilation - through education, civilizing and protection.[31] Such a program, after most of the land was taken and incorporated into commercial productivity, was most infamously enacted in an official capacity by Robert Muir's young brother-in-law and protégé, Archibald Meston. A man of many talents; as plantation manager, correspondent, and politician, he was the architect of the first Queensland Aboriginal Protection Act. Like a typical capitalist, he also had no qualms in exploiting his charges for personal gain. As the brains behind a travelling show from 1892-1893, a variety of early Australian cross-cultural events were re-enacted along with displays of Aboriginal culture.[32] This was an interest he had acquired, largely due to his association with Robert Muir as a teenager where Muir introduced him to various indigenous people in the Nerang River district. It appears to have been the origin of a life-long interest in Aboriginal culture and personal relationships with various groups and individuals throughout Queensland.

Muir's focus, however, was not with the displaced indigenous nations but on the establishment of 'perfect' conditions for the operation of market forces and the truly commercial society. Thus, in later life, he joined with J E Matthew Vincent, in condemning the Queensland administration of racism in the restriction of Polynesian labour as a corruption of both market forces and

---

[31] Linda Andersson Burnett, Collecting humanity in the age of enlightenment: the Hudson Bay Company and Edinburgh natural history museum, *Global Intellectual History*, DOI: 10.1080/23801883.2022.2074502, 2022, Bruce Buchan & Linda Andersson Burnett, Knowing savagery, Australia and the anatomy of race, *History of the human sciences*, 2019, Vol 32 (4) p122, John Gascoigne (with the assistance of Patricia Curthoys), *The Enlightenment and the origins of European Australia*, p148-151, Christopher Berry, *The idea of commercial society in the Scottish Enlightenment*, pp32-65, Onur Ulas Ince, *Colonial capitalism and the dilemmas of liberalism*, Oxford University Press, 2020, p159, Ben Huf, The capitalist in colonial history: investment, accumulation and credit money in New South Wales, *Australian Historical Studies*, 50:4 2019, P429,

[32] Archibald Meston, *Queensland Aboriginals: a Proposed System for their Improvement and Preservation*, Government Printer, Brisbane 1895, Judith Mackay and Paul Memmott, Staged savagery: Archibald Meston and his indigenous exhibits, *Aboriginal History*, Australian National University Press Canberra, 2016, p181-207.

human rights.[33] As a follower of political economist Adam Smith, who he appeared to quote on occasion, he believed that utmost vigilance needed to be exercised to prevent the same corruption of market forces that were experienced back in Scotland.[34]

Preserving Distributive Justice

According to Smith, as well as other Scottish disciples such as Hume and Henry Home, the emergence of the commercial society was a process, as there remained many elements of the feudal world that needed reform before the 'perfect' functioning of commercial society could be achieved. As Smith argued, the conditions for 'perfect liberty' of the market should be maintained to prevent discrimination against farmers, farmworkers, and landlords alike. Writing from the perspective of a society based on the agricultural industry, Smith argued that goods 'should be exchanged at their natural price' to preserve distributive justice and prevent the distortion of the market from the monopolizing tendencies of merchants and manufacturers.[35] This is certainly what Robert Muir believed he was fighting for in his campaign against the CSR monopoly, to preserve market share or 'distributive justice' for the individual yeoman farmer on the Clarence River in the 1870's.

As he and his colleagues discovered, the modern, commercial society with all its, civic, and liberal characteristics, had its limits and shortcomings in the colonies just as it did back home in Scotland. The squatter and pastoral regime that prevailed in Australia into the middle of the century, proved that the same conditions experienced back in home could be just as easily established in the colonies. Land legislation eventually ameliorated

---

[33] Letter by J E Matthew Vincent, The Polynesian Labour Question, *The Brisbane Courier*, Tuesday 22 January 1884, page 5, Letter R Muir Benowa 23 January, The Polynesian Labour Question, *The Brisbane Courier*, Friday 25 January 1885, page 5

[34] Horse teams versus bullock teams for prize ploughing, *The Queenslander*, 9 October 1875, p22

[35] David McNally, *Political economy and the rise of capitalism: a reinterpretation*, Berkeley: University of California Press, 1988, p210
http://ark.cdlib.org/ark:/13030/ft367nb2h4/

some of these problems, paving the way for the small capitalists or yeoman farmers to establish the agricultural foundation that many believed the colonies needed. It was believed that with their small enterprises and easy access to their 50-100 acres, and an urban block in the towns, the society they were creating, would be the finest example to date, of the commercial and civic society. Without monopolies and established privilege as it was in Britain, they believed they would leave the country in a better state than what they found it in.

Robert Muir, with his experiences in the Americas, had a more liberal approach than many of his contemporaries in Southern Queensland and Northern New South Wales. Having personally worked with slaves who fulfilled roles such as managers, technicians and in other skilled positions, it proved to him that race and social status was no impediment to success in a commercial society. Likewise, in his experiences on the goldfields of Victoria, he found himself in likeminded company where monopolies were shunned, fortune favoured the hard worker and wealth was indiscriminate. It provided a glimpse of what was possible as the Ballarat township began on a foundation of small business and diggers. As he declared in later life, he held the belief that a good society was one where, regardless of race, all should be extended the same opportunities. Government-backed schemes in the 1880s that aggregated large land holdings and large amounts of capital, were therefore all considered to be regressive and symptomatic of the same problems that had forced colonization in the first instance.[36]

Monopolies, both financial and political, were labelled as 'old fogeyism' by many other like-minded colonials and deemed to be part of the old pre-commercial system with its roots in feudalism. This, they believed, was all symptomatic of an earlier stage of development, one that the yeoman and small capitalist had left behind and would not be reproducing in the colonies. For these colonials, it would produce, they believed, the most advanced society yet – a liberal commercial society with genuine equality of opportunity.

---

[36] John Gascoigne with Patricia Curthoys, *The enlightenment and the origins of European Australia*, p62-65

Fighting 'Old Fogeyism' 1850s-1880s

Liberalism, as Onur Ince argues, when stripped of its many divergent threads, can be understood as contractual freedom and juridical equality. A liberal government's task, thus eloquently summed up by British PM Lord Melbourne 1834-1841, was 'to prevent crime and to preserve contracts.' Its inherent shortcomings in the nineteenth century, however, can be seen in oppressive labour laws, the use of farm leases back in Britain and contracts for indentured labour.[37] This 'bare bones' approach was redefined in the colonies, away from its roots in British politics, the aristocracy and endemic inequality and social stratification.

Gregory Melleuish thus argues that Australian colonial liberalism could be basically understood as the 'notion of the inalienable dignity of man, his need for self-development and right to govern his own affairs.'[38] Such ideals flourished in a climate of reaction against imperial 'capitalists' using their political influence and enormous resources to reinstate British servitude and dependency. Memories of enclosure, commercial barbarism by the East India Company, the American wars, and the unrepresentative pastoral regime that sparked Eureka, had cast a less than positive light on the relationship between capitalism and British liberalism.[39] It's lingering shadows in Australia in the 1850s, inspired democrats and radicals into action against the nearest thing to the British upper classes – the conservative order of the pastoralists, and their financial and political backers who had enjoyed a half a century of dominance. As it was often declared, colonial political activists were loyal subjects of the empire, but as their words and deeds demonstrated, there was much about the

---

[37] Onur Ulas Ince, *Colonial capitalism and the dilemmas of liberalism*, Oxford University Press, New York, 2018, p5, Margaret Slocombe, Preserving the contract: the experience of indentured labourers in the Wide Bay Burnett districts in the nineteenth century, *Labour History*, No113 November 2017 103-131, p103.
[38] Gregory Melleuish, *A short history of Australian liberalism*, Centre of Independent Studies, St Leonards NSW, 2000, p8
[39] Onur Ulas Ince, *Colonial capitalism and the dilemmas of liberalism* pp74-112

empire that they did not like or want to reproduce in the Australian colonies. What most were looking for was just a fair go.

This indeed was a loud and recurrent theme expressed during the miners' movement in the 1850s amid their campaign for civic government and political rights.[40] It was here that Robert Muir stood alongside Chartist J B Humffray at a large gathering of miners and storekeepers at Ballarat in April 1855 declaring 'that for a people to be well governed they must govern themselves.'[41] But it was also an ideal standing on a strong protectionist foundation - a reaction to most being excluded from enjoying all the benefits of a commercial and liberalised society back in Britain. Thus, as one eloquent speaker expressed it at a political protest meeting in Ballarat in 1857: 'we have come out 16,000 miles to avoid this Toryism and old-fogeyism and are we to meet with it again?'[42] It echoed similar language at another protest meeting a year earlier where C F Nicholls declared "we did not come 16,000 miles to live under the same mal-arrangements as at home. Our duty was to leave the country better than we found it."[43] It comes as no surprise therefore, that the first decade of the gold industry in Victoria, was driven by the miners, extending favourable conditions to individual diggers, and keeping the large interests out. Reforms like miners' right, access to private property and the preservation of the rights of the small capitalist enterprises and partnerships, were protected by law and the institution of a court of mines run by the miners themselves.[44]

Protection was a powerful theme that endured through the century with the establishment of new enterprises such as the sugar industry. Thus, twenty years later similar feelings continued to be expressed as far away as Queensland. Small sugar producers, who

---

[40] See Graeme Cartledge, Transition from tyranny: establishing local government on the Ballarat goldfields 1851-1856, *Victorian Historical Journal* Volume 92, No. 1, June 2021

[41] *The Age* Melbourne, Tuesday April 17, 1855, page 5

[42] The Ballarat Demonstration, *The Age* Melbourne, Thursday April 30, 1857, page 6

[43] The Governor's Speech, *The Star*, Ballarat, Tuesday December 9, 1856, page 1

[44] See the 1854-55 inquiry into the Management of the Goldfields. VPARL1854-55NoA76p

had been at the forefront of a home-grown industry, were outraged by the Government's betrayal as they contemplated annihilation by acts of parliament designed to attract large capitalist enterprises from outside the colony. As a self-confessed 'bohemian' wryly commented on the first introduction of such legislation in Queensland in 1872, 'If this 'encouraging' process is kept up much longer, the old squatter's ideal will be realized, and nobody will be allowed to live in the colony except capitalists and their hired labourers. I don't think this is the sort of millennium we want. We didn't come 16,000 miles to inaugurate a new era of this sort, my intelligent reader, did we?'[45]

It was a theme strongly reinforced shortly after by New South Wales political economist Francis Gould Smith in his self-published and widely read pamphlet, *The Australian Protectionist*. Smith was advocating protection for the creation and nurturing of home-grown and self-supporting enterprises.[46] This was a message that struck a chord with many like the Muir Brothers raised on the land with all its values and experience, who emigrated for that specific reason – not to leave their home country just to find themselves in the same position as their parents and grandparents.

---

[45] Odd notes by a Bohemian, *The Queenslander* (Brisbane) Saturday 10 August 1872, page 4

[46] Francis Gould Smith, *The Australian Protectionist*, Melbourne 1877

PART II

THE SCOTTISH FARMER

Chapter 2

Scottish Tenant Farmers: and Scottish Commercialism

Robert Muir identified as a Scotsman, the son of a tenant farmer and a ploughman. On more than one occasion for dramatic effect, he broke out into brogue when speaking to journalists in Australia. He took pride in his lowly origins and farming background even after rising to high positions in commerce and society. As one of the canniest of colonial Scots, as this biography shows, there is no denying his impact on early Australia in several spheres. However, the contribution of the Scots in general to Australian colonial life, apart from their fellow Britons, is difficult to quantify. Therefore, the primary focus of this biography is narrow - on Robert Muir's immediate social group of origin, the tenant farmer and the specific formative events and beliefs that may explain his motivations and values. Nevertheless, what is clear, is that Scots saw themselves as a distinct ethnic group with a distinct culture. On the goldfields, the great melting pot of cultures, and in many other places, the Scottish flag was often prominently displayed where highland games, the tartans and the bagpipes complemented the celebration of Scottish heroes and prominent historical figures like Robert Burns.

Some historians have attempted this monumentally difficult task, crediting their impact to their unique ability to capitalise on economic and cultural networks within the British Empire. Ben Wilkie for example in his recent work *The Scots in Australia* makes a comprehensive survey on the topic of the Australian Scottish diaspora from J H Burton's *The Scot Abroad* in 1880 through to the work of T H Devine, W J M Mackenzie and McCarthy from the 1990s.[47] Those in the earlier part of this category he labels as

---

[47] J H Burton, *The Scot abroad*, Edinburgh, Constable 1881, W J Rattray, *The Scot in British North America*, Toronto, Maclear & Co., 1880, Andrew Dewar Gibb, *Scotland in Eclipse*, London, Humphrey Toulmin, 1930; Andrew Dewar Gibb, Scottish empire, London, S MacLehose & Company, Andrew Dewar Gibb,

'contribution histories' outlining the Scottish impact on Australian society by the careers and lives of the Scots while the work of the more recent historians are categorised as more abstract drawing on 'contemporary theoretical frameworks and concepts such as diasporas, transnationalism, and identities.'[48] Wilkie demonstrates how "militarism, race, religion, economic expansionism, and monarchism, the dominant ideologies of the empirical project, took on a distinctly Scottish character in Australia."[49] Linda Colley also argues that "war and empire were significant in cementing the Union between Scotland and the rest of Great Britain" pointing out that many Scots, particularly after 1745 prospered with the British union.[50]

Australian historian Malcolm Prentice, however, places more emphasis on unique sociological and cultural values Scots brought with them to Australia, formed well before their arrival. Much of this, he argues, can be traced to a specific Scottish legacy of civic virtue, religious reform, and the effects of the 'agrarian revolution.' This, he argues, brought fundamental reforms to the Scottish social structure, displacing old methods and social arrangements. Prentice points out that this mix of ideas and values unleashed by modernity from the late seventeenth century, witnessed a proliferation of learning and knowledge that permeated society to the "artisan, agricultural and middle classes (who) had strong scientific interests and a theological bent."[51] This, as Prentice reminds us, was a key ingredient in the accelerated commercial

---

Scotland resurgent, Stirling, E Mackay, 1950; David MacMillan, *Scotland and Australia 1788-1850: emigration, commerce and investment*, Oxford, Oxford University Press, 1967, Eric Richards, Scottish voices and networks in colonial Australia, in Angela McCarthy, *A global clan*, First Published I B Taurus London 2006.

[48] Benjamin Wilkie, *The Scots in Australia 1788-1938*, The Boydell Press, Woodbridge, Suffolk UK, pp2-6.

[49] Benjamin Wilkie, *The Scots in Australia 1788-1938*, p7

[50] Linda Colley, Britons: *forging the nation 1707-1837*, Yale University Press, 1992, pp 111-129, Graeme Morton, *Unionist Nationalism: the historical construction of Scottish national identity*, Edinburgh, 1830 – 1860, University of Edinburgh, Ph.D. Thesis, p9-10, Sociology Thesis Collection, University of Edinburgh, http://hdl.handle.net/1842/20035, accessed 29/7/2020

[51] Malcolm Prentice, *The Scots in Australia*, University of New South Wales Press, Sydney NSW 2008, p20

success of the Scots from 1747 – 1850 which inspired George Bernard Shaw to comment ' they transfer the 'intellectual keenness acquired in learning "the catechism" to business and get the better of everybody.'[52]

This follows a similar approach by contemporary historians of Scotland, who argue that empire is but one factor that determined a specific and highly influential Scottish culture especially after the union with England in 1707. It is argued that it was the Scottish, as a result of their own internal struggles with feudalism and an emerging modern society, who were the first to coherently articulate the fundamental nature of a new society based on commerce and private property. A recent master's Thesis 'Enlightened Agricultural Improvement in Eighteenth-Century Scotland' supports the position of Scottish historians such as William C Lehman and Bruce Lenman, who present a case for a 'truly Scottish Enlightenment,' amidst the social upheavals in the eighteenth to the nineteenth century throughout the European world.[53] This 'enlightenment' in a society based primarily on agriculture, was particularly relevant to those who worked and lived on the land. Therefore, those such as Robert Muir's grandparents and parents, who were at the leading edge of the revolutionary developments, had a keen understanding of their importance to the nation and the changes that were occurring.

For those early 'high farmers,' the project of modernisation begun by influential leaders like Lord Kames or Henry Home, involved them directly spreading the practice of agricultural 'improvement.' Kames particularly, called this a patriotic duty believing it was essential to laying a new national foundation. Capitalising on the potential that the British union could offer, it became an important project by Home during the 18th century,

---

[52] Malcolm Prentice, *The Scots in Australia*, p20
[53] Widney, Amanda M., "*Enlightened Agricultural Improvement in Eighteenth-Century Scotland*" (2019). Central Washington University, All Master's Theses. 1222. Accessed 5/8/2020, https://digitalcommons.cwu.edu/etd/1222. Lehmann, William C. *Henry Home, Lord Kames, and the Scottish Enlightenment: A Study in National Character and in the History of Ideas*. Archives Internationales D'histoire des Idées; 41. The Hague: Martinus Nijhoff, 1971. Lenman, Bruce. *Enlightenment and Change: Scotland 1746-1832*. New History of Scotland Series. Edinburgh: Edinburgh University Press, 2009.

driven in no small part by the loss of agricultural imports from the American colonies.[54] At the same time, Home actively promoted the existence of an ancient Gaelic Scottish culture in the Highlands. A key influence was the Ossian epic poetry of MacPherson that attracted interest at home and abroad influencing Scottish writers like Sir Walter Scott, and philosophers and political economists such as Adam Smith.[55]

As Christopher Berry explains, the Ossian epics, that are set from Roman times, were also widely utilised to illustrate the progressive sophistication of society through the ages, culminating in a theorised fourth and most developed commercial stage. Thus, as Peter Stein (1988) argues, the "arrival of merchants, as middle-men between producer and consumer, demanded a whole new set of contractual and legal arrangements and this created a new type of society." Of particular significance was that this was identified and quantified most articulately by notable figures of the Scottish Enlightenment such as their own Adam Smith, Lord Kames and John Millar during the eighteenth century.[56]

More importantly for Scotland, was the speed and the way these changes were implemented. Across the border in England farming methods had been in a process of 'improvement' over centuries as the empire expanded and commercial practices began to predominate. Scottish farming practices, as Davidson outlines, had failed to keep abreast of these developments. With an increasing population, its inadequacies, especially the inability to feed its population, had been exposed by famine, particularly that of 1690s, and antiquated farming methods among the many and often warring feudal clans and fiefdoms.[57]

---

[54] C B Bow, The 'final causes' of Scottish nationalism: Lord Kames on the political economy of enlightened husbandry 1745-82, *Historical Research* Vol. 91, No 252, (May 2018), p1-18

[55] Christopher Berry, *The idea of commercial society*, p42-49

[56] Peter Stein, 'The four-stage theory of the development of societies' in P Stein, *the character and influence of the Roman civil law*, London, The Hambledon Press, pp 395-409, as noted in Christopher Berry, pp 42-50

[57] Neil Davidson, 'The Scottish path to Capitalist Agriculture 2, The Capitalist Offensive (1747-1815), *Journal of Agricultural Change*, Volume 4 No. 4 October 2004, p414

This failure to adapt, contributed to the extinguishing of feudal type of arrangements among the more commercially minded landlords particularly those closest to England in the estates in the lowlands and borderlands from the end of the seventeenth century. Improvements were thus directed towards increasing productivity and profitability. Many old practices were removed or reduced, such as commons, payment in kind, sub-letting, the 'run rig' system of farming and small individual plots. They were replaced by the creation of larger commercially viable farms with long-term leases, many up to twenty years. While this began as a slow process, its implementation on most estates throughout Scotland in the latter half of the eighteenth century, was greatly accelerated by the defeat of the Jacobites at Culloden in 1747.[58]

Thus, as Davidson, another Scot of more recent times contends, the sudden arrival of this new type of commercial farming, could be better conceptualised as a bourgeoise social revolution. As he argues, the defeat of the Stuarts and their supporters, who were dependent on feudal clans for soldiers, greatly accelerated a comprehensive restructuring of society by the landlords as part of the British conditions of victory. The assumption of the Jacobite estates and the imposition of commercial English farming methods, resulted in the removal of traditional practices, and eliminated feudal obligations and co-dependencies for a large part of the rural population. Accompanied by enforceable contracts and private rather than shared property, it also established the concept of independent citizens and civil government with all the legal ramifications.[59] What had taken the English three centuries to complete from the Tudor accession in 1430 to 1700 occurred within the span of two generations, a transformation as Davidson reminds us, that 'remains unprecedented in Western European history'.[60]

---

[58] ibid
[59] Christopher Berry, *The idea of commercial society*, p45-50
[60] Neil Davidson, 'The Scottish path to Capitalist Agriculture 2, The Capitalist Offensive (1747-1815), *Journal of Agricultural Change*, Volume 4 No. 4 October 2004, pp411-460, Neil Davidson, Scotland: Birthplace of passive revolution? *Capital & Class* 34(3) 2010, 343–359, Neil Davidson, 'the Scottish path to Capitalist Agriculture 1: from the Crisis of Feudalism to the origins of Agrarian

Davidson, however, also points out that not all were losers by this 'revolution' as many of those affected were able to take advantage of the new social arrangements by becoming tenants and farmers for profit. The new methods were quickly assimilated as Scots of that era like George Robertson and James Hutton became trendsetters on modern farming practices. Their works on agriculture became standard texts valued by farmers across the United Kingdom. Robertson observed that it was the tenant farmers, who were first and most impacted, who drove a lot of the innovations to agriculture that provided the base for Scotland's leading role in the agricultural and industrial revolution:

> the labours of cultivation they more generally, perhaps more wisely, leave to the common husbandman of the country, whose toils, stimulated by necessity, and whose schemes, resulting from experience – if not in all cases more rationally formed, – seldom fail, or at least, to be conducted with more economy.[61]

As Davidson also points out, the methods of the farmers, although often not framed in scientific terms, were nevertheless recognized, and valued by eminent Scottish publications such as *Farmers Magazine*. Other publications like those of the Highlands and Agricultural Society sent representatives to the various farms and properties to discover their methods and to share their secrets with the rest of the farming community. This explosion of innovation was to a large degree, driven by the increasing levels of literacy over the same period that enabled many aspiring farmers to subscribe to such publications and in many cases submit their work or have their work assessed by more scientifically qualified people.

Transformation' (1688-1746) *Journal of Agrarian Change*, Vol 4, No 3, July 2004, p258.

[61] Robertson, George, 1829. *Rural Recollections; Or the Progress of Improvement in Agricultural and Rural Affairs*. Irvine: Cunninghame Press, in: Neil Davidson, The Scottish Path to Capitalist Agriculture 3: The Enlightenment as the Theory and Practice of Improvement, *Journal of Agrarian Change*, Vol.5, No.1, January 2005 Neil Davidson, p42-43

This created for Scottish farming families a culture of improvement that not only became deeply imbedded but was necessary for their very survival. With no land to use as collateral, the only real asset that a tenant farmer had was his knowledge, experience and success in extracting a profit from his rented land. This required an ability to plan and agility to spot and act on an opportunity when it arose, thus creating a new class of incredibly keen and highly motivated capitalist.

By the early 1800s, these skills were challenged. The defeat of Napoleon in 1812, had led to a recession across the United Kingdom with less farms to let and less employment in the sector. The cessation of war also led to a reduction of manufacturing jobs in the towns and cities and a growing problem of high unemployment. In many quarters it was causing social unrest as wages fell and prices for grain and other food commodities increased. These concerns came to a head at the Manchester Peterloo riot and subsequent massacre in 1819. Many were fearing a social crisis with the potential to be as equally catastrophic as it had been across the channel in France a generation earlier. For a newly established class of Scottish tenant farmers, just a few generations old, it was an existential crisis, particularly for those on the margins. For the sons and daughters of even the most successful and well-established, a catastrophic loss of opportunities was staring many of them in the face.

Chapter 3

Land, Cultural Change and the Challenges of the 1800s

A New Farming Class

For many of the farmers for profit, their relatively new status and class consciousness drew a line of separation between the growing numbers of landless and often homeless, labourers and agricultural workers. These were the displaced casualties of enclosure who remained in the decaying bothies and outhouses or crammed into the new villages and tenements that were appearing all over the countryside. The farmer with the lease however, occupied the farmhouse with his family. Some of these houses, built from the late 1700s with the booming profits of commercial farming, were quite substantial such as Robert Muir's home at Springbank in the 1840s.

Daily tasks that had once been shared amongst friends and neighbours were now becoming specialised. Lawrence Saunders thus paints a picture of an emerging class consciousness - where people once lived together 'in a common kitchen and ate at the same table', there was now separation. In a couple of short generations rural culture had been totally transformed and the old ways condemned by the new rural elite – the tenant farmer with a fixed contract and a home for the family. Poverty and want was no longer a shared experience, but a result of laziness and intemperance.[62] As Saunders explains, despite the hard work, life for the farmers for profit in those first two generations, had become more genteel. Better furnishings were starting to appear with internal walls displaying paper and paint as well as better and more comfortable furnishings and accessories like a harp or piano.[63]

---

[62] Lawrence James Saunders, *Scottish Democracy 1815-1840: the social and intellectual background*, Oliver & Boyd London, 1950, 46-47.
[63] ibid, 47

In many farmers' homes a maid was also employed and most of the old communal practices like homecrafts were disappearing as increased income enabled clothes to be purchased from the stores in the nearby towns. The mistress became more like a manager overseeing the hired help. The farmer also dressed in better clothes and his wife and daughter followed the fashions. Instead of the bible and religious texts being the primary reading material, the farmer was reading the technical periodicals and farming magazines and was also a member of a local Agricultural society.[64]

Hard Times from the 1820s

By the time the third generation arrived in the 1820s the easy profits that came with the improvement movement and the accompanying booms associated with the wars in Europe and America had evaporated. A letter to the Editor by poet, author and farmer James Hogg, better known as the 'Ettrick Shepherd,' in the *Quarterly Journal of Agriculture* in 1831, warned that the days of easy profits were long gone. Hogg declared from bitter personal experience, that "the achievements in husbandry of years past were over. It was no longer possible, he lamented, for the 'smallest improvements to the soil to bring substantial profits to the farmer."[65]

For a farmer to succeed in the 1830s stressed the Shepherd, it would require careful planning with all the skill of an accountant and business proprietor. As a farmer himself and member of various agricultural societies with years of experience both successful and as a failure on more than one occasion, he was able to speak with some authority.[66] His well-costed example of a first year establishment budget indicates that for a farmer to be successful in the Scottish borders, £3569:17:11 would be the necessary investment in stock, equipment and labour in order to make a comfortable profit on a large farm of five hundred

---

[64] ibid
[65] James Hogg, On the Capital required in Farming, *The Quarterly Journal of Agriculture Vol 111*, February 1831 – September 1832, William Blackwood Edinburgh, 1932, p 450-476
[66] Valentina Bold, *James Hogg and the Traditional culture of the Scottish borders*, MA Thesis, Memorial University of Newfoundland, 1990, p 28-49

acres.⁶⁷ Thus, in similar circumstances for a young man like Robert Muir in the 1840s the likelihood of leasing a one hundred acre farm in his local area on the outskirts of Ayr was remote considering the cost and the diminishing availability. In his case, by simple calculation alone, it would require at least £700 (or almost a lifetime's wages) in establishment costs his first year and this on land that was most often reserved for eldest sons or adult extended family. It was a massive disincentive to follow in his father's footsteps.

Farmers and the hope of land ownership

While there were cases where efficient tenant farmers could attain ownership of land by way of debt and contractual forfeiture, as Alistair Livingston shows, this was not the general rule.⁶⁸ However, reforms in the 1830s to restrictive trade laws along with electoral reform, heightened the hope that more comprehensive reforms were close at hand and soon would be all encompassing including land. This had always been an expectation of eighteenth-century Scottish reformers. Philosophers such as Lord Kames and Hume viewed the exclusive ownership of land by a small minority guaranteed by law of entail and primogeniture, as *the* major impediment to a free and open commercial society.⁶⁹ Likewise, for agrarian middle-class Scots, access to land was viewed as the gateway to enjoying the benefits of the liberal and commercialised world into which they and their forebears had been pushed. Much more than an asset, it was the basis upon which the political system rested and was also the foundation on which the world of high finance sat. Without it there was no way to exert any political influence or improve their circumstances beyond the level of modest savings, leaving nothing of substance to pass on to their

---

⁶⁷ On the Capital required in Farming, *The Quarterly Journal of Agriculture Vol 111*, February 1831 – September 1832, William Blackwood Edinburgh, 1932, p 450-476

⁶⁸ Alistair Livingston, *The Galloway levellers – a study of the origins, events and consequences of their actions*, M Phil, University of Glasgow, 2009, p19

⁶⁹ Neil Davidson, 'The Scottish path to capitalist agriculture 3: the enlightenment as the theory and practice of improvement', in: *Journal of agrarian change*, Vol. 5 No.1, January 2005, p50-52

children. The inability to gain access to land in a popular pamphlet by an anonymous author circulating out of Edinburgh in 1845, called this problem the 'master evil' – greater even than the corn laws and the disenfranchisement of the working classes.[70] The author reminded the readers of the words of Lord Kames in the previous century of the injustice of the law of entail and the evils of excluding land from the free market:

> A number of noblemen and gentlemen among us lay in wait for every parcel of land that comes to market ... and the same course will be followed till no land left to purchase ... every entailed estate in Scotland becomes in effect, a mortmain, admitting additions without end, but absolutely barring alienation; and if the Legislature interpose not, the period is not distant when all the land in Scotland will be locked up by entails, and WITHDRAWN FROM COMMERCE.[71]

Springbank Farm

An event that emphasises this injustice during Robert Muir's formative years, was the passing of William Paterson who had returned to Scotland in 1829 after a long career in Jamaica as a Lawyer, plantation and slave owner. He died in Ayr during 1832 leaving a large inheritance to his son and nephew and instructions to create two estates: the Paterson Estate and the Montgomerie Estate.[72] The Muir's home at Springbank Farm was part of the Paterson Estate as listed in the Ayrshire Ordinance Survey 1855-1857 - one of many small farms in the surrounding district.[73] Most of these properties appear to have been acquired by forfeiture in the mid-1840s on the conclusion of a long-running legal case

---

[70] A landed Proprietor, *The emancipation of the soil and free trade in land*, John Johnstone Edinburgh, 1845, p4
[71] Lord Kames, Sketches, iii, p305, in: A landed Proprietor, *The emancipation of the soil and free trade in land*, p8
[72] Paterson William 1833 (Wills and Testaments reference SC6/44/6, Ayr Sheriff Court) National Records of Scotland.
[73] Scotland's Places, Ordinance survey name books, 1855-1857, Ayrshire volume 62, OS1/3/62/7

between the two heirs, and the estate taking advantage of losses incurred by the previous owners in the railway bust of the same year.[74]

There is no doubt that the change of ownership would have caused some consternation in the Muir household with an event like this often the catalyst for catastrophic family disruption. While it usually resulted in an increase in the price of the lease and the imposition of terms that boosted the return to the landlord, it often meant the loss of the family home and the breakup of the family. This was a growing concern for many farmers and farm workers affected by similar trends as farms continued to be consolidated into larger holdings during the 1830s. This was a tactic increasingly employed by landlords to counter expected losses with the coming repeal of the Corn Laws and deal with ongoing economic uncertainty. In response, large numbers of farmers and particularly their children, chose to emigrate to preserve their status and their savings while also creating a legacy for their families.[75]

The Muir family appears to have not escaped unscathed by these events. As the records indicate, they joined the ranks of many others in similar circumstances seeking solutions for them and their children. The loss of Springbank farm thus appears to have occurred during these troubles, leading to their dispersal to varying parts of the country and the world. The 1851 census shows no record of Robert's parents David Muir or Christian Muir and no official record of the death of either parent. Although a notice in the *Glasgow Herald* shows David Muir aged 64 died unregistered at Barskimming Mains near Mauchline Ayrshire in March 1853, matching dates in Robert Muir's own correspondence. David Muir, however, who was far sighted, anticipated many of the calamitous changes. He not only enrolled his children into occupations other than farming, but he also encouraged them to emigrate. This was

---

[74] *The Scottish Jurist*, Vol. V1, Edinburgh, 1834, p232, Centre for the study of the legacies of British slavery, UCL Department of History 2021, https://www.ucl.ac.uk/lbs/physical/view/1995968559 accessed 15/6/2021
[75] The Ettrick Shepherd (James Hogg) To the editor of the Quarterly Journal of Agriculture, On the habits, amusements and condition of the Scottish peasantry, *The Quarterly Journal of Agriculture Vol 111*, February 1831 – September 1832, William Blackwood Edinburgh, 1932, p263

without doubt to avoid the developing social, political, and cultural crises while retaining the culture and values associated with rural living.

For over twenty years after his marriage, the (David) Muir family had staunchly avoided the new urbanising industrial economy choosing to maintain their roots in the village and the kirk. Like many of their station and class, the cities were viewed as places to be avoided, with raging pandemics, poverty, overcrowding and unchecked vice. Stewart Mechie paints a bleak picture held by many farmers, of the living conditions suffered in Glasgow and even in the nearby town of Ayr. The epidemics of 1837 – 1844 had hit them hard as well as the failure of the social elites and government to adequately address it.[76] It was a trend that influential people like James Hogg saw as a calamity for the rural culture and lifestyle and fought hard to preserve the old ways and customs.

The Best are all Leaving

Hogg, as a poet, tenant farmer and activist, made it his mission to preserve as much of the old culture in song, verse, and prose as well as organising celebrations of traditional culture[77]. He travelled widely organising sporting events and other traditional activities in a passionate attempt at preserving local Scottish culture that he believed was disappearing. In a more commercial world, he believed it was being replaced by something less personal, meaner, and less respectful.[78] As time elapsed, he became increasingly negative, maintaining that improvement, while increasing incomes for a few, had for most part stripped the rural areas of its heart and soul. He lamented in 1832, 'before the revolutionary war ... a borderer would sooner have laid down his head in the grave of his fathers. ... But now all the best are leaving it; all the industrious,

---

[76] Stewart Mechie, *The Church and Scottish social development*, Oxford University Press, London 1960, p30-33

[77] Valentina Bold, *James Hogg and the Traditional culture of the Scottish borders*, MA Thesis, Memorial University of Newfoundland, 1990

[78] The Ettrick Shepherd (James Hogg) To the editor of the Quarterly Journal of Agriculture, On the habits, amusements and condition of the Scottish peasantry, *The Quarterly Journal of Agriculture Vol 111*, February 1831 – September 1832, William Blackwood Edinburgh, 1932, p256-263

diligent, and respectable men who have made a little competency to carry them to another country, are hastening away as if a pestilence were approaching them.'[79]

Marjorie Harper's research suggests that this is correct, arguing that for many during that period it was not an 'exodus of the poor' but an attempt to deal with the corrosive effects on their families by farm consolidations, poor harvests, and low prices. For example, William Beattie of Broomhill in Aberdeenshire wrote in 1836 to his brother George at Bon Accord in Alberta Canada complaining of rent increases. While his son John a year later stated 'we are losing greatly every year' inquiring into the possibility of purchasing land for farming. A year later another son wrote again to his uncle after a poor harvest, stating that 'streams of emigrants are going to America this year.'[80] Needless to say, a positive picture of the conditions in Canada led to the emigration of the family three years later.[81] Many of these farmers and labourers as Harper points out were not impoverished Highlanders but could be more accurately described as middle class; 'Hogg's heart and soul', with the means to pay their own way and employ labourers on arrival to assist with the establishment of their farms in the 'new world.' For many younger people it was not uncommon for parents who remained in Scotland to purchase land for them in America or Canada to provide a future legacy them that was not possible in Scotland.

As Harper , in much the same vein as E G Wakefield also argued, the exodus of people in this category was not due to a lack of savings but was as much to do with a growing inability to invest profits at home.[82] Alexander Buchanan thus reported from Quebec in 1840 through to the mid-1850s on many new arrivals from Scotland who 'were in good circumstances' and that many were 'respectable farmers and agriculturalists in comfortable circumstances ... who had emigrated to join friends.'[83] Many

---

[79] ibid, p259
[80] Marjorie Harper, *Adventurers, and exiles: the great Scottish exodus*, Profile Books Ltd London, 2003, Kindle Edition, loc 1816,1820, 1826
[81] ibid
[82] ibid, loc 1839
[83] ibid

farmers and farm workers appear to have been caught in the process of rising farm lease costs. Behind that was the consolidation of properties, leading to larger farms, lower margins, greater risk, less availability and falling prices with little wriggle room when the harvests were bad or the seasons unfavourable. The 1840s offered no reprieve to the financial and social pressures bringing ever closer the repeal of the Corn Laws. This occurred in 1846, and with it, an expected calamity in the price of grain. Following closely on its heels, came a roller coaster decade of financial setbacks that affected most sectors of the economy. It all began amid the first great stock market crash of 1847-1848 that saw the savings of many evaporate and large companies go to the wall.

A calamitous decline in cash and available funds was, for farmers, made worse by a series of poor harvests and the growing potato crisis that engulfed Ireland and parts of Scotland. To make matters worse, a trading crisis that engulfed most of continental Europe was triggered by the failure of the large Russian merchant house Harman & Co and the revolution in France.[84] This created an international funding crisis as bills of exchange failed to be honoured. Banks and large trading houses failed across the UK and Europe. The next two years were years of woe, financial hardship and severe shortages of food and money effecting the price of crucial shipments of grain and the prices of bread in an increasingly interdependent world.

At the head of all the matters worrying farmers in the 1840s was, like their landlords, the proposed changes to the corn laws. With the legislation artificially supporting prices, the vulnerability of the landless farmer to fluctuations in the grain market was becoming obvious as protests and debate in parliament continued to keep the issue in the foreground. William Van Vugt's 1988 study suggests that this became a major reason for many agricultural workers and farmers to emigrate in the period leading up to the

---

[84] D. Morier Evans, *The Commercial crisis 1847-1848*, Letts & Son and Steer, London, 1849, p48

repeal of the Corn Laws in 1846 and after.[85] R E Prothero portrayed this period as an 'agricultural panic' that lasted into the 1850s.[86] According to Marcus Lee Hanson's 1940 work *The Atlantic Migration*, many farmers were 'gripped with terror' as they contemplated and saw their wall of protection eventually removed.[87] For many, this may have been the last straw in a long line of setbacks and changes. However, as Scottish historians have documented, the rural lowland localities never existed in a state of quiet and passive acquiescence as the agricultural and industrial revolutions gathered momentum.

Rural Resistance
Many took a stand with outright violence, through literature and in the church. Beginning with the leveller's revolt in Gallway in 1724, resistance occurred sporadically well into the next century.[88] And despite the success of many rural farming families in negotiating the route to a commercial society, there lay a large degree of animosity towards the aristocracy that was deep seated and went back generations. This can be seen as Gerard Whatley points out, in the writings of Robert Burns around the end of the eighteenth century, as he expressed his 'rage against the sufferings of the small tenant farmer.'[89]

Burns was of the same generation and locality as Robert Muir's grandfather, John Muir. He was known to William Muir, very likely John Muir's brother, who features in his works as a close friend

---

[85] William E Van Vugt, Running from ruin? the emigration of British farmers to the USA in the wake of the repeal of the Corn Laws, *Economic History Review*, 2nd ser., XLI, 3 (1988), pp 411-428

[86] R E Prothero, *English farming: past and present*, Longman's Green & Co London, 1917, pp370-371

[87] M L Hansen, *The Atlantic Migration*, Cambridge, Harvard University Press, 1940, pp264-265

[88] Christopher Whatley, 'How tame were the Scottish lowlanders during the eighteenth century'? In: T M Devine ed., *Conflict and stability in Scottish society, 1700-1850*, John Donald, Edinburgh, 1990, pp1-30, Christopher Whatley, Scottish society, 1707-1830,

[89] Christopher Whatley, *Scottish society 1707-1830*, p288, Christopher Whatley, It is said that Burns was a radical: contest, concession and the political legacy of Robert Burns ca 1796-1859, in: *Journal of British Studies* Vol. 50, No. 3, July 2011, https://www.jstor.org/stable/23265422 Accessed: 07-04-2020

and owner of the Tarbolton Mill. This was situated close by the Muir's 1840s home at Springbank. His body of work, like that of Hogg, often illustrates the profound feeling of alienation that was developing amongst the rural farming population at the time in Southwest Ayrshire with well-known rhymes as 'a man's a man for a' that!' It is not surprising therefore that some elements of this would have passed along the Muir family line.

By the 1840s it was the church where much of the protest was centred. Fundamental changes in the role of the church and the heritors that supported them, led to the 'Great Disruption' of 1843 and the formation of the Free Church of Scotland. The effects of this were felt at all levels of Scottish society.[90] At the heart of the matter was the inability of the Scottish society to come to terms with rapid population growth. The established Church had failed to provide adequate seating and extend programs to accommodate the growing numbers of parishioners and their changing circumstances. Complicating matters was the blurring of civil and religious responsibilities that often crossed over in the provision for seating, payment of the ministers' salaries, administration of the law and local government. Reforms to local government in the early thirties ameliorated some of these issues in the larger nearby population centres such as Ayr and Kilmarnock. Further away, however, in localities like Tarbolton and Mauchline where the Muirs and Paterson's lived, local authority remained largely centred in the Kirk and with the local landowners and where the problems of access continued to fester.

Patrons, who had long been responsible for the financial maintenance of the local religious and social infrastructure, rather than build more churches, had instead, instituted self-protecting measures to minimise their financial burden. Strategies were implemented such as pew rents and delaying maintenance. Adding to ever increasing outrage, unallocated teind funds, which should have been used for church and parish upkeep, were often used for private projects such as mansion building. This was driving a wedge between the ruling elites, the established church, and the rest of the population. The divide was only widened by the

---

[90] Callum Brown, *The social history of religion in Scotland since 1730*, Methuen, London, 1987, pp 89-128

insistence of wealthy heritors and patrons who often did not reside locally, in appointing the local minister who increasingly was an ally in the maintenance of local law and order.[91] The effect of 'pewing' or the installation of fixed seating, however, was in many rural communities, a final cause for social division and often extreme animosity. The compulsion to pay for a seat emphasised the levels of status of the community, segregating the various classes – the lairds, the tenants, the tradespeople and servants all clearly identified and sectioned off with wooden barriers, with many simply locked out due to lack of room or poverty.[92]

Robert's father David Muir, like many others across lowland Scotland, was swept up in the evangelical revival of the early 1800s. Riding on the momentum of these and other social grievances, tenant farmers and farm workers were outraged against the religious monopoly of the established church and their connection to the aristocracy. This then fed other grievances like the lack of availability of land to let or purchase, lack of commercial opportunity and basic employment and accommodation. At his death bed scene early in 1853, described by his son Robert not long after arriving in Australia, David Muir clearly was within the fold of the dissenters being attended to by the minister of the Mauchline free church. This association had begun at least two decades earlier, as records for the birth of the youngest children in 1835 indicate a continuing association with the nearby free church at St Quivox.

Thus, viewing society as a place that offered little in the way of a place and a secure future for themselves and especially for their children, it is no surprise that tenant farmers, like the Muirs and the Patersons with the means, began to consider emigrating. By the early 1800s there were several schemes for Australian immigration that were targeted specifically at the increasingly disenchanted and disenfranchised rural population. The Muir family found them particularly attractive over those directed at North America due to

---

[91] Callum Brown, *The social history of religion in Scotland since 1730*, p94
[92] Callum Brown, Protest in the pews: interpreting Presbyterianism and society in fracture during the Scottish economic revolution, in T M Divine ed., *Conflict and stability in Scottish society 1700-1850*, John Donald Edinburgh, 1990, p91-92

the possibility of retaining their social status and rural lifestyle without sacrificing the trappings of civilization.

Chapter 4

The Wakefield Scheme and Rev John Dunmore Lang

Edward Gibbon Wakefield

The first of these schemes was that devised by Englishman Edward Gibbon Wakefield. It was a plan for colonial social engineering, transplanting the most productive elements of British society in South Australia. In Wakefield's estimation, the creation of civil government and commercial dynamics could be quickly stablished through planned releases of large tracts of land for sale at a set price, in pre-determined locations. By selecting the 'right' mix of people, such as experienced tenant farmers and agricultural workers, British social dynamics could then be quickly established along with accompanying British civil government, regulations, and culture. This would then, as he saw it, prevent the slide of the white immigrant populations towards lawlessness, poverty and ultimately a state of barbarism worse than the indigenous populations. His scheme was thus designed to endow the settler and the process with careful oversight, bearing in mind British practices and laws with respect for citizenship, private property, and civil government.[93] While it only resulted in a small percentage overall, mainly to South Australia, these basic elements underwrote much of the emigration policy to Australia over the course of the nineteenth century.

For some, it was viewed as a safer alternative to the more popular destinations in Canada, which in the 1830s, were experiencing

---

[93] Jack Harrington, Edward Gibbon Wakefield, the liberal political subject and the settler state, in *Journal of Political Ideologies*, 20 (3), pp333-351, Douglas Pike, *Paradise of dissent: South Australia 1829-1857*, First Published Longman's Green and Co London 1957, pp 79-83

periods of social unrest and ethnic tension. More than just another immigration scheme, however, Wakefield's vision became accepted by politicians at the highest level of government. Promoted as the solution the looming social problems associated with a great excess of labour and capital, it was expected to ameliorate the type of chaos that was occurring in France.[94] Wakefield's scheme, named 'systematic immigration,' therefore, sought to transplant the capitalist dynamics underpinning British society. The emigration of landowners and workers would create a social and economic 'hinterland' in Australia with reciprocal trade in raw materials and finished products restoring social and economic equilibrium.

More importantly for those in agriculture of the yeoman class, who were displaced and out of work, it would offer benefits not available in Britain such as land ownership, enfranchisement, and real investment opportunities for the many who had a modest amount of savings. It was a utopian vision where the existing regime in Britain would not be threatened and British youth would flourish in the perfect climate of South Australia or 'Australia Felix' as his utopian vision preferred, away from the corrupting influence of the penal colonies of Tasmania and New South Wales.[95] The scheme was passionately advocated by Newcastle religious dissenter, philanthropist and entrepreneur George Fife Angas, a director of the South Australia Company and committed to changing the world by colonisation through the combination of

---

[94] Duncan Bell, John Stuart Mill on colonies, in *Political Theory*, 2010, 38:34, p38-40, Onur Ulas Ince, https://www.academia.edu/1067870/ *Capitalism, colonisation and contractual dispossession: Wakefield's letters from Sydney*, 2018 p5-11, accessed online 8/7/2021, in Onur Ulas Ince, *Colonial capitalism and the dilemmas of liberalism*, Oxford University Press, 2018, Ince quoting Shaw's *Great Britain* identifies the question of falling profits to be "a problem of primary importance in British political economy." Shaw, "Introduction," pp. 11-13, Onur Ulas Ince, https://www.academia.edu/1067870/ *Capitalism, colonisation and contractual dispossession*, p21

[95] Michael Radzevicius, *Edward Gibbon Wakefield and an Imperial utopian dream*, Ph.D.., University of Adelaide, 2011, P106-7

these means.[96] Angas believed that it would be 'a new starting point in life, for myriads of his fellows trodden down by competition, persecuted for conscience's sake, or struggling to be honest'.[97]

The South Australian Company, like Wakefield, also advocated a later scheme for New Zealand for similar reasons, promoting the civilizing influences of 'industrious and virtuous settlers.' It offered, as Wakefield argued 'for the first time in the history of modern colonization' a well-managed experience that would ameliorate the problem of isolated settlers descending into savagery. As he stated, it was designed to displace the lawless squatters, the abandoned sailors, the runaway convicts, the pirates, the worse-than-savages', who had perpetrated horrors on the local aboriginal communities.'[98] It was also viewed as an improvement on schemes with Government sanction to New South Wales already in motion, that were increasingly labelled as nothing more than programs to dump unwanted human refuse on the colonies.[99] The 'fair price' concept that was a cornerstone of the scheme, promised to give exclusive access to land to those with sufficient funds to establish themselves.' While discouraging the less desirable elements it would facilitate a better functioning of economic activity by providing jobs for skilled workers who in turn

---

[96] Rob Lin, Scenes of early South Australia: the letters of Joseph Keynes of Kyneton 1839-1843, *Journal of the Historical Society of South Australia*, vol 10, 1982

[97] E. Hodder, *George Fife Angas: Father and Founder of South Australia*, (London, 1891), p. 105, Marilyn Arnold, *Promoting emigration to South Australia from Britain 1829-C1850: the importance of newspapers and other literature to the South Australia colonisation project*, Ph.D. Thesis 2019, Flinders University, Adelaide SA.

[98] Douglas Pike, Paradise of dissent: South Australia, 1829-1857, Melbourne University Press 1967, First Published, Longman's, Green & Co London, 1857, *The Land of promise being an authentic and impartial history of the rise and progress of the new British Province of South Australia*; Smith, Elder & Co London, 1839, P207, Pat Moloney, Savagery and civilization: early Victorian notions in: *New Zealand Journal of history*, 35,2 (2001), p170-171

[99] Emigration, *The Sydney Gazette, and New South Wales Advertiser*, Tuesday 9 June 1835, page 2

could save enough to become landowners and employers themselves. It was attracting a great deal of interest from aspirational agricultural labourers and 'the better class of farmers and numbers of the most respectable and influential families.' They were taking advantage of the opportunity to become landowners and proprietors and workers, avoiding the corruption, sickness and deprivations of urban life that was engulfing more of the next generation.[100]

For the Muir and Paterson families, this was viewed as the perfect opportunity for the growing numbers of younger family members. As tenant farmers and highly skilled agricultural workers, they belonged to the most prized class of immigrant, guaranteeing an immediate boost in social status with a virtually limitless field of opportunities. The first in Robert Muir's family to take up the offer of a new start, was his older sister Marion. Migrating with a large party of relatives in 1838, that included a large group on the Paterson side, she arrived in South Australia on the 'Fairfield' in April 1839.[101] Marion had applied as a skilled agricultural worker, where she was classified as 'dairy-maid' in her application for free passage. Her agent was noted as William Rankine, the leader of the party and her uncle on her mother's side.[102] They would then join with others also related, arriving later and others already in the colony like her Uncle Alexander Muir. Leading this group were the Rankine brothers John and William. John Rankine, a medical doctor, appears to have also been one of the major financial backers of the party having been the majority shareholder of the Albion Steel Works in Glasgow. His brother William had been a sheep farmer from Barr in South Ayrshire. Settling in South Australia, they purchased land with a number of other Scots, south

---

[100] Douglas Pike, *Paradise of dissent: South Australia, 1829-1857*, Melbourne University Press 1967, First Published, Longmans, Green & Co London, 1857, p75-77

[101] Dianne Cummings, *Bound for South Australia, passengers 1836-1888* (slsa.sa.gov.au) accessed online 14/7/2021.

[102] Margaret J Roberts, *Reach for the far horizon: Sloan and Muir family history*, Margaret J Roberts Bendigo, 2000, p19

of Adelaide at a place they named Strathalbyn where a town and several commercial and farming enterprises were quickly established.[103] Among the first to purchase land in the district, they were acutely aware of the significance of their mission and appear to have had no desire to return and were committed, as the later diaries of Matthew Rankine indicate, to making South Australia their permanent abode.[104]

The utopian ideal espoused by Wakefield appeared to have been an inspiration to Marion's younger brothers who followed her a decade later. Younger brother David Muir was especially motivated over the ongoing land reform movement as the colonies made a transition towards a more diversified economy from the 1850s. In 1860 he travelled from Ballarat to Melbourne to present a long letter to the editor of the *Herald* in opposition to the upcoming Land Bill. Coming from a farming family that was of a class that were inter-generational tenants, it provides insight into the utopian ideas circulating among landless immigrant farmers.

The letter contained suggestions designed to prevent many of the problems that had forced their decision to emigrate like fair access to land, protection, labour costs, local government, technological improvements, and the role of the state in private and public property.

The proposed bill, as Muir pointed out, was intended amongst other things, to discourage speculators and monopolists but in his opinion was doomed to fail. His proposal, he argued, would ban speculators for life under a system of government ownership and flat rate rental of 2s per acre. This would then attract bona-fide farmers to arable land while allowing for subsistence plus a little surplus that could be sold to buy luxuries. Anything more than that he deemed to be a 'an artificial state of existence.' Such a state existed in Melbourne he pointed out, with

---

[103] Nancy Gemmell, *Old Strathalbyn and its people 1839-1939*, National Trust of South Australia, Adelaide 1988
[104] Matthew Rankine 1829-1917, *The diaries of Matthew Rankine 1854-1868*, State Library of South Australia,
https://catalog.slsa.sa.gov.au:443/record=b2173363~S1

'people dying of starvation in arguably the richest city in the world.'[105]

Rev John Dunmore Lang

A decade after Marion had successfully established herself in South Australia, the immigration narrative had evolved from the agrarian utopian ideal of Wakefield to a much wider field of enterprise offering a diversity of opportunities for the 'yeoman farmer,' skilled mechanics and tradesmen. This was the main thrust of Scot, Rev J D Lang's campaigns throughout England and Scotland from the 1830s and the second half of the 1840s. Lang's main interest was, in addition to solving the capital and labour problems that were highlighted by Wakefield and his supporters, to ensure that all the colonies of Australia moved beyond their reputation as a dumping ground for criminals and the unwanted excess of Britain. As Rosemary Lawson pointed out, Lang was also on a mission of religion and morality as he attempted to effect 'a great moral reformation.'[106]

Unlike Wakefield who had never been to Australia, Lang was a man of direct experience having travelled widely in the Australian colonies and had personal experience with many of the aboriginal inhabitants and the various locations and conditions. It was Lang's vision that would exert more influence over the Muir brothers than the Muir sisters who clearly preferred the security of relatives and a society that was more in keeping with conditions at home. Lang made his presence known in Scotland, touring widely throughout the countryside making an appearance in Ayrshire in 1831 where he spruiked the advantages of a life in Australia for tradesmen and skilled 'mechanics' who were not able to afford the passage and expenses involved in emigration.[107] This is most likely where Robert's father David Muir was first inspired to direct his children into skilled occupations. Lang who toured Scotland again in the

---

[105] A Colonist, 'The Land Bill,' *The Herald*, (Melbourne) Thursday August 9, 1860
[106] Rosemary Lawson '*Dr John Dunmore Lang and Immigration*,' Ph.D. Thesis Australian National University Canberra, 1966, p10
[107] Rosemary Lawson *Dr John Dunmore Lang and Immigration*, p13-14.

1840s, offered a perfect solution for his children and their prospects, away from the troubles of Scotland.

The influence of Lang therefore, emerges later in the choices that the Muir brothers made - not so much in the schemes he proposed, but in the opportunities and possibilities that he promoted. Presenting the untapped potential of Northern New South Wales and Queensland which he called Cooksland, it was sold as ideal for the growing of cotton and sugar cane and almost anything else.[108] This was relentlessly advertised throughout Scotland and the United Kingdom by public meetings, literature, and intense lobbying of government members during the 1840s. It coincided precisely with when Robert Muir was contemplating an uncertain future beyond his engineering apprenticeship.

One highly detailed publication from the respected Rev Lang was practically a bible on the region and its prospects. Filled with detailed surveys, reports from officials and personal accounts of his travels, in the opinion of Rev Lang, it was the Clarence River and surrounding area that offered enormous potential for prospective immigrants in 1847. Supported by a reproduction of the 1839 report of the Deputy Surveyor General Perry, the whole Northern Rivers area was represented as suitable for the cultivation of 'wheat, maize, the vine, tobacco, sugar, indigo and many other articles of consumption and even export.'[109] As well as being sparsely populated it also was shown to have access from the open sea by steamers and other coastal shipping. Readers were reminded that Captain Perry's visit there three years later by coastal steamboat confirmed his early assessment highlighting the fact that it continued to be sparsely populated and conditions were as good if not better than his earlier survey.[110]

Lang's schemes were thus perfectly targeted at farming families like the Muirs as Lang wrote in 'Cooksland':

---

[108] John Dunmore Lang, *Cooksland in North-Eastern Australia; the future cotton field of Great Britain: its characteristics and capabilities for European colonization, with a disquisition on the manners and customs of the aborigines*, Longman Brown Green and Longmans, London, 1847, John Dunmore Lang DD, *The Australian Immigrant's Manual, or a Guide to the Gold Colonies of New South Wales and Port Phillip*, Partridge and Oakey, London 1852, pp42-60

[109] John Dunmore Lang, *Cooksland in North-Eastern Australia*, p42

[110] ibid, p47-48

Their stout sons and daughters, for whom it is so difficult to find a proper outlet, suitable to their habits and feelings, under existing circumstances in Great Britain or Ireland, would be a treasure to their parents on their arrival in Australia, and would soon be all settled as independent colonial farmers on their own account ....

There are numberless respectable persons, of all classes in the mother-country, with small capitals, of from £100 to, £500 each, for which they can find no profitable employment in business, without the utmost hazard of its entire loss, and with rising families of sons and daughters, for whom the prospect at home, in the present overstocked condition of every profession and branch of business, is sufficiently gloomy, who, I am confident, would find it their interest, in every sense of the word, to emigrate as small farmers to such a country as Cooksland.[111]

The idea that the colonies were free of the social and political monopolies was also a major selling point, with Lang by the 1840's also widely promoting a vision of the colonies as free, democratic and self-determining political entities.[112] The concept of freedom from aristocratic overlords was also a major benefit, particularly in Ireland where the process of farm consolidation was gathering momentum. For those with their own source of funds, like the Muir boys, who by the 1850s had already accumulated some independent sums and entered the merchant class, it all created the expectation that they would maintain their status and possibly improve their position once they arrived. Their social status was important to them having, in the case of the Muir family, come from lowly origins and improved their position with each succeeding generation. It had been maintained in many cases by intermarriage, as in the case of his father's family and his current family and close ties with in-laws such as the Patersons, his mother's family.

---

[111] Ibid, p225
[112] John Dunmore Lang, *The Australian emigrant's manual or, a guide to the gold colonies of New South Wales and Port Phillip*, Partridge and Oakey, London 1852, page x

Chapter 5

Muir & Paterson Farming Dynasties

The Muir and Paterson families have a long history in Southwest Ayrshire as agricultural labourers and farmers. It extends back at least four generations to 1753 just after the defeat of the Jacobites at Culloden. The first traceable ancestor is Peter Muir who appears on a baptismal record for his son John at the Stair parish church 8 April 1753. This occurred during the period of rural reconstruction after the Jacobite instability.[113] The records state that Peter Muir was a resident of 'Stepends,' a small group of farm buildings containing two cottages – the property of the Boswell family - owners of the Auchinleck Estate in Southwest Ayrshire. This would have been a basic form of housing typical of many such cottages at the time. Joined together, each residence would have consisted of a single room, 15-16 feet wide and 18 feet long. Robert Hope describes such buildings as having a dirt floor, small windows, and a dunghill, often in close proximity – living conditions that persisted into the nineteenth century.[114] The inhabitants were primarily subsistence farmers utilizing many of the old cooperative feudal methods of grazing and cropping. It was a way of life that had changed little for hundreds of years. A survey in 1856 shows the cottages still existing under the same ownership – Sir James Boswell, son of Lord Auchinleck.[115] They remained as a remnant of the past and a reminder to the older folk of the

---

[113] 08/04/1753 MUIR, JOHN (Old Parish Registers Births 614/ 10 18 Stair) National records of Scotland, Page 18 of 145

[114] Alexander Fenton, 'The housing of agricultural workers in the nineteenth century' in T. M. Devine, *Farm servants and labour in Lowland Scotland 1770 – 1914*, John Donald Publishers, Edinburgh, 1984, p 192

[115] National Records of Scotland, Scotland's Places, Ordinance Survey Name Books, Ayrshire OS Name books, Ayrshire Volume 03, OS1 3/3/95, Christopher Whatley, *Scottish society 1707 – 1830: beyond Jacobitism, towards industrialisation*, Manchester University Press, Manchester, 2000, p70-71.

profound social and demographic changes that had occurred in their lifetimes.

While many point to the 'highland clearances' as a typical outcome of rapid modernization of Scottish society during the nineteenth century, it had also been transformative for the lowlands of Scotland for the greater part of the previous century. Many lowland Estates such as those where Peter Muir resided, had already been undergoing commercialization for some time, displacing many of the small communities. T M Devine thus points out that that the decline in rural lowland populations was matched by an increase in the larger towns and villages as manufacturing, trades, mining and other industries emerged over the course of the eighteenth century. This provided a diversity of work and the evolution of new trades and occupations that were not available in the highland regions, thus obscuring the most dramatic effects of modernization.[116]

The Muir family, however, maintained continuity within the rural industry and environment. In the new social hierarchy, a cottar family in the mid-1700s like the Muirs, enjoyed a relative security of tenure as a tenant on the estate working as a farm servant with the security of an arrangement with the landlord in the form of a lease that could be from six months or longer particularly as the commercialization of agriculture began to predominate. In other cases, the arrangement could be that of a class of agricultural workers like a 'mailer' who rented the cottage and a small tract of arable land while hiring out their labour and services to surrounding farmers.[117]

With agriculture thus becoming increasingly commercialized by the aristocracy, for the Muir family, these changes set in motion a twin set of values that would remain deeply imbedded within the family line. The first was the appreciation of improvement techniques for profitable farming and secondly, a resentment of monopolies, particularly that enjoyed by the established aristocratic order that had extinguished much of the older established methods

---

[116] T M Devine, *Clearance and improvement: land power and people in Scotland 1700-1900*, John Donald Edinburgh 2006, p140-145

[117] Alexander Fenton, 'The housing of agricultural workers in the nineteenth century', p 192 - 194

and lifestyles. What fuelled the resentment was that most of it had been done legally by instruments like the laws of entail and primogeniture which guaranteed the aristocracy ownership of most of the Scottish property and with it control of the political system.

On the estate, in keeping with the Scottish commercialization initiative after Culloden, Lord Auchinleck's initiated changes that included levelling and beautifying the grounds and constructing Auchinleck House. His program of improvement was also applied to the farming land to increase its profitability. This completely changed the appearance of the countryside with the creation of small farms and enclosing the fields with hedgerows, ditches, and dykes. To facilitate more efficient movement, roads and bridges were also constructed to enable produce to quickly reach the growing urban centres.[118] Much of this occurred during the 1760s and 1770s as it did on many Scottish estates. It also indicates the success of John Muir as a teenager and young adult during this time in assimilating and excelling at the new practices.

Farming was becoming a vocation and a career rather than a way of life as it had been for previous generations. Security of tenure was based on securing a long-term lease to make a decent living, by ensuring the landlord enjoyed a profitable return. This meant that farmers and agricultural workers who could not turn out a profit to cover and exceed the costs of improvement, were not likely to be offered a lease and were more likely to be evicted if unable to adapt to the new commercial conditions. For young aspiring farmers, this involved the acquisition of the new skills such as animal husbandry and agricultural methods that incorporated all the available land on a more flexible year-round system. This was achieved following the lead of modernizers and improvers like Lord Kames and John Cockburn of Ormiston with scientifically based methods using different fertilizers and lime, crop rotation, the use of root crops as fodder, and the appropriate methods of soil improvements to ensure higher yields over longer periods.[119]

---

[118] Christopher Whatley, *Scottish society 1707-1830: beyond Jacobitism, towards industrialisation*, Manchester University Press, Manchester U.K., 2000, pp70-72
[119] Christopher Whatley, *Scottish society 1707-1830: beyond Jacobitism, towards industrialisation*, p69-71

This made many of these projects highly profitable and possibly the most notable innovation was the introduction of the small plough, or 'swing plough' replacing the old Scots plough that required more than one person and a team of oxen.[120] This technology would be a major catalyst for the Muir family and the direction life would take them and their descendants. Thus, after an apprenticeship of over ten years, by the 1780s, John Muir can be identified as a farmer that specialized in ploughing using the new technology that could be operated by one person with two horses. By age twenty-two, as the baptismal records for his third son Robert indicate, John Muir had left the Auchinleck estate and had taken up a position on another Boswell property at Barbieston, about eight miles away to the west, where his son Robert was born in March 1775.

The property contained a small cottage with a few acres of land in much the same arrangement as his father working as a farm labourer and a ploughman.[121] A year later John Muir had progressed, acquiring the contract to farm the nearby property at Corsehill near the village of Coylton in the parish sharing the same name, only ten miles from where he was raised. This began an association spanning three generations with the parish of Stair and the nearby localities of Tarbolton, Mauchline, St Quivox, the village of Stair and the picturesque Barskimming Estate. This is a part of Ayrshire, that along with the Highlands, has had a huge influence on the development of Scottish identity. Steeped in religious and political history it is commonly associated with the poet Robert Burns, William Wallace, the covenanters and Robert Bruce, with a long history of resistance to tyranny. Raised in similar circumstances to Scotland's famous bard, Robert Muir's father David also the son of a tenant farmer, spent many hours of his early life in Stair, Tarbolton and the larger town of Mauchline.

---

[120] Gavin Sprott, 'The country tradesman' in T M Devine ed., *farm servants and labour in lowland Scotland 1770 – 1914, 1984,* John Donald Publishers, Edinburgh, p 146 - 147

[121] Scotland's Places, National Records of Scotland, ordinance survey name books, Ayrshire OS name books 1855-1857, Ayrshire Volume 3 OS1/3/3/57, National Records of Scotland, Scotland's People, 12/03/1775, Muir Robert, Old parish Registers, 614 10/35 Stair, page 35 of 145

For Grandfather John, farming in his own right would have represented a great improvement in status for his growing family as well as a huge improvement in living and working conditions over the one roomed cottage on the Auchinleck Estate. The farm is thus described in the 1855 ordinance survey, some seventy years later, as 'a neat low farmhouse one storey high partly slated and partly thatched - the out offices in the same style.[122] The farm, like most in the area would have been mixed with dairy, cattle and crops on around one hundred acres, the most common and optimal size for a sound and profitable agricultural enterprise for a large family to manage themselves. This was often typical of South Ayrshire where dairy became predominant towards the end of the eighteenth century.[123] He had obviously thrived in the new environment having also purchased two plough horses on which he paid the required tax of four shillings and was probably the holder of a twenty-year lease on the farm.[124] In addition he had also added a cart to his growing list of assets and most likely also a couple of horses with which to pull it.[125]

By the end of eighteenth century after forty years of commercialization, farmers like John Muir were becoming small proprietors and managers of thriving agricultural enterprises. As longer leases also became more common, farmers began to diversify and experiment. Thus, in the Southwest of the county of Ayrshire, dairy and cattle was becoming a local specialization.[126] With the support of improvement-focussed landlords who invested heavily on local infrastructure such as farmhouses, hedgerows, drainage, roads and bridges etc, the arrangement was highly beneficial to ambitious young men like

---

[122] Scotland's Places, National Records of Scotland, ordinance survey name books, Ayrshire OS name books 1855-1857, Ayrshire Volume 17, OS1/3/17/31

[123] T M Devine, *Clearance and improvement: land power and people in Scotland 1700-1900*, p117-118, R H Campbell, Agricultural labour in the Southwest, in T M Devine ed., *farm servants and labour in lowland Scotland 1770 – 1914*, 1984, p 59-61

[124] Scotland's Places, National Records of Scotland, Historical Tax Rolls, Farm horse tax rolls, 1797-1798, Volume 1, E326/10/1/229

[125] Scotland's Places, National Records of Scotland, Historical Tax Rolls, cart tax rolls 1785-1798, cat tax volume 1, E326/7/1/18

[126] R H Campbell, *Agricultural labour in the Southwest*, p 58 - 59

John Muir who were willing to take on the risks of managing their own piece of land leased as it was. It became highly profitable especially leading up to and during the American and French wars in the early stages of the nineteenth century. In just two generations under the new arrangements, the labourer and servant had become 'a keen businessman, a man of substance, influential and respected in local society.'[127]

It was during this period, that many aspects of the commercial society envisaged by Scottish theorists such as Adam Smith, Ferguson and Hume started to come to fruition as social transactions slowly became monetised. As more became educated, skills like bookkeeping, mathematics, history, reading and writing were becoming inculcated in the following generations facilitating a working knowledge of banking and political economy. The farmer was actively participating in Agricultural Societies, managing budgets, and negotiating loans and contracts with wholesalers and middlemen. These were the skills passed down to the next generation – John Muir's fifth son David Muir.

David Muir, like most of his siblings before him, was born at Corsehill farm or Crosshill as it was also known, in 1786 as shown on the baptismal entry, as it was also for some of David Muir's first children.[128] David Muir's birth registration entry reads 'David Muir lawful son of John Muir at Corsehill was baptised by Mr Steele January 8 1786, the first entry for the year.[129] Life for David however would prove to be more challenging and less stable than it did for his father whose success appeared to have been achieved with support from Lord Auchinleck who very likely saw him as a valuable asset in his program of modernisation. It would take David Muir much longer to find his own way, staying and working with his parents periodically until he was in his early thirties.

---

[127] Laurance James Saunders, *Scottish democracy 1815-1840: the social and intellectual background*, Oliver and Boyd, Edinburgh, p37-38

[128] Scotland's Places, National Records of Scotland, ordinance survey name books, Ayrshire OS name books 1855-1857, Ayrshire Volume 17, OS1/3/17/31.

[129] 08/01/1786 Muir David, *National Records of Scotland*, (Old Parish Registers, 614 10 48 Stair), page 48 of 145

For a young man like David Muir, trained in most aspects of modern farming, this would mean attending one of the many hiring fairs held at the larger towns which were becoming the most popular means of obtaining a contract or a position. These were held at appointed times during the year usually in the spring or autumn and coinciding with other festivals such as Whitsunday and Martinmas. These were events that quickly evolved to be much more, incorporating all the aspects of a festival day with races, performances, stalls of all descriptions and also a place where a future partner may be met as was the case with the parents of the poet Robert Burns.[130] It is also likely that it was at such a fair where David Muir at age twenty-six met his wife and Robert's mother Christian Paterson aged nineteen.

David Muir and Christian Paterson were married in the Stair parish church 6 December 1812 at the height of the second British American war.[131] This time of international unrest was a boon to the agricultural industry as prices and labour costs soared to an all-time high not to be matched for decades. Milk and other forms of dairy such as cheese were in high demand in the nearby town of Ayr and at the growing urban and manufacturing centre of Glasgow. Other produce such as pigs and grain that would have been raised and cultivated with much of the surplus supplied to the armed forces. There was plenty of well-paid work to be had in this time at the height of the so aptly named 'Agricultural Revolution.'[132]

The Paterson's like the Muirs, were originally farmers at Crofthead for most of the eighteenth century and early nineteenth,

---

[130] Michael Robson, the border farm worker in: T M Devine ed., *Farm servants and labour in lowland Scotland 1770-1914*, p 79-82, Jean Aitchison, 'A study of the servant class in South Ayrshire 1750-1914', Ph.D.., thesis, University of Glasgow June 1998, p35-40, Published by ProQuest LLC 2018 No 10992089, accessed online 25/1/2021, Enlighten: Theses https://theses.gla.ac.uk/ research-enlighten@glasgow.ac.uk

[131] National Records of Scotland, Scotland's People 06/12/1812 Muir, David, (Old Parish Registers Marriages 614/ 10 130 Stair) Page 130 of 145

[132] J D Chambers & G E Mingay, *The industrial revolution 1750 – 1880*, B T Batsford Ltd London, 1966,

passing the lease from father to son.[133] Listed in the 1855 survey of the County of Ayr as the property of the Duke of Portland, it was then in the 1850s, a large property near Tarbolton in the County of Ayr. It remains today in 2021, a well-appointed farm with a bed and breakfast set in picturesque surrounds.[134] Situated about five miles from Corsehill where the Muirs were farming, less than a mile from the village of Tarbolton and about five miles from the town of Mauchline, it was certainly in a location where a young couple would cross paths and in easy proximity to the Stair parish church where people would gather.[135]

According to the tax records for 1797-1798 Alexander Paterson, Robert's maternal grandfather, was levied for four horses or two teams of ploughs indicating a greater than average operation than the usual two or a single team.[136] Christian's father Matthew Paterson is also recorded at her baptismal in 1793 as 'portioner in Mauchline,' a reference to a long family association to Skeoch, a

---

[133] James P Wilson, The Monk's Road to their lands, AANHS Collections, 2nd Series, Vol.1, 1950, p142

[134] https://uk.hotels.com/ho731566432/crofthead-farm-house-mauchline-united-kingdom/?pwaDialogNested=media-gallery see page 63

[135] National Records of Scotland, Scotland's People, 11/03/1762 Paterson, Matthew, (Old Parish Registers Births 619/ 10 106 Tarbolton) page 106 of 272, Alexander Paterson in Crofthead, his son Matthew was baptised March 11th, 1762

[136] National Records of Scotland, Historical Tax Rolls/ farm horse tax rolls 1797-1798, Volume 1/ E326/10/1/211

nearby farming location with a long association to the Paterson family. They were known in the district as bonnet lairds with a relatively small private holding that had long since been divided amongst the heirs.[137] Her father Matthew, who had remarried after her mother had passed away in 1797, was listed as assessed for five farm horses for the years of 1797 and 1798 for his leased farm at Barskimming Mains, just a mile away, indicating a substantial operation in the same manner as his father Alexander.[138]

David Muir and Christian Paterson, however as middle children, family assistance would play less of a role in assisting their way in the world. By age twenty-seven and twenty respectively, their first child arrived, a son named John. John was born in Mauchline in September 1813, the largest town in the district where David was working as a labourer.[139] Their situation would have been a rented room in the town while David offered his services to district farmers. By March 1819, six years later at age thirty-three as the baptismal record for Marion their third child indicates, their small family was separated with Christian living with her in-laws at Corsehill, or Crosshill as it was also known, along with James their third child born in April 1821 also at Crosshill.[140] David, however as the records show, appears to be resident in the parish of Monckton and Prestwick in the town of Ayr some 5-6 miles away. This would indicate a live-in labouring position on a farm highlighting the precarious and insecure nature of work and family for many mothers and younger children who stayed with their in-laws and grandparents who were in more secure situations.

---

[137] National Records of Scotland, Scotland's People, 16/07/1793 Paterson, Christian (Old Parish Registers Births 604/ 20 124 Mauchline) Page 124 of 365, National Records of Scotland, James P Wilson, The monk's road to their lands, p142

[138] National Records of Scotland, Historical Tax Rolls/ farm horse tax rolls 1797-1798, Volume 1/ E326/10/1/200

[139] 19/9/1813 Muir, John (Old Parish Registers Births 604/ 30 82 Mauchline) page 82 of 165, National Records of Scotland

[140] 11/04/1821 Muir, James (Old Parish Registers Births 606/ 30 19 Monkton and Prestwick) page 19 of 410, National Records of Scotland

Two more children followed, William born sometime in 1823 and Robert, the subject of this biography, born unrecorded in 1826.[141] Sandwiched between these two was the birth of David Jr, christened in the nearby parish of St Quivox in September 1825.[142] It appears however that David died unrecorded sometime between 1825 and 1831, his name given to one of the set of twins, named after their parents David and Christian, born and baptised at St Quivox in March 1831.[143] The last two births (not recorded) were Matthew Paterson Muir and Alexander in 1834 and 1836 respectively as indicated in the 1841 census.[144]

From 1821 the family fortunes appear to have taken a turn for the better - both parents appeared to have secured more permanent arrangements on the estate of the Oswald family of Auchincruive on the outskirts of Ayr. St Quivox Parish records for 1834 show David Muir as a family head residing at Mossblown farm, which still stands today, a large complex with a well-appointed farmstead and numerous outbuildings within walking distance of the nearby town of Ayr. The family resided there until sometime in the early 1830s. There is also a suggestion also that the family finances were boosted to some extent, laying the foundations for David Muir to accumulate enough savings to secure passages for his two eldest daughters to South Australia and apprenticeships for the older boys. The use of the middle name Paterson from 1823 with the birth of William suggests that this may well have been due to some inheritance money coming to his wife Christian or some other beneficial arrangement with her family.

Following their tenure at St Quivox, they then took up residence at Springbank near Tarbolton about two miles distant

---

[141] Not to be confused with Robert Muir born October 1828 (Dalry Associate) – father also David Muir. 1841 Census has this family recorded as weavers by occupation. Dalry is also located near Glasgow in a different part of the county.

[142] 18/09/1825 Muir, David (Old Parish Registers Births 612/1 20 66 St Quivox) page 66 of 387, National Records of Scotland

[143] 06/3/1831 Muir, David & Christie, (Old Parish Registers Births 612/1 20 106 St Quivox) page 106 of 387, Scotland's People, National Records of Scotland.

[144] Scotland's People, 1841 Muir David, (Census 619/ 2/ 1) page 1-2 of 17

towards the end of the 1830s as indicated by the 1841 census.[145] Springbank farm, which also exists in 2021, a few miles from the busy Prestwick Airport, was a property of similar size and scope to the Mossblown farm and like many Southwest Ayrshire farms was a family run enterprise with three employed labourers providing assistance.[146]

The 1841 census indicates a large family with the parents and five children thirteen and under living in the family home and very likely assisting with the work. The eldest child John and his wife Mary were in attendance with their daughter and stepson James Stirling who appear to have been visiting for the census. For the rest of the family, William aged eighteen, was listed as an apprenticed joiner and James who is listed as an apprentice merchant, would have been offering limited assistance. Robert aged thirteen therefore would have been his father's right-hand man on the farm learning all the skills associated with ploughing, horse management and mastering the skills of modern farming.

[145] National records of Scotland, Scotland's places, ordnance survey name books, Ayrshire OS name books 1855-1857/ Ayrshire volume 54, OS1/3/54/9, National records of Scotland, Male heads of families 1834 for Parish of St Quivox, CH2/319/1, pp54-56, accessed oldscottish.com

[146] Springbank farm Between the A719 and Ladykirk Burn, seen just before landing at Prestwick © Copyright M J Richardson and licensed for reuse under this Creative Commons Licence.

This is not forgetting the five younger members who would have all been working on the farm in some capacity in addition to attending school. The eldest daughter Marion whose stated occupation was dairymaid, had emigrated to South Australia three years earlier with her mother's stepsister, aunt Jane Rankine (Paterson). This left their mother Christian responsible for the dairying with the assistance of eldest daughter Janet and farm servant Jane Clare, possibly of Irish extraction, aged twenty.[147]

This was a common arrangement for many agricultural labourers who often were able to make a good living and advance their status through thrift, good management, and entrepreneurial skill. As R H Campbell explains, many farms like Springbank were too small to provide a decent living for skilled workers, and so most of the labour requirements were met by the immediate family often complemented with an unmarried servant living in.[148] For much of the nineteenth century arrangements like these changed little as John Spier observed later that century, 'the farmers in most cases do a great proportion of the work; even the wives do the bulk of the cheesemaking ... They work and work very hard ... The dairy farmers themselves, wives, sons and daughters, ... were all year round being worked like slaves.'[149]

With his occupation listed as 'agricultural labourer' it is thus, highly likely that Robert's father David occupied Springbank under a sub-tenancy arrangement while working as a ploughman both on the farm and as a ploughing contractor in the local area. R H Campbell describes this practice named 'bowing,' as specific to Southwest Ayrshire where a local farmer who had leased more than one farm but also had dairy cattle, would prefer to outsource the dairy operation based on a set payment per beast, while he supplied the capital and the supplies such as fodder and feed. As Campbell explains this became a common method for many lesser sons of small farmers to be able to acquire their own lease after a period of

---

[147] MacFarlane's Lantern No. 121 - March 2012, Scotland's People, 1841 Muir David, (Census 619/ 2/ 1) page 1-2 of 17
[148] R H Campbell, *Agricultural labour in the Southwest*, p63, *Report on the present state of agriculture in Scotland* arranged under the auspices of the Highland and Agricultural Society, Edinburgh, W blackwood & Sons, 1878, p62
[149] ibid

bowing and so achieve a degree of social mobility.[150] In this case it appears highly likely that this was the case - with the Paterson family who had a history of holding multiple leases at the same time, also holding the lease over the farm while David Muir and his family occupied the farmstead. This would be a reasonable assumption considering the closeness of the two families, the addition of Paterson as a middle name for two of the Muir children - William in 1823 and Matthew 1830 - and that members of both families emigrated together to Adelaide South Australia in 1839 under the Wakefield Scheme.

Arrangements like these were typical of the continued adherence to the clannish nature of Scottish society but with unique adaptations to the ever-encroaching modernisation of society. Family arrangements such as these often continued in the communities established in the colonies. Such an arrangement would prove lucrative for a hardworking family like the Muirs, particularly with the highly respected skill of David as a ploughman in the district. As a ploughing judge for local competitions his reputation not only had the support of the local farmers but also of the landowners and the local agricultural societies.[151]

As an 1845 article in the Ayr Advertiser suggests, the competitions were not only to show off skills and techniques, they were also an occasion where all classes in the district agricultural communities gathered, socialised and assessed innovative practices and designs. All received recognition from the smith who made the plough to the local dignitary and landowner who in many cases was also the parish heritor, magistrate, and landlord. The 1844 Tarbolton event in which David Muir was a judge, was held on the Montgomerie (Coilsfield) estate on the East Carngillan farm of tenant farmer Mr George Andrew, where all the competitors and spectators were entertained along with local dignitary Mr Burnett of Gadgirth representing the Highland society.

As the ploughing matches indicate, they were community events that reinforced and encouraged collegiality and fraternity with new traditions based on the commercial success and continuous improvement. The Agricultural Societies, and the

---

[150] ibid, p87-88
[151] *The Ayr Advertiser* 1844, Tarbolton ploughing match, page 1.

tenant farmers themselves, as Davidson explains, were a major influence in driving the changes in the rural areas and in the agricultural industry and were emulated by those who emigrated like the Muir brothers wherever they settled.

For a ploughman like David Muir conditions were particularly attractive as a highly specialized craft where many, after a two-year apprenticeship, were inducted as a brother into the 'Horseman's Word' – a secret society modelled on the masons with secret rituals and meetings where a secret word was imparted that worked magic on horses when whispered in their ear. The ploughman, therefore, at least in his own estimation, as a well-known ballad portrayed, was really in charge:

the king that wears the crown
the brethren of the sacred gown
the dukes and lords of high renown
Depend upon the ploughman.[152]

Although, in many respects the 'brains' behind the application of modern farming techniques, the ploughman rarely received any credit. Unless he was a substantial and innovative farmer, his name rarely made the pages of the newspapers, or the membership lists of the more prestigious organisations like the Royal Highland Agricultural Society of Scotland. Those pages, for those who wished to peruse them, were for the higher classes such as the landowners and urban elite who took credit for many innovations implemented successfully by hands-on operators. Ploughman farmers like David Muir were more likely to be associated with a local farmers and agricultural club such as the St. Quivox club where 'matters effecting the culture and management of the farm and dairy' were discussed by farmers and other interested parties.[153]

---

[152] T M Devine, *The Scottish clearances: a history of the dispossessed 1600-1900*, Penguin UK 2018, p193-4

[153] See for example RHASS 1840-49, archive.rhass.org.uk, *Directory for Ayr, Newton, Wallacetown, St. Quivox, Prestwick and Monkton, 1845-1846*, compiled by Charles Lockhart, printed at the Ayr Observer Office, accessed online 18/2/2021 deriv.nls.uk

However, for the women who ran the dairy on many Ayrshire farms, the monopoly they enjoyed over milking and cheesemaking in the county lowlands, reduced their conditions to that of 'black slaves.' Hours were long and the work laborious. The amounts paid to many unmarried daughters as T M Devine shows, were a pittance under a regime of 'family tyranny.' This was surely the motivation for Robert's unmarried sisters to emigrate to Australia in advance of their younger brothers.[154] Their father's advice years later to the 'boys' in Australia just before his death in 1853, ignored the 'girls' who had migrated years earlier and suggests a lingering resentment of his daughters for leaving, their thankless toil for most of their adolescent and early adult lives, typically unappreciated and unrecognized.

It was thus at Springbank farm where most of his childhood and adolescent life was spent where most of the values evident in Robert Muir's later life were formed. Determined by forces often far from home, the reality of Scottish society and its commercialisation, nevertheless, taught early lessons to the adolescent Robert Muir like the importance of hard work, financial skill, and the need to master technology and agriculture to succeed in life like the three generations before him.

---

[154] T M Devine, *The Scottish clearances: a history of the dispossessed 1600-1900*, p195.

Chapter 6

Turbulent Teenage Years

Life at Springbank for Robert Muir was filled with many fond memories, some of which are alluded to in letters to his fiancée just after arriving in Australia in 1853. He thus wrote nostalgically shortly after arriving in Victoria,

> it is a busy time at Stoneyfield[155] getting in the crops, and I think I could enjoy being in the midst of it. It would recall the artless days of childhood when the fragrance of the hay field and the merry chorus of the haymakers made us think we had all on earth we could desire.[156]

Not surprisingly, Springbank was the name he gave to the farm established on the outskirts of Ballarat in 1855. By the end of the 1840's however, family circumstances would be irrevocably changed. The mother had passed away, the father had remarried, and most of the children had left. William and Robert were working in the Americas, while eldest child John, who had been sent to Glasgow well before 1840 to serve an apprenticeship in the Ironmonger's store of Alexander Stirling, was in the process of establishing his own business. The second daughter Marion also had left, emigrating to South Australia as a single woman and second eldest son James had died. This left eldest daughter Janet, Matthew, David, and Alexander with their father, while Christie, David's twin, was living in Glasgow with her elder brother John

---

[155] Stoneyfield refers to a locality now in Monkton and Prestwick close to Springbank farm.
[156] *The Age* (Melbourne) Thursday 13 August 1857, page 6

assisting him with his shirt manufacturing business in 1849.[157] However, the census of 1841 indicates that this may have been planned well in advance anticipating a change of direction for the family away from the insecurity and hard labour of Scottish farming.

David apparently had no desire to see his sons follow the same uncertain career path as himself, sending them to the other side of the world with his blessing. It would be there that he hoped the security that was out of reach in Ayrshire could be achieved. For him, it would only be in the last decade of his life that his occupation is shown as 'farmer' eventually leasing a property in his own right. Interestingly, it came after most of the 'free' family labour was no longer available to him.[158] It came with a recognized status as the marriage of his daughter Christie in 1853 indicates. His title is shown as Esq. and occupation is listed as 'farmer' but still landless and with nothing of permanent value to pass on to his family. However, his initial decision to direct eldest child John away from agriculture and in placing him amongst the commercial world of Glasgow, proved to be the catalyst for the rest of the brothers in changing their status and direction in life.

Eldest son John was initially placed as an apprentice merchant with Glasgow ironmonger James Stirling who was friend of his father's older brother William Muir, a farmer at Campsie in Stirlingshire. John obviously flourished in this position which resulted in a long and close association with their son Alexander Muirhead Stirling who was of a similar age. On the death of Alexander in 1838, John Muir at age 27, married Alexander's wife and his cousin Mary (daughter of William Muir) and assumed responsibility for her son James who would accompany the Muir brothers to Australia in 1853.

An opportunity for John to enter business in his own right arose in 1849, as one of many new entrepreneurs that emerged from the commercial crisis that prevailed from 1846-1849 that had laid waste to many enterprises across the United Kingdom and across

---

[157] *Glasgow Herald*, 29 October 1849, 'Shirt Cutters Wanted' page 2, Friday 27 July 1849, 'Shirt Cutter Wanted' page 2

[158] *North British Daily Mail*, Thursday 17 February 1848, page 4, 'Marriages'

Europe.¹⁵⁹ Commencing a shirt manufacturing company and haberdashery business based in Glasgow, Muir & Co became the genesis of Muir Brothers and the extension of business to the Australian goldfields. However, on his death in July 1874, the listed assets in his will, although substantial at almost £15,000 did not include any land or real estate. However, a small farm near the town of Campsie – Mary Muir's childhood home - of fifty acres is listed under his wife's name at the time of his death in 1874 indicating an inheritance from her father.[160]

Unlike his elder brothers who all progressed into the emerging urban world of commerce, Robert, as his future exploits suggests, attained his goals by the utilisation of skills and knowledge he developed on the farm. This indicates a close and personal relationship with his father as a trainer and a mentor. As his later activity in agriculture indicates, it involved a highly developed knowledge of animal husbandry in addition to plant hybridization, cultivation and ploughmanship. Without any registered qualification in this area, most of this knowledge would have been developed by personal experimentation and experience as well as knowledge passed down from earlier generations under the guidance of experienced teachers. Thus, despite his commercial success on the goldfields in Australia, his most memorable achievements occurred when he returned to agriculture and to the land utilizing inherited skills. Nevertheless, his father saw fit to expand his knowledge taking note of his obvious talent for things mechanical. This resulted in him being placed in an engineering apprenticeship in the nearby town of Ayr.[161] This would have commenced around 1840, and at the age of fourteen, and well-conditioned by years of farm toil, the physical side of the job would present no obstacles. Additionally, the mental aspects would not either, as the young teenage Robert Muir emerged at the end of it

---

[159] *The Commercial Crisis 1847-1848*, D Morier Evans, Letts & Son and Steer, London 1849.
[160] Scotland's People, 1874 John Muir (Statutory Registers 500/ 76) Deaths in the Parish of New Kilpatrick in the County of Dumbarton, page 26, Scotland People, 1874, Muir John, (Wills and Testaments reference SC65/34/19, Dumbarton Sherriff Court, pages 320-330)
[161] Alexander McRobbie, The real Surfer's Paradise, Pan News Pty Ltd, Surfers Paradise Qld 1988, p28

with a thirst for adventure and with a strong sense of self-assurance and confidence.

In one of the rare studies of engineering apprenticeships of the 1840s, William Knox offers a window into a world often characterised by bullying, physical harassment, and often exploitation but also of fraternity and the strict maintenance of customs and status.[162] It was not the ideal place for the physical or mentally frail, but one where the resilient and confident would thrive. Thus, by 1843 as a government study found, the tradition of 'indoor' apprenticeships was a rarity or in rapid decline depending on the district and the industry. A young person entering a trade was no longer bonded to a tradesman but was considered a part of the 'outdoor' system.[163] As a relatively new trade, engineering was a quintessentially modern occupation and so had none of the traditions associated with the older 'indoor' apprenticeship which had been strictly controlled by guilds with their secret traditions and rituals. It would instead foster a sense of independence, requiring working long hours in addition to walking or riding to and from his place of work.

For a young teenager like Robert Muir this had profound implications. It meant that he was not required to live under the same roof as his master or employer. This meant that unlike the old system, where the apprentice became a member of the household for the term of his tenure, he was sustained by his parents and went home at night, receiving a small token wage that increased year by year.[164] For Robert therefore, it maintained the strong link to the church and family and their guiding influence. It also enabled a sense of control over his destiny and more importantly, control over his money.

For a devout evangelical Protestant, as Weber argued many years later, Christian values went hand in hand with the idea of hard continuous physical labour, thrift, restraint, pleasure

---

[162] William Walker Knox, *British Apprenticeship 1800-1914*, Ph.D. Thesis, unpublished, University of Edinburgh 1980.
[163] William Walker Knox, *British Apprenticeship 1800-1914*, p11, Second report of the Commissioners on Trades and Manufacturers, BPPX111, 1843, p26
[164] William Walker Knox, *British Apprenticeship 1800-1914*, p11

postponed and saving.[165] And, as his later correspondence indicate, his protestant religious values were certainly front and centre, at least into his twenties. It also meant that he followed more than one occupation, being trained in engineering while working the farm on the weekends, a trait he appeared to be very adept at throughout his life. Thus, the connection with farming was never broken remaining a reliable and basic source of income throughout his life.

Although widening the scope of interaction for a young fourteen-year-old lad, indications are that the workplace selected therefore would not have been outside of the bounds of acquaintances and fellow church members. John Foster's 1974 study reveals that many employers of apprentices, especially if they were parents of female children, were careful to maintain class and cultural affiliation by taking on boys from respectable families of a similar status and preferably from the same church – a strong characteristic of non-conformists.[166]

There is no reason to doubt that this was not the case with Robert, who at twenty-six and not long arrived in Australia, was unmarried and retained many aspects of a strong evangelical upbringing and respect for customs. This is indicated by his letters to fiancée Flora Cameron as he writes:

> When I pray to our Father in Heaven, I ask him earnestly for two things in particular – first that he may give us grace and faith in the atoning blood of our blessed saviour to enable us to meet him above and sing hallelujahs to his praise and glory; and next I earnestly desire him to spare us a while here for each other before he calls us hence.[167]

It would appear therefore that the church maintained a strong influence over the Muir family and especially the conduct of the

---

[165] Max Weber, *The Protestant ethic and the spirit of capitalism*, first published 1905, Unwin Hyman, London 1930
[166] John Foster, Class *Struggle and the Industrial Revolution*, (Weidenfeld and Nicolson, London, 1974) P-167 in William Walker Knox, British Apprenticeship 1800-1914, p18
[167] The Star (Ballarat) Thursday 13 August 1857, page 2 Supreme Court

children most of whom remained devout members of the church. Notably, eldest brother John appears to have taken on a mentoring role upon the death of their father David in 1853, sending regular communications and spiritual advice to the family in Australia. In Australia, William married into the family of Rev. Adam Cairns, the leader of the Chalmer's Presbyterian Church in Melbourne.[168]

For a devout family such as the Muirs, an apprenticeship in the 'wrong environment' would pose a risk for a young person to be quickly led astray so the placement would have been made very carefully. As Knox points out, apprentices had a bad reputation over many centuries for public disturbance and petty crime. With modernisation providing greater freedoms and less scrutiny and oversight after hours, some were calling outdoor apprenticeships 'the most destructive demoralising thing that was ever introduced into the land'. As one respondent to a survey on crime stated: 'I have known in printing offices myself from that unhappy practice, five out of a dozen that have been either hanged or transported.'[169] Much of this reputation extended back to the disturbances leading up to the civil war, especially in London where the Earl of Essex mobilized 8000 apprentices to his army in 1642.[170]

Robert Muir, as a fourteen-year-old, entered the engineering trade in what Knox describes as a period where roles, and wages and technology were entering an extended period of contest that intensified as the century progressed.[171] However, as late as 1850 many engineering companies continued to promote their services using the old title of millwright, a term derived from the manufacture of milling equipment. However, with the proliferation of steam technology increasing numbers also advertised themselves as general engineers – makers of steam engines and equipment for farming and other heavy and laborious tasks.[172] For some of these firms, as Knox points out, their

---

[168] Muir, W. P., (1993). *A journal and cash book belonging to William Paterson Muir*, [manuscript], State Library Victoria
[169] Report on the Police of the Metropolis, BFPVI, 1828, p. 115 in: William Walker Knox, *British Apprenticeship 1800-1914*, p23
[170] Brian Manning, *The English people and the English revolution*, Penguin Books Harmondsworth UK, 1978, p216
[171] William Walker Knox, *British Apprenticeship 1800-1914*, p313-346
[172] Ayrshire Directory 1851-1852, *Ayr Advertiser*, 1852, Advertisement p15

contracts, particularly in a harbour town like Ayr, included not only milling and farm equipment but also extended to bridges, docks and construction. Nevertheless, as specialization was beginning to define the trade between fitting and turning, Robert's skills were strongly biased towards the older fitting aspect of the trade. The fitter, as Knox explained, in an age without proscribed tolerances, was the person who corrected inaccurate workmanship and assembled and adjusted the manufactured product to working order using hammer, file and saw.[173]

The emphasis on assembly and engineering in Robert's early education and training, is demonstrated in his work in the establishment of the first brewery in Grafton in August 1861. However, his 'fitting' skills were most successfully employed later with breakthroughs in sugar processing with crushing equipment innovations, the design and construction of a new battery in 1880, and Sutton's Sutton Pan Evaporator. These devices were demonstrated around Southern Queensland and the New South Wales Northern Rivers district from 1879 and 1880 by the Muir Brothers, Robert, Matthew, and David.[174]

For Robert, however, in 1845 and nearing the completion of his engineering apprenticeship, a long and prosperous career beckoned. With almost fifteen hundred rail projects in progress and in planning, an engineer would have no trouble in finding a position. Railways were touted as an instrument for bringing moral and social revolution and universal peace as international projects would ensure that the globe itself would soon be girdled. At home in Britain grandiose schemes such as the London underground were well under way with extensions to existing lines proposed in all parts of the Kingdom. Unlike the earlier boom and bust in the 1820s, this massive extension was supported by the innovation and wide acceptance of joint stock companies.

The 'railway mania had sucked in the money of people from almost all walks of life – 'men without houses or homes, clerks at

---

[173] William Walker Knox, *British Apprenticeship 1800-1914*, p336-337
[174] *Northern Star* (Lismore), Saturday 14 August 1880, page 2, *Northern Star* (Lismore) Saturday 8 March 1879, page 2, *Clarence and Richmond Examiner* (Grafton) Tuesday 22 September 1903, 'The early history of Grafton – August 1861', page 8

small salaries in banks and merchant's establishments, (had) openly established themselves as buyers and sellers.' At the top of the heap company directors made fortunes and at the bottom speculators operating in back alleys buying and selling on 'paper' only, as soon as new projects were announced, added to the mania. Unfortunately, it was, as one commentator called it, 'mostly smoke.' Almost half of the proposed projects failed to materialise, triggering the first great stock market crash from 1847-1848 as deposits due on many of the new projects failed to be paid.[175] For a newly qualified engineer like Robert Muir, it was a huge blow and with agriculture not an option, it forced him to look elsewhere for opportunities.

---

[175] D. Morier Evans, *The Commercial crisis 1847-1848, Letts & Son and Steer*, London, 1849, p10-30

PART III

THE AMERICAS

Chapter 7

Emigration: Canada or America?

In 1846, on completion of his apprenticeship and with the country in economic turmoil, at age nineteen, Robert decided not to wait at home for opportunities. With his brother James who had trained as a merchant, now aged twenty-five, they followed many before them of their class and background. Canada was by far the most popular destination during this period, as those with agricultural experience were leaving economic uncertainty to take advantage of the vast amount of good farming land. With many Scottish communities and religious adherents there, who shared their Free Church brand of Presbyterianism, two eager young men in their early twenties would be assured of success.

Canada, as T W Acheson's (1972) study reveals, also benefited greatly from skilled migrants from Scotland from the nineteenth century, stating that they were the leading influence in 'number and importance' in the establishment of manufacturing industries in the provinces of Ontario and Quebec.[176] As Acheson notes: 'they came from an industrializing society in the mid-nineteenth century and came prepared … to function in and to give leadership to the fledgeling Canadian industries.' Their technological superiority offering advantages over other ethnic groups as well as the local population.

Canada certainly made a lasting impression on a young Robert Muir. Making landfall in Nova Scotia, he was particularly taken with the Labrador Peninsular and the Newfoundland Coastline – his first sight of a foreign shore. Memories of this important milestone remain in the suburb of Labrador on the Queensland

---

[176] T W Acheson, Analysis of the industrial elite in: *Canadian Business History*, 1497- 1971, D S McMillan ed., Toronto 1972, quoted in R A Cage ed., *The Scots abroad: Labour. Capital, Enterprise, 1750-1914*, Croom Helm Ltd, Beckenham Kent UK, p64

Gold Coast with its similar coastline and mountainous hinterland which he so named thirty years later.[177] Canada was certainly a suitable destination for James Muir with entrepreneurs and merchants like Isaac Buchanan giving priority to Scottish immigrants both as workers and customers.[178] However, with the technological and manufacturing boom not yet delivering fortunes, it was clear that their stay there would be temporary in so far as Robert was concerned. While no disagreement between the brothers is evident, indications are that James was persuaded by his enthusiastic younger brother to look elsewhere for better opportunities more in keeping with his newly acquired engineering skills.

It was not long therefore, for his attention to be drawn to the southern states of America - the sugar and cotton industries and the employment of new technologies like steam power. Little is known of this venture, but it appears that it did not end well. The movements of the brothers can be traced from the various letters that Robert Muir wrote to local Australian newspapers in the 1860s and 1870s. He describes his experiences in the West Indies and a short probation in America where he learned the skills of sugar production.[179]

In one letter to the local paper while living on Harwood Island in the Grafton district in 1864, he argued that the Northern Rivers and especially the Clarence valley, was highly favourable for sugar growing. Robert reveals that this conviction was based in his experience in Louisiana where he was employed in the Mississippi Delta, the Red River district near Alexandria and also in Texas.[180] His sojourn there would last approximately two years but proved

---

[177] Dawn Hasemann Rix, *Labrador: the early pioneers*, D.H.R. Publishing, Main Beach Queensland, 2002, p7
[178] David S Macmillan, Scottish enterprise and influence in Canada, R A Cage ed., *The Scots abroad: Labour. Capital, Enterprise, 1750-1914*, Croom Helm Ltd, Beckenham Kent UK, p63
[179] Sugar Cultivation on the Clarence River, *Clarence and Richmond Examiner and New England Advertiser*, Grafton NSW Tuesday 5 July 1864, page 2
[180] Sugar cultivation on the Clarence River' *Clarence and Richmond Examiner and New England Advertiser* (Grafton), Tuesday 5 July 1864, page 2, 'About American cane planting and culture', *The Queenslander* (Brisbane Qld) Saturday 25 November 1876

to be a place that did not match well with his expectations of success. His arrival in 1846-7 landed him in an industry that was run on vastly different methods to those he had been raised with, and on an economy of scale well beyond the resources of an individual farmer. It was also an industry coming to grips with the difficulties of growing sugar cane in a climate that was less than ideal and working conditions that were very different to those back in Scotland.

Once considered ideal for cotton in the eighteenth century with its fertile soil, many prospective growers had left in despair. The humid climate was largely to blame with high moisture levels rendering the area highly incompatible. By the end of the century many of these problems were being addressed as sugar cane also began to emerge as a potentially lucrative proposition. The main drawback again was the climate which could periodically be subject to the cold fronts of winter that blew the bitter cold of the northern prairies as far south as Louisiana.[181] Thus, on arrival he discovered a developing industry driven by a high degree of experimentation and innovation and of course, supported on the foundation of slavery.

Richard Follett's account of the state of the industry during this period describes a very different world to that of Scotland. There the plantation owner occupied the top level of society. Living in similar style to a monarch, he possessed vast tracts of land and controlled large populations of workers, the majority of them slaves.[182] On the brink of the civil war William Howard Russell of the London *Times*, from the plantation house of John Burnside's 6000-acre plantation on the outskirts of Baton Rouge, described a striking green vista that spread to the horizon of vast open fields without hedgerows, of the finest agricultural land.[183] This vision of success and obvious prosperity was a result of many years of innovation driven by shrewd and relentless experimentation. When Robert Muir and his brother arrived, a great deal more had already

---

[181] Richard Follett, *Marketing the old South's sugar crop, 1800-1860*, Revista de Indias, Vol. LXV, No 233, pp 117-146
[182] Richard Follett, *The sugar masters: planters and slaves in Louisiana's cane world 1820-1860*, Louisiana State University Press, Baton Rouge, 2005, loc97
[183] Richard Follett, *The sugar masters*, loc93

been accomplished with the introduction of steam technology. After a difficult half century, the most successful were declaring in the 1840s that they had improved their initial yields fifteen-fold.[184]

Over time the plantation owners had developed some interesting methods in dealing with the fast response times dictated by the rapid changes in the seasons. And, despite the evolution of technology, most continued to favour less costly work gangs that could be quickly deployed in planting and harvesting. Descriptions of this cruel but efficient practice are graphically described in Solomon Northrop's account as a slave working in the sugar house on the Red River in the 1840s, in the same time and vicinity as Robert and James Muir.[185] It was a far cry from the conditions of home where workers were employed under contracts and vastly different conditions.

It is very likely that Robert, as he later elaborated in Australia at Benowa, would have gained experience on such a plantation, possibly that owned by the Wise family, one of the families that took advantage of cheap land after the war of 1812. It was in this district that technology such as the steam granulating pan, a forerunner of the Sutton Pan that revolutionized production in Australia for open pan producers, was developed and utilized to great effect.[186] The greatest lesson he would have learned however, would be what Robert Russell concluded, 'free labour cannot compete, in the manufacture of sugar, with better organized slave labour.'[187]

By the middle of the 1840s this was more than just an opinion, it was becoming reality in many successful plantations. Slaves were crucial in the manual tasks where work gangs endured high levels of regimentation and depersonalisation toiling under the overseer's lash. But at the same time, many were also being trained in technical skills, delivering substantial value to their owners,

---

[184] Richard Follett, *The sugar masters*, loc109
[185] Solomon Northup. *Twelve year a slave: narrative of Solomon Northup a citizen of New York, kidnapped in Washington City in 1841 and rescued in 1853 from a cotton plantation near the Red River in Louisiana*, Derby & Miller, Auburn, 1853, pp208-223, accessed digital online version 5/8/2021,
[186] Richard Follett, *The sugar masters*, loc240
[187] Richard Follett, *The sugar masters*, loc1397

providing a major competitive advantage.[188] Mills which were becoming modernized, were employing the latest technology like conveyor belts, steam boilers, evaporators, and vacuum systems, requiring engineers, mechanics, and skilled operators.

A growing number of slave masters like Tean Deballiievre, from the 1830s were so convinced of the compatibility of slavery, that most of the tasks on their plantations were delegated to highly trained slaves. Deballiievre for example had his slave Franquois trained as his accountant while others in the development and expansion of his estate were trained as sugar production overseers, brickmakers, masons, ploughman and carpenters with all displaying a high level of competence and dedication.[189] As Follett argues, this made a mockery of Adam Smith's dismissal of slave labour as counterproductive as forced labour and efficient management proved to be a highly profitable mix. But it showed firsthand to a prospective plantation owner and sugar producer that the ideal of the independent yeoman farmer would not be achievable in America in competition with no labour costs and such highly capitalised and well organised concerns. It would thus remain for Robert Muir, merely an introduction or an apprenticeship into the art of sugar making that would be further developed by experiencing for himself how it was done with free labour in the emancipated dominions and colonies of the Caribbean a few years later.

By the time 1847 had ended, he would leave his brother James and return to Ayr after receiving notice that his mother had passed away. There are no records of this tragic event but it can be assumed with some degree of certainty to have occurred sometime around 1847, for his father, as the public record shows, had remarried in July 1848, to Lillias Allan at Tarbolton.[190] As he states in another Australian letter to a local newspaper in 1874, describing his credentials as a sugar grower and producer, he made several trips to and from America and also the West Indies while taking

---

[188] Richard Follett, *The sugar masters*, loc1462
[189] Richard Follett, The sugar masters, loc1846-1857.
[190] Muir, David, (Old Parish Registers Marriages 619/30 417 Tarbolton) page 417 of 572, National Records of Scotland.

Emigration: Canada or America?

up several positions, including a two year stint on the Orange Grove Estate on Trinidad, all in the production of sugar.[191]

During the hiatus periods, it can be reasonably assumed, he spent farming with his father, assimilating all his knowledge on cultivation, livestock, and finance. It was also likely that he spent every available spare moment researching the possibilities of sugar cane and sugar production in Australia after attending one or more of J D Lang's presentations on Cooksland, the future sugar and cotton production centre of Australia. It is also where he honed his skills as an expert ploughman which were often demonstrated to many in Australia both as a manufacturer of ploughs and as a competitor. With the death of their mother Christina, Robert also took more responsibility for the two youngest boys, David, and Alexander. This appears to have been at the request of his father as an extension of his Christian duty as he reminded his boys in Australia 'to remember the one thing needful' on his deathbed.[192] By 1849 however, it was time to move on. News had come from America that his brother James had died in August of 1849. James

---

[191] Will sugar growing pay in the Southern Districts? *The Queenslander Brisbane*, Saturday 16 May 1874, P5

[192] Supreme Court Cameron V Muir, *The Star* (Ballarat) Thursday 13 August 1857, page 2

appeared to have ended his days on the Ashford estate of the Wise family – a local minor sugar dynasty. He appears to have achieved a respected status among them and judging by the gravestone in their private cemetery was also loved and valued by the family.[193] After settling his brother James' affairs in Alexandria Louisiana, he continued on to Trinidad and the Orange Grove estate where he had found a position as an engineer and overseer.

Robert was one of a comparatively small number that made the journey in the 1840s, as places like Trinidad were certainly not high on the list of desirable locations. The large stream of migrants of the previous century had slowed almost to a stop. There were no more stories like that of his family's Springbank landlord, William Paterson of Ayr, who returned with a fortune and took an elevated position in the community. From 1841 to 1850 according to the returns of the Colonial Land and Emigration Commissioners, only 661 people had made the journey across the Atlantic.[194]

---

[193] See page 80, *James Muir (unknown-1849)* - Find A Grave Memorial Old Wise Cemetery in Woodworth, Louisiana - Find A Grave Cemetery accessed online 4/8/2021

[194] Donald Woods, *Trinidad in transition: the years after slavery*, Oxford University Press for the Institute of Race Relations, London, 1968, p81

Chapter 8

Trinidad and Useful Lessons for The Victorian Goldfields

The turbulent 1840s gave rise to many utopian schemes promoted as offering solutions to unemployment and the unstable social conditions. Among them were those that extolled the value of technology and skilled tradesmen like engineers who would be the leaders of a new utopian world where machines would free people to live a life of ease and comfort.[195] Schemes such as these offered hope to young Scottish men like Robert Muir in the troubled 1840s. One particular scheme promoted by J A Etzler, an anti-slavery campaigner, claimed that his utopian society, that he was creating on tropical Trinidad, would yield an abundance in food and facilitate the development of the arts and individual talents. It would be the salvation of the labouring poor of Great Britain where the slaves would be the machines and steam technology would create a communal fortune in sugar. A wooden railway was proposed under the auspices of the Trinidad Great Eastern and South-Western Railway. Unfortunately, for those attracted by its promise, it all collapsed along with many others in the manic investment bubble during the second half of the decade.[196]

However, as fantastical as it seemed, in the troubled 1840s, schemes like Etzler's rekindled the dream of days gone by for intrepid young men like Robert Muir, who attempted to take advantage of the economic climate and make a sugar fortune. Its main attraction was that it offered the possibility of gaining access to land at a low price considering the depressed state of the market. Still, with Trinidad in a state of flux, this would not be easy as the

---

[195] Donald Wood, *Trinidad in transition: the years after slavery*, Oxford University Press London, 1968, P84-89
[196] Donald Wood, Trinidad in transition, p87

large population of emancipated slaves provided major competition to the outsider, as they also were beginning to gain access to land and to live independently.

The passing of the 1846 Sugar Act that removed protection, had inflicted a terrible blow on the industry on Trinidad. It was the main cause of the collapse of Eccles Burnley and Company, a Scottish company connected to William Burnley, the owner of the Orange Grove Estate and largest sugar producer. Burnley was connected through his son, a director and a major supplier and agent for Trinidad sugar. It had a dramatic flow-on effect resulting in a mini-collapse of the West Indian sugar industry as prices crashed and plantations were abandoned. Selwyn Cudjoe portrays a disaster as 'estates that had been bought with their slaves in 1829 for £63,500 were resold eighteen years later for £3,000.'[197] For an enterprising young man like Robert Muir, therefore, it represented a tempting opportunity especially for a person like himself with some valuable experience already acquired through his time in Louisiana.

Of the 661 Britons who emigrated to Trinidad during the decade, most were like Robert Muir, Scots leaving for a position on the estates. It was an arduous existence where only the tough could thrive, and Robert was clearly one who was blessed with a tough and resilient constitution. Conditions, as Donald Wood explains, were harsher than those they had left. But for a hard worker, promotion was often guaranteed due to the colour of their skin. Those who succeed, as Governor Lord Harris wrote, 'probably is a person whose constitution has enabled him to survive many contemporaries.' It was also, for many British young men, a great leveller as ideas of racial superiority were challenged. Fed a hard dose of reality from the first day on Trinidad, Lord Harris thus painted a bleak picture where 'the overseers are scarcely lodged and fed as well as the negroes, and the coolie on his arrival is certainly no worse off than the lad who comes from a

---

[197] Selwyn R Cudjoe, *The slave master of Trinidad: William Hardon Burley and the Nineteenth Century Atlantic World*, University of Massachusetts, Amherst, USA, 2018 p333

comfortable home in England or Scotland.'[198] For Robert Muir particularly, this led to the development of a less racist outlook than most of his peers when confronted with such bias in Australia.

Working conditions were equally harsh and also no special allowances were made. With slavery abolished there was no colour bar and the majority of those coming from Britain were, as Woods describes, as humble and obscure as the Africans, the Americans, and the small-islanders or creoles. All worked together on the estates.[199] Robert Muir thus briefly describes himself working in the boiling house on the Orange Grove Estate as well as out in the fields as a planter.[200] It is highly likely that he was one of the many recruited for their skills in 'improved methods of cultivation' – a measure that had been encouraged by Lord Harris in response to low profits by the plantation owners and high labour costs in the latter parts of the 1840s.[201]

There were, however, many lessons and skills to be learned on the Orange Grove Estate of William Burnley in addition to the practical skills of the sugar industry. There was also a political aspect that could not be ignored. Although the emancipation of the slave population had occurred over a decade before Robert's arrival, the transition to a free existence was proving to be less than smooth. It offered a unique insight into the travails of a population recently freed from tyranny. This would provide a unique perspective in his sojourn on the goldfields of colonial Victoria a few years later as the diggers sought to establish civil government after the arbitrary rule of the commissioners.

By 1849, when he first took up residence, the industry was at its lowest ebb, and social and political turmoil was a regular occurrence. The emancipation was really nothing more than a purchase of the freedom of the many slaves on the island by the British government, compensating the plantation owners and leaving most of the Africans to fend for themselves. It resulted in

---

[198] C.O 295 Vol 163, Harris to Grey, 1 July 1848, in Donald Wood, *Trinidad in Transition*, p81
[199] Donald Wood, *Trinidad in transition*, p81.
[200] Will Sugar Growing Pay in the Southern Districts? *The Queenslander*, (Brisbane) Saturday 16 May 1874, p5
[201] Donald Wood, *Trinidad in transition*, p81

the scattering many of them all over the island who were following a subsistence lifestyle as squatters. Their rights remained largely undefined as the government continued unchanged and largely unrepresentative consisting of a single house of crown nominees. It was dominated to a large extent by William Burnley, the owner of the Orange Grove Estate where Robert was engaged. For many of the black and brown population, both Burnley and his plantation had become the central focus of mounting anger.

The main reason was that his employer had failed to embrace change. He had cultivated an infamous reputation for frustrating any attempts to modernise the economy or the political and social structure of the island. One commentator in the local paper the *Trinidadian* described him 'as cunning as the fox, and as much principle, compassion and feeling as the vulture, the alligator, and the shark.'[202] Over the decade Burnley, who had never accepted emancipation, waged a long but unsuccessful battle against rising labour costs proposing many failed schemes to entice Indians, African Americans, as well as local immigration within the West indies itself.

One of the schemes designed to attract a better class of worker, lay in the same set ideas espoused by Edward Gibbon Wakefield, that had attracted Robert's sister to South Australia in 1839.[203] Burnley, who was acquainted with Wakefield personally, believed that selling land at a 'sufficient price' was thus an excellent way to entice British labourers to the island as it could act as a deterrent for Africans to ever become landowners.[204] It was most likely the reason why Robert later chose Trinidad over the slave states of Southern USA, as it could offer an opportunity to purchase land. Additionally, it would function as an important classroom in establishing how an independent producer purchasing one of the many derelict estates, could make a profit with free labour. However, as he later discovered, he was just a pawn in a larger scheme by the local sugar monopoly designed to prevent land ownership by small operators of any colour.

---

[202] Selwyn R Cudjoe, *The slave master of Trinidad*, p299-300
[203] Selwyn R Cudjoe, *The slave master of Trinidad*, p156
[204] Selwyn R Cudjoe, The slave master of Trinidad, p156-160

By the time Robert Muir arrived in Trinidad in 1849, the impending disaster Burnley predicted with emancipation and the later sugar act, had resulted in not so much the end of the sugar industry but a fundamental change in the social and political structure of the Island. It would not be long before Robert would find himself engulfed by the turmoil that would erupt a few months later and further solidify his later attitudes towards land ownership, monopolies, and political economy in Australia. While Burnley had seen off many modernisation projects like the railway, which met its end in the British speculation bubble 1846-1848, he continued to fight a spirited but losing battle against the forces of modernity and change.

With the start of 1849, battle lines were being drawn. Resistance to paying rates and taxes imposed by an unrepresentative Legislative Council was becoming widespread among the creole population. With worker unrest also gaining momentum, it was not long before a declaration was made by representatives, that they would no longer obey oppressive labour laws.[205] While this was occurring, Burnley himself was busy trying to put an end to a proposed postal service by the Governor Lord Harris throughout the island.[206]

For many this was the last straw and so by September 1849 Burnley himself was becoming the prime focus for the growing anger of the African population, particularly those that laboured on the plantations including his own. His latest scheme to bring more Indian workers to Trinidad was met with outrage over the threat imposed on their hard-fought wage rates. It sparked a large demonstration of over 6000 people with a large and vocal female element organised by the leaders of the African community in conjunction with many of the leading citizens. Organized to coincide with the debate in the Legislative Council over amendments to the laws pertaining to debtors both small and large, it attracted the large crowd outside the chambers. A large majority of all persuasions viewed the measure as retrograde. But what stirred up the crowd even more were new debtor legislations where small debtors would have their heads shaved and be forced to wear

---

[205] Selwyn R Cudjoe, *The slave master of Trinidad*, p315
[206] Selwyn R Cudjoe, *The slave master of Trinidad* p316

canvas prison garb and endure the lash. This was seen as particularly harsh and degrading towards women.[207]

As soon as it was apparent that the legislation would be passed, the mood outside quickly darkened. A riot then broke out with sporadic violence spreading throughout the island. Some elements began attacking Burley's lordly mansion with plans to burn it down.[208] A disaster was averted however by a sudden change in the weather. The employees managed to put out most of fires and limit the damage, something I am sure Robert Muir would have been involved in. As the violence spread into other parts of the island an increasingly paranoid Burnley began to describe it as a revolution.

The growing democratic climate, however, did little to stop Burnley and his supporters from further diabolical attempts to curtail the growing political solidarity of the black and brown populations. The last, and possibly most devious and reminiscent of the license fee Robert encountered on the goldfields of Ballarat just two years later, was the poll tax proposed in the second half of 1850. It was labelled by Des Sources, the editor of the *Trinidadian* as unconstitutional and described as 'taxation without representation' considering that the proposals for a new constitution had not been discussed or ratified.[209]

But with a liberal minded Harris now running the island, progress toward a more cohesive, multicultural society was gathering pace. Rather than fight progress, Harris commenced an experiment as early as 1846, selling land in affordable one acre lots in areas of high population. It proved to be extremely successful and led to the creation of the first towns and permanent villages outside of the main city, Port of Spain. Most of these however, were in the cocoa growing district, away from the sugar plantations and located in areas difficult to police and away from the influence of men like Burnley. By the time of Robert's arrival, a few were exhibiting structures such as churches and police stations as many more locations were marked for survey in an ongoing

---

[207] Selwyn R Cudjoe, *The slave master of Trinidad*, p320-322
[208] Selwyn R Cudjoe, The slave master of Trinidad, p327
[209] Selwyn R Cudjoe, *The slave master of Trinidad*, p351

program.[210] However, for Robert Muir and others like him, the prospect of earning enough to buy sufficient land for cane growing or even a derelict plantation remained well out of reach. There were very few of his station that were able to accomplish this feat due to the punishing climate and the length of time, but mostly because of the land policy dictated by the Plantation owners.

Much of this was based on their manipulation of Wakefield's 'sufficient price' concept in the legislative council. With the price of unalienated land subject to British government legislation, the quantity was not. This provided an opportunity for Burnley and his supporters to force an increase from a minimum of 320 acres to 680 acres later in the decade. Thus, as Donald Wood put it 'no capitalist in their right mind would consider buying a square mile of virgin forest for sugar cultivation in the depressed conditions of the 1840s.'[211]

For Robert Muir raising the land qualification was a step too far that would set any plans for land ownership back years. At an empire wide rate of £1 an acre he may have been able to scrape enough money together over five to ten years to purchase 320 acres of virgin scrub but doubling that put any dream of owning any well out of reach. He would have to his sights elsewhere for better opportunities. It did for him, however, add another layer of outrage at the injustice of monopolies maintaining their positions at the expense of others, defying the principles of fairness, free trade and a liberal society.

---

[210] Donald Wood, *Trinidad in transition*, p94
[211] Donald Wood, *Trinidad in transition*, p94

Chapter 9

Glasgow, Muir Bros and Australia

The perfect opportunity soon presented itself when correspondence arrived from his brother John inviting him to come home as he had a business proposition. John's clothing business in Glasgow had been performing well and he had been able to increase turnover by shirt and clothing manufacturing rather than just operating primarily as a merchant. With the discovery of gold in Victoria, along with the emigration of Janet, and Matthew to South Australia earlier in 1851, it was viewed as an ideal opportunity to expand even more and for the younger brothers to relocate. This was reinforced by a glowing report from the goldfields early in 1852 from brother Matthew who joined a party of friends and relatives in a venture at Bendigo. As there was little hope for any of them to ever follow in their father's footsteps or to maintain their status in Glasgow, extending the business to the Australian colonies was viewed as a risk worth taking.

Robert's Brother William had also returned to Glasgow possibly some time earlier where he had also entered into business with brother John. The business operated under the name of Muir & Co in premises at 38 Queen Street Glasgow as wholesale clothiers, slop and shirt manufacturers, in a large multi-story building with an impressive front façade.[212] John Muir lived close by in a substantial house located on 12 Ure Place long since demolished and now currently part of the grounds of the Strathclyde University.[213]

The business had prospered since its commencement in 1849, securing a financial accommodation with the large local merchant house and commercial banking company, Dennistoun Brothers.

---

[212] *Scottish Post Office Directories, Glasgow 1851-1852*, National Library of Scotland, p230, accessed online 6/8/2021 https://digital.nls.uk/83871241
[213] Scottish Post Office Directories, Glasgow 1851-1852, National Library of Scotland, p230, accessed online 6/8/2021 https://digital.nls.uk/83871241

When the Australian branch was established in Melbourne and Ballarat it would be a relationship that would have profound consequences on the brothers' fortunes that nobody at the time could have foreseen. At the time, it was a strong endorsement of Muir & Co, having secured the backing of such a large and respected organization that was linked into international banking and commerce at the highest level. It opened many doors in Australia once business was established.

Dennistoun Bros, in addition to consigning large shipments of tobacco, sugar and other bulk staples from the USA and around the world, also extended letters of credit and bills of exchange for export. Muir & Co would be one of the first clients of the Australian branch commencing with a shipment of clothing and haberdashery that the Muir brothers brought with them in October 1852 on the Malabar. The company was formally established in Melbourne in 1853 by Robert Sellar, a Dennistoun relative by marriage, and well-known Australian merchant James McCulloch then a junior partner. McCulloch later became a Premier of Victoria.[214]

The lack of any 1851 census record indicates that Robert arrived back in Scotland sometime late in 1851 or early in 1852. His arrangement for joining the firm of Muir & Co appears to have been organized while in the Caribbean as on his return he did not proceed to his father's farm but remained in Glasgow where he took up residence with his brother John. His youngest sister was also living there just prior to her marriage to David Foyer, a farmer.[215] While he resided there he was trained in the operations of Muir & Co. This arrangement continued up until October 1852 when he embarked on the Malabar for Australia. Letters published

---

[214] *Biography of Robert Sellar Merchant*, 1828-1900, Angus & Rosemary's miscellany of Malvern, accessed online 6/8/2021, http://www.the-malvern-hills.uk/other_history_robert_sellar.htm, Geoffrey Bartlett, McCulloch Sir James, *Australian Dictionary of Biography*,
https://adb.anu.edu.au/biography/mcculloch-sir-james-4075, accessed online 6/8/2021
[215] *National Records of Scotland* (Census 644/1 140/ 18) page 18 of 29, 1851, John Muir, Muir, Christina, (Old Parish Registers Marriages 644/1 440 272 Glasgow) page 272 of 562, *National Records of Scotland*. Father David Muir is shown as 'farmer Barskimming'.

in the Age indicate a close and congenial relationship with his brother John and his sister-in-law Mary as well as their children especially his niece Christina who referred to him as a 'brick'.[216] It was, however, a relationship that soured considerably as the 1850s progressed, due to the financial turbulence encountered later in the decade.

The brothers, William aged 29, Robert 26, David 22, and Alexander 17, left Greenock in October 1852 for Australia on what would be a very long and eventful journey that ended at Melbourne in March 1853. Also with them was James Stirling, stepson of their brother John. The brothers travelled in relative comfort enjoying the privacy of first-class cabins.[217] This placed them all in an esteemed and privileged position among the passengers, at the highest level, giving them the exclusive use of a cook and a steward who attended to their meals and other needs. For the other less fortunate ninety percent, it would be a long hard voyage, with a daily grind of scrubbing floors, cleaning and doing all the other daily domestic chores they would normally do at home.[218]

It did not take long for Robert to get acquainted with the rest of his fellow immigrants, especially the female passengers, forming a close relationship that would prove to be particularly eventful on arriving in Australia. Another Scottish family, the Camerons, were travelling intermediate, which on the scale of class, was above steerage but below the first class enjoyed by the Muir brothers. They were travelling in a family group that included the father Duncan, a son, four daughters and an aunt.[219] According to reports, the Muir brothers were among the principal persons on board.[220] The four daughters of Duncan Cameron caught Robert's eyes from the very first, but it was Flora who became the focus of his attention. This was particularly so as she was in a state of grief

---

[216] Breach of Promise of Marriage, *The Age* (Melbourne) Wednesday 12 August 1857, page 6

[217] Law Report, *The Argus*, (Melbourne) Wednesday 12 August 1857, page 6

[218] *Shipboard: the Nineteenth century emigrant experience: class distinctions*, State Library New South Wales, Class distinctions | Shipboard: the 19th century emigrant experience | Stories | State Library of NSW, accessed 8/8/2021

[219] Supreme Court Wednesday 12th August, *The Star* (Ballarat) Friday 14 August 1857, page 2

[220] Law Report, *The Argus* (Melbourne) Wednesday 12 August 1857, page 6.

for much of the voyage due to the illness and eventual death of her older sister. Robert was very supportive, supplying a ready ear and spiritual consolation for the very religious young lady.[221]

The Camerons were of a similar background and social status to himself having been tenant sheep farmers in Argyleshire in the northern Scottish Highlands. Although Duncan Cameron claimed to have at one stage to have owned over 400 sheep in Scotland, their circumstances in Australia were ambiguous. Unlike many of his station who had emigrated, four years hence he remained a tenant farmer living with his son who owned a farm at Donnybrook about thirty kilometres north of Melbourne.[222]

Deeply religious, sensitive, and delicate having never been exposed to the rigors of farm work, Flora Cameron conveyed a sense of class unlike that of Robert's sisters who had been raised to work on the farm and in the dairy with all the physical toil that it involved. In a letter, Flora is described as having good looks, an amiable temper, a quiet and loving disposition with a beauty of mind and goodness of heart.[223] Portrayed as the most eligible of the sisters, it appeared that Robert was the victim of a clever on-board match-making project by a conspiring aunt, an elder sister and an opportunistic brother.[224] With four single girls and four single and very eligible young men, it presented a perfect opportunity in an environment where the proceedings could be almost totally managed. Considering the disparity in their status while on the long six-month voyage and the likelihood of success with the brothers' commercial venture, it was not long before an engagement in principle was arranged between them by January 1853 – half-way into the voyage.[225]

It was a semi-sincere charade that would endure for the best part of two years while on the voyage and in Victoria by correspondence after they had arrived. Although often filled with

---

[221] Supreme Court Wednesday 12th August, *The Star* (Ballarat) Friday 14 August 1857, page 2
[222] Law Report, *The Argus*, (Melbourne) Wednesday 12 August 1857, page 6, Supreme Court, The Star (Ballarat) Thursday 13 August 1857, page 2
[223] ibid
[224] Supreme Court, *The Star* (Ballarat) Friday 14 August 1857, page 2
[225] Supreme Court, *The Star* (Ballarat) Thursday 13 August 1857, page 2

religious and romantic platitudes, his letters also reveal mixed feelings however, that occasionally indicated his true state of mind. Thus, as he wrote in 1854 'I know dearest, your love for me was not the result of my appearance or my position in the world or I would be very sorry' and earlier, 'God has intended us for each other; but if not, his will be done.'[226] More significantly, the engagement was never officially sealed with a ring as was the usual custom and both parted on arrival at Melbourne without contact. Rather, it was an understanding that appeared to have been facilitated by ongoing business arrangements with her brother and as another letter indicated, a rather open-ended commitment to follow through with the marriage after he had established himself after a few years.

---

[226] Letter dated 3 April 1854, Supreme Court, *The Star* (Ballarat) Thursday 13 August 1857, page 2.

PART IV

THE VICTORIAN GOLDFIELDS

Chapter 10

Trading at Bendigo Amid the Red Ribbon Protests

After embarking at Melbourne in March 1853, the brothers announced their arrival with a public thankyou letter to Peter MacVean, the surgeon who accompanied them on the voyage.[227] Robert, David and Alexander shortly after, proceeded on to the diggings at Bendigo loaded up with as much produce as they could carry – about 15% of the consignment that came with them on the voyage. The remainder was placed into the hands of a local retailer, Wharton, Caird & Little with premises in Melbourne, to sell on consignment for them while the Melbourne branch was being established. William and step-nephew James Stirling remained in Melbourne as commission agents leasing premises at 86 Collins Street. They advertised themselves amongst other things, as a branch of the Glasgow operation: Muir Brothers & Co Wholesale Slop Manufacturers, General Importers and Commission Merchants.

Their first major shipment of over 40 cases and bales of clothing and other goods from brother John arrived in May 1853.[228] The Melbourne operation was diverse, selling anything on commission such as consumables and large vehicles such as drays to the steady stream of hopeful diggers heading out of Melbourne. William, as manager, took a different direction entirely to his brothers, forging long-lasting commercial relationships with the political and business elite of Melbourne. It was a fortunate association with the Australian Freehold Association and the

---

[227] *The Geelong Advertiser and Intelligencer* Tuesday 22 March 1853, page 2
[228] *The Argus* (Melbourne), Saturday May 21, 1853, page 6

banking fraternity in 1854, that stood him in good stead in later years.[229]

The goldfields venture meanwhile, was bolstered with the addition of brother Matthew who had arrived on the Bendigo goldfields with relatives from South Australia the year before.[230] Matthew, from all indications, appeared unenthusiastic about the hard manual grind of gold digging. Having arrived with his sister Janet in South Australia in 1851, he had for a couple of years, gotten involved with the early founders of Strathalbyn - the Rankines and her husband's family, the Sloans and their farming projects. Family accounts reveal that Matthew became heavily involved in the layout of the township, the farms and the church, being elected to the first Committee of St Andrews Church.[231] By the end of 1852 he had left with a party of eight that included his brother-in-law Colin McFarlane, cousin Matthew Rankine, and brother-in-law James Sloan, for Bendigo to try their luck. It did not take him very long to decide not to return with the successful diggers to South Australia but to remain with his brother Robert. Muir Bros had more appeal to a person of his talents than the mud and dirt of the diggings and commerce held out the greater likelihood of success. This was clearly where his talents lay, managing several enterprises on behalf of the brothers until the 1870s.

The two youngest brothers, Alexander and David, however, were more interested in striking it rich and had purchased an expensive mining kit which was valued at £100. This would have included tents, digging equipment, clothing, food and everything required for an extended stay.[232] Approaching Mount Alexander on their long journey to the diggings, they would have been encouraged by signs of civilization with massive road works, construction gangs and drays loaded with road material going back

---

[229] Public Companies, Australian Freehold Association, *The Age*, Saturday 23 December 1854, page 2, The Argus, (Melbourne) Friday 12 August 1853, page 1.
[230] Insolvent Court, *The Star* (Ballarat) Friday 28 February 1858, page 2
[231] Margaret J Roberts, *Reach for the far horizon: Sloan and Muir family history*, Margaret J Roberts, Bendigo, 2000, p87
[232] Insolvent Court, *The Star* (Ballarat) Friday 26 February 1858, page 2

Trading at Bendigo Amid the Red Ribbon Protests

and forth and bridges being constructed. This was in response to a series of protests and a petition over the state of the roads and access to the goldfields the previous year.[233] Arriving on the Bendigo diggings they found it was as lucrative as they expected. In a short space of time all the goods they had carted with them were sold realizing a pleasing profit of £300. This was sent back to William in Melbourne and a second consignment was despatched.[234] With such a promising start a store was constructed on the White Hills diggings.[235]

Nevertheless, after such a good start to their venture, the unpredictable nature of goldmining began to test their resolve. The good rains of autumn were patchy going into winter and by August, the much-needed water sources needed for washing the paydirt either did not run as well as they did the year before or were flooded. The better funded and organized had started to leave for

---

[233] *Resident Commissioner Castlemaine to the Chief Commissioner of the Goldfields, weekly report to 9 July 1853*, C53/7249, VPRS 1189/P0000/00087, Bendigo, *The Argus* (Melbourne) 22 July 1852, page 4, Mems from the Mount, *The Cornwall Chronicle* (Launceston), Wednesday 28 July 1852, page 472, *Petition To La Trobe and Members of the Executive Council, from the Gold Diggers and others residing at the Bendigo Goldfield.* VPRS 1095 P0000/5 1852/2760

[234] Insolvent Court, *The Star* (Ballarat) Friday 26 February 1858, page 2

[235] C J Russell 1840-1860 artist, *White Hills Bendigo (original art) Sept 1853*, State Library Victoria, accession No. H36532

more conducive locations or return to Melbourne until conditions improved. That left many diggers scattered across the northern goldfields – almost 60,000 according to one correspondent, with many of them gathering in the Bendigo and Mt Alexander area with little spare cash to spend on clothing or other merchandise after the license fee was paid.[236]

By July, under constant pressure to pay the monthly thirty shillings license fee, a growing number of unlucky diggers were finding themselves in dire economic circumstances. This was the source of increasing levels of dissatisfaction with the quality of life they were experiencing under the local commissioners. By the end of June, many were calling for the license fee to be reduced to a more affordable level, urged on by the newly arrived 'Captain Brown' from New South Wales. Brown was perhaps the most radical in the growing movement, announcing that conditions were very soon going to worsen as he had heard that Governor Fitzroy had signed a bill at the end of 1851 to cover the cost of bringing 400,000 more immigrants to compensate for the labour shortage caused by the gold rushes.[237] This added a sense of urgency to the ongoing campaign being run by the respected Captain Harrison for social reform to bring the goldfields to a state of local sustainability and independence. His vision was what the Muir Brothers were hoping for, a chance to purchase land and establish themselves. Harrison was advocating the creation of townships that could be surrounded with farming lots available from 20 – 160 acre lots thus allowing for the miners to experience the same degree of permanence and civilization that people enjoyed in Melbourne and Geelong.[238]

The location of the Muir Bros White Hills store, however, proved to be a bad choice for a variety of reasons. Firstly, most of the commercial activity was centred around the Government

---

[236] Bendigo-No1, *The Argus* (Melbourne) 9 July 1853, page 3, *The Senior Assistant Commissioner in Charge at Sandhurst to the Resident Commissioner at Castlemaine, weekly report to the 27 August 1853*, D8889, VPRS 1189/P0000/00087

[237] Bendigo- No1, *The Argus* (Melbourne) Saturday 9 July 1853, page 3, *Sydney Morning Herald*, Tuesday 23 December 1851, page 2 'Legislative Council 22 December 1851'

[238] Bendigo, *The Argus* (Melbourne) Saturday 9 July 1853, page 3

Camp a mile or so distant, and as the local Commissioner pointed out, was not organized in any orderly manner. Competition for the best locations was intense, outpricing newcomers such as themselves. While there was a call to bring some order and have streets surveyed and a township created, it was contentious due to competing interests and so remained under discussion.[239]

Perhaps the most pressing reason was that their chosen site was in the middle of where meetings and rallies were called to discuss the these and other issues of the day. They would not have failed to notice that the almost daily proceedings were becoming larger and increasingly hostile to the police and the officers of the Goldfields Commission. At a large gathering on Saturday July 1, on a wet and windy day, a crowd of about 2500 gathered to compose a petition to the Governor for the lowering of the license fee and other associated matters. It was interrupted by a riot where a prisoner was rescued, and the police pursued back to their barracks under a hail of missiles.[240] A few weeks later, not far from their store, police armed only with batons, were wounded in a shooting by armed criminals in the interception of a dray of sly grog.[241] However, another meeting a few weeks later was most likely the catalyst for a decision to seek greener pastures. A massive gathering engulfed the area as over 6000 diggers carrying a variety of banners were led in by a band of musicians that had marched to their location from many of the outlying areas.[242]

Over the next couple of weeks conditions worsened as pressure was put on many of the store holders who were deputised to issue

---

[239] *The Chief Commissioner of the Goldfields to the Honourable the Colonial Secretary suggesting expediency of establishing a township at Sandhurst*, C53/8096, VPRS 1189/P/0000/000086

[240] Bendigo-No1, *The Argus* (Melbourne) 9 July 1853, page 3, *The Resident Commissioner Castlemaine to the Chief Commissioner of the Goldfields, 53/934, Extract from Assistant Commissioner Panton's Report dated 2 July 1853*, 53/932, VPRS 1189/P0000/00087.

[241] *The Senior Assistant Commissioner in Charge at Sandhurst to the Resident Commissioner at Castlemaine, weekly report to the 27 August 1853*, D8889, VPRS 1189/P0000/00087

[242] *The Senior Assistant Commissioner in Charge at Sandhurst to the Resident Commissioner at Castlemaine, weekly report to the 27 August 1853*, D8889, VPRS 1189/P0000/00087

licenses, to join the diggers in their campaign against the government. This was due primarily by a resolution carried at the meeting that the store-holders should join with the protest by placing a red flag or placard outside their premises with a notice reading 'no licenses taken here.'

The resolution however, incited acts of intimidation on traders like themselves, particularly those who were either unsupportive of the action or refused to wear the 'red badge' worn by the protestors.[243] This was only highlighted by the desperate actions of Captain Brown as a nearby store-holder was assaulted for not contributing to the miners' fighting fund. With a temporary improvement of conditions and the arrest and prosecution of the 'Captain,' tempers subsided a little but the brothers had resolved to move on to places that may provide less risk and greater opportunities.

With news of a rich discovery at Mt McIvor about thirty kilometres to the southeast, the four brothers decided to leave with many others equally hopeful to try their luck at the new diggings.[244] It was a hard and difficult journey across undulating and often steep terrain driving a dray and horses loaded up with all their stock and belongings. *The Argus* correspondent at McIvor describes the straggling crowd 'seen daily coming in with their heavy swags, trudging along weary and worn … numbers also returning from the Goulburn where scarcity of water has nearly stopped operations.'[245] On arrival they found the place in a state of turmoil and uncertainty after the recent robbery of the McIvor gold escort on the road to Kyneton by bushrangers and the wounding of some of the guards.[246]

Although some spectacular finds were reported, one weighing seventy-two ounces, the opposite problem prevailed. With too much water making it virtually impossible to do any digging with

---

[243] *Chief Commissioner of the Goldfields reporting apprehension of Capt Brown, one of the diggers' delegates, D53/8799 3 September 1853*, VPRS 1189/P0000/00087
[244] Insolvent Court, *The Star* (Ballarat) Friday 26 February 1858, page 2.
[245] McIvor and Goulburn Diggings, *The Argus* (Melbourne) Wednesday 7 September 1853, page 4
[246] The Escort Robbery, *Geelong Advertiser and Intelligencer* Monday 25 July 1853, page 2.

safety, it was a problem that would affect the ability to sell their produce within an acceptable time frame and profit margin. Here as well, they found the agitation against the government and the Goldfields Commission was in full swing with many of the agitators there also identifying themselves and their tents with red flags and red ribbons attached to their hats. Matters were also complicated by the confused messages coming from the government camp about police protection and the license fee. Announced by notices nailed to trees and local buildings, it implied that both would be both discontinued pending the results of conciliation with the government on the matter.[247] With so much uncertainty in the air, it was decided to sell off all the remaining stock as quickly as possible and return to Melbourne, which they did in September, leaving with a small profit of £53.[248]

---

[247] McIvor and Goulburn Diggings, *The Argus* (Melbourne) Wednesday 7 September 1853, page 4
[248] Insolvent Court, *The Star* (Ballarat) Friday 26 February 1858, page 2,

Chapter 11

A New Start at Ballarat

Their decision to return was validated by William and James Stirling in Melbourne who had been to the large meeting held in the Protestant Hall on Thursday 4 August 1853 about the issues on the Bendigo goldfields. Present were many like themselves, linked to the Melbourne commercial establishment, who were heavily invested in selling goods and chattels to the miners. The Argus correspondent described it as, 'crowded to excess' with local residents, miners' representatives from Bendigo, the Mayor J T Smith and Lieutenant Governor La Trobe.[249]

At stake, according to the miners, was the viability of gold digging, which was threatened by the inability of many to afford the license fee and the possibility of a violent clash between the miners and the Government. It was emphasised that despite the large amounts collected from the diggers, there was little visible return. Benefits that people would ordinarily expect from being taxed like roads and other services enjoyed in the established towns and cities were not being provided. The points made by the miners' delegates: Jones, Captain Brown, George Thompson, and Dr Owens, were underscored with the implied threat of violence, as Jones summed up by requesting a suspension of the license fee for the month of September. It came with a warning: 'the gold-diggers had declared their determination to resist it even by force of arms.' Others like Dr Owens were calling for the establishment of civil authority like Melbourne where people could go about their business without being harassed by police on every street corner.[250] The threat of a confrontation however, between the diggers and the Government was a very real possibility according to Lieutenant

---

[249] Grievances of the Gold Diggers, *The Argus* (Melbourne) Friday 5 August 1853, page 4
[250] Grievances of the Gold Diggers, *The Argus* (Melbourne) Friday 5 August 1853, page 4

Colonel Valiant's report on his arrival at Bendigo with the 40th Regiment early September.[251] The prospect of being caught in a war zone was sufficient reason for the Muir Brothers to leave and never return to Bendigo or any of the other northern goldfields as the brothers set their sights on Ballarat as a source of easier opportunities with less risk to life and limb.

The results of the subsequent Government investigation into the miners' grievances triggered by the recent events, was published on November 1st, 1853, just before the Robert and Matthew left for Ballarat. Its release was eagerly anticipated by almost everyone in the colony and was generally well received. Its most important finding for the miners was that it recognized that the license fee was unaffordable for many and so legislated a significant reduction to a reasonable 40s for three months replacing 30s for one month.[252] While it did not fall to the ten shillings per month that the miners were requesting, it did fall far enough to increase the appeal of digging once again to the large numbers now coming to Victoria from overseas and within the Australian colonies.[253]

Significantly, the report acknowledged that the basic problems in the northern fields were the lack of new gold discoveries, the unprecedented stream of population and the lack of an inclination to settle down.[254] As the brother's experienced first-hand, the White Hills and McIvor experiments while not altogether complete failures, had exposed the 'shifting' nature of gold digging and the associated difficulties involved in getting the location right. Although up to 60,000 miners were in the district as the protestors pointed out, many of them were scattered far and wide in obscure gullies and creeks all over the district. It consequently forced storekeepers, in some cases, to become roving tinkers like the

---

[251] APPENDIX C. Letter from Lieutenant Colonel Valiant to the Colonial Secretary Melbourne, Victoria, 10 October 1853, *Report of the Select Committee of the Legislative Council on the Goldfields*, VPARL1853-54NoD8gfieldscommreport.
[252] Carboni Raffaello, *The Eureka Stockade, the consequence of some pirates wanting on the quarter-deck a rebellion*, Carboni Raffaello, Melbourne, 1855, p5
[253] *Report of the Select Committee of the Legislative Council on the Goldfields*, VPARL1853-54NoD8gfieldscommreport.
[254] *Report of the Select Committee of the Legislative Council on the Goldfields, 1853.*

NSW Commissioner Hardy who highlighted these problems in the collection of license fees.[255]

At Ballarat, however, the 'healthy tendency to settlement' was progressing as the Government hoped it would. The new scale of fees as well, were directed at encouraging the diggers to take out licenses for longer periods and thus encouraging the creation of permanency. As the Goldfields Inquiry report stated: 'by granting such advantages, and by making the proposed reduction to those who take Licenses for the longer period, your Committee trust that ere long the evils hitherto attendant upon the wandering and unsettled habits of the Miner, may be removed.'[256]

For the Muir brothers, and particularly for Robert, Ballarat also held out far more potential for the attainment of achieving the goal of gentleman or yeoman farmer. The Government report indicated a very different environment at Ballarat to that of Bendigo where the nature of mining was more conducive to small scale puddling ventures that were widely dispersed across the district. This was obvious from the tone and evidence tendered by the Ballarat delegates to the recent inquiry - there was no revolutionary and violent rhetoric. Rather, the aims of Sylvester and Dr Carr who were the Ballarat delegates, were about securing local independence through the creation of local government and a municipality. Their evidence was a reinforcement of an earlier petition that the Ballarat locals had presented to the Government in September calling for local government, roadworks, liquor licensing and making land available for permanent settlement.[257]

In addition, for a group of entrepreneurs like the Muir Brothers, Ballarat also offered the ideal opportunity to establish themselves in a growing township that was already surveyed. Moreover, awash with government money being spent on infrastructure as well as a booming gold industry, it would have appeared as an opportunity too good to resist. At the end of August with an estimated

---

[255] J. R. R. Hardy, *Squatters and gold diggers, their claims and rights*, Piddington, Sydney, 1855
[256] *Report of the Select Committee of the Legislative Council on the Goldfields, 1853*
[257] *Report of the Select Committee of the Legislative Council on the Goldfields 1853*, item 1610 – 1623 p74, 1343 p60, *The Argus* (Melbourne) Tuesday 6 September 1853, page 4

population of just over 10,000, tenders were being called and a significant amount of construction was already under way in the district.[258] A new courthouse and gaol, new police barracks, military barracks, stores, kitchens and other significant buildings in Ballarat were part of a government building boom. It was clear that this was indeed destined to be a major and permanent centre of population.[259]

The main attraction, however, was the spectacular results from the shafts being sunk along the Yarrowee valley and the Eureka leads, all situated within a one-to-three-mile radius where yields had increased four-fold in just a few weeks. One claim worked by a party of five in the Canadian Gully reported 826 ounces alone on 26 August while another nearby reported 919 ounces for the week.[260] The Prince Regent's Gully, just over a mile from the Government camp and the township, was highlighted as being the richest of them all, just as new areas were also being opened up at Winter's Flat and Magpie Gully.[261] The reports that were coming from the press from early August 1853 were suggesting that these were not lucky finds but could be a viable long-term propositions. Thus for a firm like Muir Brothers trading in large quantities of dry goods and haberdashery, it offered the right conditions for establishing a new venture.[262]

More importantly, there was less dissatisfaction in the air and few instances of the monster protest meetings at Bendigo and across the Northern Goldfields.[263] The resident Commissioner's reports for July and August indicate that compliance rates were

---

[258] *Department of the Commissioners of the Goldfields, return on the number of licenses to dig issued at the various goldfields, also the estimated population for July 1853*, VPRS1189/P/0000/000086

[259] *To the Senior Assistant Commissioner Ballarat, from Henry Bowyer Lane Clerk of Works 6 June 1853*, (copy ne ref allocated) VPRS1189/P/0000/000086

[260] *Resident Commissioner Ballarat to the Chief Commissioner of the Goldfields, Weekly Report to 27 August 1853, (copy) C8771*, VPRS1189/P/0000/000087

[261] *Resident Commissioner Ballarat to the Chief Commissioner of the Goldfields, Weekly Report to 23 July 1853*, 53/31, C7874, VPRS1189/P/0000/000086

[262] *Resident Commissioner Ballarat to the Chief Commissioner of the Goldfields, Weekly Report to 6 August 1853*, (copy) C8111, VPRS1189/P/0000/000086

[263] *The Chief Commissioner of the Goldfields to the Honourable the Colonial Secretary, weekly report to 20 August 1853*, D 53/8790, 53/372, VPRS1189/P/0000/000087

very high, even before the reforms, as more were taking out their licenses than in previous months. At the Creswick Creek diggings, the inspectors had reported that there was one hundred percent compliance.[264] While supportive of their Bendigo colleagues, the Ballarat diggers were clearly led by men who were happy to work with the officials in discouraging disturbances. Offering themselves as deputies and encouraging the payment of licenses by posting notices to that effect around the diggings, they maintained a sense of industrious order as they waited for the results of the government inquiry.[265] Thus, on arrival the Muir brothers found the favourable reports were substantiated with more than a few Government buildings in various stages of completion on the township which was dwarfed in size and scope by the busy diggings along the river flats.[266] The locality on the 'flat' was a sea of tents and mining activity, while a permanent road to Buninyong was in the process of being constructed to replace the temporary track that was being taken over by mining claims.[267]

More importantly, they also discovered that there were many good sites available to lease very close to the diggings and the population had grown only slightly, as many of the unlucky diggers in other locations had not yet rushed the area. There was, as they quickly discovered, room for an opportunist firm like Muir Bros to get established early. The brothers acted quickly on the good news, transporting themselves and approximately £1800 worth of stock to Ballarat securing a site at the epicentre of activity. On the intersection of the new Main Road and the Melbourne Road, it was within a stone's throw of the now famous Prince Regent's lead and less than 100 yards from Bakery Hill where the Eureka rallies were

---

[264] *Resident Commissioner Ballarat to the Chief Commissioner of the Goldfields, Weekly Report to 23 July 1853*, C8771, VPRS1189/P/0000/000087

[265] *Resident Commissioner Ballarat to the Chief Commissioner of the Goldfields, Weekly Report to 23 July 1853, 3 September 1853*, 53/191, C8771,53,250 D11093 VPRS1189/P/0000/000087

[266] Insolvent Court, *The Star* (Ballarat) Friday 26 February 1853, page 2

[267] *Resident Commissioner Ballarat to the Chief Commissioner of the Goldfields, Weekly Report to 24 September 1853*, D11096, *53/105* VPRS1189/P/0000/000087

A New Start at Ballarat

held.²⁶⁸ It proved to be a successful venture, making an almost 100% profit on their goods in less than twelve months.²⁶⁹

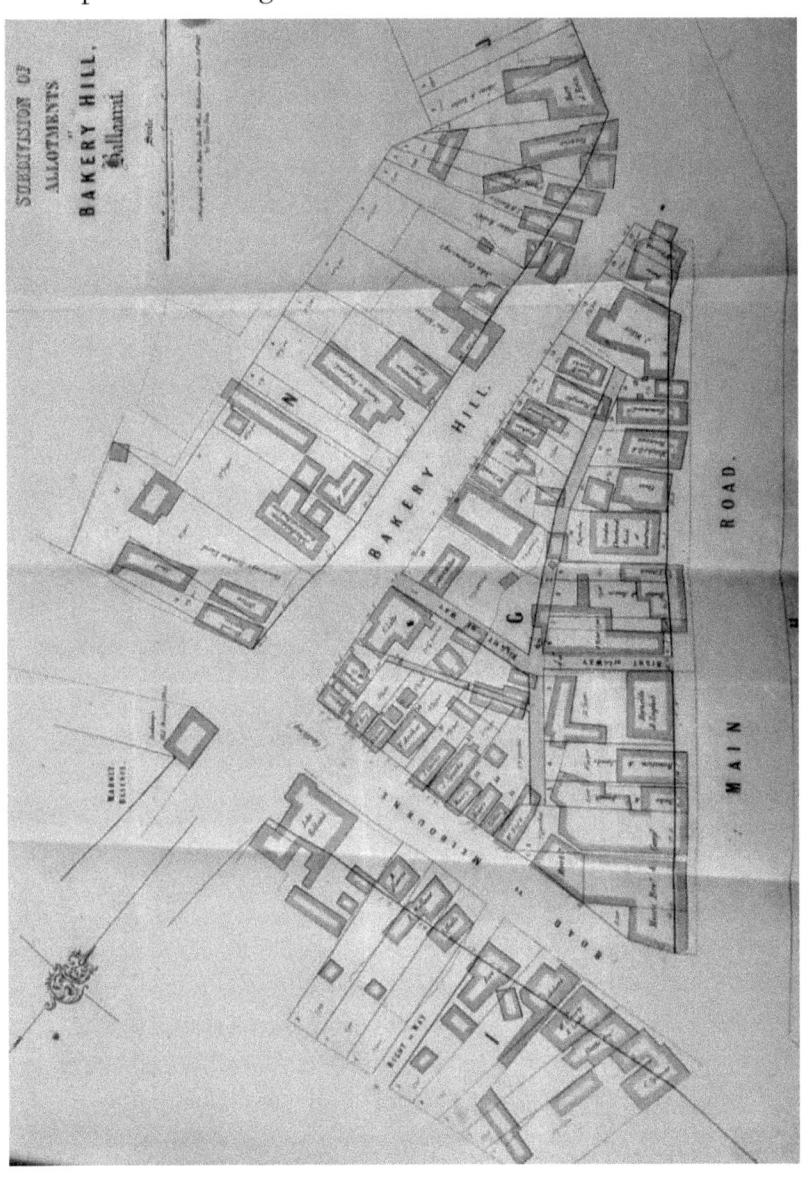

---

²⁶⁸ Map of Bakery Hill precinct 1857 with Muir Bros site on the corner of Main Road and Melbourne Road, Victorian Public Records VPRS 2500 P0000/1 Ballarat Municipal Council Letters Inward January-Dec 1857
²⁶⁹ Insolvent Court, *The Star* (Ballarat) Friday 26 February 1853, page 2

A New Start at Ballarat

Shortly after arriving, their confidence in the future of Ballarat was further supported by proposals, despite a furious campaign against it, to wind down administrative functions at Buninyong, which had served as the main legal and administrative centre for the district, and relocate them to Ballarat.[270] The confidence of the brothers was bolstered further by the proclamation of a notice of intent from the Government early December, to also enforce the termination of pastoral licenses where they may infringe on mining activity.[271]

As December began, the news of the astounding wealth being achieved along the Canadian Gully and the Gravel Pits lead attracted many more traders and storekeepers to the area, quickly occupying the vacant lots along both sides of the new road to Buninyong.[272] Thus, Muir Brothers, under the local management of Robert and Matthew had arguably secured *the* prime location at Ballarat with a wide frontage on all access roads to Melbourne, Geelong, Buninyong, and to the Township of Ballarat, setting themselves up for an exceedingly prosperous and successful four years. It would have appeared to them, with so many advantages in the new location, that the fickle nature of the goldfields had been left far behind at Bendigo.

---

[270] *To His Excellency Charles Joseph La Trobe Esquire Lieut. Governor of the Colony of Victoria, the Humble petition of the Landholders and Inhabitants of the Town of Buninyong*, 8 November 1853, Dec 19/53, VPRS 1189/P/0000/000088
[271] *Chief Commissioner of the Goldfields to James Cloke Solicitor General enclosing copy of Proclamation relative to Termination of Pastoral Licenses in Vicinity of the Goldfields*, 53/607, VPRS 1189/P/0000/000088
[272] *Resident Commissioner Ballarat to the Chief Commissioner of the Goldfields Weekly Report to 3 December 1853*, 53/12677, VPRS 1189/P/0000/000089

Chapter 12

Off the Leash and finding a voice

The more stable conditions at Ballarat were vast improvement to that of the Bendigo field. There, basic civic services barely existed as a coherent plan for permanent settlement remained under discussion. Relocating to an area that had more advanced facilities and provided more certainty, would have been a great relief to Robert Muir and his brothers. They had risked not only their own fortunes but also that of their brother John back in Glasgow. For John Muir, it was an even greater gamble, fully trusting his business to the entrepreneurial skill of his much less experienced younger brothers. Unfortunately for all of them, it wouldn't be long before the relative tranquillity would be threatened as the miners' movement gathered a new impetus and local troubles began to raise fresh concerns.

As 1854 commenced, it was clear that a new feeling was in the air and once again it was like in 1853, ignited at Bendigo and quickly spread across the goldfields. The first stirrings of change interestingly, came with the survey of the proposed Sandhurst township in response for some order to be imposed on the haphazard growth of stores around the Government Camp. On arrival there to discuss proposals in December 1853, the survey party led by the Colonial Secretary and Andrew Clark, the Surveyor General, found themselves embroiled in a new series of rallies and protests based on civic issues. With concessions on the license fee achieved, the new focus was on securing political, social and individual rights – or the integration of the mining communities into the social and political framework of the rest of the colony.

The agenda was earlier declared publicly by the newly formed 'Diggers Congress' in December 1853 at Bendigo at a large rally of over 2000. The congress included diggers on the Ballarat fields like Henry Hollyoake, brother of well-known English chartist George Hollyoake, who attended as representatives.[273] The issues were subsequently followed up with the Melbourne survey party at a gathering in Bendigo where local elder Angus MacKay declared that constant unrest would continue until the franchise was extended to the miners as well as all the privileges enjoyed by the other members of the community.[274]

Ballarat however, clearly had progressed much further in this direction, with plans for the ongoing development of the township now well advanced, although the political dimension was yet to emerge to the degree that it had in Bendigo. In February 1854 notices were thus gazetted for roads to be improved and laid out for the Ballarat township, and an updated and precise description of boundaries were advertised.[275] By July 1854, a campaign to have a hospital erected on the township was well under way, led by the Resident Commissioner Robert Rede, the arch-villain of Eureka. This was part of a wide ranging civic initiative begun in the latter part of 1853, to implement systematic sanitation measures and other local regulations for weights and measures and licensing already in place in other colonial towns.[276] All this was music to Robert Muir's ears and despite the incessant rumours and unrest, it was confirmation that he and his brothers had made an excellent decision in relocating to Ballarat.

At Ballarat Robert was the elder brother and person in charge of the local business. He was also managing the day-to-day running of things. Without the telegraph, which would not make an appearance until the end of 1856, he was endowed with a great amount of trust and personal discretion to take advantage of the

---

[273] *Report by Resident Senior Commissioner Sandhurst to Colonial Secretary* 24/12/1854, D53/12.922, D12.295, VPRS 1189/P0000/Unit 000089

[274] Frank Cusack, *Bendigo: a history*, Heinemann Melbourne, 1973, p99, Bendigo, *The Argus* (Melbourne) Thursday 19 January 1854, p5

[275] *Description of the boundaries of the Ballarat Township Reserve*, W K Wright, Chief Commissioner of the Goldfields, (Memo no ref) Gazetted Feb 54, VPRS 1189/P0000/Unit000090

[276] *Resident Commissioner Ballarat to the Chief Commissioner Melbourne, 11 July 1854*, 54/170, VPRS 1189/P0000/000091, *Chief Commissioner's Report to Colonial Secretary W/E 10/12/1853, C53/9933, A C Cruikshank application for Inspector of Weights and Measures & Slaughterhouses 4 October 1853*, VPRS2500 P0000/89/C53/9933

vast number of opportunities. Ballarat was far enough away to avoid any immediate oversight of William in Melbourne and with four to six months delay in the exchange of information with John in Glasgow, Robert was left with a free hand. Any doubts the brothers may have entertained about his abilities, however, were dispelled after the first financial year's accounting. The books showed a huge profit of £3153.[277] And there was every sign that the large profits would continue for the foreseeable future, as there was no sign of the gold diminishing in their highly lucrative location. Nevertheless, from the start of 1854, there were worrying signs of increasing levels of social disturbance as the locality began to be keenly contested by rival factions of English and Irish. Reminiscent of their White Hills experience, the Muir Brothers found themselves once again at the epicentre of mayhem that periodically spilled over into all the surrounding areas.

Not long after setting up in November 1853, violence broke out close by between Irish and English diggers over a disputed claim. A drainage ingress issue, which greatly inflamed matters, extended the ongoing confrontations, raging for almost twelve months. A serious outbreak of the dispute in March 1854, involved over 1000 combatants, a shooting and an attempted rescue of a prisoner by the angry mob. With the police overwhelmed, order was only restored by the intervention of the military. The disturbances continued thereafter on and off until the Eureka Uprising twelve months later.[278] The Brothers discovered to their dismay that they were wedged between the two warring factions. To the north east was the territory of the Irish known as the 'Tipperary Mob.' Their territory extended from the rear of their premises at Bakery Hill, along the rather patchy Eureka Lead for approximately 2 miles. Controlling the richest leads and inspiring a great deal of ethnically

---

[277] Insolvent Court, *The Star* (Ballarat) Friday 26 February 1853, page 2
[278] *The Geelong Advertiser and Intelligencer*, 27 August 1853, Supplement, page 1, Meetings at Ballarat, *Resident Commissioner Ballarat to the Chief Commissioner of the Goldfields, Weekly report to 10 December 1853, 53/202*, VPRS 1189/P/0000/000089, *Resident Commissioner Ballarat to the Chief Commissioner of the Goldfields, Reporting a Serious Disturbance that had taken Place at the Ballarat Goldfields* 14/3/1854, 54/2796, 54/59, VPRS 001189/P0000/Unit000090, Weston Bate, *Lucky City*, p51-55, p276 notes

based envy, were the English whose run of amazing luck seemed never ending. Their claims extended from below the Commissioner's camp along the river running north to south, passing immediately by front of the store.[279]

Not deterred however, by the end of 1854, amid all the conflict, Muir Bros. had completed their first major project of the Ballarat enterprise – the construction of a large permanent structure on their prime allotment. It was described by the local correspondent for the Melbourne Age as 'a splendid warehouse of magnificent proportions ... constructed of corrugated iron ... on the flat near the gravel pits, by the Muir Brothers.'[280] Named the Exhibition Mart, with a frontage of 80 feet on Main street and 160 feet on the Melbourne Road, it was the largest of its kind on the diggings and possibly in the district, providing the financial base from which

---

[279] Carboni Raffaello, *The Eureka Stockade, the consequence of some pirates wanting on the quarter-deck a rebellion*, Carboni Raffaello, Melbourne, 1855, p, Diggings News, *The Age* (Melbourne) Friday 9 March 1855, page 5, Advertising, The Star (Ballarat) 25 September 1856, page 3
[280] Ballarat, *The Age* (Melbourne) Saturday 30 December 1854, page 4

they rapidly expanded during the next three years.[281] The building was extended and renovated with large advertisements a central feature of every Saturday newspaper, before it was sold in 1857. The site can be found in Ballarat today on the opposite side of Stones Corner on Main Road, as a multi-fronted business and office building, now modernised, at the eastern end of the Bridge Mall.[282]

It was a prudent decision made amid growing tensions between competing commercial interests on either side of the Yarrowee River. On the western side was the township where the freeholders lived and where most of the Government funds were being spent. On the eastern side was the spectacular prosperity of the rich gold leads and the accompanying growth of the commercial interests servicing the diggings. With the recent removal of administrative functions from Bunninyong to the Ballarat Township however, a distinct impression was emerging that the township was the future. Being aware of the fickle nature of gold digging, which could end at any time, visionary local investors like Robert Muir, would have therefore, been foolish to ignore its growing importance. This, therefore, was where Robert privately directed his attention as a developing set of conflicting issues around its location created both headaches and opportunities.

Sitting high and dry on the western escarpment, it was the freeholders who were the primary beneficiaries of emerging civic developments during 1854. This growing sense of privilege and difference, was creating a divide that would in just over twelve months later, take up a large proportion of Robert Muir's time and resources and challenge loyalties and priorities. In September 1854, however, he found himself in a campaign with other storekeepers in the diggings, against landowners in the township. A titanic struggle for local hegemony and trade had broken out between the two factions. Drawing in the colonial government as the arbitrator, it was here that Robert began his career as a local advocate arguing

---

[281] *Lucky City*, Weston Bate, p101.
[282] 2022 photograph of Exhibition Mart Site with Bakery Hill in the background, p112

the case for his fellow storekeepers on government land on the 'other' side of the river.

The new local township boundaries recently established, determined that the eastern border was the Yarrowee River. This immediately created a problem for storekeepers who had erected stores and other trading establishments on crown land on the western side. With some of them permanent structures, they were deemed too close to the surveyed and sold lots in town, just over one hundred metres away. A movement quickly developed within the township to pressure the Government stop the encroachment of lessees with their competitive advantage getting any closer.[283] This was quickly countered by a deputation of the leading storekeepers in the diggings comprised of their leading men such as Robert Muir. Their main argument was that the stores merely followed the mining activity for convenience. This came with the added assumption that the rich leads under excavation were all headed in the same direction – into the township and there was nothing anyone could do to stop it.

There was even speculation that much of the private township land may have to be purchased back by the Government and the Government camp re-located. A compromise was subsequently reached where Hotels would not be constructed inside a half a mile from the township boundary and stores a quarter of a mile. This conveniently left the exhibition Mart just compliant by approximately 100 yards. However, this rule was overturned early in 1855 by strong lobbying by Robert and his fellow storekeepers on the new Geelong Road, as the mining threat continued to expand, threatening to engulf the Government Camp.[284] Meanwhile, amid all the unrest, Robert Muir, with a large and ever-increasing cash surplus burning a hole in his wallet, was eying opportunities on enemy territory on the other side of the river. However, rather prudently, he decided to bide his time as other concerning matters began to assert themselves.

The visit to Ballarat in August 1854 by the new Lieutenant Governor Charles Hotham and his wife, had generated an

---

[283] Ballarat, *The Banner* (Melbourne) Friday 22 September 1854, page 7
[284] Ballarat *The Age* (Melbourne) Wednesday 21 February 1855, page 3

exceedingly positive mood. A rousing speech to one of the largest crowds ever seen had raised hopes that improvements to the diggers living and working conditions was close at hand. It led many to assume that the positive dialogue begun with his predecessor La Trobe, would continue after the events of 1853. Discussions and negotiations, characterised by brinkmanship on both sides, had nevertheless, been productive, delivering the October 1853 Bill that reduced the license fee and amendments to the Gold Act. La Trobe had also indicated, before he left the colony, that more reforms would follow. Matters under discussion were the appointment of local magistrates from the ranks of the goldfield's residents and the appointment of Goldfields nominees to the legislative council.[285]

The visit followed a rally in Geelong where Hotham proclaimed that he would not neglect the peoples' interests, a gesture that inspired hope, particularly among the diggers and storekeepers on the eastern side of the river. Seeing so many government buildings under construction in the township over the past twelve months, had created a growing impression that the Goldfields Commission was more interested in the preservation of their jobs and comfort than the needs of the miners. It was an enduring issue that formed a large part of the evidence presented to the 1853 inquiry and the Royal Commission instituted in November 1854. So, despite the rousing acclamation of the new Lieutenant Governor, it was becoming clear, as 1854 unfolded, that he was on borrowed time to address the concerns of the goldfields population.

---

[285] Ballarat, *The Age* (Melbourne) Monday 13 November 1854, page 5

Chapter 13

Capitalizing on the Eureka Chaos

Barely a few weeks after the official visit, Robert would have noted with dismay that things did not transpire as the diggers were expecting. The reforms to the 'gold laced gentry and useless officials' resulted in one or two from Ballarat being dismissed. But expected changes that would lighten the administrative burden and encourage the further development of local mining did not eventuate.[286] There were also none of the encouragements to buy land and settle down that dominated the inquiry the year before. Matters had taken a decidedly hostile turn as inspections were stepped up, forcing the Muir Brothers at the Exhibition Mart and the other main road storekeepers along with the diggers, to endure the indignity of police entering their premises twice a week. These harsher measures were an ultimately futile attempt to address a perceived financial crisis due to the drop in revenue with the fee reduction and other budgetary shortfalls.

Meanwhile at the Exhibition Mart, a noticeable drop in business from the Irish diggers on the Eureka lead, contrasted with the ongoing activity and continued prosperity on other parts of the diggings. The brothers would have had many discussions with Carboni Raffaello, the well-known author of the first account of the Eureka Stockade over its dire state. Raffaello referred to them as his neighbours, 'to whom I am personally known long ago having been their neighbour on massacre hill Eureka.' Muir Brothers after the rebellion, were appointed by Raffaello, as authorised distributors of his book at ten shillings a copy, a service gratuitously executed, contributing half a crown to local charities from the proceeds.[287]

---

[286] Weston Bate, *Lucky City*, p55-56.
[287] Carboni Raffaello, *The Eureka Stockade; the consequence of some pirates wanting, on the quarter-deck, a rebellion*, Melbourne 1855

Matters deteriorated further as September progressed with the arrest of a digger for being a day overdue with his license renewal. It was however the arrest of Frank Carey and the six-month sentence over the sale of two glasses of ale had the diggers incensed.[288] For many on Eureka, talking over a drink was all there was to do, as the digging on the Eureka lead had stopped. As Weston Bate reminds us – 'for a five- or six-week period in September and October … not a hole was bottomed.'[289] As October began, the burning of the Eureka Hotel and its aftermath created an indelible impression that the justice reforms suggested by La Trobe before he left the colony, were as far away as he was. The following investigation reinforced a profound sense that the local law was with the evildoers as the victim was painted as the perpetrator of the affair. Thus, as the month wore on, Robert and his brothers could not have ignored the growing crowds appearing almost daily just a hundred metres from his door and their increasing sophistication and level of organization. There was a sense that change was in the air especially with the announcement that a Royal Commission was appointed to inquire into the management of the Goldfields.

The Ballarat Correspondent for the Age voiced the feeling of many that began with the miners in Bendigo and the Ovens twelve months before, that the Goldfields Commission era was drawing to a close – that 'the system itself is vicious and ought not to be allowed to exist any longer.'[290] However, this did nothing to halt the scaled up license inspections that were imposed on the successful as well as the increasingly destitute Irish diggers on the Eureka lead. In addition, the heavy-handed approach was now being extended to the storekeepers and builders of permanent structures on crown lands as well. One incident that raised the ire of many storekeepers was the unreasonable removal order of a building on a lot where a permanent structure had been erected. The seller was given just 24 hours for its removal or face prosecution.[291] This, more than anything else, reinforced the

---

[288] Weston Bate, *Lucky City*, p56.
[289] Weston Bate, *Lucky City*, p55.
[290] Ballarat, *The Age* (Melbourne) Saturday 4 November 1854, page 5
[291] Ballarat, *The Age* (Melbourne) Monday 13 November 1854, page 5.

tenuous nature of living under Goldfields Commission administration. It very likely became a catalyst for Robert Muir to consider more secure and permanent arrangements.

Although the Exhibition Mart was in a highly sought-after location and the profits were guaranteed by the continued prosperity of the Canadian Gully, Red Hill and Prince Regent leads, there were more pressing disincentives to further expansion in the diggings. The increasing lawlessness that was accompanying the political agitation and the unrest sparked by the increased surveillance and license inspection, was complemented by increasing local crime. Irish gangs or 'the Bakery Hill mob' as they were commonly known, based in close proximity, were proving to be a major headache for proprietors in the wake of the robbery of the Bank of Victoria and the hijacking of a detachment of soldiers and theft of their armaments.[292]

The notorious events of the week leading up to Eureka where the brothers found themselves beset by incidents on all sides, would have pushed all of the local storekeepers into fits of despair. Violence that had been threatening to explode, broke out on the river flats immediately behind the Exhibition Mart, in front of the Government Camp and along the road in front of the store. Melees involving troopers, police and diggers heightened a sense of chaos, as missiles were thrown, volleys of shots were fired by diggers, the police and troopers, and prisoners were taken to the camp. The Government quarters began to look more like an army barracks under siege, with sentries and sandbags protecting key buildings. Barricades were also erected and instructions were given to set fire to the houses behind it if an invasion was mounted from the diggings while the famous stockade was constructed alongside the Melbourne Road just a mile away.[293] Its construction provoked a skirmish among the miners themselves involving those gathered at the stockade and a group against the stand against the government,

---

[292] Ballarat, *The Age* (Melbourne) Monday 13 November 1854, page 5, Ballarat, *The Age* (Melbourne) 4 December 1854, page 5.
[293] Ballarat, *The Age* (Melbourne) Monday 4 December 1854, page 5

who rushed the stockade under the cover of darkness the night before the final tragic altercation.[294]

Nevertheless, while the chaos of Eureka gathered momentum and raged around the Exhibition Mart, opportunities were there to be had. The township, which had fallen out of favour because of the mining threat, offered great possibilities for future expansion as well as independence from the reach of the Goldfields Commission. It was also prudent bet each way on the fate of both the township and the diggings and the eventual possibility of owning the Exhibition Mart land as well. In addition, to the west, not far from town, agricultural land was finally being offered for sale but because of the troubled state of things very few were in the buying mood and land sales were being cancelled due to a lack of interest.[295] Thus, despite the turmoil, with the amazing profits continuing to mount, Robert went on a highly speculative buying spree. Betting on the future of the township and with his newly found experience as a leader in the proximity dispute, he also saw an opportunity to influence its direction. With the Exhibition Mart as valuable collateral Robert thus managed to acquire some highly strategic and valuable properties both out of town and in the Township.

The first of these was a small purchase of 34 acres at Dowling Forest adjacent to the present site of the Ballarat Racecourse, towards the end of 1854. In February following, he purchased an adjoining 171 acres and named it Springbank Farm, a nostalgic reference to the brothers' childhood home back in Ayrshire. The farm which had been paid for in cash, was then placed under the management of the two younger brothers, David and Alexander, who began immediately to clear and prepare the property for cropping and the raising of stock. The two brothers lived on the property in a tent for the next two years while this was

---

[294] Ballarat, latest from the riots, from the correspondent of the *Geelong Advertiser*, November 30th, *Colonial Times* (Hobart) Wednesday 6 December 1854, page 2
[295] Ballarat, *The Geelong Advertiser and Intelligencer*, Saturday 2 December 1854, page 4

Capitalizing on the Eureka Chaos

accomplished.[296] Under the management of David, the farm became well known as a model of modern commercial farming with a reputation for being the best in the district. Within a short space of time, they had established high quality crops of wheat, oats, barley on almost one hundred acres in addition to 26 acres of potatoes, enough to provide a sizable proportion of the needs of the Ballarat township.[297]

---

[296] Insolvent Court, *The Age*, (Melbourne) Thursday 25 February 1858, page 5.
[297] Advertising, Growing Crop, *The Star* (Ballarat) Tuesday 8 December 1857, page 3.

This first major decision however was made without consultation with Brother John in Glasgow who was only informed after the fact by William in his regular dispatches regarding the business. While John, in Glasgow, early in Robert's career on the Goldfields attempted to counsel his younger brother, his advice may have been noted but does not appear to have influenced his future actions as William's diary suggests.[298] It appears to have been the beginning of a rift between the younger Robert and his eldest brother that only grew in intensity, as indicated by the many abusive letters sent to William in Melbourne from Glasgow. It did little to deter the younger brother however, as he continued at a furious pace, making decisions based on his own judgement, expanding from haberdashery into many other areas of commerce like grocery, liquor, hardware, and machinery. Shortly after the land for Springbank farm had been purchased, Robert branched out again, this time in the township purchasing a vacant half acre allotment for £660. Located in the central business precinct on the corner of Lydiard Street, and Dana Streets, it was quickly outfitted and opened as a grocery and liquor store in March 1855. It was further developed during the year to include offices, living quarters, a basement and a lane way providing rear access from Dana Street.[299]

This was under Robert's management while the Exhibition Mart remained under the management of brother Matthew. Once the grocery store was completed an iron store was erected adjoining it and both were immediately stocked with around £5000 worth of goods supplied to their Melbourne branch from Glasgow and secured by a mortgage over the two stores and the farm and a letter of credit from Dennistoun Brothers in Melbourne. This

---

[298] Robert Muir letter to Flora Cameron 1 June 1853, Supreme Court, *The Star* (Ballarat) 13 August 1857, page 2

[299] Advertising, *The Star* (Ballarat) Monday, 8 March 1858, page 3, 2022 side and frontage photographs of Muir Bros land on corner of Lydiard and Dana Streets now the site of numerous business offices with existing cobbled laneway left centre on top photograph. Ballarat Town Hall tower on Sturt Street at right rear (see page 120), Advertising, *The Star* (Ballarat) Thursday 1 January 1857 page 1

EXHIBITION MART!

MUIR BROTHERS & CO.

HAVE just opened later arrivals of Summer Stock. Intending purchasers are respectfully invited to inspect the undermentioned goods before purchasing, as they will be offered much under usual prices. Great care having been taken in their selection, they will be found admirably adapted for the season, and so assorted in style and in quality as to suit all purchasers.

SHAWLS.
Grenadine, Tissue, Barege, Lama, Crape, &c., &c.

MANTLES.
All the novelties in Moire Antique, Watered Silk, Satin, French Glacé, Gipuire and Lace; these comprise the newest shapes, and are trimmed in most fashionable styles.

OPERA CLOAKS IN WHITE, PINK, AND SKY COLORS.

SILKS
Black and Colored Moiré Antiques, Watered Silks, every other said quality, in French Glacés; also, a magnificent assortment of Brocades, Damasks, Figured Silks, Checked, Striped, and Robed Glacés.

FANCY DRESSES.
Plain, Checked, Striped and Robed, Bareges; Norwich Lustres, Grenadines, Printed Muslins, &c., &c.

BONNETS, MILLINERY, ETC.
A superb assortment of Drawn Silk, Satin, Crape, Tulle, Lace, &c., &c. Crinoline Bonnets in endless variety.

STRAW GOODS.
Dunstable, Rice, Chip, Tuscan and Leghorn; Bonnets and Hats in newest shapes; Girls, Boys, and Infants' Hats in Tuscan, Leghorn, Straw, Beaver, Paris, Felt, Braid, and Cashmere, &c., &c.

Infants' Braided, Cashmere, and Satin Cloaks, Pelisses, and Dresses. Ditto ditto Hats and Hoods. Baby Linen and Underclothing.

GENT'S. CLOTHING, ETC.
Suits of Fancy Doeskin, Fancy Tweeds, &c., &c. Coats, Vests, and Trousers, in Black Cloth, Fancy Doe, Tweed, Alpaca, Drill, Cricketing and Flannel, &c., &c. Tweed Jumpers, and Grey American Shirts.

Panama, Cabbage Tree, French, American, and English Felt Hats, in black, brown, drab, and fawn. Gent's. Black and Drab Paris Hats.

Dress Shirts—Plain, Cluster, Plait, and Embroidered,—carefully cut to fit close to the body.

SUITS MADE TO ORDER.

A SPLENDID STOCK OF FANCY TWEEDS, &c., JUST OPENED.

| MUIR BROS. & Co., WHOLESALE WINE, SPIRIT, AND PRODUCE MERCHANTS, LYDIARD-STREET, TOWNSHIP. | MUIR BROS. & Co., AGENTS FOR THE NORTHERN ASSURANCE COMPANY. LYDIARD-STREET, TOWNSHIP. | MUIR BROS. & Co., MERCHANTS, 86, FLINDERS-STREET, WEST. MELBOURNE. |

arrangement was successfully concluded and paid for in full before the year's end indicating another highly successful venture.[300]

By the middle 1856, plans were well advanced for the erection of permanent buildings on Springbank farm which were completed early in 1857. It was a comprehensive project that encompassed all the needs of a large enterprise with commodious living quarters that Robert initially intended for his permanent home and that of his promised, Flora Cameron.[301] Built entirely in kiln-fired brick, which was sourced from clay deposits discovered on the site, it was described as costing a very large sum and designed for comfort and style with no expense spared. It would be a just reward for the hardship brothers David and Alexander had endured and the remarkable work they had done to establish the farm over the previous two years. The main house had four rooms, a slate roof, spouting and gutters and a large veranda. Inside it was well finished and painted throughout with wallpaper as well as a separate kitchen, cellar, oven and a separate servant's apartment. There was also a large brick barn, stockyards, stables, piggery, and outhouses.[302]

With this barely completed, tenders were again called to construct a hotel or 'bush pub' on the nearby boundary at the base of Mt Blowhard and the intersection of the major roads that converged from the developing communities to the west of Ballarat.[303] The aptly named Mt Blowhard Hotel would complete a picture of rural cooperative existence pictured by the brothers and described in David's letter to the Herald in 1860. Based on the clan structured life at home in Ayrshire where farms and families worked together and shared their resources like the Muirs and the Patersons, it would be a place where locals could gather and conduct business and

> **To Carpenters and Bricklayers.**
> SEPARATE TENDERS are requested (labor only) for the works required in erecting a Bush Public House for Messrs Muir Brothers. Plans and specifications can be seen at our office on or after noon of 25th instant. Tenders returned by the following Saturday evening. Lowest or any tender not necessarily accepted.
> BACKHOUSE & REYNOLDS,
> Architects,
> Armstrong-street, Township.

---

[301] Letter to Flora Cameron, Ballarat 9 May 1854, Breach of Promise of marriage, *The Age* (Melbourne) Thursday 13 August 1857, page 6
[302] Advertising, *The Star* (Ballarat) Monday, 8 March 1858, page 3.
[303] Advertising, *The Star* (Ballarat) Wednesday 25 March 1857, page 3

support other local functions. For almost ten years it served as the post office, electoral office and as a meeting place for organizations like the Agricultural Society and the District Roads Board. But this time, instead of the landed gentry, the farmers would be the owners and the decision-makers and the drivers of politics both local and Colonial.

The management of the hotel was placed in the experienced hands of James McNee who lived there with his wife Margaret, the owners of McNee's Crow Dining Rooms next door to Muir Bothers Exhibition Mart on Main Road, while the license was owned by David Muir who chose to live in Ballarat.[304] Robert, however, remained the manager of all the other operations. Having achieved all his business objectives, Robert Muir then turned his attention to developing a career in local politics, something that he had been involved in from when he had first established the Exhibition Mart.

---

[304] Advertising, *The Star* (Ballarat) 23 August 1856, page 3

Chapter 14

Establishing Law and Order and Local Government

The tyranny of the Goldfields Commission and its final act of overreach in December 1854, had stirred up the diggers against the unrepresentative rule by Commissioners. However, its removal did not mean the absence of conflict. Differences of opinion quickly emerged as electioneering began for the two Legislative assembly seats promised in the wake of the recent Royal Commission. Allegiances quickly coalesced between the supporters of Lalor, the acknowledged leader of the uprising, and those of J B Humffray who had adopted a moderate approach. Although the role of Robert Muir in the Eureka Uprising is unclear, it is noted by Carboni Raffaello, that Muir Bros were remembered as friends in his account soon after and that they were sympathetic to the cause. Muir's allegiance, however, appears to have been squarely behind the majority moral force faction led by J B Humffray.

His colleague James Oddie, who was elected to the position of Chairman of the first Municipality at Ballarat, was a vocal supporter of Peter Lalor, the 'Commander in Chief' of the stockaders, and his official nominee to the Legislative Council in November 1855.[305] There are, however, few, if any, indications that Robert Muir offered Lalor any support, but many confirming a strong association with the Victorian Reform League and J B Humffray after the tragic events of December 1854.

The politics of Peter Lalor were most likely a strong reason for Robert Muir's political preference for the agenda of Humffray. Lalor, who led the 'physical force' faction at Eureka, was viewed as antagonistic to the 'moral force' position of Humffray by virtue, as some have suggested, of his family connections in Ireland. This was a point highlighted during a subsequent election campaign in

---

[305] Victoria, *The Courier (Hobart)* Saturday 17 November 1855, page 2

1857 where Humffray reminded constituents that he was hijacked at gunpoint and prevented from dissuading the promotors of violence from doing anything rash. After, Eureka it also became clear to many, that although Lalor was a major protagonist in the removal of the oppression of the Goldfields Commission, he was not necessarily as eager to support a democratic process based on natural rights. Instead, he promoted the concept that ruled back in Britain that led many to emigrate in the first place - that land ownership should be the guarantor of the electoral franchise.

For many, this was too reminiscent of conditions that had existed back home in Britain and the current system that was dominated by squatting interests. Lalor's position became a liability for him after it was exposed during campaigning for the Legislative assembly at the end of 1856. It was revealed by his opponents that Lalor supported the 'fourth clause' guaranteeing voting rights in multiple electorates to relevant landowners. At a very hostile meeting where he was called to resign at Ballarat on that and other issues, he was roundly condemned and also reminded of disparaging comments he had made on Chartism, democracy, and an Australian republic. [306]

J B Humffray, on the other hand, had a more liberal approach, having been active in dialogue with all the parties on both sides of the conflict. As Carboni reminds us, he had a unique ability to address the interests of the many combative factions including the government: "he has as many friends, but not *one friend* because it is his policy ever to keep friendly with the redcoats and gold-lace, at one and the same time as with blue-shirts and Sou'-westers.[307] Thus, unlike Lalor, he was a figure that many looked to for direction after the chaos of Eureka. As a political figure he stood on a platform of local unity, natural rights, and local development. This became the focus of a new organization created after Eureka called the Victorian Reform League that attempted to unite the miners and township residents in the various districts behind a common cause of social integration and the protection of diggers' interests.

---

[306] Mr Lalor's Vote, *The Star* (Ballarat) Monday January 12, 1857, page 2
[307] Raffaello Carboni, *The Eureka Stockade*, p31

Unifying individuals such as Humffray were essential in the healing and restoration process that occurred in the wake of the Eureka uprising as many of the 'troubles' that plagued the community continued long after. With the removal of the local governing arm of government – the Goldfields Commission – there was an urgent need for local people to show leadership in the community. In this Humffray found a strong ally in Robert Muir who had a high level of respect in the diggings and a rapidly growing notoriety in the township as a reformer with a strong public speaking ability and an interest in establishing local infrastructure and commerce.

Seeing the opportunities in this development, Robert had quickly associated himself with the Victorian Reform League. In the aftermath of Eureka, the Reform League and the moral force faction had reasserted control from the physical force proponents as local leaders like J B Humffray, Weeks, C F Nicholls, H R Nicholls began to take a more active role in the establishment of civic government and local development. As a local businessman, Robert's first concern was the growing problem of law and order in the district and its effect on trade. Secondly, he also saw the commercial opportunities that a local government could unlock for local enterprise with the establishment of local services, utilities and civic infrastructure. His initial interest, therefore, was spurred, like many others, by the growing unsettled state of the community and a crime wave that was under way as the police force and officials connected to the Goldfields Commission were retrenched or redeployed elsewhere within the public service.

Aggravating matters was the large contingent of soldiers enforcing martial law, which were proving to be source of unnecessary trouble and friction with many residents. Skirmishes were becoming a regular occurrence. Matters escalated a few weeks after Eureka at a live show at Hanmer's Theatre where drunken soldiers were harassed by a jeering crowd. Tempers were white hot after a soldier who wounded one of the patrons after firing into the crowd, was fatally whipped by one of the bystanders.[308] The local expression of rage overflowed in response to an ongoing

---

[308] Ballarat, *Colonial Times* (Hobart) Saturday 6 January 1855, page 2

intimidation campaign by police and soldiers after subduing the miners at the stockade. Many locals were subject to a variety of intimidatory 'pranks' like demanding to be included in local 'shouts' at the hotels and needlessly obstructing access and other work in the district.[309] Patrols also remained at high levels and rather than using the law, rowdy parties were addressed by 'dishing out just deserts' as a local correspondent described it.'[310]

Other incidents involved large crowds that escalated into out-of-control riots with one notable altercation saw a party of redcoats badly beaten by a party of fifty Cornish miners. A pickpocket sparked a huge public disturbance that involved mounted police and a crowd of irate locals that numbered into the hundreds.[311] As Easter approached effective policing continued to remain at a low level. This led to crimes becoming more brazen such as the 'audacious scoundrel' who attempted to walk away with the cash box at the Charlie Napier Hotel. Adding to that there were persistent reports of collusion between the soldiers, local Vandemonians, and criminals which in turn, sparked talk of the application of 'lynch law' and vigilante responses to counter the threat.[312]

Matters came to a head with the emergence of a group of bushrangers, the latest episode in a crime wave that was beginning to effect communities in Ballarat and as far as the outskirts of the better resourced areas of Melbourne and Geelong.[313] Protection societies were becoming a popular measure to counter the growing problem which was described as having revolutionary undertones.[314] Following measures adopted in the other large mining towns of Castlemaine, Bendigo, and Maryborough, the

---

[309] Ballarat, *The Age* (Melbourne) Thursday 1 February 1855, page 5
[310] Ballarat, *Colonial Times* (Hobart) Saturday 13 January 1855, page 2
[311] Ballarat, *The Age* (Ballarat) Thursday 1 February 1855, p5
[312] Ballarat, *The Age* (Melbourne), 1 February 1855, p5, Ballarat, Ballarat, *The Geelong Advertiser and Intelligencer*, Wednesday 15 August 1855, page 3, Creswick's Creek, *The Age* (Melbourne) 1 February 1855, page 5, Lynch Law at Ballarat, *The Age*, April 11, 1855, page 5
[313] Ballarat, The *Argus* (Melbourne), Thursday 19 April 1855, Page 6, Ballarat, *The Age* (Melbourne), Friday 13 April 1855, page 5, Ballarat, *The Geelong Advertiser and Intelligencer*, Thursday 12 April 1855, page 2.
[314] Creswick's Creek, *The Age* (Melbourne), Thursday 1 February 1955, page 5

residents of Ballarat also banded together. At Ballarat there were divided interests with different agendas. One group led by a Mr Goodman supported the local squatters and some of the local businesses. It was considered a 'silly freelance' operation that was more politically motivated opposing the local diggers and miners east of the river.[315] Robert's allegiance, however, was with the more progressive Reform League that followed a more inclusive and consultative approach to the problem that included the miners and most of the landowners in the township.

The Victorian Reform League, in the absence of any governing body, had taken it upon themselves to operate as a quasi local government addressing the needs of the district after the demise of the Goldfield Commission. A makeshift office was hastily arranged in the Star Hotel where a committee selected from both diggers and local landowners was formed. With significant interests in both the diggings and now the township, Robert Muir, like Humffray, was viewed as a figure that could unite the feuding factions and collaborate and communicate effectively and so was elected to lead the local committee.

Robert Muir's announcement was brief, outlining the purpose – to compile evidence of the unsafe condition of Ballarat and to 'devise a means for the better protection of life and property' quipping rather cheekily that the only objectors would be 'those gentlemen who, though too lazy to work, were not too nice to plunder.'[316] J B Humffray, as the next speaker declared that this was a necessary step in managing their own local affairs and should be further extended into a petition for the establishment of a municipality for the district. This would, he explained, secure two important political rights, 'the raising of local taxation and expending the same for the benefit of those who pay it.'[317] The main objective, as a correspondent reported, was to place the police 'under the management of those who understood local requirements' and so remove any repeat of the indignities and harassment that had led to the Eureka rebellion.[318]

---

[315] Ballarat, *The Geelong Advertiser and Intelligencer*, Thursday 10 May 1855, page 2
[316] *The Age* (Melbourne) Tuesday April 17, 1855, page 5
[317] *The Age* (Melbourne) Tuesday April 17, 1855, page 5
[318] *Mount Alexander Mail*, Friday 4 May 1855, page 3

Establishing Law and Order and Local Government

Shortly after, Robert Muir, along with J B Humffray, presented the newly compiled and printed report to the community for action which included a petition to the Governor for more police and the control of the police to be exercised by the local community.[319] The Governor, however, was unwilling to cede control of the police, proposing a compromise. As many police that could be spared from other districts would be despatched while endorsing current protection measures, suggesting that those taking part enrol themselves also as special constables with the police to quell the disturbances.[320] Although the advice took months to arrive, the 'Crow Club' vigilance society, which was officially titled 'The Ballarat Voluntary Protection Society,' was formed in April 1855 and proved highly effective by instituting regular patrols with the police especially at night. It restored a sense of community and of safety which was sorely needed during those unsettling few months after Eureka. The club met at the Crow Tea Rooms next to the Exhibition Mart on the Melbourne Road. The well-known tea rooms were owned and operated by Robert Muir's friend James McNee who later managed Muir's Mt Blowhard Hotel.[321]

The protection society was conceived as more than simply a group of concerned citizens but appeared to have taken on many of the other community and political issues. It was closely linked with the movement for the application for municipality status as well as keeping the Government to account on the findings of the recent Royal Commission into the Goldfields and the proposed political franchise for the miners. Robert Muir was heavily invested in both campaigns and was recognized as the community leader most able to successfully execute their objectives. This new-found local assertiveness, however, was staunchly resisted by the local squatting interest and in the Legislative Council.[322]

This only strengthened the resolve of the people of Ballarat to pressure the government to honour the promise of four Goldfields appointees to the Legislative Council as a promised first instalment of enfranchisement, and to support their friends in the Council. At

---

[319] *The Age* (Melbourne) Tuesday April 17, 1855, page 5
[320] Ballarat news, *The Age* (Melbourne) Monday June 4, 1855,
[321] Ballarat, *The Age* (Melbourne) Tuesday 17 April 1855, page 5
[322] Ballarat, *The Geelong Advertiser and Intelligencer*, Thursday 10 May 1855, page 2

a meeting on Wednesday 10 May, several resolutions to that effect were made and a memorial to the Colonial Secretary was drafted. The meeting was called by the Reform League with Robert Muir once again voted as chairman and included speakers, James Oddie, C F Nicholls, H R Nicholls, Thomas Bath, John Rolf and J B Humffray. Their actions were successful with both Lalor and Humffray appointed to the Legislative Council later in the year.[323]

The application for a municipality was initially made to create a local government body like many that existed back in Britain where policing was under local control. However, as the government was unwilling to oblige, the application was put aside while the public safety crisis was in the process of being dealt with. By August, the mission had been accomplished, and matters were much more tranquil. The gangs that had plagued the district 'coincidentally' had ceased their activities along with the removal of the soldiers. Thus, as the Geelong Advertiser reported, the Protection Society was disbanded. It was followed immediately by a petition to the Governor requesting him to declare the district of Ballarat a municipality.[324]

The initiative in this was taken by H R Nicholls and his business associates who were in the process of commencing a very extensive drainage project to facilitate mining ventures along the Yarrowee River. Their aim was to include the soon to be alienated commercial properties on the eastern side of the river with those on the western side to create one large municipality.[325] With mining prospects for individual miners becoming unprofitable, this provided hope in the form of long-term employment as well as the prospect of securing land under miners right and accessing the regularly flooded land for mining.

It was, however, backed by the continuing and widely held belief held by many on the eastern side of the river, that mining should hold pre-eminence over any township rights. This came on the back of speculation that the existing mining leads would extend

---

[323] Ballarat, *The Geelong Advertiser and Intelligencer*, Thursday 10 May 1855, page 2
[324] Ballarat Mining Intelligence, *The Geelong Advertiser and Intelligencer*, Thursday 9 August 1855, page 2
[325] White Flat Drainage and Mining Company, *The Star* (Ballarat) Saturday 6 September 1856, page 2

under the township and possibly result in the relocation or removal of many of the existing buildings and infrastructure. People from the township and the diggings remained bitterly divided on the issue throughout most of 1855. Not surprisingly it resulted in the drafting of two competing petitions for the municipality, with one dominated by H R Nicholls and his supporters and the other supported by those sympathetic to the existing township.

Despite having a foot in both camps, Robert Muir believed in the pre-eminence of the Municipality having become a landowner himself. In fact, he doubled down on what many saw as an unfair advantage enjoyed by many storekeepers including himself, who were proprietors on crown land. For an annual fee of £10 anyone could set up shop and commence trading, drawing away patronage from the township by the lower prices enjoyed by the substantially less capital investment. As also a large property owner on the township many saw this as a betrayal and a reversal of his previous position of supporting the leaseholders the year before.

Once the competing petitions were resolved at a joint meeting, Robert was immediately called upon by his new township colleagues to arrange and chair another meeting to address the problem of premises erected on crown land within the boundary of the coming municipality.[326] It was proposed that a memorial be drawn up and presented to the Governor that any offending buildings be removed.[327] Robert Muir was clearly positioning himself for a position on the coming municipal council, a betrayal which created enemies in the local mining community and their township supporters who dogged his progress and attempted to undermine his and the Muir Brothers reputation over the next two years.

This interest in local government was also likely a result of brother William in Melbourne who was reported to have had a great interest in the welfare of the district. It was a passion of his that was well known among the political and commercial elite in Melbourne who were urging him to stand for one of the two Legislative Council seats promised by Sir Charles Hotham in the

---

[326] Ballaarat, *The Argus* (Melbourne) Monday 20 August 1855, page 7
[327] Ballaarat, *The Argus* (Melbourne) Monday 20 August 1855, page 7

Establishing Law and Order and Local Government

wake of the Eureka rebellion.[328] William had become well established in commercial circles in Melbourne, serving as Chairman of the Melbourne Chamber of Commerce during 1856 alongside MLA's such as William Westgarth who had a long association with Ballarat and the miners and their protests.[329] Deciding ultimately not to run as a candidate, William, as a secondary preference, very likely as a shrewd piece of business strategy, encouraged his younger brother, who was already located in Ballarat, to pursue a seat on the proposed municipal council. This would provide an excellent opportunity to be informed on local projects and possibly be able to benefit commercially as well. The municipality petition was finally approved on December 24, 1855, and a meeting to decide the composition of the new council was set for Saturday 5 January 1856.[330] What was clear from the candidates standing for election was that this would be a council for Ballarat West exclusively. The candidates presented included those who were amongst the first landowners after the 1852 township survey, like P W Welsh and later purchasers James Oddie who was elected chairman.

As a newcomer to the township Robert only had his recent reputation to speak for him. It was enough, however; his hard work during 1855 in bringing a restoration of civic normality to the district, elevated him to the second highest vote of 126 behind one of the original diggers, now land agent and auctioneer, James Oddie on 132. His alliance with J B Humffray had also proven to be a wise move, situating himself with arguably the most influential man in the district. Over the course of the next two years, it would be a partnership that would continue to initiate many projects in the community.

J B Humffray represented the local progressives who had a vision for Ballarat that was more than bringing order and safety. They were focussed on making the region a productive and economic powerhouse. The wealth that was being dug up from the

---

[328] Ballarat, *The Age* (Melbourne) 11 June 1855, page 6, Ballarat, *The Geelong Intelligencer and Advertiser*, Saturday 3 November 1855, page 2
[329] Commercial, *The Argus* (Melbourne) Friday October 1856, page 4
[330] Ballarat, *The Geelong Advertiser and Intelligencer*, Monday January 7, 1856, page 3

ground informed a growing belief that they were in the vanguard of the Colony with the power to influence many aspects of colonial society. Thus, once elected to the Legislative Council in 1855, at the very first meeting of the newly expanded Council in December 1855, Humffray was on his feet requesting a progress report on the application for Municipal Institutions, the Court House and whether a circuit court would be established at Ballarat and the steps taken in the construction of the Electric Telegraph from Geelong to Ballarat.[331]

---

[331] Legislative Council: Notices of Motion and Orders of the day, *The Age* (Melbourne) Thursday 13 December 1855, page 4.

Chapter 15

R Muir Municipal Councillor

Once created, the Municipality of Ballarat began with nothing. There was no money readily available for offices, stationery, or furniture, all this had to be purchased without any assistance from the Government. With various ideas presented for funding, the most logical to the new councillors and many others, was the proceeds from the sale of crown lands within their jurisdiction. However, applications to the Colonial Government for approval proved unsuccessful. This forced the newly elected councillors to guarantee the establishment and running costs themselves, taking out a personal loan for £1000.[332] Despite this high degree of solidarity however, divisions were developing from the very beginning that would cause Robert more than a few headaches in the coming months.

The first and most worrying was the persistent issue of mining on private property within the township borders and whether mining should take precedence over the surveyed lots and buildings in the township. To the relief of the township residents, the talk of dismantling the Government camp and digging up the township had died down since the hysteria of the previous year. Hope had been bolstered by several township landowners led by original purchaser Thomas Bath, who had formed an influential clique based on increasing evidence that mining would extend south rather than into the township. With discussions already in progress for a large extension of the township in that direction, they were demanding that the sites of many of the new projects such as the Court House and the Gaol be in their immediate vicinities. This effectively created two powerful cliques called the

---

[332] *Ballarat West Council Minutes, 15 February 1856*, VPRS 13007 P0001

southside and the northside groups divided by the main boulevard of Sturt Street.[333]

Robert, however, was a member of neither, having properties in various locations, with the Exhibition Mart on the government land on the diggings, the farm on the northwest side of town, and properties in the township all on the south side. For him, the major task was resolving the continuing proximity issue of trading establishments on crown land. As leader of the 'central committee,' and displaying a high degree of duplicitous imagination, he managed to carefully steer the outrage at the competitive advantage enjoyed by the main road traders towards the hotels, the most popular and lucrative establishments. Having earlier represented the interests of that group against the township, he now sat on the other side of the fence serving in the new municipal council and the owners of private land. It was an issue that continued to simmer during 1856 culminating in October with an ultimatum notice to relocate to the township. Signed by the Ballarat West hoteliers and shopkeepers, it declared that a petition to the Government was in progress to have their liquor licenses revoked. A £5 reward was offered in an advertisement in the local paper for anyone brave enough to leave a copy of the petition with any store on the Main Road in the diggings.[334]

The reason for this stunt was obviously based in the increasing likelihood that the Main Road properties would soon be sold to the existing occupiers. Once converted to freehold they could be the basis for the creation of a second municipality in Ballarat East, a proposal that was already under consideration. This would then deprive Ballarat West of valuable rates revenue. For Robert himself, he would not lose either way as the properties were eventually alienated as promised early in 1857, allowing him to secure the improved lots where the Exhibition Mart stood, for

---

[333] To the Editor of the Star (by an uninterested Burgess) *The Star* (Ballarat) Tuesday 23 September 1856, supplement, page 1, The Municipal Elections, *The Star* (Ballarat) 14 January 1857, page 2, The Municipal Elections, *The Star* (Ballarat), Wednesday 14 January 1857, page 2

[334] £5 reward, *The Star* (Ballarat) 4 October 1856, page 4.

£250 in September 1857, many times less than its improved value of over £3000.[335]

This highly politicized project provided valuable experience for the now 29-year-old local councillor. It would be a good proving ground for his next major project for the township of Ballarat West, the Market Place. However, this time there were forces at work amongst the diggers not impressed with his 'defection' to the township. Appointed to lead the committee on the establishment of the market, it was not hard to see that the original site selected was totally unsuited as it occupied the floodplain of the Yarrowee River. While this would be an ideal location for the diggings and provide many patrons to Thomas Bath's hotel and his own businesses which were a short 100 yards away, it would be a muddy quagmire for two to three months of the year.[336] Not wanting to be denied, the ardent supporters on the eastern side of the river, supported by Councillor Carver, who appeared to be against almost anything that Robert Muir proposed, then chose another smaller site adjacent. This too was considered unworkable by Taylor, the Government surveyor.[337]

Taylor suggested another site nearby which had been earlier discarded due to an illegal vote earlier in the year by only three councillors. Robert Muir then decided to put the matter to the people at a public meeting to decide on that, and an alternative that he had selected in the township's west currently used as a stone quarry. He was opposed in the press by an anonymous letter writer calling him both an eloquent councillor and vindictive.[338] Arguments against the stone quarry were based on a dubious mining assay report and the cost to fill it in.[339] However, Robert Muir was not deterred, 'finding' a complainant who was persuaded to write a letter to the council over the dangers of blasting and quarrying to the nearby houses. It was a clever move

---

[335] Insolvent Court Wednesday 24th February 1858, The Estate of Muir Brothers, *The Star* (Ballarat) 26 February 1858, page 2, Insolvent Court, *The Age* Melbourne, Thursday 25 February 1858, page 5
[336] The Market Place, *The Star* (Ballarat) Saturday, 19 July 1856, page 2
[337] The Market Place, *The Star* (Ballarat) Saturday, 19 July 1856, page 2
[338] Open column, *The Star* (Ballarat) Thursday 24 July 1856, page 3
[339] Letter to the Editor, Quartz reef Township, *The Star*, (Ballarat) Thursday 31 July 1856 page 3

labelled as irregular during the following year's council elections.[340] After Robert Muir had successfully persuaded the ratepayers to support the quarry option, the marketplace became a deadlocked issue for most of 1856 and 1857 as progress became stalled by a lack of co-operation. Councillor Carver and his allies among the diggers on the east side of the river who owned properties adjacent to their preferred location, successfully thwarted any attempts to commence works on the project.[341]

Despite this setback, Robert took to his role as a civic leader and innovator with great relish. It was an outlet for his obvious energy, creativity, and ability to influence by persuasive argument and he quickly moved on to other projects. One of the first, and closest to his heart, was the formation of the Agricultural Society which was becoming a necessary development with agricultural land being released in ever increasing quantities. From 1855 the countryside surrounding Ballarat was becoming more like that of their British origins. Land was progressively being cleared, fences and hedgerows installed, and crops and livestock were beginning to appear. A local correspondent for the Age thus predicted that the Ballarat district would soon be competing for first place in Agricultural honours.[342] For Robert, this would be an opportunity for the first time to put on display the skills of the farmers and farm workers free of the landed monopoly back in Scotland who exercised control of the industry by patronage and administrative control of the agricultural societies.

With his father David back in Ayr having enjoyed a high reputation among the local farming fraternities as a ploughman and a ploughing judge at local competitions, the skills learned at home in Ayrshire more than qualified him for a leading role. This was acknowledged by his colleagues at Ballarat who voted him to chair the first meeting for the establishment of a local Agricultural Society on Friday 7 June 1856. He was then later elected as secretary. The association was launched shortly after with a

---

[340] The Government Quarries on the Township, *The Star* (Ballarat) Tuesday 19 July 1856, page 3
[341] The Municipal elections, *The Star* (Ballarat) Wednesday 14 January 1857, page 2
[342] Diggings Intelligence, *The Age* (Melbourne) Saturday 14 July 1855, page 3

ploughing match at a suitable property and a £5 subscription from attendees and prospective members.[343]

It was held at Baird's farm at Greenfields near Lake Burrumbeet on Thursday 10 July 1856 with Secretary Robert Muir presiding as judge. A large crowd of over 300 were present on the sunny but icy day with a heavy frost rendering the ground very difficult to work. This was no obstacle to the Muir Brothers whose ploughman John Wales took out the first prize for ploughing with horses. The award was, as the correspondent described it, 'a beautiful gold medal' and the prize for ploughing with bullocks was won by James Christie who was ploughman for Eason Brothers.[344] The next major decision was the selection of land for the premises for sheds, yards and exhibitions which the society occupies to this day (2021) on a site selected by Robert Muir and his fellow members and presented to the Legislative Assembly for approval by local MP J B Humffray in November 1856.[345]

With the creation of the Agricultural Society, it was also suggested that the rural areas could also derive great benefit from creating their own local branch of the District Roads Board. As land was beginning to become available, the increasing number of farms had created a desperate need for the formation of district roads as well. A previous attempt to create district councils had proved unsuccessful due to the sparse population and the resistance to paying rates and tolls. This then led to the Central Road Board System that was totally reliant on Government Grants under the suggestions of a local committee.[346] By 1856 and the huge influx of people with the goldrushes, the Government was once again encouraging rural districts to form their own local Roads Board. It was thus strongly recommended that Ballarat take

---

[343] Ballarat Agricultural Society, *The Age* (Melbourne) Friday 13 June 1856, page 3
[344] The Ploughing Match, *The Star* (Ballarat) Saturday 12 July 1856, page 2, Ballarat Agricultural Society, *The Star* (Ballarat) Saturday 16 August 1856, page 2
[345] Ballarat Agricultural Society, *The Star* (Ballarat) Tuesday 18 November 1856, page 2
[346] Bernard Barrett, *The civic frontier: the origin of local communities and local government in Victoria*, Melbourne University Press, Melbourne 1979, pp 72-75, 89-93

advantage of the recommendation and form their own local board. The power to levy rates and tolls would then facilitate forming the district roads so badly needed to get their produce to market and to enable travel within the district.[347]

A meeting of interested candidates was held on Friday 24 October 1856. Twenty-two nominated for the position and nine were elected, with Robert Muir finishing third on the ballot.[348] Robert was incredibly invested in this as demonstrated by the conduct of the meeting. Initially elected to chair the meeting he stepped down after incorrectly assuming that he would be appointed rather than elected to the ongoing position. Although he was later elected to the position of president of the Board.

At much the same time it was determined by the Council that the matter of a fire brigade that was raised at one of its first meetings should be explored as a matter of urgency. Recent fires in the township and the diggings, including one that had destroyed Abraham's 'Beehive' department store in September, just a few metres away from the Exhibition Mart, had resulted in substantial loss of life and property.[349] The matter, however, appeared to be urgent for more than the one obvious reason. The other was that as protective clothing manufacturers and resellers, there was an ongoing opportunity for their own merchandise to be sold to the officers. This proved to be the case with Muir Brothers often winning tenders to supply jumpers, coats, and other protective garments. The first meeting for the formation of the fire brigade was held on Tuesday 10 June 1856 and was led by Robert Muir. Although not well attended, it was clear that a lot of work had previously been done to raise subscriptions. A total of £334 was reported as well as a £20 donation from the Municipal Council. This was then allocated for the purchase of an engine, a task allocated to W S Gibbs and Robert's brother William in Melbourne.[350]

---

[347] The Ploughing Match, *The Star* (Ballarat) Thursday 10 July 1856, page 2
[348] District Roads Board, *The Star* (Ballarat) Saturday 25 October 1856, page 2
[349] Ballarat, *The Age* (Melbourne) Monday 10 September 1855, page 6, The Fire at Ballarat, *The Age* (Melbourne) Tuesday 4 December 1855, page 5
[350] Ballarat, *The Geelong Advertiser and Intelligencer*, Saturday 14 June 1856, page 3

As 1856 continued to unfold, Robert's confidence increased in proportion. Having achieved an incredible amount in such a short time and occasionally against some strong and sustained opposition, he was developing a reputation as a person who could get things done. His political instinct was also becoming more finely tuned to issues that could be useful and those that could be unprofitable. One such situation that was developing in the Ballarat District was that of education. It had the potential of dividing communities and creating enemies as the National school system was in the process of being established throughout the colonies of Australia. Locally, those in favour of the denominational system had sought to combine their desire for a Presbyterian School at Dowling Forest. Using the newly formed Agricultural Society to air their plans and grievances with the national system it was beginning to sow disagreement and dissention.[351]

Robert had a keen interest in education serving on National School boards in later life. Nevertheless, despite being a product of the Presbyterian system himself, he wisely chose not to become involved even though it would be in an area quite close to the Muir Bros farm also at Dowling Forest. It would seem, unlike his brother William who enjoyed a close association with the Chalmers Presbyterian Church in Melbourne, that Robert's interest in religion had waned considerably. He received no honourable mention in the committee to erect a Presbyterian Church in Ballarat and was never mentioned among the ranks of the leaders of the religious community both in Ballarat and elsewhere over the course of his life. This is reflected in his letters to his fiancée where he states that his only spare time in the week was a Sunday, obviously not spent in church, describing himself as feeling 'very wicked ... and too much engrossed with this world's wealth and vanities.'[352]

The lack of spare time became more acute as Robert embarked on yet more ventures on behalf of the newly incorporated town of

---

[351] Ballarat Agricultural Society, *The Star* (Ballarat), Saturday 16 August 1856, page 2
[352] Breach of Promise, Letter to Flora Cameron Ballarat 16th October 1854, *The Age* (Melbourne), Thursday 13 August 1857, page 6

Ballarat West. Muir Brothers had become more than a local business, they had become a local institution, operating as an agency for other business such as banking, insurance, and even extending finance on occasion to loyal customers. The first foray into the financial market was the appointment as Ballarat agent for the Australian Freehold Association in January 1855. It was a perfect ideological fit for landless immigrants such as Robert and his brothers, offering a solution to many who could not compete against developers and sharks through co-operative purchase arrangements.[353] Following a few weeks after, Robert himself was one of the leading initiators of a bank to cater to the local farming community, chairing the meeting for the first local Commercial and Agricultural Bank in Ballarat.[354] Shortly after Muir Bros were appointed as agents for the international insurance company Northern Assurance Company (fire and life)[355]

With so many interests and with such a high degree of enthusiasm for the prospects of Ballarat, Robert was in increasingly high demand as a speaker and as an organizer for new initiatives. In August 1856, as the gold continued to be dug up in prodigious quantities, there was a growing confidence in the future of Ballarat as a leading city of the land. There were soon calls for a local Chamber of Commerce to be established originating with Charles Rodier, a future Mayor of Ballarat East, following a similar move in Geelong earlier in the year. This was inspired by a new mining boom that was just beginning south of Ballarat based on the 'frontage system.' Devised by members of the new Court of Mines and promoted by James Baker, a local engineer and entrepreneur, it was expected that a huge expansion of trade and industry would follow in its wake. To take advantage of the opportunities, a body of likeminded local businessmen was needed to lobby the government for increased infrastructure spending on necessary projects, particularly, the rail and the telegraph and the formation of streets on the worked-out parts of the diggings.[356]

---

[353] Ballarat, *The Age* (Melbourne) Wednesday 17 January 1855, page 6
[354] Ballarat, *The Geelong Advertiser and Intelligencer*, Thursday 7 February 1856, page 2
[355] Advertising, *The Star* (Ballarat) 25 September 1856, page 4
[356] Ballarat Chamber of Commerce, *The Star* (Ballarat) 7 August 1856, page 3

Robert was called upon to chair the meeting. In characteristic confident style he extolled the virtues of Ballarat declaring that 'it would be second to none in Her Majesty's dominions' he then handed the meeting to J B Humffray, MLC who was present offering his support. Robert was then elected to the committee of seven. Following this a meeting was called for the election of permanent committee members and Robert, who received the most votes, was automatically selected as president. However, he chose to decline the position, advising in writing, due to expected absences. It resulted in R B Gibbs stepping into the role as second highest on the ballot.[357]

The calls on Robert Muir's optimism in the future of Ballarat just kept coming. Only a few weeks after setting in place the arrangements for the Chamber of Commerce, local identity J Daly esq, the local Gold Department warden, had crystalized his ideas on harnessing the creative local talent and expertise for the benefit of the mining industry and other associated and future enterprise. His grand idea was named the Ballarat Industrial Institute inspired by the great crystal palace exhibition in London in 1851. For Ballarat, as a local journalist described it, it would be an organization dedicated to the periodical 'exhibition of articles used in the arts and sciences in connection with the mining, manufacturing and general interests of the district.'[358] Robert, as an early proponent of the Agricultural Society, found this to be equally appealing as an essential institution for promoting progress, innovation and commerce. Thus, he was appointed to the office of treasurer, one of four other permanent office bearers that included Daly the president. The elected members also included the Chairman of the Municipal Council James Oddie and newly elected MLAs J B Humffray and Peter Lalor, the one-armed hero of Eureka.[359] One of Robert's first tasks was the application to the Government for a £3000 grant to erect a building comprising of a

---

[357] Chamber of Commerce, *The Star* (Ballarat) Saturday 6 September 1856, page 2.
[358] Ballarat Industrial Institute, *The Star* (Ballarat) Thursday 23 October 1856, page 2
[359] Ballarat Industrial Institute, *The Star* (Ballarat) Thursday 23 October 1856, page 2

large auditorium and offices and the allocation of five acres of land at a site selected opposite the hospital on the northern end of Sturt Street. The development was approved in January 1858 after Robert had left the district.[360]

The new year of 1857 came with a decided change in the mood of the township, the diggings and for Robert himself. The council elections were underway for three redundant positions among the seven members and the lobbying had gotten to a childish level. Robert who was not one of them, would not have been oblivious to the bitter factionalism that had arisen over the course of the 1856. Having experienced a taste of it during the market square and the dirty tricks that were played, including some of his own, he had, very noticeably kept well away from the contest. He endured the nomination meeting in uncharacteristic silence. New candidate W C Smith, a future Chairman and member of the Legislative Assembly standing as a reformist candidate, and the chairman James Oddie, were in a full-blown feud over accusations that Oddie had been given preferential treatment for the street to be metalled in front of his premises.

This was typical of the level of pettiness that had arisen during the year that had created many grievances that were not settled. Perhaps the most childish of them all was the persecution of Councillor Carver, who represented the eastern diggings interest, over his new water closet. While the very latest technology, Alexander Dimant, the town's inspector and a personal friend of the chairman James Oddie from their previous lives in Geelong, refused to give it official sanction. Dimant operating as the feared enforcer of the new civic regulations, launched a protected legal case against the unfortunate councillor that attracted both ridicule and entertainment for the best part of a year.[361] More sinister was a previous meeting by Oddie and his chief supporter and South Side, power broker Thomas Bath, who had locked out W C Smith in a blatant attempt to secure a majority for the 'southside' faction and the removal of Robert Muir's adversary and eastern

---

[360] Industrial Institute, *The Star* (Ballarat) Thursday 7 January 1858, page 3, Industrial Institute, The Star, Thursday 7 January 1858, page 3
[361] Municipal Council, *The Star* (Ballarat) 6 December 1856, page 1, Municipal Council, Municipal Council, The Star (Ballarat) Saturday 27 December, page 2

sympathizer, Carver, from the council. Carver, eventually deposed, departed the council in acrimony with parting shots at his many enemies but specifically singling out Chairman James Oddie, and Robert Muir in a bitter public speech.[362]

Robert's silence during the council elections of 1857 is notable – there were no speeches, and he was not called upon to chair any meetings. This was most likely due to matters on his mind that engrossed him for weeks, as he explained in a letter to Flora his fiancé.[363] He was evaluating his life and the direction that it might take as storm clouds were gathering as issues both known, and unknown were emerging from the shadows of the past.

---

[362] Municipal elections, *The Star* (Ballarat) Saturday 17 January 1857, page 2
[363] Law Report, Cameron V Muir, *The Argus* (Melbourne) Wednesday 12 August 1857, page 5-6

Chapter 16

1857: A Turning Point

The year had barely commenced when the first of many setbacks presented itself. It had begun on the voyage to Australia as alluded to earlier. As a young eligible bachelor of twenty-six, he was inexperienced in the mating game having spent much of the previous ten years in mainly male company away from home in far flung places. The shipboard romance with Flora Cameron that had resulted in a hasty engagement, appeared to end once the ship docked in Melbourne. Robert left without as much as a goodbye. He did, however, leave a letter to be passed on to her. It was an unconvincing missive with a strong past-tense emphasis where he asserted that he would not break his promise to her, loaded with a strong indication of pre-existing doubts. Filled with religious platitudes to his very pious fiancé, it was also an obvious attempt to reassure her that his religious commitment, which had quickly dissipated once arrived, would ensure that he kept his word.[364]

He left with mixed feelings however, and amidst the loneliness of the Bendigo Goldfields he reached out to Flora five weeks later to test the state of feeling that existed regarding his reputation with her and her family. He once again expressed his doubts about whether the match was a real and sustainable one, stating 'God has intended us for each other; but if not, his will be done. We will try with what lies in our power to be husband and wife soon, but the consummation lies with him who directeth all things.'[365] The correspondence was then maintained for the best part of eighteen months, facilitated and encouraged by Flora's family and friends

---

[364] Law Report, Robert Muir to Flora Cameron Ship Malabar 7th March 1853, *The Argus* (Melbourne) Wednesday 12 August 1857, page 6
[365] Law Report, Robert Muir to Flora Cameron Bendigo 13 April 1853, *The Argus* (Melbourne), Wednesday 12 August 1857, page 6 Wednesday 12 August 1857, page 6

who kept in regular contact with Robert and updated them on his progress. This was first through a Cameron family friend, Mr Cunningham while at Bendigo, and later another family acquaintance, Alexander McKersie who had done business with the brothers in Ballarat and Melbourne. The Camerons were very satisfied that Robert had indeed succeeded beyond their expectations and would be an excellent match.[366]

As the year 1855 commenced, and Robert, finding himself heavily committed to the reconstruction of the Ballarat community, decided that it was time to end the charade. After writing two letters in the month of January 1855 expressing no indication of his state of mind, he followed with the bombshell on 12 February 1855, that he was ending the relationship. He stated 'I cannot any longer disguise my true feelings. … It is impossible to act the hypocrite any longer.' Asking Flora to show the letter to her father and her aunt, who was probably the matchmaker, he asked for any reply to be their last correspondence. He also accompanied the fateful letter with one to Duncan Cameron, her father, declaring 'I have much wronged you and yours and can scarcely dare hope for your forgiveness, but this crisis is inevitable and the sooner the better, for I feel that in truth, honour and justice, I could never act otherwise.'[367] Robert, in the same letter, gave Flora three months to think matters over but received no reply within the specified time. Assuming the matter was finally behind him, he resumed his usual duties with a huge load off his mind.

Despite the descent of the Municipal Council into petty politics, Robert continued to show leadership on essential projects as 1857 progressed and refused to be distracted. For him the most important problem to be solved for the township, was the water supply. He had first raised this as an important issue in March the previous year only to discover that it was another controversial issue beset by the a variety of private, personal and financial interests.[368] It's progress had been regularly thwarted despite the

---

[366] Supreme Court, Cameron V Muir, *The Star* (Ballarat) Friday 14 August 1857, page 2.
[367] Law Report, Cameron V Muir, *The Argus* (Melbourne) Wednesday 12 August 1857, page 5-6
[368] Council Minutes 13 March 1856, VPRS 13007/P0001

persistent attention brought to the matter by Robert Muir and Councillor James Stewart, the Doctor famous for the amputation of Peter Lalor's arm.

Damming the swamp to increase the water level also had met with resistance. A first attempt was demolished by person's unknown under cover of night and the assumption of the water pumps by the council was resisted by the owners and the water carters who made a very decent living from it.[369] Despite resolving all these issues in the council's first six months, progress continued to be slow as new excuses continued to be raised to slow or even stop progress. The ambitious plans, however, were well advanced, based on piping water from 'the swamp' the only permanent water source in the district, into the township streets. This would save the residents a great deal of expense while adding significantly to the Council's income. It would also put an end to the water cartage business which ran under license bringing water on order to the township and all over the diggings from the series of pumps installed the previous year. [370]

However, with most of the objections removed, it soon became clear that the final obstacle was the Chairman of the Council, James Oddie. Claiming absolute loyalty to Peter Lalor as the hero that removed tyranny from the goldfields, he insisted that Lalor was the best and only representative to take up the cause of water supply to the government. Matters became very heated after Robert Muir expressed exasperation with Lalor's tardiness in pursuing their application for the £10,000 grant for the water supply made many months prior. With the approach of summer and the possibility of more fires, it was becoming a matter of urgency. A meeting was called where it was decided to deputise a trio of councillors to make a direct approach to Melbourne. This resulted in Oddie storming out of the meeting leaving it to Robert Muir to propose that he would lead the approach as he also had personal business in

---

[369] Nicola Cousen, *Dr James Stewart: Irish doctor and philanthropist on the Ballarat Goldfields*, Ph.D. Thesis Federation University Ballarat 2017
[370] Ballarat Water Supply. Report upon the most desirable means for obtaining the necessary supply of water to the township of Ballarat, *The Star* (Ballarat) 30 August 1856, page 4

Melbourne to attend to.[371] Unfortunately for him there would be many trips to Melbourne over the course of 1857, most for personal reasons.

Around the same time came a letter from a Mr Jones, a Melbourne solicitor, demanding £2000 compensation for ending his engagement to Flora Cameron. After two years it was a shock. However, in a most businesslike manner he replied with an offer to renew the engagement while also stressing that his heart would not be in it. Giving Flora thirty days to respond he declared that failing any acknowledgement he would deem himself free of any obligation.[372] Despite some vacillation on the parts of both protagonists, Flora was convinced by her brother to recommence the action raising the damages to £5000. This was due to an inheritance of £470 that Flora had come into at the end of January from her uncle which would, as her brother explained, be more than enough to mount an extended case in the courts if necessary.

The case was set for trial on Tuesday 11 August 1857 and became sensational news in Australia and in Britain appearing in many of the prominent newspapers. Locally it generated a considerable amount of interest drawing quite an audience at the trial itself. Robert however, called no witnesses and did not take the stand. However, his actions were carefully noted and described as trivializing the whole affair. The local correspondent from the *Ballarat Star* noted the familiar relationship between Robert and his council, Aspinall, and the jokes being shared between them over the course of the two-day trial. Robert's character and actions were exposed in the most negative light being described as a heartless, relentless recreant. Many would have found it hard not to laugh as he was also described as a bully, instructing his solicitor to advise Flora's father Duncan Cameron, himself no stranger to the civil courts, that he would contest the case. He was also painted as lacking compassion and without regard for the health and well-being for his fiancée who allegedly was confined to her bed for almost twelve months due to shock.

---

[371] Municipal Council, *The Star* (Ballarat) 9 January 1857,
[372] Supreme Court, Cameron V Muir, Robert Muir to Flora Cameron, Ballarat 28 March 1857, *The Star* (Ballarat) Tuesday 13 August 1857, page 2

In his defence, Aspinall argued that a concerted attempt had been made by the Camerons to embarrass and discredit his client in public, complaining that much of the personal correspondence between Robert and Flora had been published in the press. He also argued that a great deal of the evidence was an exaggeration designed to elicit sympathy. Aspinall reminded the court that there was no proof provided of Flora's illness and eluded that the relationship was engineered and insisted upon to secure a financial advantage for the wider Cameron family. He argued that Robert had acted honourably and had notified all parties of his changed state of mind and in no way wished to condemn Flora to un unhappy life.[373] The verdict awarding £2000 thus appeared to be a reasonable outcome – less than half of the £5000 originally claimed indicating some doubt as to truthfulness of the plaintiff.

This case clearly marks a fork in the road in the life of Robert Muir and on the surface has all the hallmarks of an act of career suicide. However, his manner at the trial indicates a man who was not overly concerned at the outcome, maintaining a level of humour and banter with his defence lawyer Aspinall. With a great deal at stake, particularly his reputation and the relationship with his brothers, it would seem, with such a cavalier attitude, that he was, like a good chess player, had already planned his next series of career moves. Certainly, a marriage into a family like the Camerons, for Robert Muir, who viewed them as a nasty self-serving lot, was a fate to be avoided at any cost.

The ruling came with profound consequences, leading to Robert leaving the family firm of Muir Brothers and dissolving the partnership in so far as he was concerned, almost immediately. A notice to that effect was posted in the press Friday 28 August 1857.[374] A week after that he resigned from the Ballarat West Council, his letter of resignation dated Wednesday 2

---

[373] Supreme Court, Breach of Promise of Marriage, Cameron v Muir, *The Star* (Ballarat) 12th August 1857, page 2, 13 August 1857, page 2, Law Report, Cameron v Muir 11 August 1857, *The Argus* (Melbourne) 12 August 1857 page 5-6, Breach of Promise of Marriage, Cameron V Muir, *The Age* (Melbourne) 13 August 1857, page 6, Supreme Court, Cameron V Muir, Wednesday 12 August 1857, *Bendigo Advertiser*, Friday 14 August 1857, page 3.
[374] Advertising, *The Argus* (Melbourne) Friday 28 August 1857, page 7

1857: A Turning Point

NOTICE is hereby given, that the CO-PARTNERSHIP heretofore existing between the undersigned, WILLIAM PATERSON MUIR, MATTHEW PATERSON MUIR, ROBERT MUIR, DAVID MUIR, JOHN MUIR, and JAMES STIRLING, carrying on business at Melbourne and at Ballarat, in the Colony of Victoria, under the firm of "Muir Brothers and Company," has been, so far as concerns the said Robert Muir only, this day DISSOLVED by mutual consent.

Dated this 19th day of August, 1857.

WM. P. MUIR,
MATTHEW P. MUIR,
By his Attorney, Wm. P. Muir.
JOHN MUIR,
By his Attorney, Wm. P. Muir.
DAVID MUIR,
ROBERT MUIR,
JAMES STIRLING.

Witness to the signatures of Wm. P. Muir, Matthew P. Muir, John Muir, and Robert Muir—Wm. Linton, Clerk.

Witness to the signatures of David Muir and James Stirling—J. W. Parson.

September 1857.[375] Shortly after he also resigned his other positions - the District Roads Board, the Agricultural Society, the Chamber of Commerce, and the Industrial Institute. He was then totally unencumbered by leadership and involvement in the Ballarat community. However, this 'sudden' withdrawal from public life had many indications of a carefully planned exit with the assistance of younger brother David. As a twenty-two-year-old with some experience, David became his replacement on the District Roads Board as a member, and on the board of the Agricultural Society.

Leaving the family partnership proved to be a lucky break as Muir Brothers survived him by less than six months. By February following, the company was declared insolvent. Much of this was not due so much to paying out Robert his stake in the partnership but to the failure of Dennistoun Brothers in Scotland. The large international Scottish company with a reputation that many thought was beyond doubt, had gotten badly exposed to the prevailing American financial and economic downturn and the failure of the Liverpool Bank where they were a major shareholder. This resulted in Muir Brothers, who through no fault of their own, being caught short by almost £7000 in a series of interconnected

---

[375] Municipal Council West, *The Star* (Ballarat) Wednesday 2 September 1857, page 2.

contracts both in imported goods from Glasgow and some local transactions where bills could not be honoured and collected.[376]

This resulted in all the Muir Brothers properties except the grocery store on Lydiard Street Ballarat, the Mt Blowhard Hotel and the Melbourne warehouse on Flinders Street being sold as part of the insolvency arrangement.[377] Robert, it seemed, had also been acting outside of his responsibilities and thus worsened an already bad situation. An audit of the Ballarat businesses by James Stirling, organized by William, had discovered 'great recklessness' in the conduct of the business, with many bad debts on the books that were called good. One bad debt of £4000 for goods held and sold on commission by Schofield, a local merchant, had resulted in the loss of almost half the total amount of Muir Brothers stock.[378]

Robert, however, had disappeared from public view and did not appear to have any intention of remaining in Ballarat to assist with the chaos that he had created and left for his brothers to resolve. In that intervening period from 1857 until 1860 there are indications that Robert had just wiped his hands of his association with Muir Brothers and made a clean break. It would appear however, that true to his character, he had been incredibly active elsewhere, assessing several promising options - travelling to northern New South Wales and had also taken a voyage back to Great Britain.

There are no indications that the £2000 awarded to Flora Cameron was ever paid and a strong likelihood that it wasn't. Indications are that on resigning from his various official and commercial entanglements, it seems he had also closed and finalised his financial arrangements as well. Bank accounts appear to have been closed and all his financial assets converted into cash, gold sovereigns and loose gold nuggets which could be traded on the market. After the trial he practically became a ghost, departing

---

[376] The Messrs Dennistoun Brothers Failure, *The Star* (Ballarat) Wednesday 10 February 1858, page 2
[377] Insolvent Court, *The Age* (Melbourne) Tuesday 13 July 1858, page 6, Law Report in the Estate of Muir Brothers, *The Argus*, Thursday 25 February 1858, page 6, Insolvent Court, Muir Brothers, *The Age* (Melbourne) 25 February 1858, page 5,
[378] In Re Muir Brothers, *The Star* (Ballarat) Saturday 20 March 1858, page 2,

1857: A Turning Point

the district almost immediately, leaving no hint of his whereabouts and making no further contact with his Ballarat associates. A memorial dinner for his old council colleagues in 1905 confirms a total lack of knowledge of his history on leaving Ballarat in 1857 and no knowledge of his death nearly twenty years prior.[379]

His departure from the family business would have been conducted on a commercial basis paying him out for his share of the company's valuation prevailing at that time. Based on later financial reporting, it could have returned to him a sum anywhere between £4000 and £6000 plus any private funds. A subsequent story thus indicates that he may not have paid the Judgement against him. Vacating the country eighteen months later, he apparently had converted his share into gold, departing with 50 gold sovereigns stored in a belt, and gold nuggets in a large wallet. On prevailing valuations, this would amount to around £6000. There was certainly enough to provide for his travels between 1857 and 1860 and some large purchases that he made during this time. The most substantial was a large consignment of brewing equipment and supplies that was purchased on arrival in London in 1859.

It was here that disaster struck that could have left him destitute and destined never to return to Australia. On arrival at Plymouth England on 2 August 1859 after departure from Melbourne in April 1859 on the Prince of Wales, he travelled to London and found himself in a coffee house in High Street Poplar where he had rented an upstairs room. Here he encountered a woman and was engaged in a conversation. Unfortunately, he had fallen foul to a notorious thief. After learning he had returned from the goldfields and had a quantity of gold sovereigns with him, the woman engaged the talkative Scotsman while shouting him to some drugged coffee. After falling asleep, she presented herself as his wife to the proprietor, and with another accomplice, went to his room and stole the 50 gold sovereigns. Luckily for him the gold that was hidden in a satchel remained undiscovered. Fortunately, the landlord noticed the suspicious behaviour and reported the

---

[379] The Jubilee of the City Council, *Ballarat Star*, 19 December 1905, p.1

incident to the police, resulting in the recovery of most of the sovereigns.[380]

---

[380] Thames, *Daily News* (London) 5 August 1859, page 6

PART V

GRAFTON AND BENOWA

Chapter 17

A New Beginning on the Clarence River

Concluding his business in Britain, Robert returned to Australia. His brother William in Melbourne thus noted in his diary on 7 June 1860, 'Robert is in town.' He then added that Robert advised him that he was returning to Ballarat. This was most likely an attempt to persuade his brother David to join his new enterprise in Grafton NSW. It would seem from William's journal that Robert had already recruited Matthew into assisting him with the venture. William notes on two occasions, on 7 June and 10 July 1860, that Robert has left Matthew in charge at 'Rabbit Island.'[381] Rabbit Island is a small island at the mouth of the Clarence River near Grafton in New South Wales, currently used in 2021 as a weather station. It was likely a reference to a staging place where the brothers may have camped in preparation of the upcoming Robertson Land Acts that were being debated in the New South Wales parliament. Presumably the brothers were there hoping to benefit from the 1860 movement advocating for free selection of land before survey. The expected decision was keenly anticipated by many farmers who had already established potential sites among themselves, waiting on the results of Government meetings and petitions both locally and in Sydney.[382]

The island is located close to Harwood Island where Robert selected land in 1860. The most plausible explanation of their activities there could be that Matthew was taking part in the informal negotiations with other prospective selectors on behalf of his brother. While he was also marking out and clearing the expected selection, Robert would have been busy setting up business in Grafton. The intended purpose for the lot was to grow

---

[381] William Paterson Muir, *A journal and cash book belonging to William Paterson Muir*, SLV accession No 14302
[382] Latest Sydney, *Clarence and Richmond Examiner and New England Advertiser*, (Grafton) Tuesday 6 November 1860, page 2

cotton, cashing in on the growing cotton shortage that was developing with the hostilities in the United States. This form of family and friends' cooperation, commonly known as dummying, or peacocking, was beneficially used later in Queensland as the brothers assisted Robert in the purchase and establishment of the Benowa Estate in the 1860s and 1870s.[383] Despite the loose ownership arrangement, the forty acres selected on Harwood Island after the act was passed, was always acknowledged as belonging to Robert Muir as an advertisement noted in the subsequent sale of the plot: 'portion 108 – containing 40 acres of rich agricultural land situated on Harwood Island, formerly in the occupation of R Muir.'[384] An earlier court case over the property also confirms that Robert Muir was the owner in a previous sale despite the official selection being made by Thomas Hutchins in February 1862. It is a good example of dummying, showing how land in early colonial times often existed in a parallel economy. In this case it passed through various hands by word-of-mouth agreements until it was eventually surveyed and sold in 1867.[385]

Robert had been active in the district almost immediately after his exit from Muir Brothers. Departing Ballarat in 1857, it appears that his intention was to establish a diversified enterprise based on real estate, brewing, hospitality and agriculture. However, it appears also, that it was always his intention to explore the possibilities of growing cotton and the region's much touted suitability for sugar as well. It is likely that his interest had been stimulated through a personal relationship with Rev J D Lang's son George in the relatively small Ballarat West township business clique. George Lang was manager of the local Bank of New South Wales, and coincidentally, was also involved in a protracted legal case from 1855 to 1857.[386] Lang, no doubt, would have stimulated

---

[383] John Elliott ed., *Letters to Bundall*, Boolarong Publications, Southport Qld 1993, p68-71

[384] Advertising, Choice Riverbank Farm on Harwood Island, *Clarence and Richmond Examiner and new England Advertiser*, Tuesday 11 June 1867, page 3

[385] Grafton District Court, *Clarence and Richmond Examiner and New England Advertiser*, Tuesday 11 August 1868, page 4

[386] Lang and Drake's Case, *Geelong Advertiser and Intelligencer*, Saturday 29 March 1856, page 2, *John Dunmore Lang 1799-1878 chiefly autobiographical: cleric writer traveller statesman, pioneer of democracy in Australia*, an assembly of contemporary

much discussion locally regarding his father's quest to publicise and attract settlers and entrepreneurs to the immense possibilities and opportunities that were to be had on the Clarence River and Southern Queensland. Interestingly, after a short period of incarceration in 1857, he continued to promote his father's passion for 'Cooksland,' working as a correspondent in Brisbane and later as an agent for Lang's Moreton Bay Immigration and Land Company both locally and in Scotland during 1860 and 1861.

For Robert Muir, like George Lang, Northern Australia would have presented as the ideal opportunity for someone running from a troubled past. Possessing all the relevant knowledge and skills outlined by Lang senior, one could therefore, successfully make a new start. Thus, having spent some time in the district from the end of 1857 and through 1858, he was convinced of its potential. Writing in a letter to the local newspaper in July 1864, he declared he had formed the conviction from the first time he came on the river, that 'its banks at no distant day would be clothed with wealth producing sugar-cane.'[387]

The earliest public evidence of his presence in Grafton was in October 1861 where it was reported that a man in the employ of Mr Muir of Dobie Street suffered a severe injury from a horse.[388] It can be deduced therefore, that what existed in 1861 would have been the product of some years of planning and establishment activity. It could therefore be assumed that his trip to England in 1859, was for the purpose of purchasing the brewing equipment that arrived in Grafton from Sydney in August 1861. It was installed in a large building that Robert had constructed close to the wharf and the ferry in the centre of Grafton on ten acres of cleared scrub.[389]

---

documents, compiled and edited by Archibald Gilchrist, Volume 1, Jedgarm Publications Melbourne 1951
[387] Robert Muir Letter to the Editor, Sugar cultivation on the Clarence River, *Clarence and Richmond Examiner and New England Advertiser*, Tuesday 5 July 1864, page 2
[388] Accidents, *Clarence and Richmond Examiner and New England Advertiser*, Tuesday 15 October 1861, page 2
[389] The Early History of Grafton August 1861, *Clarence and Richmond Examiner*, Tuesday 22 September 1903, page 8, Advertising, *Clarence and Richmond Examiner and New England Advertiser*, (Grafton), Tuesday 21 April 1863, page 3

The building also accommodated a public house that was described as 'new' in January 1862, commanding the principal landing place for all parties visiting Grafton from down the river.[390] Nearby Robert had also built a weatherboarded cottage with a veranda. Advertised for rent 1863, it was described as neat and well finished, pleasantly situated on the bank of the river.[391] With such an extensive building project it could be assumed that he would most certainly have been in Grafton well before 1860 to have selected and purchased the land for the brewery, public house and cottage and organized the arrangements for their construction.

After receiving delivery of the brewing equipment, the plant was in full operation by October 1861.[392] It was announced in the local newspaper that Mr Muir's brewery was in full operation and in addition to Mr Frazer's new flour mill across the road from him, would be of great benefit to the district.[393] The brewery began offering ales manufactured from English malt and hops at five gallons minimum and later ales in bottles as well as new yeast and grains, all delivered to any part of the river.[394] The hotel was advertised for lease once it was completed in 1862.[395] The cottage, in a manner similar to the residence at Springbank Farm at Dowling Forest Ballarat, was typically furnished with some of the best fittings available providing a degree of comfort and sophistication not usually seen in a town like Grafton. Some of the

---

[390] Public House to Let, Advertising, *Clarence and Richmond Examiner and New England Advertiser*, (Grafton) Tuesday 28 January 1862, page 3

[391] Advertising, *Clarence and Richmond Examiner and New England Advertiser* (Grafton) Tuesday 26 May 1863, page 3

[392] *The Armidale Express and New England Advertiser*, Saturday 26 October 1861, page 3

[393] Local Intelligence, Grafton, *The Armidale Express and New England General Advertiser*, Saturday 26 October 1861, page 3, The early history of Grafton, *Clarence and Richmond Examiner* (Grafton) 22 September 1903, page 8, Robert Muir is identified as the founder of the first brewery as well as a pioneer of the sugar industry locally as well as in Southern Queensland.

[394] Advertising, Grafton Brewery, *Clarence and Richmond Examiner and New England Advertiser* (Grafton) Tuesday 26 November 1861, page 1, Tuesday 18 November 1862, page 1

[395] Advertising, Public House to Let, *Clarence and Richmond Examiner and New England Advertiser* (Grafton) Tuesday 28 January 1862, page 3

pieces such as a 'bean tree' chiffonier, Arabian bedstead, and spring couch, were described as the most substantial in Grafton and the equal of anything in Sydney.[396]

As was the case in Ballarat, Robert Muir had more than one enterprise in play, a strategy that proved to be successful over the course of his life. When one area of business was in decline there was always another that kept an income coming in. Farming was thus, the one basic skill that he never relinquished that underpinned his ability to retain a degree of financial liquidity. Thus, while the cash business of the brewery was operating from 1861 to 1863, there was also the property at Harwood Island that housed a small piggery and was the source of other produce such as potatoes.[397] The piggery was particularly useful providing a steady turnover of stock as well as bacon which was sold at the brewery.

The cultivation of maize however, had been the primary reason for many earlier settlers coming to the district from the 1830s. With such an amenable climate, most of the fertile land surrounding the river was soon cultivated to full capacity destined for markets in Sydney and the other southern states. As free selection gathered pace in the colonies, the popular horse feed was increasingly sown elsewhere leading to overproduction and a substantial reduction in the price.[398] With maize in decline cotton was viewed as a crop with far more potential for a good return on the average forty-acre lot. It is likely that this is what his brother Matthew, as mentioned in William's diary in 1860 was in the process of preparing the ground for. Plots such as these were made available on very easy terms under the Robertson Land Acts of 1861.[399]

The American Civil War had created a high level of excitement over the possibility of growing cotton in northern New South Wales and Queensland. The blockade of southern American ports

---

[396] Advertising, Superior Household Furniture, *Clarence and Richmond Examiner and New England Advertiser* (Grafton) Tuesday 28 April 1863, page 3.
[397] Advertising, *Clarence and Richmond Examiner and New England Advertiser* (Grafton), Tuesday 22 April 1862, page 1
[398] History of Clarence, Mr D McFarlane, *Daily Examiner (Grafton)* Thursday 30 October 1924, page 6
[399] *An Act for regulating the Alienation of Crown Lands 18th October 1861* claao1861n26270.pdf (austlii.edu.au), accessed online 15/10/2021

had sent prices soaring to unbelievable heights turning the attention of farmers once again to Lang's earlier predictions. Alexander Cameron, an Ulmarra farmer quickly saw an opportunity and convinced many to get on board. Having been an overseer on an American cotton plantation himself, he was able to convince many others that fortunes were to be made.[400] In Grafton, an association had been formed offering prizes and other inducements such as a government bonus. Based on local experimentation by respected locals, the Rev Selwyn and Mr Havenden the Chief Constable, the samples they produced looked very promising indeed.[401]

Robert, who always had an open ear for a business opportunity, had found many likeminded Scotsmen in the Ulmarra district. He had become particularly close with Alexander Meston another local farmer and owner of the local Commercial Hotel and a large amount of local farming land.[402] Born in 1803 in Scotland of an old pioneering family, he was the brother of Robert Meston who sat in the first New South Wales Parliament as the member for New England.[403] Back in Scotland the family claimed a direct link to William Meston who held Dunnottar Castle for Bonnie Prince Charlie in the war of 1745.[404]

Unfortunately, a flood in 1862 had inundated most low-lying areas of the river putting plans of a fast windfall into chaos.[405] By 1863 however, with the war still raging in America many Clarence farmers decided to try their luck once again. Robert appeared to have decided to go all in with this plan, being equally convinced of the success of sugar the other potential cash crop, an idea held in reserve should cotton fail once again. It seemed that J D Lang's

---

[400] Cotton growing, the first crop on the Clarence, *Daily Examiner* (Grafton), Friday 2 June 1922, page 4
[401] Meeting at the Clarence on the Cotton Question, *The Sydney Morning Herald*, Saturday 20 April 1861, page 16
[402] Advertising, Choice Riverbank Farm, Harwood Island, *Clarence and Richmond Examiner and New England Advertiser*, Tuesday 11 June 1867, page 3
[403] Local and General, Death of Mr Meston, *Logan Witness* (Beenleigh) Saturday 1 November 1890, page 2
[404] Mr Francis Crystal Meston, Pioneer and Centenarian, *The Richmond River Herald and Northern Districts Advertiser*, Friday 10 January 1930, page 2
[405] Sugar on the Clarence, *Sydney Mail*, Saturday 24 October 1868, page 10

schemes to entice respectable classes of yeoman farmers and skilled tradesmen to Australia was finally paying off. It had been long coming, making a huge impression in the tiny hamlet of Grafton in 1847 promoting 'Cooksland.' His idea was similar to that of Angas in South Australia in the 1830s - a separate colony free of convicts and the emancipated, populated with respectable protestant yeoman farmers and mechanics.

Lang had presented this not only as a financial opportunity but also as a moral imperative. His aim was to replace the prevailing American monopoly of cotton and sugar production that were dependent on huge slave plantations. His vision was of small independent farmers who could grow their ten acres of cotton with a variety of other crops and livestock worked by them and their families. As early as 1845, Lang had been offering samples of Australian grown cotton to the Manchester manufacturers and merchants with a generally favourable response to the quality of the crop.[406] Robert, having experienced the tumult of Trinidad ten years earlier would have no doubt, like many other progressive thinking people, would have understood that the days of slavery were indeed numbered and without any Burnley style monopoly in Grafton, it seemed there was a real chance of success.

While Lang's messianic zeal for an Australian cotton industry finally bore fruit with the Manchester tycoons, his yeoman vision did not. It was quickly neutered by the new government of Queensland in the early 1860s throwing open the lands to anyone selecting a minimum of 320 acres to a maximum of 1280 acres, for the cultivation of cotton. With the Lancashire mills no longer able to reliably import from the Southern States of America, a new source was urgently needed. Thus, as most of the investment was taking place across the border in the newly declared colony of Queensland, it was roundly condemned by Lang who saw the industry being dominated by large capitalists from the very outset and a direct threat to his vision of small farms run by owner-operator yeoman farmers.[407]

---

[406] J Farnfield, Cotton and the search for an agricultural staple in early Queensland, *Queensland Heritage* Volume 2, Issue 4, May 1971, pp 20-25
[407] Select Committee on Immigration July 1860, in Michael Jones *Country of five rivers* p58

By 1863 there were established plantations with crops ready to harvest such as the Caboolture Cotton Company north of Brisbane and the Manchester Cotton Company in the south as well as many smaller farms around Ipswich.[408] Very large investments had been made in the potential of a cotton windfall at the expense of the American growers. What sparked Robert's interest was the Manchester Cotton Company, the most substantial and serious of them all. Personally endorsed Sir George Bowen, the first Governor of Queensland, it had been organized by Thomas Bazley, Manchester MP, Chairman of the Board of the Manchester Cotton Company and eleven other shareholders contributing £1000 each.[409]

Despite this discouraging development over the border, in Grafton, the mania had taken hold. The Sydney Chamber of Commerce and associated merchants in communication with contacts in England, were actively sounding out local farmers in 1861 in the Clarence district for the planting of cotton in the coming growing season.[410] Delayed by a wet couple of years, the first local crop was planted in September 1864 on the Coldstream, an arm of the Clarence River followed by a smaller experiment on three quarters of an acre by Angelo Zanelli that yielded at the very viable rate of £36 an acre.[411] This was ample evidence for Alexander Meston who followed soon after along with Robert Muir and many other local farmers. Both Muir and Meston successfully planted and harvested in 1864, over 10 acres each. Meston harvested 1498 lbs and Robert Muir 843 lbs, receiving an export bonus of £18 14s and £10 10s respectively in 1866.[412]

---

[408] J Farnfield, Cotton and the search for an agricultural staple in early Queensland, *Queensland Heritage* Volume 2, Issue 4, May 1971, p23

[409] Robert Longhurst, *Nerang Shire: a history to 1949*, The Albert Shire Council Nerang Qld, 1994, pp24-28

[410] 'Cotton Growing in the Clarence River District', Letter to the Editor by Charles William Goodes, *The Sydney Morning Herald*, Wednesday 1 May 1861, page 2

[411] Cotton Growing, First crop on the Clarence at Ulmarra in 1864, *Daily Examiner* (Grafton) Friday 2 June 1922, page 4

[412] Cotton, *Clarence and Richmond Examiner and New England Advertiser*, Tuesday 20 November 1866, page 2

A future as a small mixed farmer however was not what Robert had in mind. Unfortunately, this would have been his fate had he remained farming his forty-acre plot on Harwood Island. More importantly, with the activity of large-scale projects across the border in Queensland there was little prospect of ever competing equally with them. The large amounts of money they could command and their ability to produce in large quantities kept the prices low enough to make it difficult for the small operator. It was a dilemma that obviously preoccupied him while in Grafton. However, once familiar with the Queensland projects under way, Robert was very quick to realize that by spending very little he could easily capitalize on the obvious lack of experience and the large amounts of money behind them.

Chapter 18

Business Setback Cotton Queensland and Sugar

There was no shortage of curious onlookers from the Grafton region and in Sydney who had travelled to Queensland to see for themselves and assess the extent and viability of the various cotton schemes. They returned with glowing reports.[413] It is highly likely that Robert Muir was one of those, making the acquaintance of Edmund Henry Price, one of the shareholders of the Manchester Cotton Company shortly after he arrived in Brisbane in April 1862 as the 'resident director.'[414] For Robert Muir, this was the first link in a chain of decisions and events that resulted in a long and illustrious career in Queensland and the sugar industry.

Having very early on thrown his lot in with the Ulmarra and Harwood Island farming communities, it was not long, as an eligible bachelor, that he caught the attention of a potential marriage partner. Jane Meston, almost fifteen years his junior and the daughter of Alexander Meston, became quite enamoured with the enthusiastic and entertaining newcomer with big plans and with an obvious ability to carry them out. They were married in March 1863, Robert aged thirty-six and Jane twenty-two, at the residence of her father Alexander near Ulmarra.[415]

A few weeks later, Robert placed the brewery and the hotel in the hands a manager, Timothy Crowley, and put all his household effects up for sale as well as the farm produce - a large quantity of corn, potatoes and pumpkins, from the remaining land in

---

[413] Cotton in Queensland, *Empire* (Sydney), Monday 7 April 1862, page 8.
[414] Robert Longhurst, *Nerang Shire: a history to 1949, Albert Shire Council*, Nerang Qld, 1994, pp26-27
[415] Family Notices, *Clarence and Richmond Examiner and New England Advertiser* (Grafton) Tuesday 10 March 1863, page 2, Family Notices, *The Queenslander* Saturday 14 May 1870, page 1, Family Notices,

Grafton.[416] He announced he was moving to another part of the river, presumably to keep an eye on his latest investment - the Clarence entrance works and plant cotton. Moving in with his wife's parents upon the conception of their first child Matthew, where none of the chattels would be needed was a perfect solution.[417] At the same time, he also advertised all the Grafton real estate and the land for lease and notified that he was commencing a new business buying and selling farm produce for cash, making weekly deliveries to settlers along the river.[418] Things were looking very rosy indeed at that stage, as further possibilities with the potential for sugar, an industry he had vastly more experience with than anyone else on the river, was also beginning to be seriously considered. The plan, as his 1864 letter on sugar potential suggests, appears to have been to expand his land holdings in the Ulmarra, Rocky Mouth (now McLean) district and explore the potential for sugar and cotton as Lang had so long promoted. His business in Grafton would remain operating under management.

However, it appears that he had invested too heavily in the Clarence River, entrance & harbour project. Designed to establish Grafton as a new economic regional centre, in a few short months it had all gone up in smoke. It was the largest project to come to Grafton up to that time, attracting a great deal of local investment while substantially boosting local economic activity. After years of publicity and government debate, once approved unfortunately, it was in financial trouble almost from the outset, leaving many local suppliers of goods and services exposed.

Almost immediately after Robert Muir delegated his Grafton business, word began to circulate about John White, the contractor engaged to complete the highly anticipated development. It was a huge undertaking, widening the bar and deepening the channel as well as constructing various harbour and wharf installations around the river mouth and at Ulmarra upriver. Its cost was estimated to

---

[416] Advertising, *Clarence and Richmond Examiner and New England Advertiser* (Grafton), Tuesday 28 April 1863, page 3.
[417] Birth – Muir, *Clarence and Richmond Examiner and New England Advertiser*, Tuesday 8 December 1863, page 2
[418] Advertising, *Clarence and Richmond Examiner and New England Advertiser*, Tuesday 12 May 1863, page 4

be over £120,000 and considered vital to the future of the colony through the development of the local resources which were expected to boom in the following years.[419] Failure to pay for fifty loads of timber in June 1863, was soon met with an avalanche of claims over the following weeks.[420] By August news arrived from Sydney that John White was filing for bankruptcy. As the local correspondent sadly observed, there were many local suppliers and wage-earners who were invested in the project with supplies and other services, who were badly hurt by this development.[421]

Robert Muir was unfortunate to be one of those casualties. It would appear, he had learned little from his earlier misfortunes in Ballarat, relying heavily on credit to fund the rapid expansion and diversification of his new business as well as speculating heavily on the relatively unknown John White from Sydney. Thankfully for him it did not result in the same dire outcome, as his fellow creditors, but it forced him to exit his commercial enterprises in the town of Grafton and focus exclusively on the potential of cotton and sugar production.

A deed of assignment for all the property, buildings and stock was thus drawn up to local auctioneer Thomas Fisher to sell for the benefit of his creditors.[422] He walked away from an enterprise that had been years in the planning with virtually nothing. All the proceeds of the Muir Brothers partnership was gone, including his stylishly furnished home in Grafton. Having earlier sold the expensive furnishings in March, he left with a small amount of cash, plus the land on Harwood Island and the cotton crop that was yet to be harvested.

---

[419] Legislative Assembly Wednesday 8 October 1862, Clarence River Breakwater, *Clarence and Richmond Examiner and new England Advertiser*, Tuesday 14 October 1862, page 3, New Wharf, *Clarence and Richmond Examiner and New England Advertiser*, Tuesday 17 March 1863, page 2

[420] Small Debts Courts, *Clarence and Richmond Examiner and New England Advertiser* (Grafton) Tuesday 2 June 1863, page 2

[421] Ulmarra, New Insolvents, *Clarence and Richmond Examiner and New England Advertiser* (Grafton), Tuesday 4 August 1863, page 2

[422] *New South Wales Government Gazette* Friday 21 August 1863, Issue No 163, page 1840 (R Muir Deed of Assignment) see page 168

NOTICE is hereby given, that by a certain indenture of assignment, bearing date the fifth day of August, one thousand eight hundred and sixty-three, and made between Robert Muir, of Grafton, in the Colony of New South Wales, brewer, of the first part; Thomas Fisher, of Grafton, in the Colony of New South Wales aforesaid, storekeeper, and Edmund Potts, of Grafton, in the Colony of New South Wales aforesaid, storekeeper, of the second part; and the several persons Creditors of the said Robert Muir, who have executed or shall execute the said indenture, of the third part; the said Robert Muir did bargain, sell, assign, transfer, and set over unto the said Thomas Fisher and Edmund Potts, their executors, administrators, and assigns, all the property, Estate, book debts, credits, and effects of every description of him, the said Robert Muir, upon certain trusts therein expressed, for the benefit of all the Creditors of the said Robert Muir: And further, that the said indenture was duly executed by the said Robert Muir, and by the said Thomas Fisher and Edmund Potts, in the presence of, and attested by Rowland Brodhurst Hill, one of Her Majesty's Justices of the Peace for the said Colony: And further, that the said indenture is now lying at the office of Mr. W. H. Pigott, solicitor, Prince-street, Grafton, for inspection and execution.—Dated this fifth day of August, A.D. 1863.

Signed by the said Robert Muir, Thomas Fisher, and Edmund Potts, in the presence of
ROWLAND B. HILL, P.M.

ROBERT MUIR.
THOMAS FISHER.
E. POTTS.

2822—1   £1

While his new enterprise as a local merchant and carrier may have provided a steady income, it was much less than before. However, it increased his circle of contacts, making him a familiar face to many local settlers all along the river from Grafton to the heads. I am sure, as a quick-witted conversationalist, as he was remembered as by some, he had many debates about the viability of cotton and sugar as the next big cash crop with his customers and friends.[423] For cotton particularly, in 1863 the sky appeared to be the limit as prices continued to climb to crazy levels due to the ongoing blockade by the Yankees of the southern American ports.

To the north, in Queensland the promising cotton project under Edmund Price from Manchester had every chance to succeed. It had the backing of the Queensland Governor who had personally selected the best available land on the Nerang River and the Colonial Secretary Robert Herbert, had invested £1000 of his own money into the scheme.[424] Within twelve months there were

---

[423] Lena Cooper's Manuscript, in *Letters to Bundall 1872-1879*, in John Elliott ed., Boolarong Publications Southport Qld, 1993, p298
[424] Robert Longhurst, *Nerang Shire: a history to 1949*, Albert Shire Council, Nerang Qld, 1994, page 29-30

reports of some very fine cotton being grown on the property the equal of any grown anywhere in the world. Unfortunately, that would be the high point of the project. A disastrous flood in 1864 restricted the amount of usable ground and was a major contributing factor in the final harvest in 1865. The company went into liquidation a few months later heavily weighted by Price's extravagant living.[425] It was a huge failure along with the other projects at Caboolture and elsewhere that failed. As the Colonial Secretary noted in his correspondence to his mother, the variable climate, floods, hail and local pests that few had anticipated, defeated them all.[426]

However, Price was a resourceful and according to some, also a deceitful man. While the company enterprise was beset by mounting problems, Mr Price had been making private business arrangements of his own. Making several land applications, he created a new estate he had named 'Bundall' on the opposite side of the Nerang River. While the Accountants were pouring over the mess left in his wake on the Manchester Cotton estate, Price forged ahead with the development of his own business after successfully applying for an extension of time for his 1280 acres selected in 1862 under the Cotton regulations.[427] Within twelve months the Bundall Estate was named as one of the best in Queensland, astutely selected on ground well above the high-water level in a locality that includes today's Sorrento.[428]

Most of this progress however was due to the work of Robert Muir, who had been appointed as the manager in the latter part of 1864. Leaving his wife and new-born son with his father-in-law at Ulmarra in New South Wales, he arrived amid a bitter armed standoff between Price's overseer and the new management of the Manchester Estate. Robert ignored the loaded guns, and the physical altercations, focussing on the possibilities in establishing

---

[425] Robert Longhurst, *Nerang Shire: a history to 1949*, Albert Shire Council, Nerang Qld, 1994, page 33

[426] Knox, Bruce Ed., *The Queensland years of Robert Herbert, Premier: letters and papers*, Brisbane, University of Qld Press, 1977, p79

[427] Robert Longhurst, *Nerang Shire: a history to 1949, Albert Shire Council*, Nerang Qld, 1994, page 33

[428] Robert Longhurst, *Nerang Shire: a history to 1949*, pp 30-34

sugar cane and his own enterprise.[429] Most likely, he was also the motivation for the expansion into the production of sugar on the estate which was originally intended to be a model cotton plantation. It can be deduced from the complex court case over the provenance of the Harwood Island property, that Robert became permanent on the Nerang River with his brother Matthew around April 1865 after selling his 40-acre lot on the Clarence River in February 1865. [430]

Almost immediately on arrival at Bundall, he registered his own interest in 640 acres adjacent under the terms of the Queensland Sugar and Coffee Regulations of 1864. His allocation dated 16 April 1865 in the Albert and Logan region is noted in the Parliamentary Papers for 1865-66 as among the first twenty to do so along with his brother Matthew who selected 320 acres later in the year presumably in the interests of a family partnership.[431] The terms as an initial three-year leasehold, were very generous at a shilling an acre per year paid in advance. The selector could then, after spending £1 per acre on genuine coffee or sugar cultivation for one twentieth of the total acreage, would qualify to convert to freehold at the same rate. This was a huge gamble, speculating with his now limited funds, on his ability to develop a profitable operation in less than three years. It was something that many other contenders, far more highly capitalized and resourced, had failed to accomplish.

By mid-1866 his brother David had joined the business, recreating the old firm of Muir Brothers or Muir & Co as they were also known as, after the inclusion of his father-in-law Alexander Meston in various ventures. Things had not gone well for the younger brother. Nevertheless, for a time after the dissolution of Muir Brothers in Ballarat, David had emerged in a reasonable financial position. He had married Margaret McNee, the widow of

---

[429] Central Police Court, *The Brisbane Courier*, Thursday 9 November 1865, page 2
[430] Grafton District Court, *Clarence and Richmond Examiner and New England Advertiser*, (Grafton) Tuesday 11 August 1868, page 4
[431] Michael Jones, *Country of five rivers: Albert Shire 1788-1988*, p67, J U McNaught Brisbane 1882, *Manchester Cotton Co's Estate comprising 36 scrub farms*, John Oxley Library, State Library of Queensland, see next page

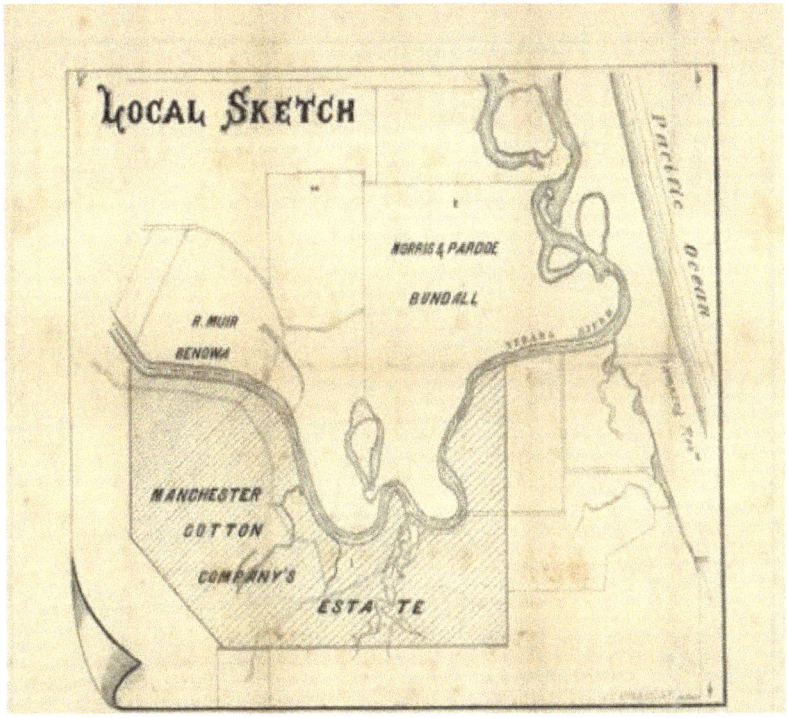

James McNee, owner of the Crow Tea Rooms in Ballarat and later manager and licensee of the Mt Blowhard Hotel. His commercial acumen however, left much to be desired with scandals and legal actions surrounding his management of the business. In April 1865 he filed for insolvency arresting what he claimed to be a decline in business. Settling the estate, David left with virtually nothing having been leveraged to almost 100% of his assets. He continued as the licensee until he transferred the publican's license to John Boone in June 1865, his last business transaction in Ballarat before he joined his brother Robert the following year.[432] Following this, David's affairs in Ballarat came to a tragic end with the death of his wife Margaret who passed away on 21 December 1865 at their home at the Mount Blowhard Hotel where they were permitted to reside after the failure of the business.[433]

---

[432] New Insolvents, *Leader*, (Melbourne) 15 April 1865, page 5
[433] Family Notices, *The Ballarat Star*, Saturday 23 December 1865, page 2

Over the course of the next twelve months the brothers, along with some hired help, had cleared and planted at least fifty acres of land with sugar cane on their own properties, while Robert also continued as the manager of operations on Price's property next door. This provided an opportunity to experiment with sugar production free of charge, from a range of cane varieties planted on Price's estate in 1865. An account of his endeavours in early March 1866 attracted a lot of excitement after a sample was handed to the Brisbane Courier.[434] By the following year Robert had begun crushing mature cane with a home-made mill of his own basic design. It was described by the Queensland Guardian as:

> Two short blocks of wood placed on top of the other and the under one is a tub to collect the juice. The cane is placed between the blocks and the upper one is brought down over the other by a very powerful lever. The juice is conveyed to a series of pots and the boiling process is affected. [435]

These first samples of sugar from 'ribbon canes' attracted a great deal of interest, described as bright and well crystalized and of a quantity that was very promising. Robert explained to the interested media that the variety selected had surpassed his expectations being based on his knowledge of frost resistant varieties in the southern states of America. He thus was confident that based on this small example, that sugar had a future in Australia.[436]

With fifty acres planted for the coming season for his employer, Robert then, with over six months to kill, wasted no time in planning for a lucrative future of his own. From his near penniless circumstances at the close of 1863 Robert had, within just over two years, once again established a reasonably healthy financial foundation. As manager of Price's plantation, he had also secured the position as local Postmaster soon after his arrival in 1865, for

---

[434] *The Darling Downs Gazette and General Advertiser* (Toowoomba) Saturday 24 March 1866, page 3
[435] *Queensland Daily Guardian*, 19 May 1866, page 5, Robert Longhurst, Nerang Shire: a history to 1949, Albert Shire Council, Nerang Qld, 1994, page 33
[436] Agricultural, *The Brisbane Courier*, Tuesday 17 April 1866, page 3.

the small but growing numbers of settlers on the Nerang River and surrounding area. This resulted in the reliable ongoing income of at least £3-400 per year.[437] In addition he had the small amount of cash from the sale of his furniture and effects, the land and cotton proceeds from Harwood Island, as well as the income from his small delivery and merchant business. It all amounted to around £1000. With the possibility of realizing over £2000 in the next few years if he succeeded in achieving good results with sugar production, his bold move was indeed showing promise as he continued the back-breaking work of establishing his own sugar plantation nearby.

Once securing the three 320 acre lots adjacent to Price's Bundall Estate, Robert then left for Ulmarra to re-join his small family over the border. Packing up enough belongings and provisions for at least a fortnight, he left with his brother Matthew in a 'covered two-horse waggonette' leaving brother David to oversee operations. According to his brother-in-law Archibald Meston, they were the first Europeans to achieve the feat of driving such a vehicle from the Logan to Casino. Meston describes their journey through unmarked territory passing by Mount Lindesay, Unumgar, Kyogle and the treacherous Beantree Crossing – 'a deep wedge-shaped creek with steep banks twenty to thirty feet in height' that had claimed the lives of several unlucky adventurers.[438]

Unfortunately, later in 1866, on his return to Bundall, Robert found matters once again in chaos. Price was in dispute again with the liquidators of the Manchester Cotton Company. With little in the way of income from the estate, Price was keeping affairs afloat by mortgaging his own property while at the same time fighting off the lawyers and liquidators of the Manchester Estate. It was a strategy doomed for disaster with the assets ending up in the hands of the mortgagor Alfred Holland, brother of one of the eventual owners a little over twelve months later.[439] Despite this apparent

---

[437] Robert Longhurst, *Nerang Shire: a history to 1949*, Albert Shire Council, Nerang Qld, 1994, page 34
[438] South Coast Memories, *The Brisbane Courier*, Monday 17 March 1924, page 10
[439] Robert Longhurst, *Nerang Shire: a history to 1949*, Albert Shire Council, Nerang Qld, 1994, page 35

reversal of fortune, Robert was quick to capitalize on the lack of knowledge and experience in the sugar industry that was still very much in its infancy. While a few pioneers had been able to grow sugar cane for many years, nobody had been able to produce consistently paying commercial quantities of sugar both raw and refined.

Chapter 19

Hon Louis Hope MLC and the Travails of Profitable Sugar

With his undeniable knowledge of the industry, Robert Muir quickly sensed an opportunity for somebody with experience as both a grower and a boiler. With a keen interest in its potential, he would have been cognisant of the obvious lack of knowledge and experience by the local pioneers of the industry. For the most part, many of the early experiments were focussed primarily on growing, as there were few in Australia with extensive experience with sugar production. Nevertheless, the lure of a lucrative cash crop such as sugarcane, had resulted in successful cultivation as far south as Kiama in New South Wales. In these early attempts, sugar was produced in small quantities as proof of its potential. From Port Macquarie in New South Wales Thomas Scott had conducted many experiments since the 1840s, while further north an even more promising project was under way by the Hon Captain Louis Hope, a well-connected Scot, successful squatter, grazier and Queensland MLC at Cleveland, just a few miles from Robert's location on the Nerang River.

To make sugar a paying proposition however there were many challenges and gaps in the knowledge and experience of those pioneering the industry. For example, as was pointed out at a conference in Sydney in 1865 sponsored by NSW politicians J D Lang and Henry Parkes MLA, labour costs were a significant disincentive.[440] However, as those with experience, like Robert Muir would have known, this was based on the British West Indies where slaves had long been emancipated and where they quickly learned to combine to force the payment of higher wages. Robert also would no doubt have not forgotten his experiences in America

---

[440] The Planting and Manufacture of Sugar, *The Sydney Morning Herald*, Tuesday 31 January 1865, page 8

with the highly sophisticated plantations and their well-trained slave workers using the most advanced equipment of the day. Thus, in the knowledge that the solutions were not as simple as the Australian experts believed, he watched with interest the flailing attempts of the local pioneers as they sought to find a way to produce sugar at a competitive price.

Hope saw part of the solution in increasing the yield from crushing, by experimenting with different types of cane. Identifying the highest yielding varieties suited for the Southeast Queensland climate, and utilizing heavy machinery to reduce labour costs was viewed as the answer. Initial results from his own earlier trials at Port Macquarie, according to persistent lobbyist and publicist Thomas Scott, were encouraging with some results indicating a yield more than 20% higher than what could be achieved in the West Indies.[441] With government backing by way of a generous land grant and the use of the resources of the Brisbane botanical gardens, Scott was positive that success with Hope's venture was a certainty. After the failure of cotton, sugar in the mid-1860s was considered a better option to boost GDP for the new colony. By 1869 there was a small experimental plot in Brisbane where seventeen varieties from varied locations, local and abroad, were cultivated and compared for their extraction quantities and climate compatibilities by the botanical gardens curator Walter Hill.[442]

But in 1866, all eyes were focussed on the Ormiston Plantation at Cleveland, where Louis Hope, as he had indicated, had made a huge investment in the second part of the solution, installing some very heavy equipment for crushing the cane and manufacturing the sugar. A journalist described the installation as first-class - a powerful mill powered by a stationary engine driven by eight horses. Steam was supplied to the mill for evaporation by a set of 600-gallon clarifiers and a host of other metal cisterns and coolers. The whole installation was contained in a large shed with a

---

[441] The Sugar Plantation at Cleveland Point, *The Courier (Brisbane)* Tuesday 1 December 1863, page 3
[442] The Grant to the Hon Louis Hope, *The Queenslander*, Saturday 29 February 1868, page 4, The Sugar Cane in the Brisbane Botanic Gardens, *The Queensland Times Ipswich Herald and General Advertiser*, Saturday 6 November 1869, page 4

corrugated iron roof. The latest technology also was employed in the cultivation of the cane fields with a steam locomotive named 'Pioneer' used for cultivation.[443] Thus with so much money and effort being expended, it was believed that success was now guaranteed. Unfortunately, much of it was wasted due to lack of experience with the boiling, evaporation and crystallizing of the extracted juice. As far the industry itself was concerned, the local growers who had done deals to supply the cane, were wary of allowing one huge operation to dominate, preferring, like the Yeoman class that many were, to retain as much of the process and the returns for themselves.

Thus, after a great deal of early fanfare over the 'blue sky' possibilities of sugar, the eagerly anticipated results from the 1867 crushing from the most prominent plantations of Whish and Captain Hope were very disappointing. The sobering fact was that prices and yields were well below the international benchmarks.[444] During the following year, McDonald, Hope's manager at Cleveland Mill, who had signed contracts for the supply of cane with many local farmers, went on a publicity campaign to explain to the increasingly nervous growers that the problem lay in the varieties of cane that were being grown and crushed. Pointing out, from his claimed experience in the West Indies, that Bourbon cane that many were cultivating, while the most common and lowest cost, was not necessarily the best for Queensland conditions.[445]

At a further meeting where the mood turned hostile, McDonald's competence and credibility was questioned when he failed to satisfactorily explain why more molasses than sugar was produced from their cane.[446] It would appear from later revelations, that it was due to McDonald experimenting with a manual

---

[443] Manufacture of Sugar at Cleveland, *The Queenslander*, (Brisbane) Saturday 10 August 1867, page 10

[444] Queensland Sugar, *The Queenslander* (Brisbane) Saturday 10 August 1867, page 10

[445] Sugar Growing at Tingalpa, *The Queenslander* (Brisbane) Saturday 14 September 1867, page 10
Different Qualities of Sugar Cane, *The Queenslander* (Brisbane) Saturday 11 January 1868, page 10

[446] The Farmers Association and the Manufacture of Sugar, *The Queenslander* (Brisbane) Saturday 19 October 1867, page 5

centrifugal machine while employed by Louis Hope. While it could be manufactured for the affordable cost of £15, it primarily produced molasses rather than facilitated the crystallization of sugar.[447] Following that a unanimous resolution was passed to renege on their agreements by activating an escape clause that Captain Hope had generously written into the contracts as a gesture of goodwill. The prime motivation was that they could do much better themselves and would retain any profits locally for the benefit of local planters. It was proposed that a limited liability company be formed and £2000 be raised to construct their own mill.[448]

By October 1869, the press was reporting that the Cleveland Plantation was in a better position due to the addition of an experienced sugar manufacturer.[449] Shortly after, Captain Hope's new sugar expert was enthusiastically canvassing the local press who reported that Robert Muir was the new expert and manager and was proudly exhibiting some very fine samples of high yielding sugar. It restored confidence among supporters, albeit a little late, in the operation.[450] Muir's stay at Hope's Ormiston mill extended for almost twelve months, supervising a refit of much of the plant while Matthew Muir remained in charge at Benowa. With virtually unlimited funds, he was responsible for constructing the large chimney that served as a local landmark for almost eighty years when it was demolished in 1946.[451]

Despite, the success at Ormiston, and that of the farmers' co-operative on Doughboy Creek shortly after, the dream of the individual grower also becoming a producer remained very much alive. It was given a boost when John McDonald Superintendent

---

[447] A Useful Machine for Sugar Makers, *The Brisbane Courier*, Friday 3 June 1870, page 3
[448] A Sugar Mill for the Doughboy, *The Queenslander* (Brisbane) Saturday 10 October 1868, page 6
[449] Sugar Growing in the Logan District, *The Brisbane Courier*, Thursday 7 October 1869, page 3
[450] Agricultural Items, *The Brisbane Courier*, Saturday 9 October 1869, page 6
[451] Old Landmark Disappears, Letters to the Editor, *The Courier Mail* (Brisbane) Friday 21 June 1946, page 2, William Boag ca 1871, *Ormiston Sugar Mill Cleveland Qld*, John Oxley Library State Library of Queensland, (see next page)

of the St Helena penal colony installed a mill designed to make the prison self-sufficient for the low cost of £120.

It was touted as an affordable milling equipment for the small farmer based on a vertical design, powered by four horses.[452] However, the breakthrough that raised the hopes of the small operator was the invention reported already at work on Robert Muir's establishment on the Nerang River. Being an engineer himself Muir had wasted no time seeking out the services and opinions of fellow engineers in the pursuit of an affordable

---

[452] The Sugar Cane in Queensland, *The Brisbane Courier*, Friday 10 December 1869, page 4

solution for the small producer but more specifically for his own circumstances.

He had engaged Brisbane engineer Joseph Collett who was persuaded to invest in the idea of a compact mill. In less than twelve months it was designed, constructed, and put to work on Muir's plantation and was producing good sugar. It was described as partly constructed of wood with four horizontal rollers powered by four horses. Collett, who retained the patent, assured the Queensland Times correspondent that the whole plant including crushing and clarifying equipment as well as a shed to contain it could be supplied and erected for £350.[453] This was the equipment used in the first crushing and production of sugar on the Benowa estate assisted by brothers David and Matthew and his brother-in-law Archibald Meston from Grafton. Meston, who had come to learn the art of sugar making as he recalled many years later, described it as a very basic operation. Without any centrifugal apparatus for separating molasses and sugar granules, as he later commented, it was largely dependent on the skill of the operator.[454]

Once the harvest was completed, Robert left the marketing of the sugar in the hands of his brothers and left for Ulmarra to take up a position as manager and later lessee of the Carr's Creek sugar mill on the Clarence River. This would be a trek of over two weeks on horseback following the shoreline and the beaches with his seventeen-year-old brother-in-law Archibald Meston. Meston, who later became a news correspondent, politician, explorer and Aboriginal Protector, is remembered also for his work in the preservation of many Aboriginal languages. He recounted the journey in a series of 'reminiscences' in newspaper articles in later life recalling the names of the local indigenous people he encountered along the way.

---

[453] Local and General News, *Queensland Times, Ipswich Herald and general Advertiser*, 20 December 1870, page 3
[454] South Coast Romantic History, Burleigh, Currumbin and Coolangatta, *The Brisbane Courier*, Saturday 9 February 1924, page 17, Nerang Memories, *The Brisbane Courier*, Tuesday 11 May 1920, page 6

However, at Benowa, as Muir had now named the property, things had finally taken on a more European and settled appearance. A comfortable cottage had been constructed along with other buildings such as a sawmill and sheds and buildings for sugar production. There had also been extensive clearing and drainage in preparation for cultivation of a wide variety of produce in addition to sugar cane. It was now suitable for his family to live in relative comfort. His work on the estate created wide publicity with an artist's sketch and a description appearing in the Melbourne, Sydney, and Adelaide Illustrated News in August 1871. Described as a 'magnificent estate' in an idyllic location high on the banks of the Nerang River, it overlooked 60 acres of sugar cane already planted and a further 50 acres almost ready. The rudimentary mill was described as producing sugar that was competitive with that produced by the best technology of the day such as steam and centrifugal processes.[455] Robert was even more pleased with the result of the first cane crushing which turned out almost one ton of dry sugar per day. Samples submitted late to the

---

[455] Benowa Sugar Plantation, Nerang River, Queensland, *Illustrated News for Home Readers*, (Melbourne) Saturday 12 August 1871, page 149-154

January 1871 Agricultural Show in Brisbane by his brothers were widely acknowledged as the best in Queensland and samples sent to his brother William in Melbourne were priced by local merchants at the premium rate of £35 - £40 per ton, justifying similar opinions also aired at the Brisbane and Sydney markets.[456] Matthew, filling the role as the manager, also advised the press, that by the next year, steam equipment would be installed, and the plant, equipment and buildings would all be extended and modernised, replacing the old primitive slab construction roughly hewn from trees on the property.[457] The Muir's success did not go unnoticed, especially over the border in the Clarence River district where a large body of small farmers who viewed themselves as Lang's quintessential yeomanry, were engaged in a struggle for an independent market niche against the large Sydney sugar monopoly, Colonial Sugar Refinery.

---

[456] Sugar, *The Brisbane Courier, Saturday* 23 September 1871, page 6
[457] Sugar, *The Brisbane Courier, Saturday* 23 September 1871, page 6

Chapter 20

CSR and the Yeoman Farmers on the Clarence

During a downturn in the world sugar market during 1865 and 1866, Jerome De Keating, owner of the La Rosa sugar Estate on Mauritius, was scouting better opportunities for sugar production in Australia. His assessment appeared to confirm the basis of Hope's proposed Cleveland operation, that large scale sugar production would only succeed in the Australian colonies by smaller farmers growing cane and selling it to a large central mill. He argued in a widely read pamphlet, that the possibility of the small farmer becoming a sugar producer was out of reach 'no matter how enterprising he may be.'[458] However, another more important reason was that the small independent operator-producer was a direct threat to the established business model of his and the Colonial Sugar Refinery, the Australian monopoly.

For many years, the Sydney Sugar Company or CSR as it was later known as, had faced little opposition, operating virtually alone in Melbourne and Sydney as a refiner, importing raw sugar and 'concrete' or solid undried sugar to be processed. After changes to the composition of the company and ongoing instability in world sugar prices, a new strategy was formed around the concept of a home-grown industry, avoiding the problems of relying on increasingly uncertain sources and conditions. The Clarence River district was viewed as an ideal place to commence. Edward William Knox, the son of one of the directors planned for three mills to be established in 1869-1870.[459] As earlier company records indicate, it

---

[458] Sugar Growing and Manufacture, *Maryborough Chronicle, and Wide Bay Burnett Advertiser*, Saturday 3 June 1865, page 4, Duyker, Edward, Mauritians, *Dictionary of Sydney, 2008*, http://dictionaryofsydney.org/entry/mauritians, viewed 03 Nov 2021

[459] www.danesinaustralia.com/colonial-sugar-refining-company-csr.html, accessed online 22/11/2021.

was always the intention to maintain their monopoly both as a destination for locally grown cane as well as the production of sugar.[460] Thus, by 1868, Melmoth Hall appeared in the district looking to establish a refinery and central mill in the district that would be supported and supplied by local cane growers. By the following year he had become well acquainted with most of the local farmers while conducting extensive product and marketing research. This resulted in contractual discussions with many of them including Alexander Meston Robert Muir's father-in-law.[461]

But in 1869, Robert Muir had made, what was viewed by some, as a breakthrough for the small independent producer. He had succeeded in manufacturing marketable quantities of quality sugar on his own estate, while those on the high-density farming areas around Grafton and the Clarence River were struggling to get established. This got the attention of the local farmers, who, despite the assurances of Melmoth Hall, were not convinced they could survive by selling their cane to a central mill exclusively. Thomas Bawden, local Grafton identity, believed that to be profitable, they needed to also recoup the returns from producing the sugar as well. Responding to what he saw as a misinformed overview of the industry in Queensland for the small independent grower, Bawden offered a more realistic assessment. He argued that it would be a long time before anyone would see sugar become the economic staple for the small yeoman farmer that many were anticipating.[462]

---

[460] B W Higman, Sugar Plantations and Yeoman Farming in New South Wales, *Annals of the Association of American Geographers*, Dec, 1968, Vol. 58, No. 4 (Dec., 1968), pp. 697-719, footnote 42 and following citations: C. S. R. Board Minutes, 26 Mar., 1867 and 30 June, 1868, Extracts from Board Minutes, C. S. R. Archives, *Manning River News*, 12 Oct., 1867, and 11 July, 1868; *Clarence and Richmond Examiner*, 14 July, 1868; E. Knox to G. Knox (Cambridge), 18 July, 1868, Knox Family Papers, Box 5 (Uncatalogued MSS 98); C. S. R. Half Yearly Report, 23 Aug., 1869; E. Knox to D. Larnach, 7 June, 1880, Knox Family Papers, Box 14

[461] Original Correspondence, *Testing Sugar Cane, Clarence and Richmond Examiner and New England Advertiser*, Tuesday 10 August 1869, page 3

[462] The Sugar Mill Question, *The Brisbane Courier*, Saturday 25 September 1869, page 7

His scepticism followed the frustrating experiments by a few brave local enterprises, who, after two seasons, were no closer to making sugar a paying proposition. A local association had been formed in 1867 following the apparent successes north of the border and letters were written to Robert Muir and Captain Hope and a few other producers to procure suitable cane varieties. There was also added optimism that the small farmer may also have a chance with an invention by a Mr Knaggs of an affordable piece of machinery that could be operated by one person.[463] But two years on, most had done the practical costings and learned from bitter experience that it was not as simple as the press was portraying.

But Thomas Bawden, was not to be discouraged from the dream of achieving success as both a grower and producer for the small operator. Like Robert Muir, he also had the benefit of years' experience in the West Indies in the sugar industry and was convinced that success with older and less sophisticated, open pan technology could be achieved by lowering expectations a little. Bawden suggested that farmers form small cooperatives and purchase the less sophisticated equipment, and that while not producing first grade sugar, they would still generate sufficient income from rum, molasses and sugar sold to the refiners. Even so, he believed that this could only be achieved with Government assistance to procure the necessary equipment priced between £500 and £1000.[464]

This made many extremely reticent to commit a large portion of their mainly 40-acre properties to a relatively untested enterprise, convinced by the failure of Bawden's Carr's Creek Mill to successfully produce anything.[465] Adding to the sombre mood, another enterprise, the Belmore mill at Ulmarra owned by another local consortium and fitted out with the latest technology, also had failed to produce any returns to the investors and was in the

---

[463] Rocky Mouth, *Clarence and Richmond Examiner and New England Advertiser*, 24 September 1867, page 2

[464] The Sugar Mill Question, *The Brisbane Courier*, Saturday 25 September 1869, page 7.

[465] Sugar Production in the Clarence District, *The Sydney Morning Herald*, Saturday 12 November 1870, page 7,

process of being wound up. This had contributed to a local crisis with the potential wastage of a large proportion of harvested and unharvested crop. With many farmers staring losses in the face it greatly discouraged any further planting.[466] Likewise operations at the Southgate mill recently constructed by CSR on the bank opposite the Belmore, had been suspended due to the mill's completion occurring too late for the previous season's harvest and their problems with the floods in 1870.[467] However, as a sign of good faith for the coming year, the problem was generously ameliorated to some extent by CSR paying the local farmers advances on their unplanted or unharvested crops. It was looking very much like sugar production as a viable industry was in a very dire position for anyone.

The success across the border among small operators like Robert Muir, however, was viewed by CSR with dismay. Likewise, the continued efforts by prominent local business entrepreneurs like Thomas Bawden was making the possibility of controlling the industry as they had done for many years, increasingly difficult. It was also noticed that plantations like Louis Hope's and Price's at Bundall, were beginning to produce good raw sugar direct to the market and avoiding the £5 import duty that was imposed on the imported product for refining.[468] These developments complicated matters for CSR, forcing them to purchase more advanced machinery for the Clarence Mills, and consider clarifying and refining locally rather than at the centrally located refinery in Sydney.[469]

---

[466] Belmore Sugar Mill, *Clarence and Richmond Examiner and New England Advertiser*, Tuesday 8 March 1870, page 2, The Belmore Sugar Mill, *The Clarence River Advocate*, Thursday 24 November 1932, page 1, Sugar Cultivation at the Clarence, *Sydney Mail*, Saturday 27 August 1870, page 10

[467] The Colonial Refining Sugar Company's Mill Southgate, Clarence River, *Empire* (Sydney) Tuesday 9 November 1869, page 4, The Sugar Industry in New South Wales, Queensland Times, *Ipswich Herald and General Advertiser*, Tuesday 8 November 1870, page 3

[468] B W Higman, Sugar Plantations and Yeoman Farming in New South Wales, *Annals of the Association of American Geographers*, Dec 1968, Vol. 58, No. 4, page 707

[469] B W Higman, Sugar Plantations and Yeoman Farming in New South Wales, *Annals of the Association of American Geographers*, Dec 1968, Vol. 58, No. 4, page 707, *Logan Witness*, (Beenleigh) Saturday 21 February 1880, page 2

For the local private mills just commencing operation, this new development was an insurmountable obstacle. On top of a lack of expertise, there was the additional burden of the lack of funds necessary to purchase the modern equipment to compete with CSR, often in the thousands of pounds. In addition, the manual separation of the liquor from cane with crude box filters and ladles were all requisite of years of experience that most in the district just did not have. This presented an opportunity for a resourceful sugar boiler like Robert Muir who, using these methods, had the expertise to maximise the older, cheaper open-pan technology to the fullest.

As he later recounted, he was tentatively approached early in 1870 by the directors of the Carr's Creek Sugar Company at Grafton, inquiring as to what were his terms and conditions for putting their mill into working order. After producing a letter of recommendation from Louis Hope, owner of the Cleveland Estate and respected MLC, guarantees were provided for his contractual arrangements.[470] This included the temporary management of the mill after the failure of their latest sugar boiler, the seventeen year old Marshall Jr, who, along with his father appeared to have made a bad situation much worse.[471] A very generous bargain was also struck with Thomas Bawden, the managing director, whereby a one-year lease was extended at no cost. In return Robert was to make the necessary alterations as well as purchasing the company's cane while retaining the proceeds of any sugar produced. Leaving Matthew again as the manager at Nerang Creek, and son Matthew in the care of a nanny, his wife Jane recently passed away, he relocated to the Carr's Creek Mill in Grafton. Muir then went to work sorting out the mechanical and procedural problems. It was not long before he was producing five to six tons of sugar weekly that achieved the prevailing premium rate of between £35 and £38

---

[470] Brushgrove, Complimentary Dinner to Mr Robert Muir, *Clarence and Richmond Examiner and New England Advertiser*, (Grafton), Tuesday 30 July 1872, page 4

[471] Sugar Production in the Clarence District, *The Sydney Morning Herald*, Saturday 12 November 1870, page 7

per ton.[472] As the local press correspondent wrote, 'the starting of the mill after alterations was an event of importance to the people and the issue was watched with considerable eagerness.'[473]

With the mill in operation Robert then went on a buying campaign purchasing any remaining crops in the district that were available and realizing for himself the proceeds of over one ton of sugar per day.[474] He immediately made an impact on the local community, attracting the attention of a visiting correspondent from a Sydney newspaper who reproduced large parts of a long interview on the merits of cane varieties and the industry itself. The correspondent even attempted to reproduce the humorous elements of Muir's obviously broad Scotch accent which he proudly turned on for his benefit.[475]

Robert, who was never reticent with an opinion, was making a huge impact in the local area based on his practical demonstrations of answers to controversial issues and problems. Not the least of these was debunking beliefs among many growers regarding the most suitable varieties and harvesting time. This was in response to debate on whether cane should be grown for two years instead of one to be fully mature. Considering the difficulties due to the recent floods, an early harvest could potentially ameliorate losses and save money. The two year opinion was held by the old school, supported by the 'father' of the industry in Australia Thomas Scott.[476] The local debate had become even more confused due to the activities of Melmoth Hall, the Colonial Sugar expert, who had his own unique opinions. However, the speed with which Robert Muir had been able to plant a crop, harvest it, and produce good sugar in under a year at Nerang Creek was creating an enormous impression among the local growers as was his own experiments with other varieties that could be harvested in under a year. His

---

[472] Sugar in New South Wales, *The Queenslander*, Saturday 23 September 1871, page 5
[473] Sugar cane on the Clarence, *Australian Town and Country Journal*, Saturday 14 October 1871, page 14
[474] Ibid.
[475] The Tourist, *The Sydney Mail and New South Wales Advertiser*, Saturday 28 October 1871, page 1114
[476] Upper Mary, The Sugar Cane in Australia No 2, *Maryborough Chronicle, Wide Bay and Burnett Advertiser*, Saturday 27 August 1870, page 2

father-in-law Alexander Meston publicised this later in the local press.[477]

Thus, with the problems experienced by the other mills in the district, this created a small window of opportunity where Robert Muir for a short time held a virtual monopoly over sugar production in the district, realizing a very substantial profit as the 1871 meeting of the Carr's Creek company shareholders suggest.[478] Thomas Bawden, the Managing Director, then convinced the shareholders that a plan that Robert had drawn up for them be immediately implemented. This involved the cultivation of the whole sixty acres of their property and the retention of Muir for another twelve months as manager.[479] This, as Robert explained, would involve a further investment of £1000 but would return a profit of £500 after recouping the investment and expenses for the next season.

Bawden believed that the survival of the company was vital for any local interest in the industry, likening the attempts to keep the company afloat, to a battle between 'Sydney and local capital.' He warned that if local farmers continued to be recruited to the Colonial Sugar Refining Company's cause, 'they would … live to regret it.'[480] While many local farmers were content to supply the Colonial Sugar mills, the large profits they were making and the obvious attempts to create a monopoly aroused a strong sense of injustice. This resonated loudly at the re-negotiations for their crop at a long and often contentious meeting with the CSR agent Melmoth Hall in August 1870. In their reduced bargaining position, he taunted them by bringing up the threats the year before to only support the failed local Belmore Mill.[481] For those in a sound financial position however, the potential to become a both

---

[477] Testing Sugar Cane, *Clarence and Richmond Examiner and New England Advertiser*, Tuesday 10 August 1869, page 3
[478] Grafton and Carr's Creek Sugar Company (Limited), *Clarence and Richmond Examiner and New England Advertiser*, Tuesday 31 October 1871, page 2
[479] Brushgrove, Complimentary Dinner to Mr Robert Muir, *Clarence and Richmond Examiner and New England Advertiser*, (Grafton), Tuesday 30 July 1872, page 4
[480] ibid
[481] Sugar Cultivation on the Clarence, *Sydney Mail*, Saturday 27 August 1870, page 10

a grower and a producer from their fifty acres was a risk worth taking. With an average of two tons of sugar to the acre at a conservative price of £35 per ton a potential profit of £1000 per season was seen to be an answer to their prayers and a better option than handing it to Sydney capitalists.

Hall, however, was not giving up the campaign to create a monopoly, increasing the incentives to the local growers by offering two prizes of £50 each and a further two prizes of £25 each to the best five to ten acres of cane supplied to the new Chatsworth Mill soon to come online. He declared optimistically that if they stayed loyal to the Colonial Sugar Refining Co. it would not be long before their sons would be 'all mounted on fine horses and their daughters were wearing silk dresses and playing the piano.'[482] Despite these rosy promises there were a small number who were convinced by the example of Robert Muir, that such a state of prosperity could be achieved a great deal sooner by branching out on their own as both growers and producers by taking a risk on a relatively modest investment. Having seen Carr's Creek mill turned to a profit with relatively primitive technology had raised the hopes of many in the district that with the initial assistance and direction of Robert Muir, it could be a relatively safe. As further confirmation, the sugar produced at the Carr's Creek Mill, earned second prize at the annual exhibition of the Clarence Pastoral, Agricultural and Horticultural Society in March 1873. Exhibited by Matthew Muir, it was highly commended for its quality and deemed competitive with the CSR exhibit which was produced using all the most up to date equipment.[483]

The first to take a gamble on Robert Muir was Leeson, a prominent local businessman and farmer. With the price of maize remaining in a depressed state, sugar cane as a viable long-term substitute was gaining in popularity especially with the attractive offers made by Colonial Sugar Refinery. However, with banks eager to lend to those with equity and assets, a relatively modest

---

[482] Sugar Cultivation at the Clarence, *Sydney Mail*, Saturday 27 August 1870, page 10
[483] Clarence, Pastoral, Agricultural and Horticultural Society, Seventh Annual Exhibition, *Clarence and Richmond Examiner and New England Advertiser*, Tuesday 25 March 1873, page 2

investment of £100 for a return of at least ten-fold in one season on a 20–30-acre crop, becoming a producer as well, was too good a proposition to ignore.

Thus, while leasing and operating the Carr's Creek Mill during the 1871 season, Robert had also been very active elsewhere, negotiating with others like Leeson similar arrangements as well as redesigning and improving the mill that was operating at his own plantation. An improved version of this was designed by Muir and presented to Leeson who, along with another private operator, the Kirk family at North Arm on the Clarence, agreed to engage Sydney engineering firm Chapman & Co that later that year. By August 1872 Leeson's mill was reported to be in operation after its construction was personally supervised by Robert Muir, and as a local correspondent described it, 'producing 15cwt of beautiful marketable sugar per day.' For well under £500 it was deemed a success combining both old and new technology of open pan and centrifuge as well as the building to contain it.[484]

At the same time the Kirk's mill, in the final stages of construction and testing also supervised by Robert Muir, was reported to have surpassed all expectations. With the superior variety of cane grown on the property, it would, as Muir explained to a news correspondent, turn out a ton a day of similar quality sugar to the Leeson Mill when in full working order. Thus, as it was pointed out, mills such as these prove that this is the best way for 'many more planters who wish to erect their own mills … and the very reasonable figure of cost will leave it to the power of one to provide his own machinery.'[485] These two private mills in addition to another operated by Mr Chown nearby as well as the Grafton Corporate mill at Carr's Creek were the *Empire* argued, 'doing more to advance the sugar industry than a hundred company mills crushing on the terms and principles of purchasing of the Sydney Company's mills'.[486]

Robert Muir had thus shaken the local industry to its core. He had proven beyond doubt that the yeoman could also be a small capitalist and in time may even become a large capitalist. So

---

[484] Clarence River, *Empire*, Monday 5 August 1872, page 3
[485] ibid
[486] Clarence River, *Empire*, Monday 5 August 1872, page 3

profound was his impact in the district, that many of the local businessmen and farmers decided that there should be a commemorative dinner proclaimed in his honour for the services rendered to the local cane growers and for the growing number who had become sugar producers as well. Mr Fuller, of Carr's Creek, had worked hard in publicizing the event as well as taking up a collection, which was generously supported, for an award that would be later presented to their benefactor. Fuller who also spoke at the dinner, noted that the local sceptics had all been proven wrong as Mr Muir had 'proved by his acts that he indeed was the poor man's friend.'

The meeting was held on Thursday 18 July and despite a race meeting being held that day, was well attended continuing until two AM the next morning. Mr William Archer, the chairman proposed a toast at the commencement of the proceedings declaring that 'he could safely say without any fear of contradiction from any quarter, that Mr Muir had been the saviour of the district.' He reminded the farmers and merchants present that with the depressed price of maize, 'utter ruin was staring many of them in the face.' He also reminded them that there had been a vocal crowd of local critics that had discouraged many, but he also asserted that Mr Muir had proved them all wrong, succeeding first at Carr's Creek, then at Leeson's and again at David Kirk's establishment. Archer then proposed a toast 'in bumpers' one of many drunk during the long celebration, for 'placing this great industry within reach of the legitimate parties – the farmers – and removing from off their necks the oppressive yolk of the large capitalists.'[487]

In response, Robert began by reminding them that his success in the district was largely due to the generosity of Captain Louis Hope of the Cleveland Mill who first engaged his services for twelve months, three years earlier. His success in turning around the fortunes of the mill resulted in a letter of recommendation that was now in the possession of the highly respected Thomas Bawden, the managing director of the Grafton Sugar Company who was largely instrumental in bringing his services to the

---

[487] Brushgrove, Complimentary Dinner to Mr Robert Muir, *Clarence and Richmond Examiner and New England Advertiser*, (Grafton), Tuesday 30 July 1872, page 4

Clarence. Further affirming the local opposition to the large capitalist CSR, Muir then with an evangelistic zeal, assured them stating that as he had been given the credit of 'being the humble instrument of removing the yoke – the oppressive weight of the capitalist – from off the necks of the yeomen, nothing would be omitted on his part to continue his course in such a good cause.' He then outlined an ambitious plan to secure the agency of a rival firm to market their sugar as well as their cane, predicting a chain of privately owned mills all along the northern rivers to southern Queensland would not be too far into the future.[488]

This was no idle dream; within ten years the Muir Bros and many others had expanded their sphere of operations into the Grafton and Clarence River district as well as into the Tweed River Valley and as far north as Mackay. For the Muir Brothers, it provided new opportunities in the Clarence District. An advertisement in the local Grafton paper suggests that Matthew Muir had moved to a location near Grafton, while Robert's father-in-law Alexander Meston had joined the brothers in a new company called R Muir & Co. The aim appears to have been to offer training to local farmers in the art of sugar production as well as promoting and providing their affordable plant and equipment throughout the district. Based on their success with Kirk and Leeson, guarantees of a 25-30% increase in production were offered due to further improvements in the

---

[488] Brushgrove, Complimentary Dinner to Mr Robert Muir, *Clarence and Richmond Examiner and New England Advertiser*, (Grafton), Tuesday 30 July 1872, page 4

centrifugal and boiling aspects of the plant.[489] Interest in the first affordable model continued with a local cane grower Arthur Scammell located at what is known today as Terranora, purchasing Muir's original first Collett model after failing to achieve satisfactory results with a mill he had designed and constructed himself.[490]

> **FOR SALE,**
> A **FOUR-HORSE POWER** and **SUGAR MILL**, complete, in excellent working order; capacity, four tons sugar per week.
> The above machinery has taken off three crops at Benowa Plantation, Nerang Creek, and is only to be parted with on account of the undersigned requiring steam power for his extended cultivation.
> Terms—Liberal.
> **ROBERT MUIR.**

[491] Shortly after, the Muir brothers were reported to be hard at work at establishing a new mill near Tweed Heads for the partnership of Pringle, Shankie and Byrne, a group of investors with no previous experience in the sugar industry. No expense had been spared on the new equipment that included a twelve-horsepower high pressure steam engine, another steam engine driving two centrifugals, and an assortment of boilers and clarifiers imported from Robert Harvey and Co of Glasgow. Its arrival was announced as a new era for the Tweed and with one of the brothers supervising the sugar production, the first samples were described as highly satisfactory. Achieving an estimated £34 per ton on the Sydney market and up to two tons to the acre, its success was viewed as the best incentive for farmers to return to sugar planting in the district. It was one of the few successful and enduring independent ventures into local sugar production, continuing until the end of the century.[492] At the same time Robert Muir doubled down on his promise to the Clarence River farmers of a line of mills along the coast from the Clarence

---

[489] Advertising, Sugar Plant, *Clarence and Richmond Examiner and New England Advertiser*, Tuesday 21 January 1873, page 1
[490] The Tweed River, *Clarence and Richmond Examiner and New England Advertiser* (Grafton), Tuesday 1 December 1874, page 3
[491] Advertising, *The Queenslander* (Brisbane) Saturday 5 July 1873, page 1
[492] Our Country Correspondence, Tweed River, *The Queenslander*, (Brisbane), Saturday 24 April 1875, page 9, m Boileau, Joanna, *Tweed Shire Council: Community Based Heritage Study - Thematic History 2004*, page 104, Microsoft Word - Bill's Version 25 Oct Heritage History.doc (zelmeroz.com) accessed 3/12/2021

to Southern Queensland, purchasing three properties listed as sugar farms along the Tweed River in August 1872.[493]

---

[493] Tweed River, *The Queenslander*, (Brisbane) Saturday 10 August 1872, page 11

Chapter 21

Keeping the Yeoman Farmer in the Game

Robert Muir was not the only or the first small capitalist and yeoman farmer who dreamed of attaining financial independence through innovations in the sugar industry. The 1870s were alight with many inspired farmers who trialled a plethora of techniques and devices to add as much value as they could to their cane crops and keep their profits in the family or among friends. Correspondents from many of the local newspapers thus regularly visited many of the new and smaller landholdings along the Northern NSW and southern Queensland coast reporting on a variety of methods and innovations. For example, a story about Pinwell's Koorooroo estate at Beenleigh not far from Benowa, details the efforts of a highly creative innovator who employed many of the methods of 'high farming' while also making technological innovations of his own. Like Robert Muir, he also introduced steam technology in 1973 and constructed his own versions of the technology later pioneered at Benowa such as the Sutton pan and carbonic clarification.[494]

A few years later the Victor Mill made its appearance creating quite a sensation at the 1876 Brisbane Exhibition. Exhibited by Messrs Shaw & Co, it was promoted as the perfect apparatus for the small farmer who wished to produce his own sugar. Powered by one horse, it could produce up to 600 gallons of juice per day and could be operated by one person and a horse driver. The yellow sugar it produced was also deemed to be of an acceptable quality for general use. At just £80, the whole setup including clarifier was deemed an excellent investment.[495] The mill, in conjunction with a 'Cook's Evaporator' was an American

---

[494] The Logan and Albert, *The Brisbane Courier*, Saturday 9 August 1873, page 6
[495] The Exhibition, *The Brisbane Courier*, Thursday 24 August 1876, page 5, Sugar making by small settlers, *The Telegraph* (Brisbane) Monday 1 September 1879, page 3.

invention heavily promoted by liberal campaigner J E Matthew Vincent the Australian agent, as a solution for the small farmer and a political foil to the feared takeover of the industry by large capital interests. Five years later it was still being touted as the solution for the small operator, but by then its time had passed as falling prices and the need to produce larger quantities to remain viable rendered it obsolete.

What made Robert Muir different was his ability to seize the moment with showmanship and entrepreneurial flair and an eloquence, as pointed out by his enemies in Ballarat, that demanded attention. It carried him and his ideas to the highest levels of Queensland society. Rubbing shoulders with Governors, Premiers, and people of commerce, his swashbuckling approach, laced with a razor-sharp wit ensured that his innovations demanded the attention of the decisionmakers. Unfortunately, his love of a contest often found him embroiled in controversy, rubbing many the wrong way and like a duellist in a romantic novel, he never thought twice on issuing a public challenge or statement to resolve a disagreement or defend his position.

At a fundamental business level, he had no sentimental attachment to the sugar industry per se, as his primary motivation was always about profit that could be obtained as quickly and efficiently as possible. It was that which more readily gained the attention of investors and followers alike over many other struggling and innovating hopefuls in the industry. In the early-1870s one of the greatest impediments to profitability was the cane disease that many were calling rust, a mysterious brown fungal growth that severely affected the quality of the canes and the quantity of juice. It was the major cause for a fall in yields and profits identified by Muir at the Beenleigh conference on the sugar industry in 1875.[496]

Having raised the issue repeatedly, he was appointed earlier in the year to a government board to inquire into such matters along with Karl Staiger the Government chemist. It was a problem that appeared to have no identifiable cause or solution puzzling the best in the business. It led to Muir's young brother-in-law Archie

---

[496] 'Rust' in Sugar Cane, *The Queenslander* (Brisbane) Saturday 29 May 1875, page 5

Meston, now a plantation manager himself residing in the Ipswich district, to write to *the Queenslander* urging Robert Muir, who he named the best authority on sugar cane, to respond with a solution. Interestingly Meston's assessment was the same as his brother-in-law's, that the problem was due to the cultivation of varieties not compatible with the variability of the Queensland climate.[497]

Following further calls for a solution, Robert Muir and Karl Staiger were deputised by the Diseases in Plants Commission to carry out a comprehensive survey of properties north and south, travelling to Maryborough, Rockhampton, and Mackay as well as throughout the south-east. The report on the investigation was widely published in November 1875.[498] It also formed a basis for a paper Muir presented to the Agricultural Society of Southern Queensland on 15 July entitled 'What I saw in the North.' The tour however, also provided intelligence on the competitiveness of his southern colleagues with the growing strength of the northern plantations.[499] Muir's conclusion, although not scientific, was nevertheless useful because it was based on what he saw and experienced as a grower and experimenter with varieties.

It became clear to him, as he wrote in his report, that the disease, while unknown as to its nature and cause, was more prevalent in the most common bourbon variety. He thus wrote, that although proving the highest yielder of juice, bourbon was a tropical variety that may struggle in the variability of a sub-tropical climate. This was backed up with the almost total absence of rust in varieties that were better suited to the sub-tropics. Sub-tropical varieties like meera and rappoe, which Muir cultivated on his own property at Benowa and by a few others elsewhere, were free from the disease. Staiger however, concluded that the problem was certainly due to a fungus that gained opportunity in cane that had been planted in depleted soil. This conclusion was roundly discounted due to the outbreak occurring in a wide range of soils both well fertilized and depleted. Although Staiger, like Muir also

---

[497] Cane Rust, *The Queenslander* (Brisbane) 30 September 1876, page 26
[498] Inquiry into the Sugar Cane Disease, *The Queenslander* (Brisbane) Saturday 13 November 1875, page 22
[499] Beenleigh, *The Brisbane Courier*, Saturday 31 July 1875, page 6

advised to avoid planting varieties that were more susceptible to the fungus.[500]

While not really solving the rust problem, which appeared to go away with the prevailing dry spell, Robert Muir with his ability to engage, discuss and debate on all matters with sugar and business in general, had used the experience to forge contacts in the north of the state and consolidate many associations in the south. The inquiry provided a perfect opportunity to visit a great number of plantations, discuss their operations and view their equipment. It provided an open door the following year as he marketed the Sutton Pan as well as his new controversial carbonic refining process. The inquiry thus represented perhaps the single most important opportunity to cement a position in the vanguard of the sugar industry from Central Queensland into Northern New South Wales, and all paid for by the Queensland Government.

At the same time, it was also an education into how the industry was trending. He was thus able to see and hear for himself the worrying signs of large-scale enterprises appearing in the north in addition to the CSR plants already in existence on the Clarence River. Even more concerning was an apparent backflip by his local MP, Phillip Nind, elected with the support of the local producers, now advocating the 'sense' of large-scale corporate investment as the future.

Making a decent profit was a dream that many of the yeoman class enthusiastically endorsed. The new project of Tooth and Cran on the Mary River, and another at Mackay however, had the potential to reduce them to subsistence farming, putting their dreams at risk. As Thomas Bawden in Grafton, a man of similar priorities, reminded them earlier, the level of technology and experience of smaller operations, which were typically on 40-150 acres with 10-40 acres in sugar cane, would never allow them to compete with the large capitalist enterprises. The white table sugars that fetched the highest prices and enjoyed the biggest market would always be out of reach due to the inability to purchase the technology or employ the manpower. Thus, for Robert Muir, having seen and heard first-hand the developments of large

---

[500] Inquiry into the Sugar Cane Disease, *The Queenslander* (Brisbane) Saturday 13 November 1875, page 22

capitalist interests in the north during the rust inquiry tour, had a renewed determination to do all he could to keep the independent yeoman farmer/producer in game. Unlike Bawden, he was convinced that easy profits could continue to be obtained from the more primitive open pan technology. With advantages such as a much lower capital costs and a knowledge of chemistry, he set out to take on the better resourced opposition. He believed that with the right skills, any small to medium independent operator could be competitive, producing a semi-refined product almost on par and certainly near enough to be acceptable to the market.

Robert Muir was in a unique position, having direct experience of sugar production in America by various means during the 1840s when revolutionary innovations were first introduced. The process he was obviously most skilled in, as his story demonstrates, was the open pan method. This traditional method involved boiling and reducing the extracted juice in a variety of large open pans over a fire. The inherent problem with this technology was the variability of temperature and operator proficiency. From the 1840s however, this was solved with the adoption Norbet Rillieux's vacuum pan system in Louisiana where Robert Muir served his 'apprenticeship' in sugar production. It revolutionised the sugar industry, enabling the highly efficient production of quality white, crystalline sugar to be produced safely and in large quantities.[501] Robert Muir, no doubt, would have been exposed to both of these technologies during his sojourn in the district during 1846-1847. The problem for the Australian yeoman farmer, however, was that twenty years later, the vacuum technology remained prohibitively expensive. Designed primarily for the large-scale production of the southern American plantations, at over £2000 for one appliance, it was a significant deterrent to any individual contemplating producing their own sugar.

Fortunately for yeoman farmers, reducing the juice was not the only field of innovation. For many operators both big and small, the 1840s also marked the beginning of an era of widespread innovation of all aspects of the industry encouraged by the appearance of periodicals like DeBow's review in 1846. Providing

---

[501] *Norbert Rillieux* - American Chemical Society (acs.org) accessed online 23/11/2021,

updated information of the latest chemical and engineering developments, it was to the benefit of many open pan producers regarding the refining process, allowing most to remain in the industry.[502] Thus, armed with this knowledge and experience, Robert Muir was ideally placed to improve the lot of the traditional sugar boiler who would, from the 1860s to the early 1880s, comprise a significant percentage of the sugar producers in the emerging Australian industry. Solving the dual problems crystallization and refining would allow the multitude of growers the option of becoming producers as well.

Despite persistent claims up to 1878, nobody had successfully produced any significant improvements. A breakthrough, however, came that year when Brisbane's leading engineer J W Sutton finally developed a machine that enabled rapid evaporation by forcing heated compressed air through the liquid, reducing the process to less than half the time while not burning the liquor.[503]

There is a strong suggestion that Muir may have been associated with the development of the original concept and approached Sutton with a proposal to manufacture a working device just as he had approached Collett, another local engineer with the affordable mill idea a decade earlier. Significantly, this came after a failed attempt in 1869 by John Falconer while employed at the Cleveland Estate of Louis Hope under the management of Robert Muir. Falconer later attempted to claim credit for the idea which he also

---

[502] Heitmann, John Alfred, *The Modernization of the Louisiana Sugar Industry, 1830-1910* (1987). History Faculty Publications. Paper 121. http://ecommons.udayton.edu/hst_fac_pub/12, page 16

[503] Local and General News, Improvements in Sugar Manufacture, *The Northern Star* (Lismore), Saturday 8 June, page 2, The Sutton Evaporation Apparatus for Sugar, *The Queenslander* (Brisbane), Saturday 1 February 1879, page 156

claimed was not original to him, in a letter to the Queenslander on 26 February 1879.[504]

Robert Muir, announced in the press in May 1878 he would be the first to extensively trial the invention at his property at Benowa in July 1878. It would be trialled along with updated clarification machinery, using his own newly patented improvement, the Icery-Muir process, as a single integrated operation.[505] A second trial of the Sutton pan was also arranged at the Coomera estate of White and Robinson later in the year.[506] Its operation at that estate was described in a letter by D McDonald, Robert Muir's predecessor at Hope's Cleveland plantation rating it as a success and a rival and possible successor to the vacuum pan apparatus.[507] Muir, after extensively testing the device during 1979 however, became less optimistic as he stated in an later letter to the press of his own, that while the device would be a handy adjunct to the vacuum pan, he would be mad to expect it to achieve the same level of excellence.[508] This opinion was likely due to the trials of the process at Benowa over the course of 1878 not living up to expectations due to the excessive amount of power needed to drive it. It led to the device being abandoned for the rest of the year while Sutton also made further modifications.

A remodelled version released by Sutton mid-1879 was immediately acquired by Muir for testing. He confirmed that the new version did indeed live up to its promise as a superior device for open pan sugar production. As an added benefit, he also found it was able to process varying grades of juice from mature as well

---

[504] Re: Sutton's Evaporating Pan, *The Queenslander*, Saturday 8 March 1879, page 316
[505] New Process for Sugar Making, *Logan Witness*, Saturday 11 May 1878, page 2, Sutton's Compressed Air evaporator, *The Week* (Brisbane) Saturday 25 October 1979, page 9, Evaporating Cane Juice, *Northern Star* (Lismore), Saturday 1 March 1879, page 3, Evaporating Cane Juice by Compressed Air, *The Queenslander*, Saturday 1 February 1879, page 156
[506] Evaporating Cane Juice, *Northern Star* (Lismore), Saturday 1 March 1879, page 3, The Sutton Evaporation Apparatus for Sugar, *The Queenslander* (Brisbane), Saturday 1 February 1879, page 156
[507] The Sutton Evaporating Pan at Work, *The Brisbane Courier*, Wednesday 26 February 1879, page 5
[508] Sutton's Compressed Air Evaporator, *The Queenslander* (Brisbane) Saturday 22 November 1879, page 667

as unripened and frost damaged cane to a high quality. He thus declared confidently 'the colour of the sugar is in every way equal to that made in other pans, but the grain is vastly superior. ... I am convinced when Mr Sutton carries out his original idea of consecrating the juice by this process, none of our sugars will find their way into the refiner's hands.'[509] While maintaining his opinion that the Sutton pan was best operated as an adjunct to the vacuum pan, for open pan producers he deemed it the most cost effective and profitable piece of equipment available. He also added, that 'when properly worked (it) can be made to make more money value out of a given quantity of juice than any other, the vacuum pan not excepted, the cost of plant and cost of working, the same considered.'[510]

Playing a significant role in solving the crystallization problem with the Sutton Pan, Robert Muir had proved that open pan sugar could be equally, if not more profitable. Furthermore, at much the same time on another front, an opportunity presented that could solve the refining issue as well. Significantly it came from CSR, the greatest threat to the yeoman farmer. In a campaign to bring the rebellious growers on the Clarence River under their control, they also sought to counter their growing technical competence. This led to the engagement of the industrial chemist Benjamin De Lissa in 1878 as part of a modernisation and refit program with a view to refining of sugar locally.[511] De Lissa was the Australian agent for the Icery patent for clarifying sugar using the mono-sulphite process. Invented by Dr Icery in conjunction with the traditional open pan method, he claimed an improvement on the existing lime procedure to remove residual molasses that many of the farmers were using in the final stage of crystallization. Many producers in the Grafton district were taught this method by Robert Muir during his visit in 1869-70. By utilizing De Lissa's Icery technology, CSR expected to create a technological advantage over the local

---

[509] Sutton's Compressed Air evaporator, *The Week* (Brisbane) Saturday 25 October 1979, page 9
[510] Sutton's Compressed Air Evaporator, *The Queenslander* (Brisbane) Saturday 22 November 1879, page 667
[511] District News, North Arm, *Clarence and Richmond Examiner and New England Advertiser*, Tuesday 5 August 1879, page 3

market as well as taking another step in creating the monopoly that they originally planned.

Robert Muir quickly spotted the opportunity when De Lissa's efforts ended in failure, being unable to produce adequate results with the Icery process for CSR in Grafton at their mill on Harwood Island.[512] The fallout from this was very damaging publicity for the new process as De Lissa and CSR engaged in an exchange of claims and counter claims that ranged from accusations over poor mastery of the technology as well as inadequate equipment provided by CSR. Nevertheless, while failing to make a less than favourable impression with CSR, De Lissa was not deterred, continuing to aggressively market its advantages in the Clarence River district, pointing out its potential to produce a superior grade of open pan sugar to the local farmers with their own mill. [513]

De Lissa had taken a huge gamble with the technology blinded to some extent by the quality of the sugar it produced but deficient in the economics and the marketable application skills. Muir, whose priority was always profit, outlined in a letter to the press, was that to achieve the results demonstrated by De Lissa, it was both very time consuming and costly. This was proven by his own experience and the many complaints raised by those who, a little later, had adopted the process in the MaKay district.[514] Thus, seeing an opportunity, he had been working on an improvement that would reduce time and increase quality and profit.

Robert Muir, as De Lissa pointed out, was quick to take advantage of his new technology, receiving free training from his brother David who was engaged at the nearby White and Robinson Plantation where the mono-sulphite process was in use. It had been instrumental for them in winning first and second prizes for open pan sugar at the 1878 Brisbane Exhibition.[515] He, very quickly, as De Lissa complained, became its greatest critic,

---

[512] Grafton, *The Sydney Mail and New South Wales Advertiser*, Saturday 30 November 1878, page 872

[513] Grafton, *The Sydney Mail and New South Wales Advertiser*, Saturday 30 November 1878, page 872

[514] To the Planters of Mackay, *Clarence and Richmond Examiner and New England Advertiser*, Saturday 4 October 1979, page 3

[515] Sugar at the Brisbane Show, *Mackay Mercury and South Kennedy Advertiser*, Saturday 7 September 1878, page 3

dissuading his neighbours Holland and Miskin and many others from taking it up.[516] Having seen his brother David utilize the technology on a neighbouring property as well as on his own, Robert Muir had plenty of time to assess its merits as had other sugar producers in New South Wales and Queensland. While there was no doubt about its ability to help produce good results at the Queensland Shows for sugar producers, it was, as CSR found, a hard stretch for any of them to make a decent profit on a full harvest nor did it offer any significant advantage to a competent sugar boiler. The correspondent thus noted in 1876 of Muir's sugar produced under the old method: 'Mr Muir of Benowa, Nerang, showed a very beautiful sugar which was so exquisitely white as to lead the initiated to imagine that it had been washed. Mr Muir has long been known and celebrated as the best sugar boiler in Queensland.'[517]

Nevertheless, for the less experienced, Muir had found a way to produce a technology that delivered a better result than De Lissa's in half the time, a saving in cost and enabling increased production and profits. Further improvements, although not revolutionary, were obtained over the Icery process with the application of a further 'carbonic' process. The key however was in the machine which he had created that could apply both processes simultaneously. Its efficacy was confirmed by Karl Staiger the government chemist. In the patent application he confirmed that by keeping the elements separate, they did not combine and form a new element, thus acting as intended by removing impurities in the sugar in their respective ways in one single appliance. This was a breakthrough, as previously multiple clarification processes needed to be applied separately in dedicated appliances. It was thus a saving in both time and expense while increasing the quality.[518]

After taking out the patent on the new operation, Muir wasted no time in getting it out into the public arena. Predictably, his first

---

[516] Sugar Refining, The Editor, from B C De Lissa, *Clarence and Richmond Examiner and New England Advertiser*, Tuesday 5 November 1878, page 2

[517] The Sugar Industry, *The Northern Star* (Lismore) Saturday 9 September 1876, page 2

[518] Muir's Sugar Refining Process, *Clarence and Richmond Examiner and New England Advertiser*, (Grafton), 15 October 1878, page 2

contact was to the cane farmers and producers in the Grafton and Clarence River district. With family in the local area in the sugar business, it did not take long for word to spread about the research and development into sugar production being carried out at Muir's Benowa plantation. By naming eminent people such as Staiger the Government Chemist and Sutton, the leading Queensland engineer of the day, any news was viewed as profit for those who were able to capitalise early.

The first to express an interest was John Small Jr, a leading Grafton businessman and sugar producer writing to Muir 19 June 1878. Robert Muir promptly responded offering to provide detailed information on the Sutton pan and his newly patented clarifying apparatus both of which he deemed to be a great improvement. He also offered to supply the new equipment and teach anyone who was interested how to use it. More importantly, he claimed an increase the value of their sugar by at least £3 per ton, approximately 10%. The cost, he explained would be about £70 delivered including tuition and a small royalty of 5s would be applied.[519] Following this, a meeting of the local mill owners Monday 22 July 1878 was held at Rush's Hotel at Rocky Mouth (now MacLean) where it was decided to invite Robert Muir to the district to demonstrate his new equipment and processes rather than accept Muir's invitation to travel to Benowa. At a further meeting on the subject a week later it was also decided that all of Muir's expenses would be met by the local association with all members strongly in favour.[520]

However, with both parties unable to meet due to pressing business and work commitments, J F Small Jr was the only person able to receive a demonstration. Travelling to Benowa in late September early October 1878, he had the benefit of receiving exclusive training in the use of the equipment. He returned as the local agent, made official early in February 1879, as promoter and

---

[519] Robert Muir to John F Small Jr 29 June 1878, Meeting of the Sugar Mill Owners, *Clarence and Richmond Examiner and New England Advertiser*, (Grafton), Saturday 27 July 1878, page 2
[520] Meeting of the Sugar Mill Owners, *Clarence and Richmond Examiner and New England Advertiser*, (Grafton), Saturday 27 July 1878, page 2

sole expert in the operation of the new process.[521] This he did without delay and without reserve sparking a vicious public debate and contest over the veracity of the process and the validity of the patent.

Small's first action was to make a public announcement in the local press on the superiority of Muir's process. He also provided samples of bulk sugar clarified by De Lissa's process at the Holland Miskin & Co Bundall plantation, and local sugar using the new Muir process as a comparison. Both samples were, as he explained from 'year old cane, more or less frosted'. The visual difference between the two was obvious confirming Muir's claim that the process using good cane would produce sugar 'almost equal to refined.'[522] Small went on to emphasize a major advantage of the new process was in the ability to produce high quality sugar from damaged, unripe and frost damaged canes, problems more endemic in the Grafton area than in the warmer and less problematic regions to the north.

The *Clarence Examiner* backed up the claims noting: 'The samples of sugar forwarded by our correspondent fully bear out what he has said concerning the Muir process. They are now at our office where we shall be happy to show them to those interested.'[523] This precipitated a savage response from De Lissa a few weeks later with a letter to the press both locally and in Sydney claiming illegal use of his patent and repudiating much of the technical and chemical validity of the claims of the Muir process. De Lissa also made some personal attacks on Muir's character calling him a liar for claiming the new process was endorsed by Staiger the Government chemist.[524]

---

[521] Country News, Grafton September 24, *The Sydney Morning Herald*, Wednesday 2 October 1878, page 6, The Sugar Industry, Local and General News, *Northern Star* (Lismore) Saturday 5 October 1878, page 2, The Sugar Industry, *Clarence and Richmond Examiner and New England Advertiser*, (Grafton), Saturday 1 March 1879, page 2
[522] Muir's Sugar Refining Process, *Clarence and Richmond Examiner and New England Advertiser*, Tuesday 15 October 1878, page 2
[523] ibid
[524] Sugar Refining, To the Editor of the Examiner, *Clarence and Richmond Examiner and New England Advertiser*, Tuesday 5 November 1878, page 2, The

Muir had never claimed that Staiger publicly endorsed his new refining process. However, there is no question that Muir and Staiger enjoyed a close professional relationship having both been appointed by the government to investigate the cane rust outbreak in Queensland during 1876. Staiger also purchased land from Muir at Labrador in a prime location, a few years later.[525] It is therefore entirely possible as J F Small claimed, that Staiger did in fact say to someone that the process effectively produced the same result in one operation that was previously done in two, most likely as part of the assessment for the patent application.[526]

Robert Muir's response was swift and creative. Publishing a notice dated 29 October in the regional letters to the editor, he pointed out that his process had been patented and had undergone all the same rigorous testing and assessments as the Icery Patent. He then challenged De Lissa to a public contest so interested parties could assess the merits of his clarifier and its procedure against that of the Icery Mono-sulphite machine. His proposal was to meet at the Beenleigh plantation, which was familiar to De Lissa having had extensive recent experience demonstrating and producing sugar with his process and where one of his machines was already in operation. This, as Muir pointed out, was more than fair as it offered a significant advantage for his opponent. However, the competitors were to be confined strictly to their respective patented machines and processes. A £20 deposit would be taken from each competitor with the loser donating their stake to the Southern Agricultural Society. The winner would be the producer who realized the highest price on the market for their sugar.[527] Needless to say, the challenge was not taken up by Mr De Lissa, saving him an embarrassing loss of face and public humiliation.

Monosulphite Process, to the Editor of *the Sydney Mail*, from B C De Lissa, *Sydney Mail and new South Wales Advertiser*, Saturday 9 November 1878, page 735
[525] Rust in Cane and the Proposed Remedies, *The Queenslander* (Brisbane), Saturday 5 August 1876, page 23
[526] Muir's Sugar Refining Process, *Clarence and Richmond Examiner and New England Advertiser*, Tuesday 15 October 1878, page 2
[527] Local and General News, 'Mr Muir's Sugar Refining Process', *Northern Star* (Lismore), Saturday 18 November 1878, page 2

However, Robert Muir was not prepared to allow his opponent to go quietly, launching an even more aggressive attack in the press two weeks later. He fired back with a devastating lesson in the history of open pan sugar refining in which, from all accounts, he was very well versed. His detailed response to the press indicated that De Lissa's and Icery's claim to the mono-sulphate patent was extremely tenuous. Quoting from reliable sources Muir thus suggested that any legal action from De Lissa could be easily defended. Alluding to contests over the patent already in motion from earlier developers in France, the United States and Mauritius, he suggested that Icery's ownership could be easily struck down with a legal challenge of his own.[528] Not deterred, De Lissa announced his intention to come to the district to deal in person with the threat as well as attempt to dissuade any considering becoming converts to Muir's new process.

His earlier warnings however, had fallen on deaf ears as J F Small, convinced he was onto a winning development, was pressing ahead with arrangements to have the machine that he had purchased from Muir to be setup and tested at Catt's mill near Rocky Mouth (MacLean).[529] Unfortunately, Small's proposed demonstration appears to have been postponed due to De Lissa's ongoing threats of legal action which, despite his losses in the public debate, he was far from backing away from.

De Lissa thus made good on his threat of legal action having Muir served with a writ while he was adjudicating as an official at a public event. This forced a resolution to the dispute, with Robert Muir purchasing De Lissa's share of the mono-sulphite patent shortly after.[530] So ended for Robert Muir, a year defined by innovation and controversy, where his reputation for sharp and sometimes unscrupulous dealing was in no way diminished. The hard-nosed and sometimes questionable approach to business that Muir had adopted in Queensland, had even begun to create

---

[528] Sugar Manufacture, *Clarence and Richmond Examiner and New England Advertiser*, Saturday 21 December 1878, page 3
[529] Grafton, *The Sydney Mail and New South Wales Advertiser*, Saturday 30 November 1878, page 872
[530] Sugar Making, Local and General News, *The Northern Star* (Lismore), Saturday 18 January 1879, page 2

problems among the previously tight relationship between him and his brothers and others such as his neighbours on the Bundall Estate and within the Agricultural Society establishment.

The letters of Julius Holland, one of the partners of the neighbouring Bundall Estate, are thus very revealing. They uncover some of the prevailing attitudes and relationships that were existing between him and the Muir Brothers during the 1870s. One episode during a release of crown land for selection at Beenleigh, shows Robert Muir engaging in dummying - the same practices that allowed him to obtain land at Harwood Island on the Clarence River in the early 1860s. By using the name of friend and associate George Black, who was in business with a relative of the Muirs, the brothers were able to increase their holdings in the area at the expense of their fellow cane farmers along the river, who were desperate to get that specific plot.

Julius Holland wrote to his manager Charles Morris expressing his outrage that David Muir had lied to him when asked point blank if he was selecting for his brother Robert. Having declined to give an answer and when later pressed on the matter, David stated that he was representing George Black, another planter who was a 'bona fide' applicant. Matthew Muir, who claimed to be representing himself, was later approached by Holland on the matter and told that that their actions were very unfriendly. Matthew agreed and subsequently withdrew his application. David, however had no such scruples and, as he had declared to Holland, he 'followed it through to the end.'

Holland then berated Morris in a letter, writing 'it seems to me that you allow and have always allowed the Messrs Muir too much consideration. It has always been one-sided.'[531] It is likely that this led to a parting of the ways between Matthew and Robert Muir with Matthew taking a separate path, selecting his own 600-acre pastoral lot shortly after.[532] He continued in the industry as a manager and sugar boiler on the nearby Logan Sugar Factory Plantation. He was also re-appointed in 1880 by the receivers, the

---

[531] Julius Holland to Charles Morris, 3 July 1876, in: John Elliott ed., *Letters to Bundall 1872-1879*, page 69-70
[532] Beenleigh, conditional purchasers – accepted, Matthew P Muir, 600a pastoral Nerang, *The Queenslander*, (Brisbane) 7 July 1877, page 29

Queensland National Bank, after the financial failure of the owners, Glasgow firm Hanna, Donald and Wilson. He remained there in that capacity until October 1883.[533] Matthew became well established and respected in the district serving on the board for the first appointed State School for Gramzow in 1879, now Carbrook in the Logan District. He also patronised the South East Queensland Agricultural Society, providing prizes for categories of draft horses and entering and winning categories in sugar production.[534] Matthew died intestate 15 March 1885 at the Goodna Asylum. Admitted in October 1883 due to a severe stroke, he suffered paralysis and loss of articulate speech, and later contracted fatal pneumonia.[535] He left a small estate worth £520 which all passed to Robert Muir in accordance with the law.[536]

With Matthew taking his own path, the task of providing a technological edge for the small operator, left David as the only family partner in the business. However, Robert Muir had little to worry about as he proved to be highly competent in the marketing and demonstration of the new process. In what appears to have been a planned and coordinated marketing strategy, David Muir was sent to the Grafton Clarence River district early in 1879, while Robert travelled north to Mackay and Maryborough later in the year to market the new refining process.

---

[533] Local and General News, Local Sugar, *The Northern Star* (Lismore), Saturday 29 November 1879, page 2, Resources of the Logan, The Logan Sugar Factory, *Logan Witness* (Beenleigh), Saturday 21 August 1880, page 3, Logan Mill, *The Queenslander*, Saturday 20 November 1875, page 22

[534] Latest Official Notifications, *The Telegraph* (Brisbane) Saturday 1 March 1879, page 2, Prize Schedule, *The Queenslander* (Brisbane) Saturday 24 July 1880, page 119, Advertising, *Logan Witness* (Beenleigh), Saturday 3 September 1881, page 4

[535] *Coroner's report into death of M P Muir*, Queensland State Archives, Item ID ITM2727398

[536] Queensland State Archives, Item ID ITM2804911, *Will Matthew Paterson Muir*

Chapter 22

Yeoman Profits with the Sutton Pan Icery-Muir Process

David Muir's first major assignment as part of Muir & Co, was to demonstrate and compare refining processes to the Clarence River mill owners. This was announced in the local press 15 February, calling for all interested parties as well as those on the Richmond River to attend.[537] The event was scheduled to be held at Catt's Mill near Rocky Mouth (Maclean) where he would be conducting the first episode, refining sugar with De Lissa's device. The De Lissa mono-sulphite part was completed on 20 February 1879 to a group of local producers. The Muir process was demonstrated a few days later on a machine that had been jointly purchased by the locals. As expected, the sugar produced by Muir's process, although late in the season and on a small experimental mill, was deemed to be very superior in quality[538]

By 26 February David Muir had completed his exercise having also decided to refine sugar with the traditional lime method. The results were advertised by John F Small Jr by in a letter to the local paper. Small, expressing a great deal of relief after putting his reputation on the line, was more than pleased with the result. The mill owners, he wrote, were delighted and he believed next season, the current one since ended, all of them will be adopting the Muir process. It clearly produced the best sugar he stated, and its quality was confirmed with a local merchant offering £31 per ton, £3 more than the other samples in the trial.[539] This then bore out the basis of Robert Muir's earlier challenge to De Lissa, that with lower

---

[537] The Sugar Industry, *The Northern Star*, (Lismore), Saturday 1 March 1879, page 2
[538] Rocky Mouth, *Toowoomba Chronical and Darling Downs General Advertiser*, Saturday 22 February 1879, page 2
[539] The Sugar Industry, the Muir Process, *Clarence and Richmond Examiner and New England Advertiser*, Saturday 1 March 1879, page 2

prices prevailing, his cost-effective innovation would still return a respectable profit.

The Queenslander also reported that his new process had generated a significant amount of interest making comparisons between his sugar and the exhibits of other mill owners using De Lissa's mono-sulphite process which were also on display. The correspondent thus reported:

> we have seen samples from several southern district plantations of open-pan sugars treated with the mono-sulphite process, which are very little inferior to the vacuum-pan sugars of the same district manufactured under the ordinary process; while those exhibited by Mr Muir appear to be superior to any.[540]

This was the highest possible endorsement confirming what he had declared many times, that a good sugar boiler could produce quality sugar as good as or very close to the quality of sugar made with the latest vacuum pan technology. This was later confirmed by growing numbers elsewhere in the Clarence District as J F Small continued to actively promote it.[541] The *Northern Star* at Lismore reported shortly after, that Small had furnished another sample, this time from a full harvest and described it as equally as good quality as Robert Muir's winning sample from the recent Brisbane exhibition. Muir's winning sample and Small's from his recent harvest were both heavily promoted and displayed in the various localities south of the border. They were described as 'equal to any refined sugars and in colour is similar to what is known as the Co's (CSR) No.1.' The correspondent thus declared 'it will be seen that the mill owners of the Clarence are not one whit behind the age in the treatment of cane juices.'[542]

As the year progressed in the Clarence River District, as was indicated to David Muir after his demonstration in February, a sizable number had adopted the new method as further

---

[540] Commercial Intelligence, *The Queenslander* (Brisbane) Saturday 9 August 1879, page 192
[541] District News, The mills, *Clarence and Richmond Examiner and New England Advertiser*, Tuesday 5 August 1879, page 3
[542] Sugar on the Clarence, *Northern Star* (Lismore), Saturday 6 September 1879, page 3

endorsements began to circulate. It was confirmed that soon after, at least three had ordered the new machine. This was in addition to the two existing at the establishments of J F Small and that of Alexander Meston and Miller on the Richmond River who were in the process of having one operational for the next season. By the end of August 1879 Robert Muir was claiming there were sixteen independent mill owners had signed up, representing a sizeable majority in the district.[543]

The earlier reports of Small's and David Muir's success with new refining process on the Clarence had also provided good publicity for Robert Muir in promoting his new process in the Maryborough and Mackay Districts just prior to the August exhibition. Robert Muir enjoyed a good rapport in both districts having visited many of the cane growing properties in 1875 with Staiger the Government Chemist, as part of the investigation into cane rust.[544] At his demonstration at the Dumbleton Plantation, as a local correspondent wrote, 'several planters present were astonished at the great difference in the colour of the sugar made by Mr Muir. One experienced planter remarked that he had seen worse sugar made by the vacuum pan.' Muir also was reported to have confidently asserted that the second and third sugars or the reprocessing of the remains, would not be deficient in quality.[545] However, Muir's penchant for showmanship and drama did generate some controversy. While the result of the sugar refined by his process was not in doubt, there had been a little massaging of the structure of the demonstration. Rather than following the same procedure as his brother David in February at Rocky Mouth, Robert settled for a comparison of two processes rather than three. Claiming to be rushed for time he made a comparison between the old lime process and his own, omitting the De Lissa process that most were using. This is what created the amazing contrast

---

[543] The Monosulphite Sugar, *Mackay Mercury and South Kennedy Advertiser*, Wednesday 10 September 1879, page 3, To the Planters of Mackay, *Clarence and Richmond Examiner and New England Advertiser*, Saturday 4 October 1879, page 3
[544] Rust in Cane, *The Telegraph* (Brisbane) Thursday 1 July 1875, page 3, Inquiry into the Sugar Cane Disease, *The Queenslander* (Brisbane) Saturday 13 November 1875, page 21 – full list of properties visited.
[545] *Mackay Mercury and South Kennedy Advertiser*, Saturday 23 August 1979, page 2

Correspondence.

To the Editor of the Mercury.

Dear Sir,—Referring to the paragraph, which appeared in your last issue, about sugars made at the Dumbleton Estate by the lime and sulphurous-carbonic process, I consider it due to Messrs. Lloyd and Walker to state that the sample of limed sugar therein referred to is much inferior to the average sugars made on that plantation. The juices from which the sugars in question were made held colouring matter which could not possibly be removed by the ordinary lime process. Unfortunately for show purposes the high class cane for which the Dumbleton Estate is famous, is, since the late rains unapproachable. This fact, coupled with the short time available for preparing exhibits, will most probably prevent Messrs. Lloyd and Walker from again taking first honours for open pan sugars at the local exhibition. Knowing your anxiety, Mr. Editor, to nothing extenuate, and having a desire that the Dumbleton bulk sugars should not be unwarrantably disparaged through my instrumentality, must be my excuse for troubling you for space.

I am, Dear Sir, Yours truly,
ROBERT MUIR.
Will's Hotel, Mackay, August 25,

between the samples. However, by processing all Dumbleton's cane, he denied them the chance to enter a sample at the local show and created an impression that they produced poor quality sugar. A letter of explanation and apology therefore was written by Muir to the local paper to remedy any negative press on the matter.[546]

This did little to deter the uptake of the Icery-Muir refining process however, as it continued to be endorsed widely by the local press. The *Maryborough Chronical* thus reported that De Lissa's mono-sulphite process had not been a local success and that an agent had been appointed for the new Muir process in the district, Mr R W Harris a sugar producer at Kirkcubbin.[547] On his own account meanwhile, Robert Muir's self-praise was backed by recommendations from the local press after a copy of his sugar account sales from Benowa for July and August 1979 along with another perfect sample, was submitted to the *Logan Witness*. It was reported that the highest prevailing prices displayed, confirming the parity of Muir's product with vacuum pan sugars as well as his care and skill as a sugar producer.[548]

---

[546] *Mackay Mercury and South Kennedy Advertiser*, Wednesday 27 August 1879, page 2
[547] Mr R W Harris, *Logan Witness*, Saturday 21 February 1880, page 2, *Maryborough Chronicle, Wide Bay and Burnett Advertiser*, Thursday 26 February 1880, page 1
[548] *The Brisbane Courier*, Tuesday 25 November 1879, page 2

A final independent endorsement for Robert Muir's refining process came at the end of 1879 establishing his combined mono-sulphite – carbonic process as the benchmark for open pan sugar production. In a response to a sample submitted to the *Sydney Mail*, by J F Small, an assessment from Fraser & Co sugar merchants at the Sydney Mart was returned describing the sugar as 'perfect in flavour, grain and complexion' valued at the premium price of £39 per ton.[549]

Sugar Making on the Clarence.

Through the courtesy of the proprietors of the *Clarence and Richmond Examiner*, we received this week a small sample of sugar manufactured by Mr. J. F. Small, jun., of the South Arm, of the Clarence River, by the combined Muir-Icery process, with a request that we should submit it to some experienced buyer in this city for an opinion. In compliance with this, we sought the assistance of Messrs. Fraser and Co., and with the following result:—

"TO THE EDITOR OF THE SYDNEY MAIL.

" Sir,—We have examined with much interest the sample of sugar sent to us by you as being the manufacture of Mr. J. F. Small, jun., of South Arm, Clarence River. It compares most favourably with the sugars of Mauritius and Queensland made under similar processes; is perfect in flavour, grain, and complexion, and would always command the best market price for that grade. We value the sample to-day at £39 (thirty-nine pounds) per ton in trade parcels, and must say the sugar reflects all credit on the enterprise of the producer.—Yours truly, FRASER and Co.

" City Mart, Sydney, December 9."

However, Robert Muir was not yet done with improving the lot of the yeoman farmer as far as the sugar industry was concerned. By the next year it was widely reported that he had created another contrivance for open-pan sugar production that dispensed with much of the labour component.[550] It was devised in conjunction with Sutton & Co in Brisbane, inventor of the Sutton Pan, and reported to eliminate practically all the brushing ladling and skimming that was normally required as well as being self-feeding, cleaning, and discharging. He announced that it would be on display at the upcoming Brisbane Exhibition.[551] A crowd of invited guests viewed the apparatus which was reported to cost no more

---

[549] Sugar Making on the Clarence, *The Sydney Mail and new South Wales Advertiser*, Saturday 13 December 1879, page 1046.

[550] Ramblings in Queensland, *Australian Town and Country Journal*, Saturday 17 December 1881, page 26

[551] Agriculture, *The Queenslander*, Saturday 17 July 1880, page 90, *Sydney Mail and New South Wales Advertiser*, Saturday 24 July 1880, page 164, Local and general News, Muir's new Battery, *The Northern Star* (Lismore) Saturday 14 August 1880, page 2

> **TO SUGAR-GROWERS.**
>
> **"MUIR'S PATENT SELF-ACTING BATTERY."**
>
> A PUBLIC EXHIBITION of the Working of the above important Invention will take place at R. Muir's Plantation, Benowa, Nurung, on SATURDAY, the 17th of July, to which all interested in the Sugar Industry are invited. 436

than £60, in a successful demonstration at Benowa on Saturday 17 July 1880.[552] A working model of the device, entered into the inventor's section at the Exhibition, won one of two prizes on offer and a mention of special merit.

Thus by 1880, Benowa's reputation as a sugar plantation and a centre of research and technical innovation for the small-capital sugar producer had become well established. Moreover, it was also becoming known as a centre for all manner of political, recreational, farming, and industrial activities and a place to visit for many touring officials and notaries. The tireless efforts of its owner Robert Muir over fifteen years had elevated him from the ranks of a struggling selector to that of a substantial landowner and employer who was well known among the political and commercial circles of Brisbane and Southern Queensland.

With his home on an elevated site overlooking the river he could relax a little and view the results of his endeavours with satisfaction. Fields of sugar cane stretched out along the winding riverbank to the not-to-distant ocean, complemented by cultivated fields of general produce. The various enterprises were a hive of activity, worked by his many employees. It would not have been too difficult to imagine him seeing himself as lord of all he could see and probably as a Lord in truth. Thus, by the end of the 1870s, having achieved an adequate level of success he began to settle into a life not to unlike that of one of the Lords of the realm back in Scotland. Enjoying a similar status and engaging in many of the similar sporting, political and social activities, he had become powerful enough to exert influence over the local political scene.

---

[552] *Brisbane Courier*, Friday 23 July 1880, page 2, *Brisbane Courier*, Thursday 15 July 1880, page 1

PART VI

POWER AND INFLUENCE

Chapter 23

Power Broker in the Electorate of Logan

By the mid-1870s Robert Muir had attained an influential position in society. It was validated by his appointment as Magistrate for the Nerang Creek district in July 1874.[553] He was officially sworn in as Magistrate for the district at a special meeting with Justice Lutwyche in his chambers on 30 October 1874.[554] Exactly how Muir came to the Justice's attention is unknown, but there is no denying that the up-and-coming sugar planter shared many similar attitudes and perspectives on society as the eminent judge. Lutwyche, like Robert Muir, enjoyed a reputation as a ferocious combatant against entrenched privilege and humbuggery of all varieties. Labelled by his peers as a 'poor man's judge,' he had fearlessly championed democratic rights against irresponsible politicians in a series of newspaper publications in the early days of Queensland separation from New South Wales. This earned him widespread acclamation and support from the public. He also denounced the same administration in 1863 for 'encouraging large capitalists and companies while restricting the man of moderate means.'[555] Enjoying a similar reputation, Robert Muir likewise, who was just as fearless in making his opinions known on the same issues, would have received the judge's enthusiastic endorsement.

While not entering politics, by the early 1870's Robert Muir had begun to assert a position of authority in the society of South-East Queensland based on his reputation as a sugar boiler and his uncanny ability to squeeze out a profit in hard times. Initially established on MLC Louis Hope's Ormiston plantation in 1869,

---

[553] New Magistrates, *The Queenslander*, Saturday 25 July 1874, page 2
[554] Current News, *The Queenslander*, Saturday 7 November 1874, page 6
[555] P A Howell, 'Lutwyche, Alfred James (1810-1880)' *Australian Dictionary of Biography*, National Centre of Biography, Australian National University, First published in hardcopy 1974, accessed online 13 January 2022

he had a baptism into the political and social workings of the new colony as his name was bandied about in the halls of parliament by the honourable member. Finally vindicated, Hope was delighted that he had proved that sugar could be the golden egg that he had often asserted. Having finally achieved the holy grail of making sugar pay, Robert Muir, the architect of Hope's success, therefore, was a name that figured prominently in the 1860s and 70s as the leaders of the new colony sought to expand its GDP and find reliable and lucrative sources of revenue. It was indeed a very fortuitous move allowing him to place one foot firmly on the bottom rung of the ladder to power and influence in the relatively new colony of Queensland.

Muir, however, unlike his earlier life in Ballarat, had taken little active interest in politics, being more than pre-occupied with establishing his plantation and doing all he could to extract a decent profit from his labours both in Queensland and in the Clarence River district. In 1873, when the Legislative Assembly elections were announced he was nothing more than an interested outsider seeking to support anyone who was willing to further his and the interests of other growers and agriculturalists in the district. He is mentioned as one of the prominent local landowners and sugar producers who spoke highly of Phillip Nind, the candidate for the new Logan electorate, which incorporated most of coastal South-East Queensland and hinterland. Nind was a local cane grower and sugar producer, owner of the Yahwulpah plantation at Beenleigh and president of the South Queensland Agricultural Society which also included Robert Muir as a committee member.[556]

As one of their number, Nind was viewed by many local cane growers, as someone who would further their interests. One news correspondent wrote, he was seen as 'a pioneer of what they trusted would ... do justice to the agricultural interest.'[557] Standing as an independent he stood for what most of them believed in. Pledging to support state education, immigration, land settlement by cultivators, he also initially took up their grievances by opposing the Polynesian Labourers Act and attacking the Government over

---

[556] *Nind Philip Henry*, Former Member Details | Queensland Parliament accessed online 14/1/2022, *The Queenslander*, Saturday 31 October 1874, page 5
[557] Electorate of Logan, *The Queenslander*, Saturday 24 May 1873, page 10

the Sugar Refineries Bill and their poor handling of the Road Trust System.[558] These were all issues that, as time went on, would draw Robert Muir into getting involved in the political sphere to varying degrees.

In less than a year, the faith that the local agricultural interest of Logan had placed in Phillip Nind was shattered. With the honourable member's plantation Yahwulpah one of several local mills that were failing due to intense local competition, he had become disillusioned with the future of the industry. This was the catalyst for him conducting a wide-ranging review of current conditions and future trends. The study would be very influential as, with an M.A. from Oxford, he was one of the most educated among them and one whose opinions carried a considerable amount of weight. Focussed on refining and its ongoing viability, it resulted in a new bill which he presented to the Queensland Parliament in 1874 as part of his only major speech in July 1874.[559] The bill was a severe slap in the face for the local yeoman farmers and small capitalists like Robert Muir. As self-made men they viewed themselves as the essence of liberal economics, the expression of a fair go, and the fulfilment of the ideal British society that Lang and others like him had so long predicted.

To them the bill was a total anathema, predicting that wide-scale small production was highly uneconomical due to the multiplier effects of capital infrastructure that had to be installed and operated on every plantation and property. Nind predicted that the future would be based on fewer large-scale operations that were technologically sophisticated, producing higher quality sugar for a much lower cost. What he clearly had in mind in 1874 was the emerging leviathan in Maryborough at Yengarie on the Mary River. In its infancy at the time of his bill, it was projected to be fully operational on a scale that would engulf most of the smaller mills in the district. There were also rumours of others like them proposed by large capitalists in the south.

---

[558] ibid
[559] Michael Jones, *Country of five rivers: Albert Shire 1788-1988*, Allen & Unwin Sydney 1988, p78

For Robert Muir, Nind's capitulation to the large capitalist interests was an act of cowardice and betrayal. Determined to not give up without a fight, he initiated a no-holds-barred campaign to stop Nind in the first instance and then to solve the problem of profitability for the yeoman farmer to preserve his role in the industry. Firstly, the technological aspect outlined in the previous chapter, resulted in a flurry of frenetic activity that produced the Icery-Muir clarifier, the Sutton pan, and the self-acting battery. The secondary focus, which made many enemies, was on a sustained political campaign that sought to remove the other barriers such as labour laws, trade restrictions and preferential treatment of large-scale enterprises.

Re-elected in June 1874 after the first result was challenged and overturned, Phillip Nind's Imported Sugar Refiners Act of 1874 was a bitter blow, especially for those supporters in his own electorate of Logan.[560] It was, as Muir argued, a poorly disguised attempt to offer direct support to Refiners Tooth & Cran of Maryborough who were struggling to compete with other refiners of imported raw sugar in New South Wales and Victoria. That it was making life extremely difficult for the smaller independent growers and producers did not seem to matter.

After an unsuccessful attempt to draw attention to Nind's duplicity on the bill before the independent growers and producers at an Agricultural Society committee meeting, Muir then turned to the press.[561] It was a huge betrayal of his local sugar growers Muir wrote, leaving the door wide open for large refiners to undercut the small producer and put him out of business. Muir argued, that while the act bound the refiners to exporting their refined sugar within three months or face a penalty, sourcing unrefined sugar from anywhere at the cheapest possible price rendered the penalty irrelevant.

---

[560] The Logan Election Disputed, *The Queenslander*, Saturday 31 January 1874, page 3, Logan Election, *Queensland Times, Ipswich Herald and General Advertiser*, Saturday 13 June 1874, page 4.
The Imported Sugar Refiners Act 1874, *The Queenslander*, Saturday 12 December 1874, page 5, The Imported Sugar Refiners Act 1874, Letter R Muir 22 December 1874, *The Queenslander*, Saturday 2 January 1875, page 5
[561] *The Queenslander*, (Brisbane) Saturday 31 October 1874, page 5

The outrage surrounding the topic became public as a series of letters began to be exchanged in the press. In one letter Nind likened Muir to Don Quixote and his followers to 'American Union thugs intent on hanging Jeff Davis from the apple tree' in a futile campaign against bribery and corruption.[562] However, in a letter in reply, Muir indicated he was thorough in his investigation of the matter, spending large amounts of time talking to MPs and particularly the supporters of the bill mentioned by Nind. This resulted in the uncovering of a corruption of process as the bill was rushed through the parliament without reading or adequate discussion. A confidential chat with his old mentor and employer, Hon Louis Hope at Parliament House, confirmed his fears that virtually nobody knew what was in the Act and passed it purely on Nind's reputation.[563]

A letter of support for Robert Muir to *The Queenslander* by R Gibson, a fellow planter on the Albert River, pointed out that Tooth & Cran's facility at Maryborough would enjoy a monopoly in Queensland because of the Act, being the only one of its kind in the colony and would threaten the very existence of smaller producers. It was a huge enterprise that dwarfed any other sugar enterprise in the colony. Twenty tons of sugar per day was produced from cane grown on the property and surrounding farms in addition to what was imported from overseas. This was compared to the one to five tons produced by the independent owner-operators. Just a few months earlier a tramway had been installed to transport cane to the crushers and three miles of pipes to convey the juice to the refinery. It was enough to strike fear into the hearts of any small sugar producer who saw it.[564]

An independent observer a week later also condemned the Act as an attempt to further the ambitions of those interested in creating wealth for themselves at the expense of the colony and its

---

[562] The Imported Suar Refiners Act 1874, *The Queenslander*, Saturday 12 December 1874, page 5
[563] The Imported Sugar Refiners Act 1874, Letter R Muir 22 December 1874, *The Queenslander*, Saturday 2 January 1875, page 5
[564] The Imported Sugar Refiners Act 1874, Letter R Gibson, *The Queenslander*, Saturday 26 December 1874, page 5, *The Queenslander* (Brisbane) Saturday 3 October 1874, page 5

development.⁵⁶⁵ A letter by Nind in reply pointed out that any shortfall between the imported raw sugar and the refined would be a benefit to the colony due to local sugar making up the difference. However, Robert Muir countered that again with more careful logic detailing how this too could be easily avoided by the refiners planning for such an eventuality by merely placing another order for the difference to arrive within the 90 days stipulated in the Act.

Having destroyed the so-called logic of the bill, he then, in typical form, issued a challenge to Nind to have the point argued by arbitration 'in the usual way' in other words by a public debate. The loser, he wrote, 'would then pay the winner a new hat which the winner would wear as a trophy of victory.' Muir then notified his size as gauge No 2, 6 7/8 inches. On the accusation by Nind that Muir had 'mounted the stump' and made braggadocios speeches against him, this also was denied, reminding Nind that the only speech made on the Act had been in his presence. The rest of the debate, he declared, had been through the letters to *The Queenslander*. He then demanded the accusations be withdrawn or substantiated with the provision of an additional hat.⁵⁶⁶ The offer, not responded to, was reiterated again a two weeks later in less jovial tones, commenting in conclusion that his unwilling combatant would be judged by the public for his loose assertions and the courage of his convictions.⁵⁶⁷

Robert Muir, as the acknowledged leader of the campaign against the bill, suddenly found himself as the leader of a groundswell of outrage against Nind in his seat of Logan and Southern Queensland.⁵⁶⁸ Having also earned a reputation for unreliability in the parliament by vacillating between the Government and opposition, the hold of the sitting member on his seat was beginning to look very shaky. In addition, an unrelenting barrage of mockery over his alleged independence

---

⁵⁶⁵ The Bonded Sugar House Act, *The Queenslander*, Saturday 16 January 1875, page 5
⁵⁶⁶ The Imported Sugar Refiners Act, *The Queenslander*, Saturday 23 January 1875, page 5
⁵⁶⁷ Correspondence, The Sugar Refiners Act 1874, Letter by R Muir 3 February 1875, *The Telegraph* (Brisbane) Tuesday 9 February 1875, page 3
⁵⁶⁸ The Bonded Sugar Refineries Act, *Maryborough Chronicle and Wide Bay and Burnett Advertiser*, 4 February 1875, page 3

from Henry Jordan, the member for Burke, was a constant drip wearing away his confidence. In his own electorate of Logan, he was also roundly criticized for his lack of interest in progress by a growing number of entrepreneurs who wanted to see a similar surge of growth to that of the United States especially with the railways.[569]

By the end of January 1875 Nind had succumbed to the pressure, his independence claims totally discredited and promises made not kept. The public humiliation over the Bonded Sugar Act was the final straw. Rumours began circulating at the height of the Sugar Bill fiasco, that the member for Logan was about to tender his resignation. After strenuously denying it in the press, it was officially announced, and writs were issued for the vacancy 1 April 1875.[570] After a bitter farewell speech to his constituents, described as 'a scurvy production against some of his friends,' he left within days for a tour of England.[571] His potential replacements were widely acknowledged as Robert Muir, Adam Black, a fellow sugar producer, and Theodore Lenneberg, local hotelier, businessman and Postmaster of Nerang Creek.[572]

The most likely winner, according to the speculators, would be Robert Muir, described by one correspondent as 'the doughty Champion in the correspondence columns of *The Queenslander* over the Bonded Sugar Act.' The same correspondent believed that he would win in a walkover due to his momentum on relevant issues, calling him 'the coming man' who would be a better fit with the prevailing direction of Queensland politics.[573] It certainly seemed like he was 'the coming man' in the first few weeks of 1875. Clearly a man on a mission to bring progress to the district, he had thrown

---

[569] Notes on the Week, *The Capricornian*, (Rockhampton) Saturday 3 April 1875, page 216, Logan and Albert, *The Brisbane Courier*, Saturday 30 January 1875, page 6

[570] Mr Nind's Reply, *The Telegraph* (Brisbane) Tuesday 26 January 1875, page 3, Logan and Albert, *The Brisbane Courier*, Saturday 30 January 1875, page 6, The Logan Electorate, *The Telegraph* (Brisbane), Friday 2 April 1875, page 2.

[571] Logan and Albert, *The Queenslander*, Saturday 10 April 1875, page 9

[572] The Nomination for the Logan, *The Telegraph* (Brisbane), Saturday 10 April 1875, page 5

[573] Brisbane Correspondence, *the Daily Northern Argus* (Rockhampton), Saturday 23 January 1875, page 2

himself headlong into the political fray commencing with the Sugar Act in the last quarter of 1874.

However, it was not to be. Writing to his supporters in a letter dated 20 January 1875, the 'coming man' advised that his arrival was likely to be delayed for some years into the future. There was still much to do in the sugar industry he explained, and his quest to bring respect to the despised southern planters and ward off their predicted demise was still to be accomplished. He also claimed that his effectiveness and credibility would be called into question if his plans for Benowa, which were yet to be brought to fruition, were abandoned for politics for which he believed he was not vain enough to make into a profitable career. Once his plans for Benowa and Southern Queensland sugar were accomplished, and he continued to enjoy their confidence, he promised he would certainly be proud to offer himself to be their representative.[574]

Despite this setback for his supporters, his political activities continued unabated. He was becoming a very familiar figure in Brisbane, circulating among the politicians and in the halls and corridors of the new parliament building. As part of a deputation to the minister for works, he offered support for the local population of Beenleigh in pressing the Government to commence the works for the approved projects for bridges over the Logan and Albert Rivers after the neglect by the previous member. Particularly urgent, was overturning the plan for the bridge over the Logan River at Waterford and erecting it at Loganholme due to the logic of its benefit to significantly more people.[575] He was there again with another deputation of local farmers and sugar growers in June 1875 with the member for Bulimba to lobby the Minister for Works on the urgent need for road works and the removal of tolls.[576]

On 20 February 1875, it was announced that he was part of a group selected by the Government to form a board aimed at improving the agricultural industry. It was aimed at dealing with

---

[574] Letter Robert Muir Benowa 20 January 1875 to John Davy JP, Adam Black Esq, H Pietzeker Esq JP, Carl Palm Esq, and other Gentlemen signing the requisition, Advertising, *The telegraph*, (Brisbane), Saturday 3 April 1875, page 1
[575] Bridging the Logan, *The Queenslander*, Saturday 20 February 1875, page 2
[576] Beenleigh, *The Brisbane Courier*, Wednesday 16 June 1875, page 7

the problem of pests and diseases and would include Karl Theodor Staiger the Government Chemist, P R Gordon the Chief Inspector of Stock, and Walter Hill, the Curator of the Botanical Gardens.[577] Locally he chaired a meeting at the Beenleigh Court House for the three accepted nominees contesting the Logan election – personal friend Adam Black, Theodore Lenneberg, and Mr C Campen who represented the interests of a growing German population. All were new to politics except for Campen, who was well known in Brisbane. Campen's candidacy however was labelled by the Lenneberg camp as being nothing more than a stunt by Black, Muir & Co to split the German vote.[578]

With sugar production the main local industry, it was clear that Adam Black had the edge on the other two as he also had the ear and support of local power broker Robert Muir. Black, who was not known for his public speaking ability, had risen to the occasion, boosted by Muir's ringing endorsement. By the time the campaign was in full swing under Muir's enthusiastic promotion, he was being touted as a future speaker of the parliament.[579] Standing for the repeal of the Bonded Sugar Act that had caused so much outrage, it was widely expected that he would win the seat. He also advocated making local roads an urgent priority and simplifying the existing land legislation. Interestingly he also claimed to be committed to the suppression of dummying, a practice of Robert Muir, in selecting land under the names of friends and relatives.[580]

The election was held on Saturday 16 April, and it proved to be even more dramatic than the last. In less than a week, calls for a new ballot were coming from several quarters. The reported result declared Adam Black the winner with 266 votes, Theodore Lenneberg second with 260 votes, Campen with 6 votes and 6 informal. Campen's involvement did indeed, as predicted, deliver victory by splitting the German vote at Yatala. After the close of

---

[577] Official Notifications, *The Telegraph* (Brisbane) Saturday 20 February 1875, page 2,
[578] Metropolitan District Court, *The Telegraph* (Brisbane) Friday 13 July 1875
[579] The Nomination for the Logan, *The Telegraph* (Brisbane) Saturday 10 April 1875, page 5
[580] Letter of Acceptance Adam Black, 2 April 1875, *The Brisbane Courier*, Monday 5 April 1875, page 1

polling, a large crowd was waiting in anticipation at the Beenleigh telegraph office for scrutineers reports to arrive. About six PM, when it was believed that the results were all in, Lenneberg arrived on horseback to a cheering crowd that had accepted the results which unfortunately were incomplete. As he was enjoying a clear lead over Black at that point, he was carried into Mayer's Hotel to the returning officer by a loud and jubilant group of supporters some of whom appear to have resorted to various forms of subterfuge in a few locations to ensure their candidate's success.[581] However, the mood quickly evaporated an hour later when another wire arrived to advise that Black had a majority and would be declared the winner.

By nine o'clock all the verified ballots were in the hands of the returning officer except for those from Brisbane and Elkana, near present day Yatala. A wire from the scrutineer advised that their official count was 38 Lenneberg, 8 Black and 1 informal. Arriving late at around midnight, the official carrying the votes in a satchel appeared in a dishevelled state covered in mud claiming he had gotten lost on the way and had dropped the package with the votes, spilling them over the ground and soiling them. After locating them all he claimed that the actual count was 39 in favour of Lenneberg and Black on 7.[582]

There was a strong whiff of skulduggery about the affair, indicating that the scrutineers for Lenneberg attempted to change the result by one vote after the results were certified and everyone had gone home for the night at Alkana. It was subsequently confirmed that on a final check before sealing the package it was supposedly found that it was one extra in favour of Lenneberg and one less for Black. This sparked a heated discussion on how the package which was secured on all sides with a seal could have become open leading to the ballots falling out onto the ground in the process of delivering them. That they were handed to James Gibson, the returning officer in that state is confirmed by Campen, the third placed candidate in a letter to the *Telegraph*.[583] The official

---

[581] Beenleigh, *The Telegraph* (Brisbane), 22 April 1875, page 3
[582] Beenleigh, *The Telegraph* (Brisbane), 22 April 1875, page 3
[583] The Logan Electorate, *The Telegraph*, (Brisbane) 20 April 1875, page 3

affidavit for the vote signed by Mr Haussman and Black's scrutineers also appeared to have gone missing.

There were reports of other irregularities from Alkana around accusations of collusion and bribery between Campen and Black that ended up in court with Campen suing Lenneberg for defamation.[584] At the Nerang Creek booth, the result was also very close sparking further reports of 'irregularities.' It came as no surprise therefore, that returning officer Gibson, advised that he would not receive, sanction, or return the result.[585] The ballots sat unaccepted under the bar at Mayer's Hotel for two full days unsupervised, before the whole package was returned unendorsed. Thus condemned, the ill-fated election for the time being would be decided by the Legislative Assembly and the Committee of Elections and Qualifications after appeals by Black.[586]

After deciding that there was no case to answer on the part of Adam Black, he was persuaded by his friends in the Parliament, against his better judgment and doubts over his constitutional status, to take his seat in the Parliament three weeks later.[587] Lenneberg, the candidate whose supporters appeared to be behind the Alkana ballot skulduggery, immediately challenged the decision based on the irregularities and called for a new election.[588] An official petition from sixty-four registered voters for an inquiry into the irregularities in election was tabled 23 July 1875.[589]

By August, after much political debate as well as public debate on the matter, it was becoming clear that Adam Black's position was less secure that he had been led to believe. Bush lawyers as well those versed in the operation of Colonial Constitutions in

---

[584] Metropolitan District Court, *The Telegraph* (Brisbane) Friday 13 July 1875,
[585] Logan Election, *Queensland Times, Ipswich Herald and General Advertiser*, 22 April 1875, page 4, The Logan and Downs Elections, *The Telegraph* (Brisbane), Wednesday 5 May 1875, page 3
[586] Beenleigh, *The Telegraph* (Brisbane), 22 April 1875, page 3, Latest Telegraphic, *Warwick Argus and Tenterfield Chronicle*, 29 April 1875, page 2, Brisbane, *Rockhampton Bulletin*, Friday 23 April 1875, page 2
[587] *The Queenslander*, (Brisbane) Saturday 31 July 1875, page 4
[588] More Election Complications, *Warwick Examiner and Times*, Saturday 22 May 1875, page 2
[589] Parliamentary, The *Capricornian* (Rockhampton) Saturday 31 July 1875, page 487

Australia as far away as Melbourne, were convinced the Queensland Government had acted unlawfully by overriding the Elections and Qualifications Committee to seat another supporting member.[590] By the end of September Adam Black had read the writing on the wall and believed his position was untenable.[591] His resignation was officially announced on 29 September 1874. Possible replacements were Theodore Lenneberg, T B Stephens, H Pietzeker, and James Savage.[592] The election was announced in the Government Gazette for the 19 October 1875 calling for nominations to be lodged at the Beenleigh Court House by 11 October.[593]

For a short time, it looked like Theodore Lenneberg and his army of fellow Germans in the Logan electorate may have won a significant victory opening a clear path for them to finally take the seat. However, it was not long before a new name appeared on the scene, Mr Frederick Shaw of Brisbane, agent for Queensland Cobb & Co and friend of Robert Muir. Muir had been busy lobbying some serious support for the cause of Mr Shaw, organizing a large meeting at Beenleigh days before the announcements were gazetted. As chairman, he presided over the meeting which included a speech by another personal friend, the well-known and widely respected editor of *The Queenslander*, Angus MacKay.[594]

Throwing the considerable political capital of Robert Muir behind Shaw, placed him into the front running for the seat. Unlike Lenneberg, Muir was a recognized heavyweight in the sugar and wider agricultural industry. His connections by 1875, extended throughout all of Southern Queensland, Brisbane and in the North, indicated by his earlier appointment to the board to inquire into livestock and crop disease and methods to improve farming practices.[595] Just a few months earlier as part of his duties on the Committee of the Southern Queensland Agricultural Society, he

---

[590] *The Brisbane Courier*, 23 August 1875, page 2
[591] Beenleigh, *The Brisbane Courier*, Wednesday 29 September 1875, page 2
[592] The Logan Electorate, *The Telegraph*, (Brisbane) 29 September 1875, page 2
[593] The Logan Electorate, *The Queenslander*, Saturday 9 October 1875, page 25
[594] Beenleigh, *The Telegraph* (Brisbane) Monday 18 October 1875, page 2
[595] Official Notifications, *The Telegraph* (Brisbane) Saturday 20 February 1875, page 2

had been instrumental in gathering most of the prominent sugar producers as well as interested bankers and politicians and newspaper men with an interest in agriculture like Angus MacKay, into Meyer's Hall at Beenleigh for an all-day conference. Topics of discussion ranged from cultivation, production, free-trade, and other related issues.[596] Facing such a juggernaut was enough to deter Lenneberg from running again leaving just one opponent, Munro an Albert River sugar planter, an advocate for roads, low taxes and an Australian Federation.[597]

Despite a strong attack on his character that involved an accusation of being a 'Government plant' Shaw easily won the seat defeating Munro his opponent 275 to 118, a shortfall of over 200 on Black's election and an indication of a strong sense of injustice that continued to simmer.[598] Shaw's win was an endorsement of his strong stand on improvement to the local roads and bridges and a commitment to implement shire councils in the electorate as the best way to achieve it.[599] Shaw, however, proved to be a disappointment to the electors of Logan, resigning less than twelve months later.[600] Thus, Muir's foray into the quicksand of politics at the colonial level was over almost as soon as it began, entering the fray merely to halt what he deemed to be a gross injustice perpetrated against the smaller owner-operator sugar producers of Queensland who were after all, as he declared so often, his main priority.

While briefly backing the successful campaign of his old friend and associate T B Stephens in 1880, chairing meetings and supporting him in various ways during his term, he was far more committed to achieving real results at a local level. On this there remained much to do in maintaining the viability of sugar production in the Logan and Albert districts amid the growing strength of the industry in the more compatible locations further

---

[596] The Conference at Beenleigh, *The Brisbane Courier*, Saturday 22 May 1875, page 6
[597] The Logan Election, *The Brisbane Courier*, Monday 18 October 1875, page 3
[598] The Logan Election, *The Telegraph* (Brisbane) Wednesday 20 October 1875, page 2
[599] *The Logan Election*, *The Brisbane Courier*, Thursday 14 October 1875, page 3
[600] The Logan Election, *The Brisbane Courier*, Saturday 13 May 1876, page 5, Beenleigh, *The Brisbane Courier*, Tuesday 2 May 1876, page 2

north. Of particular concern was the need for local infrastructure such as road and rail, a cause that he took up with equal vigour as the fight against the Sugar Act of 1874.

Chapter 24

Land Developer and Return to Local Government

With the 1875 election finally completed, Robert Muir's focus was placed squarely on the business of sugar and extracting a decent profit for himself and his fellow small producers. However, with a procession of local members between 1875 and 1880, this became difficult, time-consuming, and costly with the poor attention to local infrastructure such as roads and bridges. Therefore, much of this, like the bridge project over the Logan at Beenleigh, had to be secured by direct petition to the minister of works, an action he had been very much a part of from the beginning.

Some degree of success was enjoyed by this endeavour, resulting in the construction of the bridge over the Nerang River, just a short distance up the river from Benowa, in 1878. It was opened in December with a great deal of fanfare by an official party from Brisbane led by the Premier the Hon. John Douglas and J F Garrick the minister for lands and the local member Peter McLean. Met at the Southport anchorage by Robert Muir and a large contingent of locals, the officials were personally conveyed by Muir in his own horse and buggy to Hanlon's Hotel, then on to Muir's Benowa Plantation. Following that, the Nerang township was the next destination for the bridge opening which was announced with an artillery barrage as the party passed through a large arch of evergreens erected on the main street.[601]

For the most part, however, successes such as this were hard to come by and required a lot of lobbying, writing to the press, and organizing meetings. This became necessary for the largest project that Muir involved himself with – the extension of rail from Brisbane to the New South Wales border at the Tweed River. A

---

[601] The opening of the Nerang Bridge, *The Brisbane Courier*, Saturday 7 December 1878, page 6

safer and more accessible option than steamer, rail had long been a goal of many in Brisbane as well as those living on the south coast. Access to Brisbane by steamer was the sole form of transport for many along the Gold Coast, as it was often treacherous crossing the river mouth at Southport and at the Tweed, leading to long delays waiting for safe passage.

Writing to the *Logan Witness* in March 1881, Muir reminded the readers that this would not be easy as this was not the first such project to fall victim to Government indifference. As early as 1878, he declared, a plan for a line from the Tweed to Southport was proposed by the Sydney Sugar Refining Company, that was commencing operations in the district with a new mill and refinery. It would be the most cost-effective method of transporting the heavy equipment and later the produce to the wharf at Southport where there would be direct access to Sydney by ship.

Muir states that he met with the company's engineer, Mr Clinie to discuss the project, shortly after the announcement when he came to the district to complete the survey. He was thus advised that having assessed the terrain, Clinie was confident that the cost would be significantly less than that considered by the Government. More importantly, it would be of no cost to the government of Queensland nor were any land grants required; all that was needed were approvals and permits. But it failed through a lack of local agitation.

Thus, success in the latest endeavour would come from a united front. He was pleased that a meeting had been arranged at Nerang to promote the idea, but more would be needed with all the settlements, towns and hamlets along the proposed route getting involved. For his part, Muir promised to use his local connections and begin solicitations as well as agreeing to calling a meeting locally at Southport.[602] The meeting to kick off the campaign was held at Southport 2 April 1881; Robert Muir was elected chairman. This time the railway was made a major electoral issue and the Government threatened with a serious backlash for reneging on its earlier promise as all qualified to vote from South Brisbane to the Tweed, were urged to make sure they were registered before the

---

[602] Correspondence, Railway to the Tweed, *Logan Witness* (Beenleigh), Saturday 26 March 1881, page 3

next election.[603] In addition, to ensure its success, quite a few landowners along the route had promised to donate land to the project.[604]

This new-found interest in local government, not coincidentally, was occurring alongside Robert Muir's interest in the commercial possibilities of residential and small plots of farming land. Sugar had proven to be the lucrative cash crop that he expected and provided the means to diversify his business interests as the industry was facing a decline in Southern Queensland. So, with a healthy balance sheet, he turned his focus to the sandy beaches and vacant land just a few miles down the river and the therapeutic breezes of the elevated hinterland.

Like many of his projects he was all-in from the outset, just as he had approached the sugar industry seven years earlier. Projects that had sparked his imagination were the possibilities of residential land at Southport, growing sugar cane and timber on the top of nearby Mt Tamborine, and subdivisions on the Benowa estate. Along with the nearby seaside, Tamborine was also in the early stages of promotion as a tourist resort and sanitorium. Southport, which by 1880, had already earned the label of 'summer resort,' was particularly becoming a preferred destination for many leisure-seekers coming from Brisbane. Ever growing numbers were making the trip for a time of sailing, fishing and enjoying the beach and the sea air.[605]

Robert Muir's foray into land development began in January 1878, purchasing 53 acres of portion 62, a significant section of the nearby Labrador beach frontage. This was made with Brisbane businessman and investor John Lennon who purchased the remaining 40 acres. It was immediately subdivided and advertised for sale as some of the first seaside lifestyle lots on the Gold Coast. They were, as the advertisement declared 'sure that it only requires to be seen to be preferred, in all respects, for seaside residences, to any other land in the district, embracing a choice of hill, and lawn,

---

[603] Southport, *The Brisbane Courier*, Thursday 7 April 1881, page 3
[604] A Railway to the Tweed, The *Queenslander*, (Brisbane) Saturday 16 April 1881, page 500
[605] At Southport, *The Queenslander* (Brisbane) Saturday 31 January 1880, page 141

> THE LAND AT DEEPWATER POINT,
> ADJOINING SOUTHPORT,
> HAS BEEN SURVEYED INTO ALLOTMENTS
> AND WILL BE
> OFFERED AT AUCTION
> ON
> THURSDAY, APRIL 25.
>
> It is in contemplation to offer facilities to intending purchasers to visit the property before the day of sale, feeling sure that it only requires to be seen to be preferred, in all respects, to any other land in the district for seaside residences, embracing a choice of hill and lawn, bordered by a broad sand beach, and rendered attractive by the most beautiful semi-tropical plants, such as bread-fruit, Moreton Bay pines, &c.
>
> What constitutes especial value to this spot is the fact that Deepwater Point is the only place within seven miles where a steamer can go alongside and land passengers.
>
> The proprietors, as above intimated, prefer to give the public an opportunity to see the place and to judge for themselves, as they consider it unnecessary to dilate upon its beauties in an advertisement, wishing only to secure the sale of the land on its merits.
>
> For particulars apply to J. B. ELLIS & CO., Queen-street; JOHN LENNON; or ROBERT MUIR, Benowa, Nerang Creek.

bordered by a broad sand beach and rendered attractive by the most beautiful semi-tropical plants.'[606]

The strip of land with the backdrop of the mountainous hinterland was named Labrador soon after by Muir in memory of when he first sighted the Canadian coast in 1846 on his voyage to Louisiana. The name stuck and has been used ever since.[607] By 1881, Muir having purchased a further 212 acres of portion 14, was heavily invested in the development of the area. It was rapidly developing with roads to Deepwater Point, the main wharf for steamers from Brisbane, the proposed Grand Hotel and a proposed railway station. By then he had already placed an indelible stamp on the area having two of the most prominent streets bearing his name, Robert Street and Muir Street, which remain so to this day.[608] By 1885 he would control

---

[606] Advertising, *Logan Witness*, (Beenleigh) Saturday 23 March 1878, page 3
[607] Dawn Hasemann Rix, *Labrador: the early pioneers*, DHR Publishing, Main Beach Queensland, 2002, p7
[608] Benwell & Echlin, and Watson, Ferguson & Co. *Southport Allotments Sale on the Ground, on Saturday 30th, January Commencing at 11 A.m. Sharp*. Brisbane, Qld.: Watson, Ferguson &, Litho., 1880.
http://onesearch.slq.qld.gov.au/permalink/f/1oppkg1/slq_alma21112735400 002061, accessed 16/4/2022, Dawn Hasemann Rix, *Labrador: the early pioneers*, DHR Publishing, Main Beach Queensland, 2002, p9-13.

over 3000 acres that included 2000 acres of surveyed residential lots in Benowa, Southport and Mt Tambourine.[609]

In the more regulated and accountable commercial environment prevailing over a century later, the way this was achieved would likely be labelled conflict of interest, leading to the intervention of higher levels of government. The activities of the infamous 'white shoe brigade' of the 1980s Gold Coast comes to mind. But in the 1880s similar activity barely raised an eyebrow as entrepreneurs such as Robert Muir sought to interfere with the operations of the local divisional boards and shire councils for their own benefit. In some cases, it was actively encouraged as Brisbane politicians courted the favour of the local business elites like Robert Muir.

In 1881 the divisional roads board that serviced the Southport district was mired in controversy. Those with an interest in the growing local residential areas were increasingly at odds with each other and with many of the large landowners, farmers and sugar producers. By the middle of 1882, an influential group had formed behind the leadership of Robert Muir to actively undermine the expenditure and existence of their local board for the Nerang township. What had previously been agreed upon was suddenly labelled 'unproductive' expenditure as those with interests in Southport fought for controlling positions. This was despite the existing board having made great strides in connecting Nerang with the Brisbane and local roads, as well as substantially improving the Nerang streets and drainage systems. These were all projects deemed vital in the past few Legislative Assembly elections. Their work had been endorsed by Cobb & Co who were able to extend their service from Brisbane as far south as Tallebudgera.[610] However, what was viewed from 1875 as a vital election issue, was in 1882, labelled as a 'mistake' and misallocation

---

[609] Classified Advertising, *The Queenslander* (Brisbane) Saturday 24 October 1885, page 651, Advertising, *The Telegraph* (Brisbane) Monday 3 March 1884, page 4

[610] Country News: Nerang, *Logan Witness* (Beenleigh) Qld, Saturday 17 February 1883, page 3

Land Developer and Return to Local Government

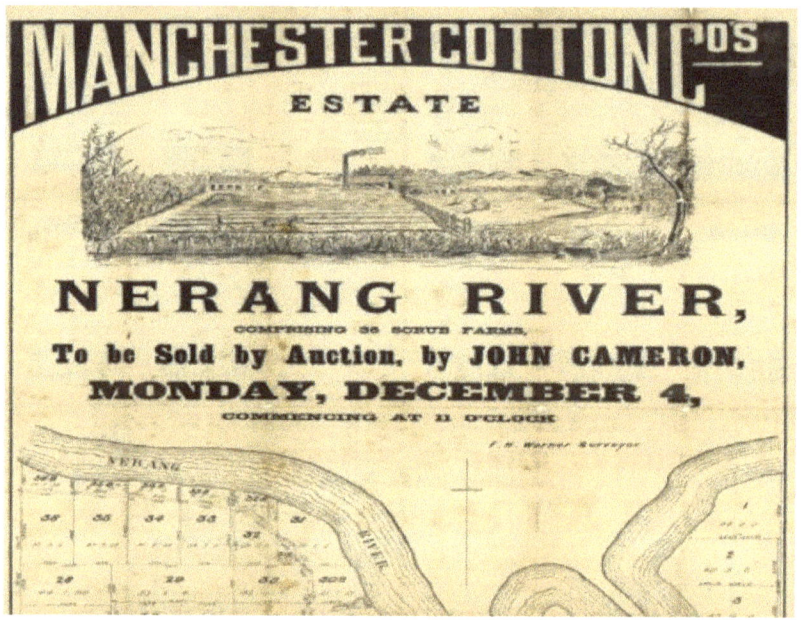

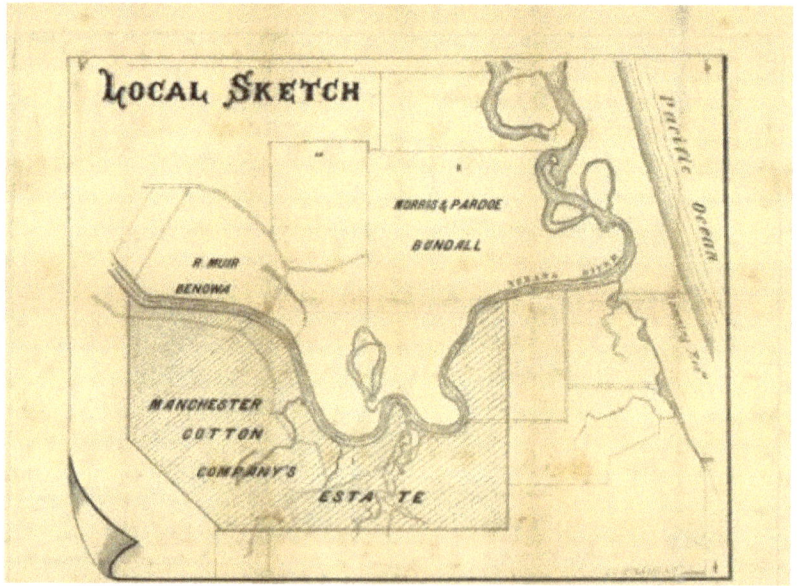

[611] J U McNaught Brisbane 1882, *Manchester Cotton Co's Estate comprising 36 scrub farms*, John Oxley Library, State Library of Queensland

of funding. The board was then challenged to put their seats to a vote to test the popularity of their decisions.[612]

Six months later they were defeated in a close and bitter election by the Muir faction. Robert Muir was then installed as the new president of No1 Nerang Roads Division replacing Mr H Smith with 76 to 64 votes and 7 informal. Muir's colleagues Stephens and Andrews were returned as leaders of the No2 and 3 divisions leaving the Southport, Labrador, Nerang districts in the hands of the land developers.[613] Within two months the real agenda was revealed as the newly elected in No 1 division were agitating to declare themselves a separate shire council, distinct from the Nerang Divisional Board with the power to spend their rates in and around Southport. Significantly, the borders of the proposed shire extended from the Nerang River to the Coombabah Creek Labrador, enclosing all the land recently purchased by Robert Muir including the proposed 'Muirlands' estate on his Benowa property.[614]

Muir's land acquisitions continued unabated during 1883, acquiring three farms on the recently subdivided Manchester Cotton Company Estate across the river. At the same time, he also purchased 733 acres on the top of Mt Tambourine. His plans for this new purchase caused a stir among his neighbours on the mountain. They were not sure of what to make of his proposal to plant 50 acres of sugar cane and the construction of a mill to process the sugar. Nevertheless, he had managed to convince more than a few that it may be a paying proposition and a chance to make some easy and guaranteed income.[615] The plans for the mill appeared to be progressing after its arrival in February 1884 on the steamer Ipswich, which he had earlier purchased and restored to working order. Muir also installed a sawmill in addition to that of Carter, a Tambourine local resident.[616] Mount Tamborine is a

---

[612] Nerang Division, *Logan Witness*, (Beenleigh) Qld, Saturday 10 June 1882, page 3
[613] Country News: Nerang, *Logan Witness* (Beenleigh) Qld, Saturday 17 February 1883, page 3
[614] Country News Southport, *Logan Witness* (Beenleigh) Saturday 21 April 1883, page 3
[615] Logan and Albert, *The Brisbane Courier*, Saturday 24 November 1883, page 6
[616] Coomera, *The Brisbane Courier*, Thursday 14 February 1884, page 6

spectacular location with views to Mt Warning and the New South Wales border to the south-west. To the east is a limitless vista of the blue Pacific Ocean and its cooling sea breezes, making it the ideal location for a resort and sanitorium. Relentlessly promoted as such by Robert Muir both locally and in Brisbane, he then created a subdivision of 212 two acre lots, naming it St Bernard's.

He even managed to persuade the newly elected liberal Premier, Sir Samuel Griffith to accompany him to the mountain to see for himself. After taking the train to the end of the line at Beenleigh, the Premier and Robert Muir proceeded in a light two-horse buggy to the top, the first such vehicle to make the journey. According to Muir's brother-in-law Archie Meston, who later entered politics himself, Sir Samuel had told him it was a hair-raising experience, as Muir, an expert but also reckless driver, got them there and back in record time. The Premier's pristine hair, he claimed, was grey when they returned.[617]

Having such high-profile supporters was a green light encouraging him to pull out all the stops. Within a year, Muir had used his influence to obtain approval for a private road from Southport to Matheson's Hotel at the foot of Tamborine Mountain and another to the top, direct to a large residence at St Bernard's already under construction. He claimed in a later advertisement that 'when the road ... is completed ladies may drive with greatest security.' He also predicted a little optimistically in 1885, that 'a year hence we safely calculate on having the iron horse running on the Brisbane, Southport and tweed line past St Bernard, distant one hour's drive.' [618]

---

[617] South Coast Memories, *The Brisbane Courier*, Monday 17 March 1924, page 10
[618] Classified Advertising, *The Queenslander* (Brisbane), Saturday 24 October 1885, page 651.

Chapter 25

The Polynesian Labour Crisis

Muir's interest in property was more than a calculated gamble and more than an investment strategy, rather, it was designed to ensure his economic survival. By the 1880s it was clear that the projected future of the sugar industry was in the more tropical northern regions like Mackay, and it would be all white. It also would be on a scale large enough to stymie any opportunities for small-scale yeoman sugar production. This was revealed in on-going speculation amongst the Queensland politicians, on Government backing for two large-scale central Mills at Racecourse and North Eton at Mackay. It was proposed that they would be supported by white European farmers as growers only, on small individual lots. It was viewed as a better way of providing a ready-made industry for selectors and settlers while preserving the British colonial ideal of independent yeoman farmers as a bastion of white British culture and values.[619]

Muir, through his contacts in Parliament House, would have been also keenly aware of the aggressive moves by CSR in 1883. Given a green light by conservatives in the Government, an investment arrangement in central and north Queensland to the tune of £200,000 was to be completed by 1888. The aim of this development was even more ambitious than the Government's, with plans to purchase large tracts of land and lease small lots to dependent tenant farmers. For the yeoman farmer, this was even more discouraging as it was too reminiscent of the prevailing conditions back in Britain on the estates. At the same time, there were also other cashed up capitalist investors particularly the Melbourne-Mackay Sugar Company that were buying up

---

[619] Kay Saunders, *Workers in bondage: the origin and basis of unfree labour in Queensland 1824-1916*, University of Queensland Press, St Lucia 1982, p144-149

properties in the Mackay district.[620]Thus as Phillip Nind had predicted, the era of individual open pan sugar boilers was coming to close. Having successfully kept the large capitalist at bay by creative innovation and relentless promotion for the best part of a decade, it was becoming clear to Robert Muir and other independent owner operators, that the future was not on their side.

Muir himself, by 1885 had moved on, fully modernising his plant and equipment, widely advertising it as 'a complete vacuum plant' producing three tons of dry sugar per day.[621]This mirrored the local trend which was reported on by *The Queenslander* correspondent that same year. Observing that the Logan and Albert sugar was at the highest quality, he attributed it to the adoption of the latest technology such as vacuum pan which had become almost universal, and the construction of a complete refinery at Coomera.[622]Much of this had been made possible by innovations that made vacuum plants more affordable. Appliances, especially those produced by Mirrless, Tait & Watson in cast iron rather than copper, had reduced the cost to as low as £300 and well within reach.[623] Meanwhile, as *The Queenslander* also reported, in the Logan and Albert districts, there was the growing phenomenon of urbanisation occurring at Beenleigh which with a steady growth in population, was expected to impact Southport just a few miles away.

This, more than anything else, the correspondent believed, was leading to the opinion that the sugar industry in the district had seen its best days and it was not likely to remain a permanent feature for too much longer. It was expected that the subdivision trend in the Logan and Albert districts into small farms for dairy and the need for other crops for the growing population would

---

[620] Kay Saunders, *Workers in bondage: the origin and basis of unfree labour in Queensland 1824-1916*, University of Queensland Press, St Lucia 1982, p147-150

[621] Advertising, *Queensland Figaro and Punch*, (Brisbane) 7 November 1885, page 22

[622] Present State of the Sugar Industry, *The Queenslander* (Brisbane) Saturday 21 November 1885, page 839

[623] Peter Griggs, *Global industry, local innovation: the history of cane sugar production in Australia 1820-1995*, p188

only accelerate.[624] In addition, a continual slide in the price of sugar worldwide due to a growing oversupply, was fuelling fears of a prolonged depression in the industry. Thus, for someone like Robert Muir who was well connected politically, it would have been foolish to ignore the growing trends. However, for him and his independent colleagues, in the short-term, the most worrying issue was the tightening regulation on Polynesian Labour which was crucial to the profitable operation of many of the small independent sugar plantations.

Recent historians, in discussing the topic of Polynesian labour in the nineteenth century Queensland sugar industry, invariably underscore that era with the indelible pencil of racism. Gaia Guiliani for example, typically argues that this was an inevitable consequence of the process of establishment of a white settler society and its imagined cultural superiority amid a sea of highly exploitable black and brown races.[625] Australian historian Kay Saunders, while not in disagreement, also suggests that economic and political developments are other contributing factors. As Saunders reminds us, the rise of militant white workers and trade unions in the latter part of the 1880s and a corresponding economic recession in many aspects of the Queensland economy, resulted in increasing competition for work of any kind. As the recession deepened, menial labouring jobs like cane cutting that had been almost exclusively filled by Polynesians, were attracting white Europeans. It would be an issue later exploited by Labor Leaders like Prime Minister Andrew Fisher, member for Wide Bay, who quite dishonestly declared, 'white men cannot get work because the Kanakas are employed in their place.'[626]

In 1884, however, such sentiments were not held by many of the independent small-capital plantation owners and employers. Content to employ anyone regardless of race, they could be better

---

[624] Present State of the Sugar Industry, *The Queenslander* (Brisbane) Saturday 21 November 1885, page 839

[625] Gaia Guiliani, Throwaway Labour, Blackbirding and a White Australia, *The Journal of the European Association of Studies on Australia*, Vol.2. No.2, 2011, ISSN 2013-6897 under the auspices of Coolabah Observatori: Centre d'Estudis Australians, Australian Studies Centre, Universitat de Barcelona,

[626] Kay Saunders, Workers in bondage, The University of Queensland Press, St Lucia Qld, 1982, page 160-163

considered as adhering to Adam Smith's anti-monopolist conception of a free market that viewed labour as a cost without any racist connotations. Being close to the Premier, Sir Samuel Griffith, however, Muir was left in no doubt as to the future of the Kanaka labourers in the Queensland sugar industry: there would be none. A major reason was the attention given to the actions of 'blackbirders' in the popular press in the early 1880s, convincing a majority in Qld Legislative Assembly that the practice would cease entirely by 1890.

The mood for change no doubt had been heightened by the horror surrounding the massacre and cannibalisation of the crew of the 'recruiting ship' the Mystery in Havannah Harbour at the island of Aboa in 1879.[627] Similarly, suspicions were raised of plantation owners disposing of their workers in all sorts of ways including murder, just prior to the expiry of their three-year indenture to avoid payment of wages. Accusations such as this were aired in the Legislative Assembly by 'reformers' such as MLA Redmond. However most, if not all, could not be substantiated.[628]

Muir himself had come under keen scrutiny for such atrocities. Like many other plantation owners, he used indentured labour, having forty-six Polynesians employed on his sugar plantation at Benowa. In January 1880, it was determined by Government inspectors, that he had breached his duty of care under the act for failing to properly register the deaths of two Polynesians who had died on his property. Claiming to have completed the necessary documentation on the matter, when produced in court it was pointed out that registration numbers were missing resulting in a technical default and a one shilling fine for each offence.[629]

---

[627] The Fate of Renton and Muir, *Mackay Mercury and South Kennedy Advertiser*, Wednesday 4 June 1879, page 2

[628] Mr Redmond's Charge Against Queensland Planters, *The Brisbane Courier*, Friday 30 May 1884, page 6

[629] Beenleigh, *The Queenslander* (Brisbane) Saturday 31 January 1880, page 134, Robert Muir (right) with overseer Hicks (left) and Polynesian workers ca 1880, Oxley Library State Library Queensland (next page)

The Polynesian Labour Crisis

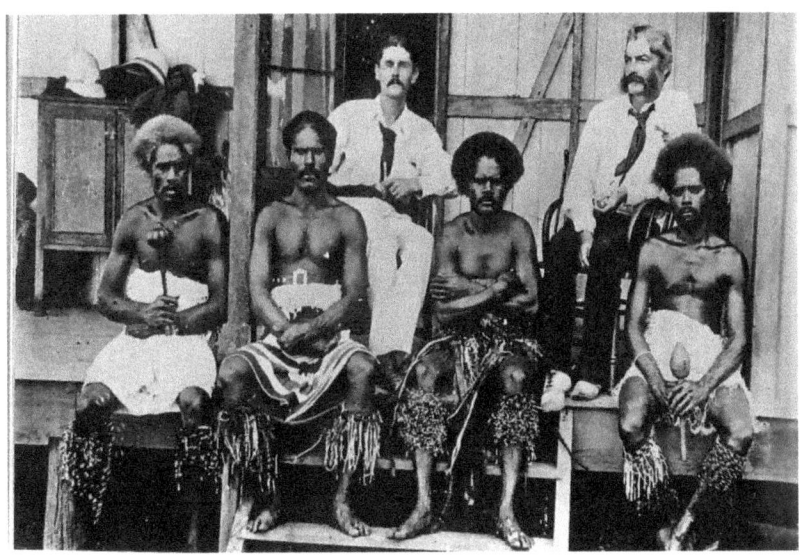

The new amendment Bill before the legislative Assembly in 1884 was also designed to place tighter restrictions on what the duties of the Polynesians could be and under what conditions they could be indentured. It was a response to the growing power and influence of the white working classes who were not impressed with the threat of lesser paid Pacific Islanders employed in a wide number of industries. Specifically, it was designed to restrict access to higher skilled and higher paid positions to white Europeans. It would also, as Robert Muir and his associates feared, hand the industry to a small number of large-scale capitalist enterprises that could afford to make a profit on smaller margins with less labour. During 1884, the issue had become strongly contested in a last-ditch attempt by those such as Robert Muir with a vested interest in maintaining the status quo. It had sparked numerous letters to the press, meetings, and political lobbying. A series of letters to the *Brisbane Courier* by J. E. Matthew Vincent esq., a liberal of a Burkean bent, lover of universal justice and opposed to the arbitrary exercise of power, muddied the waters somewhat with a self-interested campaign of his own. Vincent advocated a free trade agenda of legal equality and contractual integrity that extended to labour, worker's rights, and Government regulation of fair trading. He had earlier been viewed by Muir as a threat to the plantation owners like himself with his strong advocacy of the Victor Mill and small grower independence. The Victor Mill had been promoted for the previous five years as a solution to the 'Polynesian question' with the potential of sugar production coming from large numbers of family farms as small as 40 acres producing sugar with their own labour.[630]

Vincent's position on British liberty and worker's contractual rights struck a chord with the new Premier Samuel Griffith as well as Muir himself. Griffith, a political radical, who found himself wedged between a multitude of campaigners and issues, suggested in a published letter to Vincent, that he pursue the matter of Polynesian labour with the Secretary of State for the Colonies.[631] This caught the attention of Robert Muir whose opinion on the issue was widely known. As a prolific lobbyist and publicist on the issue, he represented the members of an association formed in March 1878 to protect the sugar industry from Government control and interference, especially regarding Polynesian labour.[632] Vincent's perspective thus resonated with Robert Muir on a personal level which he had not experienced since leaving the troubles of the Goldfields. His salient point was that Polynesian labour legislation was creating 'a pariah labour class placed under exceptional laws and withheld the rights of common citizenship.' It was, he argued, designed to keep 'the coloured man (and he the native Lord of this very soil) in a state of bondage.'[633] It was also, he continued, a violation of the natural rights of the islanders who were procured for work under Government sanction only to be treated as aliens. Vincent wrote:

---

[630] Prospects of the sugar industry, *The Week*, (Brisbane) Saturday 2 August 1879, page 17
[631] Letter A Musgrave Jr Private Secretary, Government House Brisbane 21 January 1884, The Polynesian Labour Question, *The Brisbane Courier*, Thursday 24 January 1884, page 6, Roger B Joyce, *Samuel Walker Griffith*, University of Queensland Press, St Lucia Qld, 1984, p94-105
[632] Meeting of Polynesian Employers, *Logan Witness*, Saturday 23 March 1878, page 3
[633] Letter by J E Matthew Vincent 11 January, Statesmanship or Time-Serving? *The Brisbane Courier*, Saturday 12 January 1884, page 5

It comes to this: that having brought a man here on British soil, he is unquestionably a free man: if he chooses to remain here, he has an undoubted right to do so, and to penally to prohibit another from employing him ... is to do him a criminal injustice. The truth must be admitted that the coloured man has a right to be employed, if admitted at all, in such services as his abilities qualify him for, as he may be able to secure wages more or less for the work he performs, his natural right being what he can earn and the freedom to earn it. Deprive him of this natural right and he becomes a slave, a chattel, a mechanism[634]

A few days later Robert Muir submitted a letter of his own to add his protest to that of Vincent who he described as 'the widely known champion of the British working man.' Muir asserted that the demise of unskilled labour from Polynesia could mean the ruin or at least the setback of the industry for years. Further, he maintained the proposed bill was racist by barring Polynesians from skilled positions adding that their only apparent disability was the colour of their skin. This made Queensland, he asserted, racist to a degree not seen elsewhere in Australia as he wrote to the *Brisbane Courier*:

> about thirty years ago I was proud to number amongst my friends on Ballarat "Mr Rainnie" the leading barrister in that city, the son of a negress in Jamaica and had he chosen this part of Australia instead of Victoria for a field for his talents and enterprise, our sapient law-framers would (if allowed) would have relegated Mr Rainnie to the hoe and cane-knife (sans alternative) and stripped him of his gown and wig.[635]

The proposed law and amendments he also asserted, was disingenuous in its application and permitting the engagement of islanders specifically for the three to six-month harvest season only, for a period of three years with prohibitions on any other duties was nonsense. 'Would our Premier I wonder', he

---

[634] Letter by J E Matthew Vincent, The Polynesian Labour Question, *The Brisbane Courier*, Tuesday 22 January 1884, page 5
[635] Letter R Muir Benowa 23 January, The Polynesian Labour Question, *The Brisbane Courier*, Friday 25 January 1885, page 5

sarcastically wrote, 'graciously permit a coloured brother or two lend a hand in an emergency or help clear out a waterhole ... Or would he permit the said brother to put out a fire ... or run for Dr Hockin to attend all the white men in the works after a boiler explosion.' He ended with a thinly veiled threat that it would be better for him to seek employment elsewhere in places where wise legislation was framed and industry encouraged.[636] Unfortunately, supporting Vincent's liberal free trade position, only placed Muir increasingly at odds with the firming mood in the Government and with the public who were determined to protect the privileged position of white skilled workers in the colony in a recessed economy.

Muir's bitter letter came after an unsuccessful deputation to the Premier, Sir Samuel Griffth just a few days earlier on the matter. Accompanied by Mackay MLA Hume Black, colleague and editor of *The Queenslander*, Angus Mackay, now an MLA, his local MLA, M Stephens and a small number of fellow southern sugar producers, they pled their cause for favourable amendments to the bill. With all in agreement, it was pointed out that the hysteria over the Polynesians over a couple of badly reported incidents had led to a mistaken belief that employers were cruel to their indentured labourers.

In fact, the reality they argued, was that it was incredibly difficult to procure Europeans to do any hard manual work, especially cane harvesting and working in the sugar house. The belief that the white man, unlike the Polynesian, was unsuited anatomically to the heat and the conditions, they argued, was incorrect. Robert Muir claimed, along with his brothers, that they were living proof, establishing Benowa with their own bare hands. As Muir had reported to the press over ten years before, there was no racial difference for Polynesians, from his experience, finding that 'when they first arrive in the colony ... it takes as much time to inure them to the work as it does the new white chums.'[637]Nevertheless,

---

[636] Letter R Muir Benowa 23 January, The Polynesian Labour Question, *The Brisbane Courier*, Friday 25 January 1885, page 5

[637] The Nerang River and the Southern Border, *The Queenslander* (Brisbane) Saturday 20 September 1873, page 10

it continued to be an issue as increasing numbers of out of work white labourers entered the industry after the recession began to bite at the end of the 1880s.

In the wider industry itself, the government's claim that the presence of Polynesians on the plantations disadvantaged white workers, was also repudiated based on the obvious white labour shortage. Nevertheless, Robert Muir, to keep access to the necessary workers, proposed a compromise whereby indentured workers were kept out of town and kept from doing the work of mechanics.[638] While hearing a second submission again from predominantly Northern producers a few weeks later, it was made clear that while they may have a point about civil liberties and free trade, Premier Griffith's position on the issue had not changed. The Polynesian clauses passed would remain and the workers would be kept separate from the white population while they were employed in the colony. This was in accordance with the compromise proposed by Robert Muir and other similar minded producers.[639]

Meanwhile, on his own plantation and that of others in the district, newspaper reporters portrayed a vision of happy, well-fed and behaved Islanders and owners and nothing but good feeling between all concerned. A visit to Benowa in 1885 by a correspondent from the *Planter and Farmer* revealed that the Polynesian workers there were very happy. As one interviewee stated, 'me no go back along a Tanna, me like this place bery much.'[640] On the nearby property of Riverside under the management of younger brother David Muir since 1880, the Logan Witness reported during an earlier lunch time visit, 'broad grins, a goodly consignment of meat, vegetables and roley-poley pudding.' He added that 'Cowper's gentle spirit would have cherished this

---

[638] Polynesian Labourers Act Amendment Bill, *The Telegraph* (Brisbane) Wednesday 30 January 1884, page 2

[639] The Coloured Labour Question, *Logan Witness* (Beenleigh) Saturday 2 February 1884, page 3, The Pacific Island Labourers Act Amendment Bill, *The Week* (Brisbane) Saturday 2 February 1884, page 15

[640] Michael Jones, *Country of five rivers: the Albert Shire 1788-1988*, Allen & Unwin Sydney 1988, p128

pleasant solution of the old indictment against the white man.'[641] Such a contrast to what was being portrayed in Parliament and much of the press, only confirms Doug Monroe's 1995 survey of the history of Polynesian labour in Queensland – that it was a widely varied experience that has suffered from competing interpretive perspectives.[642]

With the campaign against Polynesian labourers gaining in intensity, it was becoming apparent that his days as a plantation owner and sugar producer in Southern Queensland were numbered. He had reached an impasse, as he had on at least three previous occasions: in Ayr in 1846 on the economic crisis and family breakup, at Ballarat in 1857 and at Grafton in 1864. Thus, as no stranger to change and radical actions, it seemed he believed hard decisions would again be necessary. The suggestion in his letter to the *Brisbane Courier* that he would move away to a place that valued business investment, was no idle threat. Thus, shortly after all this transpired, he began the process of placing his properties on the market and putting them up for lease including the Benowa sugar mill. No longer able to exert the influence he once commanded, saw his popularity and influence waning as a new protectionist mood was inspiring opposition from some who remained resentful over his political and commercial activism. There were mutterings that he had forgotten his pioneering origins and that he had gotten old, incapable of hard work and out of touch with those doing it hard. They were merging with those of enemies created by his activist approach and other potentially sinister attitudes to southern sugar producers like himself that appeared to be growing year by year. However, in the mid-1870s, it was a challenge that he met head on and for a time dispelled.

---

[641] Country News, *Logan Witness* (Beenleigh) Saturday 4 September 1880, page 3
[642] Doug Munroe, The labour trade in Melanesians to Queensland: an historiographic essay, *Journal of Social History*, Spring 1995.

Chapter 26

Career Twilight – Opposition and Confrontations

Robert Muir and his family certainly were comfortable in Southern Queensland. Anyone not familiar with their hard beginnings at Benowa could be forgiven for any envious criticism, especially when the family made a visit to Brisbane, as they did on occasion. They travelled in style, conspicuously conveyed, as his granddaughter recalls her mother retelling, in a grand carriage as good as the Governors, with the policeman on duty at Queen Street saluting as they passed.[643] It had indeed been a tough beginning, even for someone so accustomed to hard manual labour and starting from scratch, as he had on more than one occasion. Despite his success, it had not been achieved without tragedy.

The Benowa plantation in the 1860s and 70s, and the district itself was sparsely populated, most of the local Aboriginal population were long gone and many of the basic elements of western civilization were yet to make an appearance. It was a hard existence for a young family as Robert himself discovered, losing his first wife Jane Meston. His partner of just seven years, she passed away in care at age 29 in May 1870 at Cleveland near Brisbane just prior to him taking the position at Carr's Creek sugar mill in Grafton in 1870.[644] Her Brother Archie Meston thus recounts a story in *The Bulletin*, that illustrated the dangerous isolation that many experienced in those early days.

On his way to Coomera on horseback in 1870 to collect two milking cows with David Muir, they encountered a lone woman and her dying baby in a slab hut in the dense scrub. Consoling the grieving mother, they assisted her as best they could by attending to some of the unfinished chores such as washing the clothes and

---

[643] Alexander McRobbie, *The real Surfer's Paradise: from seaside village to international resort*, P31
[644] Family Notices, *The Queenslander* (Brisbane) Saturday 14 May 1870, page 1

pegging them on the line, shooting some game and fixing a meal. After getting some water and firewood they went on their way promising to send help leaving her waiting for her overdue husband to return. David, no doubt, also seeking to make amends for any lingering regrets over the tragic loss of his wife Margaret in Ballarat five years earlier.[645]

Evidence of European occupation was almost non-existent in most localities apart from McGregor, the pilot at the Tweed River. The only house for many miles at the southern border, was a single room weatherboard cottage erected at Burleigh Heads by Robert Muir during 1871 while briefly returning from the Clarence River. The construction was unfortunately marred by the tragic death of a local aboriginal lad Billy Harper, the carpenter, also a well-known athlete, who was taken by a shark when a boat he was in capsized crossing the Nerang bar.[646]

Nevertheless, the original lords of Benowa alluded to by J E Matthew Vincent in his letter to *The Queenslander*, had not been entirely displaced, adapting to the European presence by eking out a quasi-traditional existence on the unused riverbank portions among the big estates on the Nerang River while taking casual employment on the estates. Most of their territory was restricted to a 'reserve' a few miles to the west of the village of Nerang occupying approximately 10 miles of river frontage that extended to the base of the Darlington Range, although it was rarely used as a permanent settlement. Almost all the settlers at some stage had employed the individuals from the local population in land clearing in the establishment of their plantations.[647]

Thus, the harmonious interaction with the local flora and fauna had been largely dismantled by the coming of the cotton and cane farmers. The flexible interactivity of the local people with the seasons and weather was replaced by fixed monocultures dependent on predictable seasons as the land was sectioned off, drained and 'improved' to conform with the principles of high

---

[645] A Bush Memory, *The Bulletin*, 24 May 1923, page 48
[646] South Coast Romantic History, Burleigh, Currumbin and Coolangatta, *The Brisbane Courier*, Saturday 9 February 1924, page 17
[647] The Nerang River and the Southern Border, *The Queenslander* (Brisbane) Saturday 20 September 1873, page 10

farming learnt from the agricultural revolution. Nevertheless, what traces there were, appeared to have been respected and left in peace by Robert Muir who chose to name the estate Benowa, a traditional Southeast Queensland name for the bloodwood tree with its distinctive red sap.

As 'Old Timer' recalled in an article to the *South Coast Bulletin* in 1947, there also remained some vestiges of Aboriginal culture enjoyed at a large camp on the Nerang River at Bundall adjacent to Muir's plantation at Benowa. The writer recalls that the fresh water and an abundance of wallabies and kangaroos as well as bird life it attracted, made it a perfect gathering place for hunting and socialising and gathering wild honey. There were corrobborees that attracted people from as far south as the Queensland border crossing the river in boats provided for them by one of the local settlers, Mr Meyer, at what would be later named Meyer's Ferry.[648]

The Talgiburri were one of the local remnant groups on the Nerang River surrounding Benowa and it appeared that some of their people enjoyed a mutually trustworthy relationship with Robert Muir as they did with others in the district. It was here, under Muir's watchful eye that his young brother-in-law Archie Meston formed an appreciation of Aboriginal culture. During his time at Benowa in 1870-1872, a teenage Archie Meston explored the area accompanied by two local aboriginal guides organised by Muir, one named Tullaman, of the local Talgiburri, and the other the aforementioned Billy Harper, son of a local aboriginal woman.[649] They travelled over a period of a few months through most of the district including a trip to Stradbroke Island after the 1870 sugar season had ended. There Meston and his guide met with the local Aborigines spending days fishing and hunting with them at Point Lookout and Amity Point.[650]

After returning to Benowa and leaving Billy Harper, Meston, Tullaman and a Richmond River Wooroowoolgen man, set out for the Macpherson Range and (Wooloombin) Mount Warning armed

---

[648] Reminisces of Early Southport, Particularly that Part Known as Meyer's Ferry, *South Coast Bulletin* (Southport) Wednesday 9 April 1847, page 15
[649] The Late F Campbell, *The Brisbane Courier*, Thursday 28 June 1894, page 7,
[650] Lost Tribes of Moreton Bay, *The Brisbane Courier*, Saturday 14 July 1923, page 18

with guns, knives, hatchets, matches and salt and two days rations, intending to live mainly by hunting and foraging.[651] Gone for a little over three weeks, this experience was the inspiration for his lifelong campaign for Aboriginal protection and preservation imparting a strong but sometimes misguided appreciation for Aboriginal lifestyles and culture. His 1895 report formed the basis of the Queensland Aboriginal Protection Act echoing the opinions of other similar minded ethnologists such as John Fraser who compiled a similar report for New South Wales.[652]

Unfortunately, his role as Queensland Aboriginal Protector shortly after, was not well remembered, due to his inflexibility and extreme measures. However, this is partly explained by his position on total isolation of Aboriginals from the white population in order to offer protection from diseases and destructive culture.[653] While clearly sharing aspects of the racist outlook of his time, he challenged many racist assumptions held in many circles, maintaining that Aboriginals were physically superior and as equally intelligent as whites, as well as holding a notorious antipathy towards the influence and presence of Chistian Missions in Aboriginal locations.[654] His brother-in-law however, appeared to have had no such inclinations. While apparently maintaining an apparently mutually respectful relationship with the local people and trusting them sufficiently to permit his young protégé entirely to their care for almost three months, his attitude was entirely consistent with that of colonisers like Wakefield and theorists such

---

[651] Nerang Memories, *The Queenslander* (Brisbane) Saturday 7 August 1920, page 42, The Macpherson Range, *The Brisbane Courier*, Tuesday 21 July 1908, page 7

[652] John Fraser, *The Aborigines of Australia, Their Ethnic Positions and Relations*, The Victorian Philosophical Institute, Melbourne 1888, John Fraser, *The Aborigines of New South Wales*, Charles Potter, Sydney, 1892, Archibald Meston, *Queensland Aboriginals: a Proposed System for their Improvement and Preservation*, Government Printer, Brisbane 1895

[653] Mark Francis, Social Darwinism and the construction of Institutionalised Racism in Australia, *Journal of Australian Studies*, Volume 20 1996, Issue 50-51, page

[654] S.E Stephens, 'Meston Archibald (1851-1924) *Australian Dictionary of Biography*, National Centre of Biography, Australian National University, published first in Hardcopy 1974, accessed online 16/2/2022.

as Lord Kames from his home country who believed in the stadial concept of human social development.

While accepting the 'brotherhood of man' regardless of race, land was to be treated as a commodity to be improved, forming the basis of the political economy on which a productive capitalist society, having attained the fourth and final stage of development, would be based. This was the very opposite of the indigenous economic outlook which always sought to live within the natural cycles, cultivating and maximising the natural resources.[655] Hard physical labour, good money management, and a strong work ethic was the prime ingredient for success and a God-ordained way of life for a civilized culture which he considered to be at the peak stage of development. Thus, like many of his kind and generation, he considered Aboriginals incapable of making 'proper productive' use of the land as God intended.[656] But, unlike his brother-in-law, Muir never made any comment or representation on white atrocities, mistreatment or injustices despite his relentless lobbying and writing on a variety of issues. Meston, on the other hand, particularly with the construction of the railways and the telegraph, reported on many individual criminal acts of violence committed by white contractors in a later investigation for the Government.[657]

Nevertheless, despite such a chasm of cultural difference, the blood-soaked frontier war between First Nations and Europeans, seemed far removed from the seemingly amicable and trouble-free relations enjoyed by the usurpers and the traditional owners in the Nerang district.[658] If there was any discord it came from the indentured labour and access to alcohol. For a few years Robert Muir, as the local magistrate, sought to stop the practice placing

---

[655] Tony Dingle, *Aboriginal economy: patterns of experience*, McPhee Gribble Penguin, Fitzroy Vic, 1988, p55-56

[656] Richard Waterhouse, the yeoman ideal and Australian experience 1860-1960, *Exploring the British world: Identity, cultural production, institutions* Melbourne: RMIT Publishing 2004, p440-459

[657] Archibald Meston, *Queensland Aboriginals: a Proposed System for their Improvement and Preservation*, Government Printer, Brisbane 1895

[658] See Henry Reynolds, *Forgotten war*, New South Publishing, Sydney NSW, 2013

advertisements in the local paper offering a reward for reports leading to the arrest of those breaching the rules.[659]

£10 Reward.

THE Undersigned Guarantees the above Reward for Information that will lead to the ultimate conviction of any person, Publican or otherwise, for supplying liquor to Pacific Island Labourers, either at Southport or Nerang.

R. MUIR,
Benowa.
MORRIS & FULLERTON,
Bundall.

Southport, October 4th, 1882.

This came on the heels of the notorious case of the shooting of Billy Tully, a local Polynesian who had completed his indenture but was showing no inclination to return home. He was making a menace of himself, spending his earnings on alcohol. According to the court reporter on the case at the Nerang Police Court on Thursday 12 June 1979, Billy had turned up in an inebriated state at the Benowa plantation looking for work and was told by Robert Muir, who was feeding cane into the crusher, to leave as he was distracting the men. Billy then approached the Muir residence with a can and a large stick and commenced to threaten Mrs Muir, the nanny, both the Muir children and those of the workers. Robert Muir was then forced to intervene after Billy attempted to kidnap one of the children and drag him into the scrub. Thereupon he took careful aim at Billy with his shotgun and fired at what he claimed was a calculated, harmless 70 yards distant to scare him away. Momentarily falling to the ground Billie then ran off never to return.

In court, it was established that Billy's posterior and upper thigh had been peppered with buckshot, a significant number of pellets being removed personally by Constable Walker. It was considered that Muir, a crack shot could not have missed as the distance was in fact 55 yards indicating that while it was calculated to injure, it was nevertheless justified in order to protect his family and the children. Billie was subsequently removed from the area and transported to Brisbane presumably to be expelled from the colony.[660]

---

[659] Advertising, *Logan Witness*, (Beenleigh) Saturday 14 October 1882, page 2
[660] Police Court Nerang Thursday 12 June, *Logan Witness* (Beenleigh) Saturday 21 June 1879, page 3

Career Twilight – Opposition and Confrontations

This incident marks a turning point in the career of Robert Muir. It is indicative of frustration that was building over the issue of Polynesian labour and the fact that, unlike many other problems such as the De Lissa patent, where he seemed to relish doing combat, he was powerless to resolve. Meting out arbitrary judgement in such a reckless manner also demonstrates an established assumption that at Benowa he was Lord and Master and could do as he pleased. Since 1866, he had been Postmaster, innkeeper, employer, and landlord over the small hamlet that was registered as a locality on the list of Queensland place names in Bailliers's Queensland Gazetteer and Road Guide in 1876.[661] Adding the title of JP completed the picture of lordly control, achieving a long-held dream of land ownership out of reach of his father, but with the added level of civic authority that was previously the exclusive domain of the patronising lairds and estate owners.

Unlike his father back in Ayr, who acted on the pleasure of the Burnetts as a judge for ploughing competitions and appearances at the local exhibitions, he now stood to receive the credit for the same competitions whether it was he who held the plough or entered the displays or his paid operator. As an enthusiastic proponent of the benefits of high farming as a capitalist enterprise, Muir was an enthusiastic supporter and patroniser of any initiatives that brought farmers and cultivators into competition with each other. Throwing his backing behind several politically backed organizations as well as renegade and breakaway associations, he found a ready arena for his competitive spirit.

In his local district the most influential was the Agricultural and Pastoral Society of Southern Queensland that had in its management team, politicians, prominent agriculturalists, as well as sugar growers and producers. It was formed in 1871 as Muir was in the early stages of establishing himself and his Benowa estate. The first meeting was convened in November 1871 and was presided over by Mr John Davy of the Beenleigh plantation of Davy & Gooding, Muir's keenest local competitors. Phillip Nind, the controversial member for Logan, was elected

---

[661] Michael Jones, *Country of five rivers: Albert Shire 1788-1988*, Allen & Unwin North Sydney, 1988, p 179-180

president.[662] Robert Muir, however, while enjoying an equally high profile appears to have shown very little interest at that time in becoming an active member but nevertheless was an enthusiastic exhibitor of his sugar. Many of his close associates like Adam Black, who later served as president, became office-bearers, as did many of his neighbours and fellow sugar growers and producers. Muir eventually joined the organization in 1874 and after the demise of Phillip Nind, accepted the position of chairman in 1875.[663]

Robert Muir, nevertheless, enjoyed a sometimes frosty and combative relationship with the organization as well as the umbrella association the ran the Queensland exhibitions. It was led by Gresley Lukin, Chief Clerk of the Supreme Court – a person who had limited knowledge or experience with sugar and who appeared to harbour a personal grudge against him. By the mid-1870s Robert Muir had earned widespread publicity for his sugar exploits, winning prizes at thirteen exhibitions in New South Wales, Victoria and Queensland. Most of these were first prize in the open pan category for both raw and refined.

This generated a groundswell of opposition based on a belief that he was cheating by doctoring the samples that he brought to the Queensland Exhibition by 'washing.' Thus, instead of a 70lb bag sample, as had been the case, the quantity for the coming 1876 exhibition was increased, at Lukin's insistence, to one ton along with a requirement for signed declarations of verified witnesses. It invited a savage response from Muir publishing a letter in *The Queenslander*.[664] Calling this nothing more than an 'out-of-the-way attempt to keep him out of the shows and exhibitions, he advised that he had shown sugar for the last time at the Queensland Exhibition. He then declared that the 'Queensland Cup' for sugar should be handed over to the Ageston Estate without competition, as they obviously enjoyed the biased support of the Queensland

---

[662] Pioneering the Logan, Agricultural and Pastoral Society of Southern Queensland, *The Queenslander*, Saturday 16 September 1922, page 11
[663] A & P Society of Southern Queensland, *The Brisbane Courier*, Wednesday 5 October 1910, page 21
[664] About Sugar, *The Queenslander*, (Brisbane) Saturday 9 September 1876, page 32

establishment. They were, he pointed out, the only vacuum pan processor in the district and the only one that had the capacity to fulfill the requirements. In his letter he explained that all his sugar is treated or 'washed' with warm cane juice, a process widely used overseas and without exception in Mauritius. The washed sample presented, he argued was therefore not specially treated and could be verified by independent witnesses. In addition, he reminded Lukin that up to the present he had won first prize thirteen times for thirteen entries under both the old conditions and new conditions. This included exhibitions local, intercolonial and at the International Exhibition where such onerous and biased rules were not applied and so had done more than enough to satisfy his thirst for competition. In presenting an analogy he argued, all exhibitors should be compelled to present larger samples such as a full herd of cattle rather than one special specimen. This would make it then possible for anyone to win a prize from a herd of 'scrubbers.'

Lukin's position which he shared with a powerful minority, appeared to be motivated by nothing more than revenge over Phillip Nind's humiliation over the Bonded Sugar Act. Around the local exhibitions, however, which Muir continued to patronise, there was no such bias. At an exhibition of the East Moreton Agricultural Association in April, a previous denial of a prize was overturned in his favour by neighbour and colleague Alexander Watt who declared that no classification was necessary and thus Muir's exhibit was well worthy of a prize.[665]

As the proposed changes were not adopted, this opened the door to Muir returning to exhibit in 1879. This he did with a great deal of fanfare taking all before him. Creating a huge impression with his new carbonised clarifying process, he vindicated himself while laying waste to those who had opposed him on the classification issue and those who had persisted with De Lissa's uneconomical clarifier. In the intervening years of 1877 and 1878 the prizes for open pan sugar were taken by White & Robertson

---

[665] East Moreton Agricultural Association, *The Week* (Brisbane) Saturday 22 April 1876, page 3

of Coomera, managed by his brother David using De Lissa's Icery Process.[666]

As a fierce combatant in any endeavour that he was involved in therefore, Robert Muir was a hard man for the established order to suppress. His willingness to question, investigate and challenge in the Brisbane and Logan districts, was second to none. This certainly extended to his most treasured and earliest skill as a ploughman, developed under the keen eye of his ploughman father back in Ayr. Despite all his diverse commercial and business interests he held a special place for his earliest acquired skill, often organizing and competing himself in ploughing competitions into his fifties. Benowa, therefore, like Springbank Farm at Ballarat was a centre of such activity during the 1870s once the estate was reasonably well established. Like almost everything that Robert Muir was involved in, they were not dull or routine affairs.

The first to be publicly recorded occurred at Oxley at an officially sanctioned competition among the local farmers. Muir, who was in attendance, showed a keen interest in the proceedings while offering a great deal of unsolicited advice. It wasn't long before he was challenged by those who doubted his self-proclaimed expertise as he stood among them – a successful sugar producer and now a magistrate and reasonably well-off businessman. Muir immediately rose to the occasion and accepted a contest between himself and another spectator, McFarlane from Brisbane. After the official program had ended the two combatants then took to the field under a cloud of wagers with Muir at long odds to win. Win he did, no doubt pocketing a substantial sum as did anyone else who was aware of his abilities.[667]

This whetted his appetite for more and another competition was announced for 1875 at his property at Benowa on Friday September 10. Convened under the auspices of the Agricultural Society of Southern Queensland, it came down to a contest between horses and bullocks for a silver cup and £7.10s to settle ongoing matters of opinion. A large festive crowd of both sexes

---

[666] Sugar at the Brisbane Show, *MacKay Mercury & South Kennedy Advertiser*, Saturday 7 September 1878, page 3
[667] Ploughing Match at Oxley, *The Queenslander* (Brisbane) Saturday 12 September 1874, page 9

attended the event which was the first of its kind in the district. Robert Muir chose bullocks and as a fifty-year-old local magistrate, was considered by many critics to be a soft contestant and again not expected to win. However, once again he took out first prize against other contestants who used horses that found it difficult going in the hard soil along the river flats. This was considered highly unusual in an industry that was becoming increasingly reliant on horses and was claimed by Muir to be a first in such competitions anywhere in the Australian colonies – a claim which he later retracted.[668] While this was in progress, some of the less interested spectators had organized a horse race which added to a general atmosphere of mayhem and high spirits as fights broke out over betting on the festivities. It was concluded with dinner and presentations at the Coomera Hotel.[669]

The debate of the merits of bullocks versus horses continued unabated however, as some were convinced that Muir was perpetrating some sort of deception or trick. Therefore, in typical style he offered a rematch reminding his detractors and critics that there was more to ploughing than horses and bullocks – the ploughman himself was also a vital part. Unlike many his age and position in society who competed with a paid ploughman, Muir chose to compete himself. His reasons for this were that to employ ploughmen to plough his fields it was only proper that he should be as equally or better skilled than them to ensure the highest standards were maintained. As he wrote 'I have ever been most sincerely of the opinion that a planter has a right to be able himself to use the plough intelligently and well, so that if any of his ploughmen making bad work put the fault on 'restive horses' or bad ploughs, all the planter has to do in such a case, is to lay hold and show them different.' He thus wrote with sarcasm to the Queenslander:

> I have been reminded that I am getting old which is most true; also, that it has a tendency to lower the status of planters and magistrates of the territory for one of their number to be

---
[668] Horse Teams vs Bullock Teams for Prize Ploughing, *The Queenslander* (Brisbane) Saturday 9 October 1875, page 22
[669] Beenleigh, *The Brisbane Courier*, Saturday 18 September 1875, page 3

ploughing like a common clodhopper; in fact, a learned judge (of ploughing) informed me that he once ploughed himself, but since they made him a judge he was above ploughing. Most fortunate and high-minded judge how fortunate to be above ploughing![670]

The challenge of a re-match was duly accepted and scheduled for 5 November at the Main Camp Flat at Coomera. His brother Matthew presided as one of the judges. The day began hot, an ominous portent of a tedious and exhausting ordeal. Unlike the prior competition it was a long and strenuous day in the field for both spectators and competitors. The only excitement was when Muir broke his plough, a home-made wooden device of his own design, after clearly struggling in the heat towards the end of the day. He was immediately surrounded with eager supporters, some with wagers on him to win. One offered to complete the job for him sparking an ugly scene as police were called to intervene before he reluctantly retired. The competition ended with Pimpama farmer Aitken taking first prize and local man Oxenford taking second. The result, however, was hotly disputed and protests were lodged resulting in a further rematch being scheduled for the following year. In the aftermath numerous letters on the matter were dispatched to the press but none were published due to concerns over perpetuating any bad feelings.[671]

The re-match occurred at Benowa on 21 April 1876 this time under the auspices of the Agricultural Society of Southern Queensland. There were nine entries including that of Robert Muir using oxen, while the rest were horse drawn. The contestants included his ploughman and overseer Hicks, later a well-known alderman and mayor of Southport, and Oxenford of Coomera also with bullocks who had lodged the protest at the previous event. Unfortunately, just prior to the commencement of the competition a telegram was received advising that the appointed judges were not able to attend leading to the selection of replacements from

---

[670] Horse Teams vs Bullock Teams for Prize Ploughing, *The Queenslander* (Brisbane) Saturday 9 October 1875, page 22
[671] The Coomera, *The Queenslander*, (Brisbane) Saturday 13 November 1875, page 6

those present. Once again, the event ended mired in controversy as C Mullen from Oxley took out first prize while Muir was second and Oxenford sixth. Muir however, caused a considerable stir expressing outrage that one of the presiding judges had placed a bet on the result before being appointed on the day and had not withdrawn it. At the urging of a very vocal group of supporters among the crowd on lodging a protest, he was advised that the result was legal as the prize had been awarded and results entered. Shortly after a great deal more of heated discussion it was revealed that another judge had no knowledge or experience with ploughing. This elicited a great deal of disgust and anger among those remaining on the field.[672]

The result was officially overturned the next day by independent arbitration declaring Muir the winner by a big margin using a more meticulous method that awarded points for different judgement categories. A storm of protest followed from all parties with *The Queenslander* weighing in on the side of the original result. Muir, however, reiterated his earlier comments that he simply wished to prove that many successful planters like himself were acquainted with the practical details of their work. Furthermore, he went on, he did this with a wooden plough he made himself, without wheels, against all comers with ploughs made by the best in Britain and the colonies and with oxen rather than horses. He said that he was not alone knowing several who could do the same.[673]

While some assert Robert Muir was a member of the old aristocracy with a lingering tendency to assert himself over the less privileged and lesser class locals, the ploughing matches that provoked so much controversy during 1875 and 1876 only confirms his lowly origin. [674] Moreover, Muir had many local supporters as the news articles indicate, many of them enthusiastic punters on his ploughing endeavours and as recipients of his

---

[672] Nerang, *The Queenslander* (Brisbane) Saturday 29 April 1876, page 1, Champion Ploughing Match, *The Queenslander* (Brisbane) Saturday 29 April 1876, page 6
[673] Departures, *The Queenslander* (Brisbane) Saturday 27 May 1876, page 32
[674] Michael Jones, *Country of five rivers: Albert Shire 1788-1988*, Allen & Unwin Sydney 1988, p157

generous hospitality which by 1880 was developing a legendary reputation. This was no doubt enhanced by the story of two travelling correspondents on a holiday adventure to the beaches of the south coast fishing and hunting, who were made welcome by Robert Muir. They were invited to stay with tumblers of rum and milk after knocking on his door at Benowa at four o'clock in the morning. Entertaining them with stories of his and his brothers' history in the district, which included a near drowning at the mouth of Currumbin Creek, he then provided them both with a warm bed until they left at three in the afternoon. Impressed by the fact that they were entertained with such willing and friendly accommodation which included horses for the rest of their journey, they ensured that part of the story received an honourable mention in the published article on their return.[675] Lena Cooper, in her manuscript on the early days of the Nerang district, also recalls time spent at Benowa as a child, especially Robert Muir telling interesting and sometimes humorous stories of his adventures on the Ballarat and other Victorian goldfields, while also entertaining them with funny Scotch ditties. Lena was of a similar age to Matthew, Muir's eldest son, attending the Nerang school where Muir was also a founding board member and Matthew in the first group of students with her three brothers in 1875. [676]

Rather than attempting to assert himself above the population like a British landlord, he was, as he wrote to *The Queenslander,* entering ploughing contests to demonstrate and celebrate his lowly origins. He was, after all, the son of a landless tenant farmer. It was also to identify with the majority of the local small farming and labouring population, many for whom he had laboured to open the door of opportunity. Alluding to Adam Smith, and Lord Kames a century earlier, he declared that agriculture was nothing to be despised or ashamed of, as it formed the basis for the wealth of the nation.[677]

---

[675] From Brisbane to Grafton Along the Coast, *The Queenslander* (Brisbane) Saturday 8 May 1880, page 588

[676] *Letters to Bundall 1872-1879 and Lena Cooper's manuscript,* John Elliott ed., Booloorong Publications, Southport Qld, 1993, p263,298

[677] Horse teams versus bullock teams for prize ploughing, *The Queenslander,* Saturday 9 October 1875, page 22

Many prominent local pioneers passed through Benowa. Alderman Edward Hicks, Southport councillor and later mayor on emigrating from England was first employed at Benowa as a ploughman, and his wife as the cook. They were engaged directly on embarking from the Royal Dane at Brisbane in 1869. Hicks shortly after was promoted to overseer of Benowa and competed against Muir in the infamous ploughing contests in 1875-1876. According to his son-in-law, Hicks later acquired his own property locally but continued to assist Muir in that role when he was absent for many years after.[678] Robert Muir was also known to be less discerning. According to Archie Meston, Muir's brother-in-law, the coming of Hicks and his wife ended the two-year tenure of Maggie MacPherson, sister of the bushranger 'the wild Scotsman' who had been engaged as a housemaid to Muir's first wife Jane.[679] Another well-known pioneer was Harry Crocker who emigrated with his brother in 1884 on the Indus. After working on the Benowa sugar plantation for twelve months, he took up farming in the Beaudesert area becoming a prominent breeder of jersey cattle as well as a member of the Beaudesert Show Committee.[680] Another was Karl Eichsteadt, remembered as a local farming pioneer whose first position, after emigrating from Germany aged 19 on the Reichstag in 1872, was cane cutting at Benowa where he was employed for six years before finally taking up dairy farming at Merrimac on the Gold Coast.[681] Likewise, his sister, Mrs Caroline Kamholz, a dressmaker, was another German immigrant who joined her brother in Queensland in 1883, her husband finding employment on the Benowa plantation for three years before selecting a property at Carrara nearby where they established a dairy farm. Her husband Karl, originally trained as a master tailor, was remembered as one of the areas 'sturdiest pioneers' involved

---

[678] Mayor of Southport, *The Brisbane Courier*, Monday 13 May 1918, page 8, Nerang Memories, *The Queenslander* (Brisbane) Saturday 7 August 1920, page 42, The Late Mr E Hicks, *The Brisbane Courier*, Friday 21 May 1920, page 8

[679] Old Time Bushrangers, *Western Argus* (Kalgoorlie) Tuesday 14 November 1922, page 1, A Meston, Bushrangers I have Met, *The world's News* (Sydney) Saturday 28 October 1922, page 21

[680] Obituary, *South Coast Bulletin* (Southport) Friday 12 May 1833, page 6

[681] Pioneer Passes, *South Coast Bulletin*, (Southport) Friday 15 January 1932, page 1

in every movement that promoted the advancement and social welfare of the district, serving as Vice President of the Nerang Show Society for many years.[682] William Baple, another local pioneer, also remembered as a dairy farmer and cane grower at Carrara, received his induction to Queensland at the Benowa plantation. Local dairy farmer Richard Crocker, a well-known sportsman and rugby player and brother of Harry, after arriving in 1884 aged 19, was another.[683]

Thus, as Wakefield and J D Lang had anticipated, Robert Muir had perfectly fulfilled the colonizing role that they, in their different ways had anticipated. The agricultural economy envisaged by Kames in the previous century, of enlightened farmers employing the techniques designed for capitalist exploitation of the land, had indeed born fruit. It had made many independent and comfortably off within Muir's sphere of influence in Southern Queensland. Excess labour from Europe in many cases had been able to follow the pioneers and establish a life and career for themselves as well.

However, in their own unique way, those Scots with farming backgrounds like Robert Muir had shown a divergent path to colonization. Their clannish ways and attitudes to land, their liberal politics, and expectations, offer a unique perspective on enlightened colonization advocated by Wakefield and Lang. Large monied patriarchal enterprises like the ones the Muir sisters were part of while sometimes successful, can be contrasted with the smaller concerns that employed combination techniques to serve their interests. This was particularly the case in the Northern Rivers of New South Wales and Southern Queensland, as pointed out by Eric Richards, where Alexander Meston and other Scots welcomed Robert Muir into their midst and supported his and their various endeavours in mutually beneficial ways.[684] As avowed liberals, they

---

[682] Mrs Caroline Kamholz, *South Coast Bulletin* (Southport) Friday 28 July 1939, page 11, Sturdy Pioneer, *South Coast Bulletin* (Southport) Friday 30 1929, page 17

[683] Mr William Baple, *South Coast Bulletin* (Southport) Friday 22 January 1932, page 7, Death of Mr Richard Crocker, *The Telegraph* (Brisbane) Saturday 13 June 1931, page 9

[684] Eric Richards, Scottish voices and Networks in Colonial Australia, in Angela McCarthy ed., *A global clan*, I B Taurus & Co London, 2012, p150-182,

had a particularly strong aversion to powerful capitalists imposing themselves on the market and denying smaller players an equal opportunity. Fighting tooth and nail to provide an open and fair commercial environment, they complied more closely to the vision of J D Lang and his yeoman ideal than the social transplantation concept of Wakefield. Robert Muir having fought hard for this against the growing might of the corporations like CSR, would have therefore noted with great satisfaction that many of his colleagues had become prosperous enough to afford the latest technology in sugar production with vacuum pan plants and his refining technology almost universal as the 1880s were coming to a close.

Eric Richards, Australia and the Scottish Connection in R A Cage, *The Scots abroad: labour, capital, enterprise 1750-1914*, Groom Helm Beckenham Kent U K 1985, p111-155

Chapter 27

The Ending of an Era

By the early 1880s, time and age were taking a toll on the yeoman's champion, coming down with a serious illness that forced him to take an extended break in a Brisbane hospital during 1881. He was welcomed home to Benowa by a small mention in local news in July 1881.[685] This signalled a change in direction as he placed more attention on the farm and especially the livestock. While he continued to enter the shows and continued to win prizes for sugar for a few more years, he began to see himself as more of a promoter of the industry in Southern Queensland. Thus, at subsequent Brisbane shows, he was becoming an attraction in his own right setting up working models of the various apparatus used in sugar production like his self-operating battery during 1880-84, and a complete working plant powered by a 5 HP steam engine that crushed cane and converted the juice into sugar in 1884.[686]

The origins of his diversification could be traced back even further to the hiatus period of 1877-78 when he withdrew from the exhibitions. During this period, while experimenting with refining techniques, he was devoting more time to the farming side of his enterprise and spending more time with his family. This brought profound changes to the appearance of Benowa itself with the appearance of a comfortable new brick home in 1872. It was complemented by the modernization of the much of the plant and equipment and the establishment of a horse and cattle stud. [687]

---

[685] Beenleigh, *The Brisbane Courier*, Wednesday 6 July 1881, page 5
[686] *The Brisbane Courier*, Saturday 16 August 1884, page 4, Prize Schedule, *The Queenslander* (Brisbane) Saturday 24 July 1880, p119, Opening of the Exhibition, *The Brisbane Courier*, Thursday 21 August 1884, page 6
[687] Benowa plantation photographed in 1872 by William Boag, Oxley library State Library of Qld. (next page)

The Ending of an Era

His focus appears to have been on training his eldest son Matthew for a similar career in farming and sugar production using the most up to date technology. In this he could boast of a high degree of success, as Matthew, at 21 years of age, took out second prize for vacuum pan refined white sugar at the Queensland Exhibition against highly rated producers in 1884, and first prize for the best collection of sugar canes. His father's renewed focus on farming had also paid dividends a few years earlier at the Beenleigh exhibition of his local Southern Queensland Association in 1878, awarded first prize for a Hereford bull under three years.[688]

By the early 1880s the dominance of Robert Muir in the southern sugar districts was being challenged. Colleagues like neighbour Alexander Watt managed to take the honours for fine counter sugar at the Melbourne International in March 1881, relegating him into second place.[689] Mounting a comeback in 1882,

---

[688] Opening of the Exhibition, *The Brisbane Courier*, Thursday 21 August 1884, page 6, Show at Beenleigh, *The Queenslander* (Brisbane) Saturday 13 July 1878, page 480, Prize Schedule, *The Queenslander* (Brisbane) Saturday 23 August 1884, page 310

[689] Sugars at the Melbourne International Exhibition, *Logan Witness*, (Beenleigh) 12 March 1881, page 3,

The Ending of an Era

he made a clean sweep of the prizes for sugar in all categories including the premier prize for any process, at the National Exhibition, as well as taking third prize for a trotting horse named Botheration. Thereafter, he appears to have put a full stop on competing for sugar honours satisfied that he had achieved all he could as an open pan sugar producer. He had proved that the old and cheaper technology was, in the hands of a competent operator, could be as good and even better than anything available.[690] But Robert Muir was clearly becoming disillusioned with the direction of the sugar industry as he searched for a new direction and focus. A major incentive to seek new challenges was the depressed state of the market that was affecting the Southern growers more acutely than their northern competitors in the Mackay and Hervey Bay districts. It had come at a time when the political and cultural mood of the public and politics had changed considerably. The southern pioneers of the sugar industry were no longer the great hope of prosperity that they were in the 70s when MLC Louis Hope and Robert Muir were considered heroes, having proven that sugar was indeed a viable industry.

The ultimate insult for Robert Muir was delivered during 1883 when a bill of exchange was returned by one of the banks. It triggered a wave of uncertainty by enemies and friends alike in the business community and speculation over his financial standing. This prompted a response by Muir on the front page of the *Brisbane Courier* explaining that the setback was due to political opposition and a bank error. He reminded the public that his financial position was beyond question with realizable assets worth at least five times the value of his liabilities. He also challenged sceptics to contact his Brisbane agent Parbury, Lamb and Raff who would open his books for inspection. He ended his statement with a defiant declaration that he was forced to make a public declaration for the benefit of his business constituents. He also stated that it was also 'in the interests of the much despised southern plantations, showing that sugar growing can be there made to pay, frost and

---

[690] The National Annual Exhibition, *Logan Witness* (Beenleigh) Saturday 2 September 1882, page 3, Prize Schedule, *The Queenslander* (Brisbane) Saturday 2 September 1882, page 4

> THROUGH unexpected circumstances, coupled with the periodic eccentricities of our monetary institutions, some of my paper was, a few days ago returned – SINCE PROMPTLY MET ON REPRESENTATION.
>
> I wish to state that I own REALISABLE PROPERTY, the estimated value of which EXCEEDS FIVE TIMES THE AMOUNT OF MY LIABILITIES, the particulars of which can be given by my agents, Messrs. Parbury, Lamb, and Raff, Brisbane, to whom I am permitted to refer anyone interested in my affairs.
>
> I make this public statement which I consider is alike due to my business constituents, and my own credit, as well as in the interests of the much-despised southern plantations, showing that sugar growing can be there made to pay, frosts and the labour obstruction tactics of the Opposition notwithstanding.
>
> ROBERT MUIR,
> Benowa, 10th July, 1883.   1272

the labour obstruction tactics of the opposition notwithstanding.'[691]

Despite his public confidence however, with the sugar industry in Southern Queensland entering its twilight years, Robert Muir had been busy elsewhere. After his bad year of 1881, when ill health and acceptance of the unfolding political reality kept him uncharacteristically quiet, he had been very active at Benowa. Significant resources of time and money were being invested into the breeding, marketing and promotion of horses in addition to his well-established reputation as a competent cattle breeder. However, it was the horses to which most of his resources were directed due to their integral role with powering the sugar plant in the early 1870s and with ploughing and other heavy work in the establishment and running of the Benowa estate.

As early as 1872 with the introduction of steam engines, his focus began to incorporate a breeding program as a way of utilizing the excess stock. The first of the stallions became well known in the district sporting the name Young Honest Tom. His services were advertised as 'the East Moreton favourite' in *The Queenslander* that year.[692] His interest in horses grew in proportion to his and his compatriot southern growers increasing fortunes. It was not long before racetracks and turf clubs were established locally at Nerang, Bundall and Pimpama offering some recreational activity for the prosperous local land owners. Robert Muir appears to have had only a limited involvement during the 1870s serving as a steward

---

[691] Classified Advertising, *The Brisbane Courier*, Wednesday 25 July 1883, page 1
[692] Advertising, *The Queenslander* (Brisbane) Saturday 9 November 1872, page 11

The Ending of an Era

at the Pimpama Christmas races in 1874 alongside other prominent figures such as George Black and J W Drewe, owner of the Pimpama Hotel.[693] By 1881 Muir had begun to seriously consider the horse business at all levels as an additional source of income to replace declining sugar revenues. This was following the lead of others in the district who were already well established, entering exhibits in the Queensland and local shows and participating in the local races. Purchasing a stud Lincoln draft stallion in February 1881 from the Clarence district south of the border, signalled an intention to also take a significant step into the field.[694]

Another purchase in April 1881, from Barnes and Smith on the Clarence River sired by Captivator, a famous draft stallion, was followed by a mass purchase of 'first class' draft horses from the same source which was driven overland to Benowa. The progress of the mob was reported in Casino, Grafton and Nerang and Beenleigh during October that year. Some were advertised for sale to interested buyers along the route with the balance forming part of the stud.[695]

From here, Muir's interest took another leap into the emerging racing industry where the main activity was centred at Eagle Farm in Brisbane. One of his most well known early racing acquisitions, was Miss Harkaway described as a freak of nature. The mare burst onto the scene untrained at the Nerang races 3 January 1882. Coming a very good second, the sky seemed the limit as the fancied horse did not let him down, coming second again at the Logan Handicap in the jumps race a few week later where she was listed as third favourite.[696]

---

[693] Pimpama Christmas Races, *The Queenslander* (Brisbane), Saturday 3 January 1874, page 10

[694] Nerang, *The Queenslander* (Brisbane) Saturday 5 February 1881, page 167

[695] Nerang, *The Queenslander* (Brisbane) Saturday 16 April 1881, page 488, Nerang, *The Brisbane Courier*, Saturday 22 October 1881, page 6, New South Wales Draft Horses, *Logan Witness* (Beenleigh) Saturday 8 October 1881, page 2, 1882 photograph of Benowa Stud farm and sugar plant Oxley Library Qld State Library (see next page)

[696] Nerang, *The Brisbane Courier*, Saturday 7 January 1882, page 6, The Logan Races, *The Brisbane Courier*, Tuesday 21 February 1882, page 3, Sporting Notes, *The Telegraph* (Brisbane) Saturday 11 March 1882, page 2

A stylish performance at an equestrian event at the Brisbane Exhibition only added to the growing reputation of Muir's prize horse which ran another second at the Coomera Christmas Races.[697] Unfortunately Miss Harkaway's promising career sadly came to an end at the Nerang races 3 January a week later, taking a serious fall at one of the hurdles. She was shot the next morning putting to an end also Muir's expectation of taking her to an anticipated first prize at the equestrian event at the upcoming National Exhibition.[698]

The loss was followed in quick succession by another setback losing his famous draft stallion King Billy. It was a reminder that the horse business was an expensive minefield where losses incurred could well have amounted into thousands of pounds judging on the prices paid at auction.[699] Not deterred however, he followed that up shortly after with the purchase of Fitzroy, another famous winner, who continued to deliver well into 1886, taking out

---

[697] The Jumping, *The Queenslander* (Brisbane) Saturday 2 September 1882, page 1, Racing notes, *The Queenslander* (Brisbane) Saturday 6 January 1883, page 14
[698] Current News, *The Queenslander* (Brisbane) Saturday 6 January 1883, page 5
[699] Country News, *The Queenslander* (Brisbane) Saturday 13 January 1883, page 47

the 'Corinthian Rack' and the 50 sovereign 'Flying Handicap' at the Southport Races in April 1886.[700] The horse stud was also increased in 1883 with a prize draft stallion from his sources on the Clarence, 'Young Muir Lad' for 250 guineas.'[701] After that came another which he named 'Young Davie,' son of Davie, the two horses representing a obvious humorous allusion to his loyal younger brother.

Added to his stock were other pedigree beasts of burden such as Spanish donkeys.[702] Following the successful conclusion of the first consignment of horses, further order was placed on the Clarence supplier and a notice placed in the Brisbane papers that another consignment was on its way. It consisted of 38 blood pedigree mares as well as 30 draft mares, colts and fillies. This was in conjunction with a further advertisement for the sale of the three farming lots on the old Manchester Cotton Estate across the river that he had earlier acquired.[703] It wasn't long before Benowa had expanded beyond draft horses establishing a reputation for breeding quality horses for all purposes as Muir continually added to his stock famous winners such as Muir Lad and Martinet.[704] Muir's self imposed exile from the exhibitions during 1877 and 1878 however, had been productive in other aspects apart from developing his part-time horse industry and experimenting on profitable innovations in sugar technology.

His foray into residential land at Southport, was showing all the signs of a developing boom. Its potential as the lifestyle resort

---

[700] Southport Races, *The Brisbane Courier*, Wednesday 28 April 1886, page 3
[701] *Clarence and Richmond Examiner and New England Advertiser*, Saturday 31 March 1883, page 4
[702] Classified Advertising, *The Queenslander* (Brisbane) Saturday 19 December 1885, page 971
[703] Advertising, *The Telegraph* (Brisbane) Wednesday 10 January 1883, page 4
[704] Advertising, *Logan Witness*, (Beenleigh) Saturday 25 October 1884, page 4

The Ending of an Era

town that it would be in the future, was becoming well established. Importantly, it would also provide a staging point for the increasing steamer traffic from Brisbane with passengers and supplies for the local industries, farms and general population. Until the railway, which in 1878 was over a decade away, steamer was the most efficient mode of transport to the area. Muir's land at Labrador was therefore subdivided into lots and advertised for sale by March 1878. Adding to the simultaneous sale of Soutport land by Frederick Bauer adjoining, and with the advantages of Deepwater Point close by as the only place where steamers could dock, it was relentlessly promoted. At the same time Robert Muir also advertised 100 head of cattle for sale at Beenleigh, which in all probability, in combination with the land sales and the horses, realized far more than the dwindling profits from sugar.[705]

That same year he purchased the Steamer Ipswich from A.S.N. Co, which was sitting idle in the Brisbane River after the demise of the river business to Ipswich with the introduction of the rail line. The Ipswich was a fast steamer 149 feet long and 18 feet wide with a light draft that had the capability of carrying 112 passengers.[706] As it was inoperable at the time of purchase, Muir had it towed to moorings at Benowa where he had the engine refurbished. He then purchased another small cutter which was later disposed of, to transport timber from his sawmill and other supplies between Benowa and Brisbane.[707]

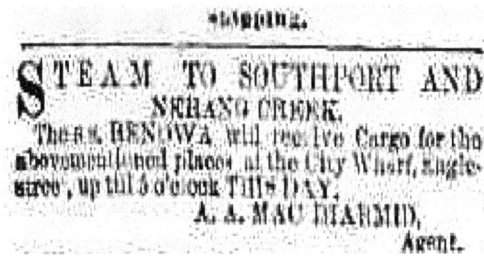

He later set about dividing the Ipswich in two to create two separate vessels, completing one of them sometime after the commencement of 1884. The forward end was named SS Benowa, the other the Scottish Prince which he

---

[705] Classified Advertising, *The Brisbane Courier*, Friday 15 March 1878, page 4
[706] Classified Advertising, *The Brisbane Courier*, Friday 15 March 1878, page 4
[707] Ramblings in Queensland, *Logan Witness*, (Beenleigh) Saturday 21 January 1882, page 4, correspondent reports two cutters owned by Muir transporting timber between Benowa & Brisbane.

not commission.⁷⁰⁸ The Benowa began operations at least by 1884 supplying timber for construction and cabinet making to the Brisbane market from the Benowa saw-mill to his timber yard in Adelaide Street opposite the Normal School.⁷⁰⁹ By April 1885, after the sale of the Brisbane premises, the Benowa became a commercial proposition on its own, operating from city wharf in Brisbane to Benowa once a week.⁷¹⁰ Like the Ipswich, its days were numbered by the coming rail extension from Beenleigh to Nerang and Southport which was put out to tender that same year. It had been a matter of discussion for some time with Muir himself having been directly involved from the outset.⁷¹¹ Nevertheless, he believed the steamer was a good investment due to its ample cargo capacity and the convenience of servicing his own needs, as well as others in the surrounding areas, directly between Brisbane and the Nerang River.⁷¹² His main interest was the convenience of the transportation of sugar direct onto the Brisbane wharf, a cost saving due to greatly reduced handling expenses.

For a property as large as Benowa with only a couple of hundred acres at most reserved for the sugar industry, general farming was another viable enterprise. Much of this was made available for cultivation from the late 1860s as the Muir brothers, like many others in the district, discontinued growing cotton. They did, however, continue to dabble in the industry by taking part in the Fiji cotton experiment in the same period. They joined speculators from Australia and New Zealand to take advantage of the cheap land and labour and the persistent high price in the wake of shortages due to the American Civil War.⁷¹³ While their cotton won an award at the Queensland Exhibition in 1873, Muir quickly

---

⁷⁰⁸ Isobell Hannah, The Early Steamers, *The Brisbane Courier*, Saturday 13 May 1922, page 16, Alexander McRobbie, *The Real Surfer's Paradise*, Pan News Pty Ltd, Surfer's paradise 1988, page 31
⁷⁰⁹ Ramblings in Queensland, *Logan Witness* Saturday 21 January 1882, page 4
⁷¹⁰ A Trip to Southport and Burleigh Heads, *The Queenslander* (Brisbane) Saturday 10 March 1883, page 372, *The Brisbane Courier*, Saturday 11 June 1881, page 4
⁷¹¹ Robert Longhurst, *Nerang Shire: a history to 1949*, p103.
⁷¹² Classified Advertising, *The Brisbane Courier*, Friday 17 April 1885, page 1
⁷¹³ Evelyn Stokes: The Fiji cotton boom I the eighteen-sixties *New Zealand Journal of History*_1968, 02_2 p165

The Ending of an Era

decided that farming his own property presented a much less risky investment.[714] Thus, in 1885, over 600 acres was occupied with the horse stud, cattle stud and a dairy with a large herd of approximately 100 head of milking cattle. With some put to breeding stock, they provided a ready supply of heifers and milk for the local market. It was also observed that Muir, like his immediate neighbour Fullarton, the owner of Bundall, had a large portion of the estate, some of which was leased, under maize, oats, vegetables and fruit produce. Between the two estates, they supplied a large proportion of the needs of nearby Southport. This particularly was viewed as the future, eventually replacing sugar.[715]

With this in mind, Robert Muir's actions after 1883, continued to show evidence of an intention to follow through on his intention to seek better opportunities elsewhere. The first step was the commencement of the sale of his most immediately realizable assets. The successful sale in 1883 of horses and two of the three Manchester Cotton farms immediately across the river, purchased in the 1882 subdivision and sale, preceded a flurry of activity that also included completing the subdivision of his lots in Southport and Labrador and those on Mt Tambourine. Meanwhile, as he and other independent sugar producers had feared, the Queensland Government announced in 1885 that a £50,000 investment in two central mills at Mackay which would be serviced by small local growers and worked by white only labour.[716] Coming on the back of a catastrophic fall in world sugar prices in 1884, it was the final straw sounding the death knell for any plans for extending the life of the Benowa plantation. By October 1885 he had announced that he was retiring from active business.

---

[714] Awards of the Jury to Queensland Exhibitors, *Queensland Times, Ipswich Herald and General Advertiser*, Thursday 6 November 1873, page 4

[715] Advertising, *Logan Witness* (Beenleigh) Saturday 23 March 1878, page 3, Ramblings in Queensland, *Logan Witness* Saturday 21 January 1882, page 4, The Present State of the Sugar Industry: the Coomera and Nerang Districts, *The Queenslander*, (Brisbane) Saturday 21 November 1885, page 839, Country News, *Logan Witness* (Beenleigh) Saturday 18 March 1882, page 2, *Queensland Figaro and Punch*, (Brisbane) Saturday 5 December 1885, page 12

[716] Peter D Griggs, The origins and early development of the small cane farming system in Queensland 1870-1915, *Journal of Historical Geography*, 23, 1 (1997) p 51

This came with an advertising campaign that extended from October through to December 1885. On offer was over 2000 acres comprising all the land, with a sale date advertised as Tuesday 15 for individual lots, the sugar mill and sawmill. Muirlands, which in October 1885 was an unsurveyed township of just over 100 acres on the Benowa property, appears to have remained a separate entity but was also included in the sale.[717] Significantly, the remainder of the Benowa property he retained, offering leaseholds.[718] For this Muir had gone to great lengths, chartering the Steamer Kate from Brisbane for three days for the exclusive purpose of transport to the sale at Southport and the return journey. The *Brisbane Courier* reports a strong response with one hundred and twenty prospective purchasers thus departed Brisbane in a carnival mood on Friday 29 January 1886 at 2 PM for the eight-hour journey. Once at Southport most spent the evening waiting to cross the Nerang bar, night fishing and enjoying the sea air. After they disembarked at Deepwater Point the next morning, they were all treated to an excellent luncheon at 11am before the sale was completed. Despite the wide publicity, a further sale had to be scheduled with almost as much fanfare, for the following March due to less than expected sales. [719]

At the Benowa Estate meanwhile, a fire sale was in progress. Opening a couple of weeks prior, it encompassed most of the furniture and effects, as well as the farm equipment and almost all the livestock. To ensure as many as possible made it to the sale, prospective purchasers were offered transportation by trap from Southport to Benowa and return. With the 'Muirlands' survey on the estate completed, lots were also offered for sale. They were described as 92 allotments fronting the river with a backdrop of

---

[717] Advertising, *Queensland Figaro and Punch*, Saturday 5 December 1885 page 12, (see page 281 & 282), Advertising, *The Telegraph* (Brisbane) Monday 30 November 1885, page 7,
[718] Advertising, *The Telegraph* (Brisbane) Thursday 4 March 1886, page 8,
[719] Commercial, *The Brisbane Courier*, Monday 1 February 1886, page 4, Benwell and Echlin, Watson Ferguson & Co, *Southport allotments for sale 30 January*, State Library Queensland, record No. 21112735400002061 Copy of the subsequent sale in March 1886, *Map of Southport showing allotments for sale at Loders Hill and Deepwater Point*, Watson Ferguson & Co Lithographers, March 1886, State Library of Queensland, record No 21240634400002061 (see page 283 & 284)

The Ending of an Era

the Dividing Range – 'the finest properties in Southern Queensland.' The sale was set to be held every day thereafter until all items for sale were sold. His accompanying announcement was that he 'was early leaving for Europe' adding a sense of finality to the proceedings.[720]

Sales, unfortunately, were slow - the Mt Tamborine (413 acres in 2 acre lots) and St Bernard lots (320 acres) first advertised for sale in 1883, remained unsold eighteen months later despite receiving a personal endorsement from the Premier Sir Samuel Griffith. The sawmill and sugar mill on the mountain also seemed to have never become operational and the SS Benowa remained unsold and in service.[721] Nevertheless by March 1886, it was reported that 144 lots at Deepwater Point had been sold, realizing £4647. The waterside lots unfortunately, which were expected to realize up to £1000 each, remained unsold, while the 220 lots sold 30 January returned a total of £7922.[722]

Most of the Tamborine lots fortunately, were sold in December 1885 as a result of the advertising campaign, while the sawmill, which had finally been readied for operation early in 1886 remained unsold at the end of the year.[723] However, despite having sold the St Bernard properties to the Tambourine Mountain Tableland Company, Muir remained embroiled in a dispute with the surveyors of the estate. It was a saga that extended over two years, frustrating attempts to have the properties ready for sale. It was testing his patience and trademark good humour to the limit.

The court case that attracted unwanted adverse attention, finalised the matter in May 1886. Amid claims and counterclaims, it seems that the property for a long period between 1883 and 1885, had gone into decay and had become derelict and overgrown among the fast-growing tropical foliage. Markers could not be located, sugar cane that had been planted nearby had also intruded

---

[720] Classified Advertising, *The Queenslander*, Saturday 19 December 1885, page 971,
[721] Classified Advertising, *The Brisbane Courier* Wednesday 23 June 1886, page 1.
[722] Commercial, *Queensland Times, Ipswich Herald and General Advertiser*, Tuesday 4 May 1886, page 2, Commercial, *The Brisbane Courier* (Queensland) Monday 1 February 1886, page 4
[723] Classified Advertising, *The Brisbane Courier*, Wednesday 8 December 1886, page 2

into the subdivision and the building constructed on the property, which was available to the surveyor, was in a filthy state. After hearing complaints from a purchaser of two lots, Muir conducted an inspection to assess the work, which included clearing the scrub and undergrowth. On seeing for himself, the normally good-natured Muir flew into a rage and ordered the surveyor and his assistant off the property, refusing to pay the outstanding account.[724]

Muir's patience was clearly wearing decidedly thin. As he had already announced, he was on a schedule to leave the district at the earliest possible time.[725] Thus, with most of the land without reserve, the indications were that he hoped to have matters finalized as quickly as possible. Having sold a third since the heavily promoted sale in January there remained 135 lots still unsold. Another sale was therefore advertised for October which was scheduled to take place at the Ipswich School of arts 23 October 1886. When it was concluded it resulted in the sale of only 48 small lots at the rear of the Grand Hotel for £650.[726]

Following this a final sale was announced. Clearly his departure was becoming a matter of urgency as the announcement of 'early leaving for Europe' a year before, was not looking as early as he had hoped. Nevertheless, having spent the last twelve months in an empty house after the sale of most of the furniture and effects, the huge sales campaign had almost reached its conclusion. All that remained were a relatively small number of lots to be sold at Labrador.[727]

---

[724] Supreme Court, *The Brisbane Courier* Saturday 22 May 1886, page 3
[725] Classified Advertising, *The Brisbane Courier* Saturday 12 December 1885, page 6, Classified Advertising, *The Queenslander* (Brisbane) Saturday 19 December 1885, page 971.
[726] Classified Advertising, *The Brisbane Courier*, Wednesday 20 October 1886, page 8, Commercial, *Queensland Times, Ipswich Herald and General Advertiser*, Thursday 28 October 1886, page 2
[727] *The Queenslander*, Saturday 19 September 1885, page 971

IMPORTANT SALE
OF
TAMBOURINE MOUNTAIN ESTATE,
FARM ON NERANG CREEK,
ONE-THIRD INTEREST IN COOMBABAH ESTATE, SOUTHPORT,
LEASE OF BENOWA ESTATE, SOUTHPORT,
SALE OF SOUTHPORT ALLOTMENTS,
STEAMER, HORSES, CATTLE, Etc., Etc.

The properties of the undersigned (Robert Muir), who is retiring from active business.

TAMBOURINE ESTATE

Contains 733 Acres on the tabletop of Tambourine Mountain, 2000ft. above the ocean, which it overlooks. This property includes the recently surveyed township of St. Bernard, containing 219 Allotments of 2 Acres each (more or less).

At all times streams of coolest water run through this property, along top of mountain, thence falling over precipices, form a succession of waterfalls of from 100ft. to 500ft. interspersed with miniature lakes—cool, deep and clear, and overhung with cedars, palms, treeferns, and vines in bewildering luxuriance and confusion.

The soil, richest chocolate, is of great depth, and the garden on the property proves it o be wonderfully adapted to the growth of all kinds of fruit (European and semi-tropical). Cedars, beech, pine, and other valuable timbers abound. The house on this property will give some idea of their size—said house 33ft. by 30ft., with detached kitchen, was entirely built out of one cedar cedar tree, and in that same tree (now to be seen on the ground) is sufficient timber left to build three more houses of equal size.

The views from this property are indescribably grand, wide, and varied; on the east the ocean, from Cape Byron to Moreton Island, with rivers like silver threads winding beneath; on the west English park-like beauties of the Beaudesert Valley, with a framing of Macpherson and 'Darlington Ranges, the lonely sentinel, Mount Lindsay standing apart and looking on this fair scene. To the sportsman—turkeys, pigeons, wallabies, and kangaroos abound.

The climate (as must be known, 2000ft. high, and near the ocean), is pure, cool, and bracing by day, at night a heavy pair of blankets is indispensable to the warmest subject; in winter frosts (except in spots) are unknown.

ST. BERNARD, TAMBOURINE,

Is within three hours' drive of Southport (to be shortened when I complete private road now under construction), over a fairly good road to Host Matheson's, at foot of Mountain, where excellent accommodation is provided. From Matheson's Hotel up to St. Bernard the visitor may either ride or drive. When the road just mentioned is completed ladies may drive with greatest security. When at the top of Mountain my house (at present unoccupied) will afford shelter, on application to Mr. Price, living on the adjoining property.

To show within what easy reach of Brisbane this grand sanitorium, St. Bernard, is, a party of well-known and leading gentlemen of Brisbane left that city at half-past 2 o'clock one Saturday afternoon lately, reached Matheson's for tea, did the whole Mountain, and returned to Brisbane next day (Sunday), being driven by two four-in-hand teams.

An alternate route is afforded by rail to Beenleigh, thence a drive of two hours to Matheson's Hotel.

A year hence we may safely calculate on having the iron horse running on the Brisbane Southport, and Tweed line past St. Bernard; distant one hour's drive.

I venture to predict that in the near future, frontages in St. Bernard will sell by the foot at big figures.

THE COOMBABAH ESTATE,

Of which I will sell one-third interest, contains about 4500 Acres, including about 135 Allotments in the best part of Central Southport, Loder's Hill, Deepwater Point, and Labrador, some of which are frontages to the Bay.

The Southport Property,

Comprises Two 5-Acre Blocks, Loder's Hill, adjoining the property of W. D. Nisbet, Esq., and near surveyed Railway Terminus; a 5-Acre Block, Loder's Hill, near residence of E. G.

Echln, Esq.; 103 Allotments, Loder's Hill and Deepwater Point, fronting the Bay, and close to Grand Hotel, in course of construction. Several of these Allotments command the grandest views in Southport.

THE BENOWA ESTATE,
1065 Acres,

Has the reputation of being not only the prettiest but the most fertile spot in Southern Queensland, situated three miles from Southport. It has a long frontage to Nerang River. Two steamers weekly plying to and from Brisbane.

This Estate is exceptionally free from frost, as evidenced by the green crop now standing after the severest winter.

It has a complete Vacuum Pan Plant, equal to 3 tons dry sugar per day. About 180 Acres are in cane, and 130 Acres are being planted with maize, and 20 Acres in oats, lucerne, potatoes, &c. The fact being that this district has been unable to supply Southport with produce, makes this property independent of the fate of the sugar industry, and being situated between the coast, and the Macpherson and Darlington ranges, extreme droughts are never experienced.

This property I would lease either as a whole or in blocks to suit farmers, or would lease the sugar-mill and saw-mill separately.

A central mill is in request, as farmers find difficulty in getting their cane crushed this season. I would be inclined to add double rollers and an additional vacuum pan, also increased general capacity of mill, to a permanent lessee, at a very low rental. I will also sell the

COOMAGULLY FARM,

47 acres, River Frontage, all alluvial deep soil, and cleared almost entirely of timber.

AT BENOWA

About 130 Horses and Brood Mares, Draught and Thoroughbred, 2 Draught Stallions, 2 Thoroughbred Stallions, 8 C. camy Ponies and Stallion (go splendidly in harness), 5 Donkeys (the pride of the Southport sands), Mail Phaeton, Four-in-hand Drag Pony Phaeton, Waggonette, with teams for each; also about 80 well-bred Hereford Cattle, and 2 Imported Bulls.

THE STEAMSHIP BENOWA,

considered the best Lighter in Moreton Bay, carries about 80 tons, drawing less than five feet of water, I offer for sale or charter; also the hull of vessel under construction (and nearly completed) in Nerang River 85 feet long, 18 feet beam; machinery ordered to send her a guaranteed speed of twelve miles an hour.

Lithographs and particulars obtainable from Messrs. M. B. Gannon (Arthur Martin & Co.,) and James Murr & Co., Brisbane; from Messrs. Stanley Harris, Geo. Andrews, and J. Stevenson, Southport, Mr. Welsh, Chairman Divisional Board, Southport; and from the undersigned, at Benowa.

TITLES PERFECT.   TERMS EASY.

Benowa, 17th October, 1885.   (Signed),   ROBERT MUIR.

Chapter 28

An Abrupt Conclusion

As he concluded the arrangements for leaving Benowa, Robert Muir's commitment to stand up for the small operator, remained undiminished. With eldest son Matthew now clearly filling his father's shoes in the sugar business, Muir re-entered the political fray once again. A small rebel group of farmers and cultivators in the Brisbane and East Moreton district were in dispute with the increasingly interventionist Brisbane City Council. The Council had refused to listen to pleas to enlarge the size of the central market, making life very difficult for the many small stall holders. With Brisbane by 1886 a large and growing urban centre, the original market that had been built over two decades earlier could no longer accommodate the increasing numbers selling their produce. Many were forced onto the street outside and into the side streets surrounding the market.

What attracted Robert Muir's attention was a by-law introduced 25 January reminiscent of the old miners' license on the Ballarat Goldfields. It was a draconian measure that made it virtually impossible for anyone transporting goods for sale in anything less than a large, wheeled vehicle, to make a profit due to the compulsion to purchase a daily license. Several politicians in the Legislative Assembly had supported the cause of the protestors by donating generously, as had Robert Muir. As one of the few who agreed to associate himself with the movement, he also accepted an invitation to officiate in an exhibition arranged by their organizational body, the East Moreton Mutual Farmers Association.[728] It would be his final political intervention but one he failed to see through to a conclusion.

---

[728] The Farmers and the Market, *The Brisbane Courier*, Monday 15 February 1886, page 5, East Moreton Farmer's Mutual Association, *The Queenslander* (Brisbane) Saturday 4 September 1886, page 32, East Moreton Farmer's

An Abrupt Conclusion

With the commencement of 1887, Robert Muir could finally see whatever future he had planned, to begin to take shape. All that was left was to finalise the sales of the remaining 82 lots of his Labrador estate and make arrangements with his agent Parbury Lamb & Co in Brisbane on other legal matters in his anticipated absence[729] However, as the month of January was ending, it seems that Muir had decided to not wait to sell the rest of his properties but to leave it all in the hands of his Brisbane agent and get on with his trip to Europe and the next phase of his life. As the final weeks of January began, the weather took a decidedly nasty turn. The humidity increased to intolerable levels, and it started to rain.

The rain was announced with a series of violent storms on Thursday 20 January which rolled over the ranges behind Benowa and Southport. It continued for three days without letup, dumping 400mm in two days. The Nerang, Albert, Coomera, and Logan rivers began to rise rapidly and within twenty-four hours had almost reached the high-water mark of the devastating floods of 1864. Punts, bridges, boats and jetties were washed away, many ending up in Moreton Bay. The Nerang bridge became completely submerged and the mail was not getting through. More of a problem for Robert Muir, however, was the telegraph, which had been put out of action from the commencement of the storms as many of the poles were either washed away or submerged.[730]

This was proving extremely frustrating as he needed to be in contact with his agents in Brisbane. Therefore, as soon as the rain stopped on Sunday 23 January, and the water began to subside, he decided that the only way to conduct his business was in person. As *The Queenslander* correspondent reports, Muir was anxious to conduct business in Brisbane in relation to his property sales and would not allow matters to be delayed. Leaving at 2PM on Sunday 23 January driving a two-horse buggy with his son Alexander

---

Mutual Association, *The Telegraph* (Brisbane) Tuesday 21 December 1886, page 4, *The Telegraph* (Brisbane) 1 February 1887, page 2

[729] The remaining allotments Muir was desperate to sell: *Muir's Southport Allotments*, Arthur Martin & Co and Hughes and Cameron Auctioneers, 1887, Image No. 18367442010-S0001, State Library Queensland, (see page 287)

[730] Southport, *The Queenslander* (Brisbane) Saturday 29 January 1887, page 167, Great inundation in the Valley of the Logan and Albert, *Logan Witness*, (Beenleigh) Saturday 29 January 1887, page 2

(commonly known as Peter), he set out in the hazardous conditions.

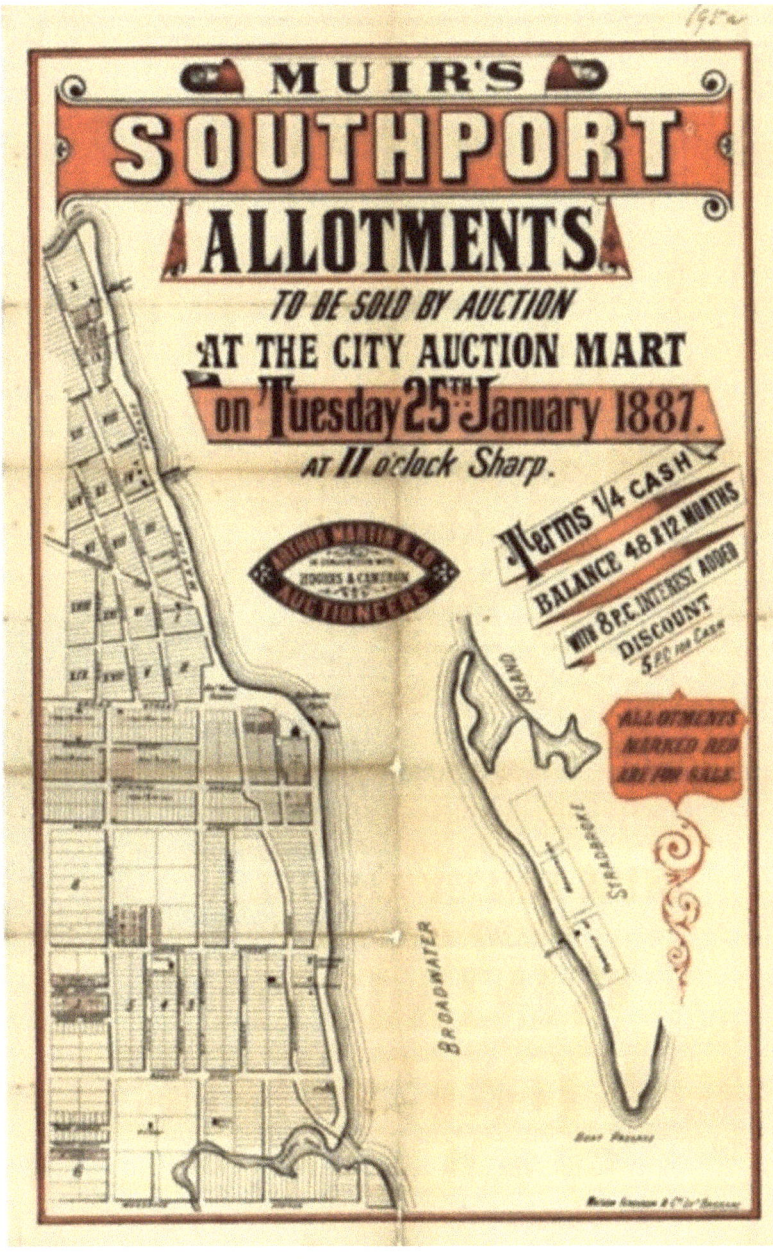

An Abrupt Conclusion

He was stopped about twenty miles into his journey at Yatala not far from Beenleigh where he was planning to take the train to Brisbane. Sam Kent, Augustus Whitehead, both sawyers, and Mr Brett, the manager of the Queensland National Bank stopped Robert Muir on the road, pointing out that the telegraph poles nearby were almost totally submerged, and the Yatala bridge had been washed away. All warned him that the road conditions ahead were too dangerous and not to proceed. However, Muir, who could see parts of the road not completely under water, despite other parts covered by a fast-moving current, proceeded, arguing that it was just minor and not to worry. After passing safely through a few puddles he encountered another and then the horse refused to go any further.

What appeared to be just another puddle like those he had easily traversed, was, as they discovered later, a gaping chasm nearly ten metres deep where a large culvert had been washed away. With horses and carriage and the occupants becoming totally engulfed in the rapidly rising torrent, the growing group on the water's edge watched helplessly. They witnessed a frantic scene as Robert Muir, who couldn't swim, clambered between the carriage and the horse in an attempt to turn its head around and reverse out. Meanwhile Peter had jumped out of the carriage and struck out for dry ground. Robert Muir seeing this, tried to reach him but was somehow struck by the horse in the panic and both father and son drowned before the helpless onlookers. It took until the next day for the bodies of Robert Muir, his son Peter and the horses and buggy to be recovered, as the water continued to be too hazardous.[731] Robert Muir's life thus ended as it had been lived, in a hurry. He and his son were officially pronounced dead on 26 January 1887 and buried that same day at the Beenleigh Cemetery on what coincidentally would be designated Australia Day fourteen years later.

His loss was keenly felt amongst many in the political, agricultural and business community, none more than Sir James Dickson who would be Minister of Defence in the new Australian

---

[731] Southport, The lower Logan, *The Queenslander* (Brisbane) Saturday 29 January 1887, page 166-167, *Coroner's Report into the deaths of Robert and Peter Muir 2/2/1887*, Queensland State Archives, Item Representation ID DR102604

An Abrupt Conclusion

Government in 1901. Dickson was a fellow Scot, and like Muir, an advocate of agriculture, and the small farming capitalist, serving as Queensland treasurer and later Premier. At the opening of the Drayton and Toowoomba Agricultural Society Show a week after the tragedy, Dickson who was in attendance with many other politicians and dignitaries, paid a special tribute to Robert Muir in his opening speech. He stated that he had known Muir for many years 'and he was one who had devoted almost a lifetime to the advancement of the Logan District and the colony generally, and in his death, he felt that he had lost an intimate relative; that the colony had lost one of its staunchest friends, and that agriculture one of its foremost men.'[732]

A short obituary in the *Melbourne Herald*, again coincidentally on 26 January 1887, credited Robert Muir as one who 'in the early days of sugar planting, helped most materially to successfully establish the industry in Queensland.' The journalist writes that in the establishment of the industry, competent boilers and sugar producers were its main obstacle until Robert Muir was able demonstrate the skills and instruct several protégé's in the technicalities of the art. He was also credited with taking a leading

> **DEATH OF A PIONEER.**
> Amongst those who have lost their lives during the late disastrous floods in Queensland we notice the name of Mr Robert Muir, of the Benowa Plantation, Nerang Creek, who in the early days of sugar planting helped most materially to successfully establish the industry in Queensland. Among the many difficulties the early planters were obliged to contend with was the impossibility of obtaining the services of really competent sugar boilers. Many men with first-class credentials from the East and West Indies were tried, but, owing to the fact that they knew nothing of the Queensland soil, and the consequent difference in the chemical components of the cane juice they were required to treat, to that to which they had been accustomed, failure succeeded failure, and planters lost heavily. Mr Muir, however, having thoroughly mastered the subject, trained a number of young men to the business, all of whom on leaving him secured first class situations in various portions of the colony. For very many years he took a leading part in all matters connected with the growth and manufacture of sugar, and his reputation as an expert was second to none in Queensland, and on more than one occasion his advice on subjects connected with the industry has been sought for and adopted by the Government. The news of his sad death will be received with regret by many persons in all parts of Australia, more especially in Queensland, where his genial qualities were known and appreciated. We may mention that in 1874 he patented a modification of the Icery process for the treatment of cane juice, an invention which enabled the planter to extract at a cheap cost a larger proportion of sugar from the cane juice than was obtainable before.

---

[732] The Luncheon, *Toowoomba Chronical and Darling Downs general Advertiser*, Saturday 29 January 1887, page 3

An Abrupt Conclusion

role 'in all matters connected with the growth and manufacture of sugar.' In addition, it was noted that 'his reputation as an expert was second to none in Queensland and on more than one occasion his advice on subjects connected with the industry has been sought for and adopted by the Government.' He was remembered as an innovator in the production of sugar and as a man whose genial qualities would be missed.[733]

Much of this could be attributed to the inherited culture of collaborative innovation learned from his immediate farming family and extended families. As direct participants in the commercialization process of the preceding two or three generations, making a profit was viewed as vital to survival in what was no longer a way of life, but an industry vital to the nation's fortunes. Likewise, innovation was also deemed a patriotic duty and actively and widely shared in an economic war of catch-up with the English and the rest of Europe. In Robert Muir's case, these inherited attributes were major drivers enabling him to personally benefit and assist the small yeoman capitalist to compete with the larger enterprises. For at least a couple of decades, he kept many of his fellow yeomen in the game, sharing any innovations that he made at minimal cost for the benefit of the small, independent producer.

Robert Muir's abrupt departure at the start of 1887 could be viewed as a political career cut short before it began. While Muir left no written notice of his intentions, indications are that, in contradiction of earlier declarations, he intended to return. Having cleared the decks of almost all encumbrances and assets that could most easily be converted to cash, and leasing the Benowa estate, indicates an intention to return after a widely publicised long trip to Europe. It is most likely therefore, with substantial cash reserves, he was finally able to enter the political arena. As he had indicated over ten years earlier, it would be to continue his fight as a liberal against racism and the growing political agendas of the trade unions and large capitalists. His plans for the Benowa Plantation were achieved by 1885 having installed all the latest technology and processes and would have also noted with

---

[733] Death of a Pioneer, *The Herald* (Melbourne) Wednesday 26 January 1887, page 3

satisfaction that most of his fellow planters in Southern Queensland had as well. Thus, it was a mission accomplished and by 1887 at the age of sixty it was time to retire or undertake a new project. It is also possible therefore, given his financial position, that he may have made plans with his son Matthew, to embark on a new sugar venture on the yet to be developed district in far north Queensland considering the movements of his sons after his death and his brother David a few years prior.

As his letters and actions indicate, Robert Muir was what Stuart Macintyre describes as a 'colonial liberal.' This is differentiated from his British counterpart, not by an adversarial stance against the established order, but by the creative imperative to create a something for the benefit of all.[734] Based on liberal ideals of fair and free trading, he envisaged a society, while typically ignorant of indigenous political economy as most were in that era, that was inclusive and did not discriminate by colour or race or status. He and his brothers therefore, beginning with the voyage on the Malabar where, for the first time they enjoyed the highest status, left for Australia with a confidence that they would arrive as members of a new ruling class with the opportunity to make such a mark on colonial society.

In the Australian colonies, he had a virtually unlimited scope to help construct a society and an industry based on these principles. They were principles born out of his unique Scottish experience with the revolutionary application of commercialization. The insecurity that it inflicted on commercial farmers such as his own family, inspired a correspondingly ferocious search for security in the colonies as it did for many other Scots. Thus, like many of modest means during the goldrush era, he found himself at the forefront of a movement to establish civil society on the goldfields and subsequently participate in the establishment of many other aspects of colonial commerce, government, and infrastructure for the next thirty years. With many Scots maintaining cultural and family networks in the colonies, it was relatively easy to make a fresh start in Northern New South Wales and Southern

---

[734] Stuart Macintyre, *A colonial liberalism: the lost world of three Victorian visionaries*, Oxford Melbourne, 1991, p12

An Abrupt Conclusion

Queensland among likeminded people. Following a nasty reminder that some old customs remained alive and well, he found a cause that allowed full expression of a lifetime of learning, observation and the bitter experiences with exclusive power arrangements. While he may have easily adopted the latest sugar production technology after a couple of seasons at Benowa, seeing himself as a champion of the yeoman class, he made a deliberate choice to bring as many of the smaller capitalists into the market as possible by fully developing the older open pan sugar production method as far as it could go.

He thus resisted attempts by powerful interests to create monopolies and reproduce the same social and political dynamics that led to him leaving his home in Scotland. Believing in government intervention to ensure a fair go for the little guy as well as all the benefits of a commercial society, he backed his words with actions, never afraid of a public contest. He would have been an asset to the administration of Sir Samuel Griffith, his talent being recognized early by Justice Lutwyche, a fellow supporter of the rights of the small proprietor and adversary of the large capitalist. Thus, his burial on what would be Australia day fourteen years later, is a remarkable coincidence. It could be viewed a marker of the end of the era of massive colonial expansion after the goldrushes as most available land was selected and the limits of capital that supported it was finally reached.[735] Time had thus expired for the liberal, small-capital agriculturalist as a new era approached where the forces of labour, large capital manufacturing, and politically sponsored racism began to mobilize at the end of the nineteenth century.[736] Unfortunately, it would be something that even he would not have been able to prevent, despite his success in silencing early advocates of big capital monopolies like Philip Nind.

His story is a chronicle of failures and successes following a restless trajectory through every colony on the east coast of Australia. It was underpinned by many enablers with a loyalty and

---

[735] Andrew Wells, *Constructing capitalism: an economic history of eastern Australia 1788-1901*, Allen and Unwin North Sydney 1989, p158

[736] R W Connell and T H Irving, *Class structure in Australian history: poverty and progress*, Longman Cheshire, Melbourne, first published 1980, p96-99

an unshakable faith in his abilities and ultimate success. So much so, that like the story of Christ in the bible, his two greatest supporters and younger brothers more than once forsook all and followed him in his (ad) ventures into some of the most inaccessible regions of Australia in search of opportunities. Many Scots like Robert Muir, with a love of civic institutions, free trade, technology, a free and democratic society and an abiding aversion to monopolies of any kind dictating and directing society, made their mark in that highly eventful half century in Australia's history.

Epilogue

Robert Muir's sudden demise presented his family with a dilemma – what was to become of the sugar plantation and the Benowa Estate? At the time of Muir's death, the Benowa plantation remained in operation with an open option to lease the sugar works, the sawmill and a large portion of the estate. According to the will, which was created in April 1887, the plantation remained in operation, but the workers, who included over 60 Polynesians, had ceased working due to the failure of wages to be paid. The will, therefore, was created and administered by John Gebbie, the retired manager of his long-time agent, Parbury Lamb & Company to resolve these issues as well as provide for his family. The assets of the estate were valued at £41,600 with debts of £20,800, a far cry from the situation four years earlier where he claimed to have a debt to asset ratio of 20%.[737] This very likely was due to prevailing weakness in the sugar industry and a relatively unsuccessful foray into land speculation which was apparently conducted with borrowed money. As his will shows, at the time of his death, land in Southport remained unsold and that it had been acquired using credit, leaving a balance of £1419 yet to be repaid. Thus, the reason for his ill-fated trip to Brisbane was the renewal of a promissory note after the recent sale of land for £887 and to finalise arrangements for sale of the balance.[738]

One can only speculate what Robert Muir's business plans were, but it seems that in consideration of his eldest son Matthew's choice of career that it was likely that it would involve a new family project in the sugar industry with his son Matthew as manager and operator. It is possible, that it would be to do with solving the profitability problem plaguing the industry due to the reliance on manual labour. From the 1870s there had been a concerted effort

---

[737] Queensland State Archives, *Item ID ITM2805900, Will: Robert Muir*
[738] Queensland State Archives, *Item ID ITM2805900, Will: Muir, Robert*

to solve this by technological means. With the first cane-cutting machinery proposed in 1873, I am sure that Robert Muir, as one of the foremost advocates of efficiency and productivity, would have been at the forefront of that endeavour as he was with the first affordable commercial mill, the self-acting battery, and the Icery-Muir process.

As many had forecast, the days of the independent estates in Southern Queensland like Benowa were numbered and Matthew, who was competent, would not take over the family business. Having taken a position as an engineer at the newly established Bingera Sugar Mill in Bundaberg just prior to the death of his father, is a strong indication that Robert Muir's plan was to decommission and sell the sugar mill after the 1887 harvest.[739] While the assets were mortgaged to a ratio of 50%, the expected residue after sale was still substantial with a potential realization in today's value somewhere in the vicinity of $10 to $30 million. This would be more than enough for his widow and children to live a comfortable life. It certainly was enough for eldest son Matthew to choose to set himself up in business after a period of employment as an engineer at the Mulgrave Sugar Mill in Gordonvale near Cairns. He became a well-known and respected member of the Gordonvale community serving on various civic bodies such as the progress association and the ambulance service. He is remembered as the proprietor of the cordial and soft drink factory, the Family Hotel and a well-known company that provided engineering services, farm machinery and car sales. Likewise, Muir's second youngest child Robert Jr, joined his stepbrother in Gordonvale in the early 1900s, where he spent the rest of his life as a farmer cultivating sugar cane, dairy and general cropping at Packer's Camp, a small community nearby.[740]

In September 1887, the administrator of Benowa Estate John Gebbie, applied to the courts for leave to sell the property in its

---

[739] Michael Jones, *Country of five rivers: Albert Shire 1788-1988*, p68-70, Bingera Sugar Plantation, *Brisbane Courier*, 16 February 1894, page 5, Clive Morton, *by strong arms, written for the Mulgrave Central Mill Company Limited*, Mulgrave Central Mill Company Limited, Gordonvale Queensland 1995, p41

[740] Queensland Government Family History Research Service, Birth Deaths marriages & Divorces, *Registration 1965/C/1629*

entirety.[741] It was advertised for sale at the offices of Robert Muir's old friend James R Dickson, 17 October 1887, concluding an era of pioneering endeavour that represented so much for the yeoman farmer and the sugar industry.[742] After the sale of the estate, His wife Elizabeth Muir,[743] nee Meston and younger sister of Jane, returned to the Grafton and Clarence River district, with her four young children, Helen, Alice, Robert and Harold, purchasing a house at Maclean.[744]

Robert Muir's brother David had left the district for Townsville before his brother's drowning, where he continued his occupation as a farmer. He died in December 1893 aged 58 with no immediate surviving family. He was born in St Quivox Ayrshire, and as reported, was married to Margaret McNee in Ballarat. By all indications he died penniless and apparently had severed all connections to his brother Robert and his family as suggested by the comments of Elizabeth Muir in her diseased husband's will.[745] Having espoused utopian ideals of co-operative land use and committed himself to the success of his family's interests faithfully for many years, it was a lonely, disappointing, and undignified end.

---

[741] In Chambers, *The Week* (Brisbane), Saturday 10 September 1887, page 26
[742] McLennan, G. G., and James R. Dickson & Co. *Benowa Estate and Plantation Nerang River / James R. Dickson & Co., Auctioneers; G.G. McLennan, Surveyor.* Brisbane: Gordon and Gotch [lithographer], 1880. Print. Accessed 21/5/2022 State Library of Queensland, (see page 297)
[743] Married Elizabeth Meston in Adelaide 15/3/1872, Family Notices *Clarence & Richmond Examiner & New England Advertiser* Tuesday 12 March 1872, p2.
[744] Family Notices, *The Clarence River Advocate*, Tuesday 1 May 1906, page 3
[745] Queensland Government Family History Research Service, *Death Registration David Muir 24/12/1893 Reg 1894/C/4001*, Queensland State Archives, *Item ID ITM2805900, Will: Robert Muir*

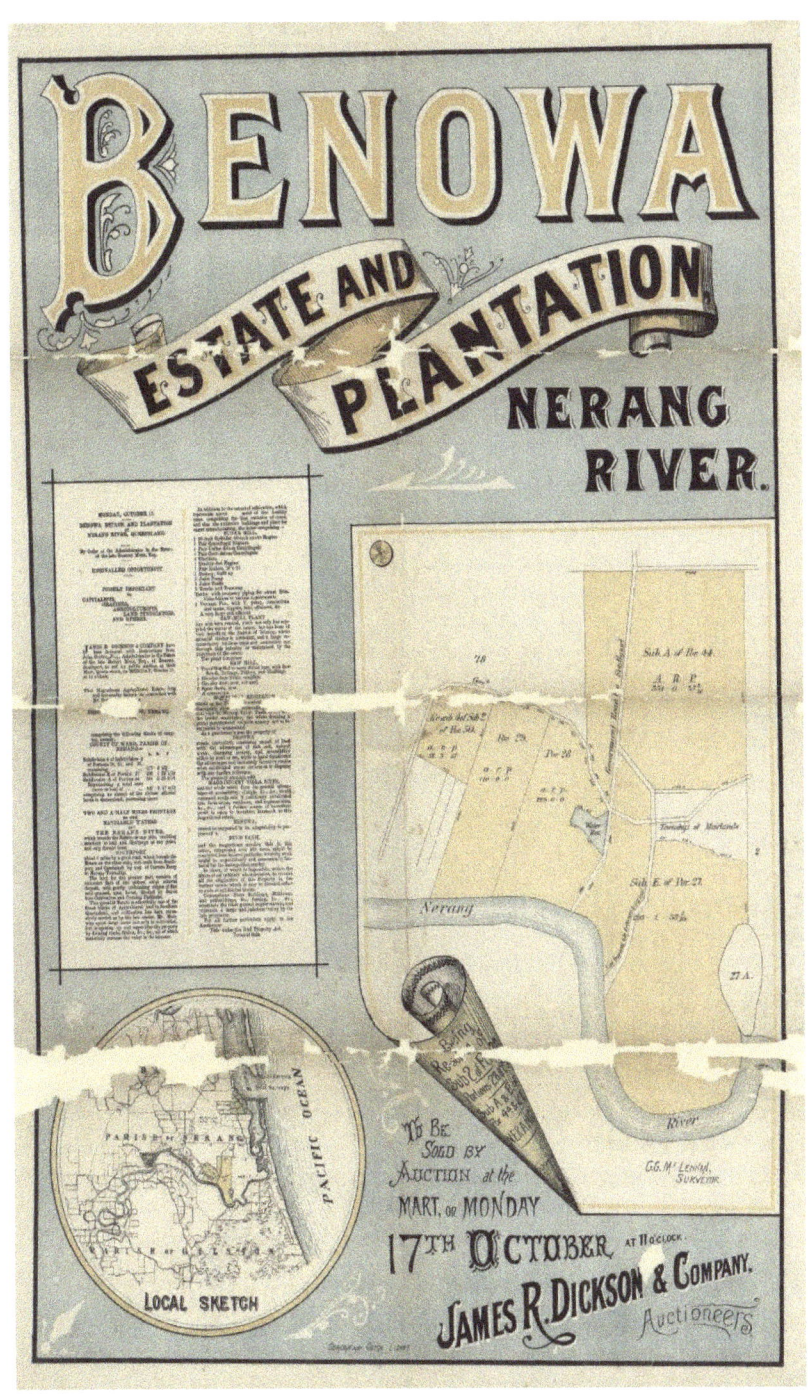

Bibliography

American Chemical Society National Historic Chemical Landmarks. *Norbert Rillieux and a Revolution in Sugar Processing*. http://www.acs.org/content/acs/en/education/whatischemistry/landmarks/norbertrillieux.html

Bernard Barrett, *The civic frontier: the origin of local communities and local government in Victoria*, Melbourne University Press, Melbourne 1979

Geoffrey Bartlett, McCulloch Sir James, *Australian Dictionary of Biography*

Biography of Robert Sellar Merchant, 1828-1900, Angus & Rosemary's miscellany of Malvern, http://www.the-malvern-hills.uk/other_history_robert_sellar.htm

D W A Baker, *Lang, John Dunmore 1799-1878*, Australian Dictionary of Biography, Volume 2, (MUP) First Published, 1967

Christopher J Berry, *the idea of Commercial Society in the Scottish Enlightenment*, Edinburgh University Press, Edinburgh, 2013

Weston Bate, *Lucky city: the first generation of Ballarat 1851-1901*, Melbourne University Press, Melbourne

Boileau, Joanna, *Tweed Shire Council: Community Based Heritage Study - Thematic History*, Report for Tweed Shire Council September 2004, Joanna Boileau Heritage Consultant

Callum Brown, *The social history of religion in Scotland since 1730*, Methuen, London, 1987
- 'Protest in the pews: interpreting Presbyterianism and society in fracture during the Scottish economic revolution', in T M Divine ed., *Conflict and stability in Scottish society 1700-1850*, John Donald Edinburgh, 1990

J H Burton, *The Scot abroad*, Edinburgh, Constable 1881
R A Cage ed., *The Scots abroad: Labour. Capital, Enterprise, 1750-1914*, Croom Helm Ltd, Beckenham Kent UK

R H Campbell, Agricultural labour in the Southwest, in T M Devine ed., *farm servants and labour in lowland Scotland 1770 – 1914*, John Donald Edinburgh *1984*

Linda Colley, Britons: *forging the nation 1707-1837*, Yale University Press, 1992

Lena Cooper's Manuscript, in *Letters to Bundall 1872-1879*, in John Elliott ed., Boolarong Publications Southport Qld, 1993

R W Connell and T H Irving, *Class structure in Australian history: poverty and progress*, Longman Cheshire, Melbourne, first published 1980

C. S. R. Board Minutes, 1867 and 30 June 1868, Extracts from Board Minutes, C. S. R. Archives

Selwyn R Cudjoe, *The slave master of Trinidad: William Hardon Burley and the Nineteenth Century Atlantic World*, University of Massachusetts, Amherst, USA, 2018

Frank Cusack, *Bendigo: a history*, Heineman Melbourne 1973

T M Devine, *Clearance and improvement: land power and people in Scotland 1700-1900*, John Donald Edinburgh 2006

T M Devine, *The Scottish clearances: a history of the dispossessed 1600-1900*, Penguin UK 2018

Tony Dingle, *Aboriginal economy: patterns of experience*, McPhee Gribble Penguin, Fitzroy Vic, 1988

Ian L Donnachie: The making of 'Scots on the make': Scottish settlement and enterprise in Australia, 1830-1900, in T M Devine ed., *Scottish emigration and Scottish society, proceedings of the Scottish historical studies seminar*, University of Strathclyde 1990-1991

Duyker, Edward, Mauritians, *Dictionary of Sydney, 2008*, http://dictionaryofsydney.org/entry/mauritians

John Elliott ed., *Letters to Bundall*, Boolarong Publications, Southport Qld 1993

D. Morier Evans, *The Commercial crisis 1847-1848*, Letts & Son and Steer, London, 1849

Alexander Fenton, 'The housing of agricultural workers in the nineteenth century' in T. M. Devine, *Farm servants and labour in Lowland Scotland 1770 – 1914*, John Donald Publishers, Edinburgh, 1984

Richard Follett, *The sugar masters: planters and slaves in Louisiana's cane world 1820-1860*, Louisiana State University Press, Baton Rouge, 2005

John Foster, *Class Struggle and the Industrial Revolution*, Weidenfeld and Nicolson, London, 1974

Derek Fraser ed., *Municipal reform and the industrial city*, Leicester University Press, New York, 1982

Derek Fraser, *Power and authority in the Victorian city*, Basil Blackwell, Oxford, 1979

John Fraser, *The Aborigines of Australia, Their Ethnic Positions and Relations*, The Victorian Philosophical Institute, Melbourne 1888
-*The Aborigines of New South Wales*, Charles Potter, Sydney, 1892

John Gascoigne (with the assistance of Patricia Curthoys), *The Enlightenment and the origins of European Australia*, Cambridge University Press, Melbourne, 2002

Andrew Dewar Gibb, *Scotland resurgent*, Stirling, E Mackay, 1950

Peter Griggs, *Global industry local innovation: the history of cane sugar production in Australia, 1820-1995*, Peter Lang International Academic Publishers, Bern Switzerland, 2011

M L Hansen, *The Atlantic Migration*, Cambridge, Harvard University Press, 1940

Marjorie Harper, *Adventurers and exiles: the great Scottish exodus*, Profile Books Ltd London, 2003

Heitmann, John Alfred, "*The Modernization of the Louisiana Sugar Industry, 1830-1910*" (1987). History Faculty Publications. Paper 121. http://ecommons.udayton.edu/hst_fac_pub/12

P A Howell, 'Lutwyche, Alfred James (1810-1880)' *Australian Dictionary of Biography*, National Centre of Biography, Australian National University, First published in hardcopy 1974

Onur Ulas Ince, *Colonial capitalism and the dilemmas of liberalism*, Oxford University Press, New York, 2018
-https://www.academia.edu/1067870/ *Capitalism, colonisation and contractual dispossession: Wakefield's letters from Sydney*, 2018

Michael Jones, *Country of five rivers: Albert Shire 1788-1988*, Allen & Unwin Sydney 1988

Roger B Joyce, *Samuel Walker Griffith*, University of Queensland Press, St Lucia Qld 1984

Margaret Kiddle, *Men of yesterday: a social history of the Western District of Victoria 1834 – 1890*, Melbourne University Press, Parkville, Victoria, 1961

Knox, Bruce Ed., *The Queensland years of Robert Herbert, Premier: letters and papers*, Brisbane, University of Qld Press, 1977

Lehmann, William C. *Henry Home, Lord Kames, and the Scottish Enlightenment: A Study in National Character and in the History of Ideas.* Archives Internationales D'histoire des Idées; 41. The Hague: Martinus Nijhoff, 1971

John Dunmore Lang, *The Australian emigrant's manual or, a guide to the gold colonies of New South Wales and Port Phillip*, Partridge and Oakey, London 1852
-*John Dunmore Lang 1799-1878 chiefly autobiographical: cleric writer traveller statesman, pioneer of democracy in Australia*, an assembly of contemporary documents, compiled and edited by Archibald Gilchrist, Volume 1, Jedgarm Publications Melbourne 1951

Lenman, Bruce. *Enlightenment and Change: Scotland 1746-1832*. New History of Scotland Series. Edinburgh: Edinburgh University Press, 2009

Robert Longhurst, *Nerang Shire: a history to 1949*, The Albert Shire Council Nerang Qld, 1994

Stuart Macintyre, *A colonial liberalism: the lost world of three Victorian visionaries*, Oxford Melbourne, 1991

Stuart Macintyre, *A concise history of Australia (fifth edition)*, Cambridge University Press, Cambridge UK, 2020

David MacMillan, *Scotland and Australia 1788-1850: emigration, commerce and investment*, Oxford, Oxford University Press, 1967

David S Macmillan, Scottish enterprise and influence in Canada in: R A Cage ed., *The Scots abroad: Labour. Capital, Enterprise, 1750-1914*, Croom Helm Ltd, Beckenham Kent UK

David McNally, *Political economy and the rise of capitalism: a reinterpretation*, Berkeley: University of California Press, 1988

Alexander McRobbie, *The real Surfer's Paradise: from Seaside village to international resort*, Pan News Pty Ltd, Surfer's paradise, Qld, 1988

Stewart Mechie, *The Church and Scottish social development*, Oxford University Press, London 1960

Melleuish, Gregory. & Centre for Independent Studies (Australia) *A short history of Australian liberalism.* St Leonards, N.S.W: Centre for Independent Studies, 2000

Brian Manning, *The English people and the English revolution*, Penguin Books Harmondsworth UK, 1978

Archibald Meston, *Queensland Aboriginals: a Proposed System for their Improvement and Preservation*, Government Printer, Brisbane 1895

John Molony, *The penguin history of Australia*, Penguin Books, Ringwood Victoria, 1987

Clive Morton, *by strong arms, written for the Mulgrave Central Mill Company Limited*, Mulgrave Central Mill Company Limited, Gordonvale Queensland 1995

Muir, W. P., (1993). *A journal and cash book belonging to William Paterson Muir*, [manuscript], State Library Victoria

Nind, Philip Henry: Former Member Details | Queensland Parliament

Solomon Northup. *Twelve year a slave: narrative of Solomon Northup a citizen of New York, kidnapped in Washington City in 1841 and rescued in 1853 from a cotton plantation near the Red River in Louisiana*, Derby & Miller, Auburn, 1853

Douglas Pike, *Paradise of dissent: South Australia, 1829-1857*, Melbourne University Press 1967, First Published, Longmans, Green & Co London, 1857

Malcolm Prentice, *The Scots in Australia*, University of New South Wales Press, Sydney NSW 2008

R E Prothero, *English farming: past and present*, Longman's Green & Co London, 1917

Carboni Raffaello, *The Eureka Stockade, the consequence of some pirates wanting on the quarter-deck a rebellion*, Carboni Raffaello, Melbourne, 1855

W J Rattray, *The Scot in British North America*, Toronto, Maclear & Co., 1880, Andrew Dewar Gibb

Matthew Rankine 1829-1917, *The diaries of Matthew Rankine 1854-1868*, State Library of South Australia, https://catalog.slsa.sa.gov.au:443/record=b2173363~S1

Reynolds, Henry; *The Other Side of the Frontier*, James Cook University, Townsville 1981

-*Forgotten war*, New South Publishing, Sydney NSW, 2013

Eric Richards, 'Scottish voices and colonial networks in colonial Australia', in Angela McCarthy ed. *A global clan, Scottish migrant networks and identities since the eighteenth century*, I B Taurus & Co, revised edition, 2012, London

- Australia and the Scottish Connection in R A Cage, *The Scots abroad: labour, capital, enterprise 1750-1914*, Groom Helm Beckenham Kent U K 1985

Dawn Hasemann Rix, *Labrador – the early pioneers*, D H R Publishing, Main Beach Queensland, 2002

Margaret J Roberts, *Reach for the far horizon: Sloan and Muir family history*, Margaret J Roberts Bendigo, 2000,

Robertson, George, 1829. *Rural Recollections; Or the Progress of Improvement in Agricultural and Rural Affairs*. Irvine: Cunninghame Press,

Michael Robson, The border farm worker in: T M Devine ed., *Farm servants and labour in lowland Scotland 1770-1914*

Deborah Bird Rose, *Hidden histories: black stories from Victoria River Downs, Humbert River and Wave Hill Stations*, Aboriginal Studies Press Canberra, first Published 1991

Royal Highland Agricultural Society 1840-49, archive.rhass.org.uk

Kay Saunders, *Workers in bondage: the origin and basis of unfree labour in Queensland 1824-1916*, University of Queensland Press, St Lucia 1982

Lawrence James Saunders, *Scottish Democracy 1815-1840: the social and intellectual background*, Oliver & Boyd London, 1950

Gavin Sprott, 'The country tradesman' in T M Devine ed., *farm servants and labour in lowland Scotland 1770 – 1914*, John Donald Publishers, Edinburgh 1984

Shipboard: the Nineteenth century emigrant experience: class distinctions, State Library New South Wales.

Peter Stein, 'The four-stage theory of the development of societies' in P Stein, *The character and influence of the Roman civil law, London*, The Hambledon Press

S.E Stephens, 'Meston Archibald (1851-1924) *Australian Dictionary of Biography*, National Centre of Biography, Australian National University, Published first in Hardcopy 1974

J T Ward and R G Wilson eds., *Land and industry: the landed estate and the industrial revolution: a symposium*, David and Charles, Newton Abbot Devon, 1971

Max Weber, *The Protestant ethic and the spirit of capitalism*, first published 1905, Unwin Hyman, London 1930

Andrew Wells, *Constructing capitalism: an economic history of eastern Australia 1788-1901*, Allen and Unwin North Sydney 1989

Christopher Whatley, 'How tame were the Scottish lowlanders during the eighteenth century'? In: T M Devine ed., *Conflict and stability in Scottish society, 1700-1850*, John Donald, Edinburgh, 1990

- *Scottish society 1707-1830: beyond Jacobitism, towards industrialisation*, Manchester University Press, Manchester UK, 2000

Benjamin Wilkie, *The Scots in Australia 1788-1938*, The Boydell Press, Woodbridge, Suffolk UK

W B Withers, *History of Ballarat and some interesting reminisces*, First Published 1870, Published in Ballarat by Ballarat Heritage Services 1999

Donald Woods, *Trinidad in transition: the years after slavery*, Oxford University Press for the Institute of Race Relations, London, 1968

Periodicals & Pamphlets

Ayrshire Directory 1851-1852, *Ayr Advertiser*, 1852

A landed Proprietor, *The emancipation of the soil and free trade in land*, John Johnstone Edinburgh, 1845

Duncan Bell, John Stuart Mill on colonies, in *Political Theory*, 2010, Vol.38 No34

C B Bow, The 'final causes' of Scottish nationalism: Lord Kames on the political economy of enlightened husbandry 1745-82, *Historical Research* Vol. 91, No 252, (May 2018

Bruce Buchan & Linda Andersson Burnett, Knowing savagery, Australia and the anatomy of race, *History of the human sciences*, 2019, Vol 32 (4)

Linda Andersson Burnett, Collecting humanity in the age of enlightenment: the Hudson Bay Company and Edinburgh natural history museum, *Global Intellectual History*, DOI: 10.1080/23801883.2022.2074502, 2022

Graeme S Cartledge, 'Transition from tyranny: establishing local government on the Ballarat goldfields 1851-1856', *Victorian Historical Journal*, Vol. 92, No.1 June 2021

Neil Davidson, 'The Scottish path to Capitalist Agriculture 2, The Capitalist Offensive (1747-1815), *Journal of Agricultural Change*, Volume 4 No. 4 October 2004
- Scotland: Birthplace of passive revolution? *Capital & Class* 34(3) 2010, 343–359.
- 'the Scottish path to Capitalist Agriculture 1: from the Crisis of Feudalism to the origins of Agrarian Transformation' (1688-1746) *Journal of Agrarian Change*, Vol 4, No 3, July 2004
- The Scottish Path to Capitalist Agriculture 3: The Enlightenment as the Theory and Practice of Improvement, *Journal of Agrarian Change*, Vol.5, No.1, January 2005

Directory for Ayr, Newton, Wallacetown, St. Quivox, Prestwick and Monkton, 1845-1846, compiled by Charles Lockhart, printed at the Ayr Observer Office

J Farnfield, Cotton and the search for an agricultural staple in early Queensland, *Queensland Heritage* Volume 2, Issue 4, May 1971

Richard Follett, Marketing the old South's sugar crop, 1800-1860, *Revista de Indias*, Vol. LXV, No 233

Mark Francis, Social Darwinism and the construction of Institutionalised Racism in Australia, *Journal of Australian Studies*, Volume 20 1996, Issue 50-51

Peter D Griggs, The origins and early development of the small cane farming system in Queensland 1870-1915, *Journal of Historical Geography*, 23, 1 (1997

Gaia Guiliani, Throwaway Labour, Blackbirding and a White Australia, *The Journal of the European Association of Studies on Australia*, Vol.2. No.2, 2011

J. R. R. Hardy, *Squatters and gold diggers, their claims and rights*, Piddington, Sydney, 1855

Jack Harrington, Edward Gibbon Wakefield, the liberal political subject and the settler state, in *Journal of Political Ideologies*, 20 (3)

Report on the present state of agriculture in Scotland arranged under the auspices of the Highland and Agricultural Society, Edinburgh, W blackwood & Sons, 1878

B W Higman, Sugar plantations and yeoman farming in New South Wales, *Annals of the Association of American Geographers*, Dec. 1968, Vol. 58 No. 4

E. Hodder, *George Fife Angas: Father and Founder of South Australia*, London, 1891

James Hogg, On the Capital required in Farming, *The Quarterly Journal of Agriculture Vol 111*, February 1831

-The Ettrick Shepherd (James Hogg) To the editor of the Quarterly Journal of Agriculture, On the habits, amusements and condition of the Scottish peasantry, *The Quarterly Journal of Agriculture Vol 111*, February 1831 – September 1832, William Blackwood Edinburgh, 1932

Ben Huf, The capitalist in colonial history: investment, accumulation and credit money in New South Wales, *Australian Historical Studies*, 50:4 2019

John Dunmore Lang, *Cooksland in North-Eastern Australia; the future cotton field of Great Britain: its characteristics and capabilities for European colonization, with a disquisition on the manners and customs of the aborigines*, Longman Brown Green and Longmans, London, 1847

Rob Lin, Scenes of early South Australia: the letters of Joseph Keynes of Kyneton 1839-1843, *Journal of the Historical Society of South Australia*, vol 10, 1982

MacFarlane's Lantern No. 121 - March 2012, http://clanmacfarlane.org.au

Judith Mackay and Paul Memmott, Staged savagery: Archibald Meston and his indigenous exhibits, *Aboriginal History*, Australian National University Press Canberra, 2016

John Medearis, Labor, democracy, utility and Mill's critique of private property, *American Journal of Political Science, Jan 2005*, Vol 49, No.1

Gregory Melleuish, *A short history of Australian liberalism*, Centre of Independent Studies, St Leonards NSW, 2000

Pat Moloney, Savagery and civilization: early Victorian notions in: *New Zealand Journal of history, 35,2* (2001)

Doug Munroe, The labour trade in Melanesians to Queensland: an historiographic essay, *Journal of Social History*, Spring 1995

Paul Sagar, The real Adam Smith, *Aeon Newsletter*, 16 January 2018, We should look closely at what Adam Smith actually believed | Aeon Essays http://aeon.co/essays/ accessed 3/6/2018

The Scottish Jurist, Vol. V1, Edinburgh, 1834, p232, Centre for the study of the legacies of British slavery, UCL Department of History 2021

Margaret Slocombe, Preserving the contract: the experience of indentured labourers in the Wide Bay Burnett districts in the nineteenth century, *Labour History*, No113 November 2017

Francis Gould Smith, *The Australian Protectionist*, Melbourne 1877

David Spring, English Landowners and Nineteenth Century Industrialism in: *Land and industry: the landed estate and the industrial revolution: a symposium edited by J T Ward and R G Wilson*, David and Charles, Newton Abbot Devon, 1971

John Stephens*: The Land of promise being an authentic and impartial history of the rise and progress of the new British Province of South Australia*; Smith, Elder & Co London, 1839

Evelyn Stokes: The Fiji cotton boom I the eighteen-sixties, *New Zealand Journal of History.ac.nz/docs/1968NZJH_02_2*

William E Van Vugt, 'Running from ruin? the emigration of British farmers to the USA in the wake of the repeal of the Corn Laws', *Economic History Review*, 2nd ser., XLI, 3 1988

Richard Waterhouse, the yeoman ideal and Australian experience 1860-1960, *Exploring the British world: Identity, cultural production, institutions* Melbourne: RMIT Publishing 2004

Christopher Whatley, it is said that Burns was a radical: contest, concession and the political legacy of Robert Burns ca 1796-1859, in: *Journal of British Studies* Vol. 50, No. 3, July 2011,

James P Wilson, The Monk's Road to their lands, *AANHS Collections, 2nd Series, Vol.1, 1950*

Theses

Jean Aitchison, '*A study of the servant class in South Ayrshire 1750-1914*', Ph.D.., thesis, University of Glasgow June 1998

Marilyn Arnold, *Promoting emigration to South Australia from Britain 1829-C1850: the importance of newspapers and other literature to the South Australia colonisation project*, Ph.D. Thesis 2019, Flinders University, Adelaide SA

Valentina Bold, *James Hogg and the Traditional culture of the Scottish borders*, MA Thesis, Memorial University of Newfoundland, 1990

Graeme S Cartledge, *From Goldfield to municipality: the establishment of Ballarat West 1855-1857*, MA Thesis (unpublished) Federation University Ballarat 2018.

Nicola Cousen, *Dr James Stewart: Irish doctor and philanthropist on the Ballarat Goldfields*, Ph.D. Thesis Federation University Ballarat 2017

William Walker Knox, *British Apprenticeship 1800-1914*, Ph.D. Thesis, unpublished, University of Edinburgh 1980.

Rosemary Lawson Ph.D., *Dr John Dunmore Lang and Immigration,*' Thesis Australian National University Canberra, 1966

Alistair Livingston, *The Galloway levellers – a study of the origins, events and consequences of their actions*, M Phil, University of Glasgow, 2009

Graeme Morton, *Unionist Nationalism: the historical construction of Scottish national identity*, Edinburgh, 1830 – 1860, University of Edinburgh, Ph.D. Thesis, 1994

Michael Radzevicius, *Edward Gibbon Wakefield and an Imperial utopian dream*, Ph.D.., University of Adelaide, 2011

Saunders, Kay, *Workers in bondage: the origins and bases of unfree labour in Queensland, 1824-1916*. St. Lucia, 1982 Qld.: University of Queensland Press.

Widney, Amanda M., "*Enlightened Agricultural Improvement in Eighteenth-Century Scotland*" (2019). Central Washington University

Newspapers

The Ayr Advertiser

Daily News (London)

Glasgow Herald

North British Daily Mail

The Age (Melbourne)

The Argus, (Melbourne)

The Armidale Express and New England Advertiser

Australian Town and Country Journal

The Banner (Melbourne)

Bendigo Advertiser

The Brisbane Courier

The Bulletin

The Capricornian, (Rockhampton)

Clarence and Richmond Examiner (Grafton)

The Clarence River Advocate

Clarence and Richmond Examiner and New England Advertiser

Colonial Times (Hobart)

The Courier (Hobart)

The Courier Mail (Brisbane)

The Daily Northern Argus (Rockhampton)

The Darling Downs Gazette and General Advertiser (Toowoomba)

Empire (Sydney)

Daily Examiner (Grafton)

The Geelong Advertiser and Intelligencer

The Herald, (Melbourne)

Illustrated News for Home Readers, (Melbourne)

Leader, (Melbourne)

Logan Witness, (Beenleigh)

Mackay Mercury and South Kennedy Advertiser

Maryborough Chronicle, and Wide Bay Burnett Advertiser

Mount Alexander Mail

Northern Star (Lismore)

Queensland Daily Guardian

The Queenslander, (Brisbane)

Queensland Figaro and Punch, (Brisbane)

The Queensland Times Ipswich Herald and General Advertiser

The Richmond River Herald and Northern Districts Advertiser

Rockhampton Bulletin

South Coast Bulletin (Southport)

The Star (Ballarat)

The Sydney Gazette, and New South Wales Advertiser

Sydney Mail

The Sydney Mail and New South Wales Advertiser

Sydney Morning Herald

The Telegraph (Brisbane)

Toowoomba Chronical and Darling Downs General Advertiser

Warwick Argus and Tenterfield Chronicle

Warwick Examiner and Times

The Week (Brisbane)

Western Argus (Kalgoorlie)

The world's News (Sydney)

Public Records
Public Records Scotland – Births Deaths and Marriages

08/04/1753 MUIR, JOHN (Old Parish Registers Births 614/ 10 18 Stair) National records of Scotland

National Records of Scotland, Scotland's People, 12/03/1775, Muir Robert, Old parish Registers, 614 10/35 Stair, page 35 of 145

08/01/1786 Muir David, *National Records of Scotland*, (Old Parish Registers, 614 10 48 Stair), page 48 of 145

Muir, John (Old Parish Registers Births 604/ 30 82 Mauchline) page 82 of 165, National Records of Scotland

11/04/1821 Muir, James (Old Parish Registers Births 606/ 30 19 Monkton and Prestwick) page 19 of 410, National Records of Scotland

18/09/1825 Muir, David (Old Parish Registers Births 612/1 20 66 St Quivox) page 66 of 387, National Records of Scotland

06/3/1831 Muir, David & Christie, (Old Parish Registers Births 612/1 20 106 St Quivox) page 106 of 387, Scotland's People, National Records of Scotland

National Records of Scotland, Scotland's People, 11/03/1762 Paterson, Matthew, (Old Parish Registers Births 619/ 10 106 Tarbolton) page 106 of 272, Alexander Paterson in Crofthead, his son Matthew was baptised March 11th, 1762.

National Records of Scotland, Scotland's People, 16/07/1793 Paterson, Christian (Old Parish Registers Births 604/ 20 124 Mauchline) Page 124 of 365, National Records of Scotland

Scotland's People, 1874 John Muir (Statutory Registers 500/ 76) Deaths in the Parish of New Kilpatrick in the County of Dumbarton

Muir, David, (Old Parish Registers Marriages 619/30 417 Tarbolton), National Records of Scotland.

John Muir, Muir, Christina, (Old Parish Registers Marriages 644/1 440 272 Glasgow), *National Records of Scotland*

James Muir (unknown-1849) - Find A Grave Memorial Old Wise Cemetery in Woodworth, Louisiana - Find A Grave Cemetery https://findagrave.com/memorial/28493189/james-muir

Public Records Scotland - Wills

Paterson William 1833 (Wills and Testaments reference SC6/44/6, Ayr Sheriff Court) National Records of Scotland

Scotland People, 1874, Muir John, (Wills and Testaments reference SC65/34/19), Dumbarton Sherriff Court

National Records of Scotland, Ordinance Survey Name Books

Scotland's Places, National Records of Scotland, ordinance survey name books, Ayrshire OS name books 1855-1857, Ayrshire Volume 3 OS1/3/3/57,

National Records of Scotland, Scotland's Places, Ordinance Survey Name Books, Ayrshire OS Name books, Ayrshire Volume 03, OS1 3/3/95

Scotland's Places, Ordinance survey name books, 1855-1857, Ayrshire volume 62, OS1/3/62/7

Scotland's Places, National Records of Scotland, ordinance survey name books, Ayrshire OS name books 1855-1857, Ayrshire Volume 17, OS1/3/17/31

Scotland's Places, National Records of Scotland, ordinance survey name books, Ayrshire OS name books 1855-1857, Ayrshire Volume 17, OS1/3/17/31

National records of Scotland, Scotland's places, ordnance survey name books, Ayrshire OS name books 1855-1857/ Ayrshire volume 54, OS1/3/54/9

National Records of Scotland, Historical Tax Rolls

Scotland's Places, National Records of Scotland, Historical Tax Rolls, Farm horse tax rolls, 1797-1798, Volume 1, E326/10/1/229

Scotland's Places, National Records of Scotland, Historical Tax Rolls, cart tax rolls 1785-1798, cat tax volume 1, E326/7/1/18

National Records of Scotland, Historical Tax Rolls/ farm horse tax rolls 1797-1798, Volume 1/ E326/10/1/211

National Records of Scotland, Historical Tax Rolls/ farm horse tax rolls 1797-1798, Volume 1/ E326/10/1/200
19/9/1813

Public Records Census - Scotland

Scotland's People, 1841 Muir David, (Census 619/ 2/ 1) page 1-2 of 17
Scotland's People, 1841 Muir David, (Census 619/ 2/ 1)

National Records of Scotland (Census 644/1 140/ 18) 1851

National records of Scotland, Male heads of families 1834 for Parish of St Quivox, CH2/319/1, accessed oldscottish.com

Scottish Post Office Directories, Glasgow 1851-1852, National Library of Scotland

Public Records South Australia

Dianne Cummings, *Bound for South Australia*, Passengers 1836-1888 (slsa.sa.gov.au)

Public Records New South Wales

An Act for regulating the Alienation of Crown Lands 18th October 1861 claao1861n26270.pdf (austlii.edu.au)

New South Wales Government Gazette Friday 21 August 1863, Issue No 163

Public Records Victoria

Goldfields Commission Reports VPRS 1189/P0000/00084-93

Report of the Select Committee of the Legislative Council on the Goldfields, VPARL1853-54

To His Excellency Charles Joseph La Trobe Esquire Lieut. Governor of the Colony of Victoria, the Humble petition of the Landholders and Inhabitants of the Town of Buninyong, 8 November 1853, Dec 19/53, VPRS 1189/P/0000/000088

Ballarat West Council Minutes, 1856, VPRS 13007 P0001

Public Records Queensland

Coroner's report into death of M P Muir, Queensland State Archives, Item ID ITM2727398

Queensland State Archives, Item ID ITM2804911, *Will Matthew Paterson Muir*

Coroner's Report into the deaths of Robert and Peter Muir 2/2/1887, Queensland State Archives, Item Representation ID DR102604

Queensland State Archives, *Item ID ITM2805900, Will: Robert Muir*

Queensland Government Family History Research Service, Birth Deaths marriages & Divorces, *Registration 1965/C/1629 Robert Muir Jr*

Queensland Government Family History Research Service, *Death Registration David Muir 24/12/1893 Reg 1894/C/4001*

All Photographs including cover courtesy of the John Oxley Library State Library of Queensland

The Author

Graeme Cartledge has an interest in local government and the history of the Victorian Goldfields. He has an MA in History from Federation University Ballarat completing a study on the establishment of the Ballarat West Municipal Council (2018). He is also the author of 'Transition from tyranny: establishing local government on the Ballarat Goldfields 1851-1856' published in Victorian Historical Journal June 2021.

INDEX

Aboriginal population
  & Archibald Meston, 253
  & Robert Muir, 253
  Nerang River activities, 253
  Nerang River existence after European settlement, 252
  Talgiburri, 253
Ageston Estate
  sugar producer (vacuum pan), 258
Agricultural and Pastoral Society of Southern Queensland, 257
Agricultural Societies
  & tenant farmers, 63
Agricultural Society of Southern Queensland
  R Muir presents paper on cane rust, 198
Alcohol abuse, 255
Allan Lillias
  David Muir remarries 1848, 79
American Civil War, 276
  & Australian cotton, 160
American Southern States
  R Muir & James Muir head for the sugar plantations, 76
American Sugar Industry
  steam granulating pan, 78
  Tean Deballiievre 1830s, 79
American Sugar Plantation
  & slavery, 78
Angas George Fife

The South Australia Co & industious/virtuous settlers, 44
Apprentices
  their bad reputation, 71
Auchincruive Estate
  Oswald family owners, 60
  St Quivox Ayrshire, 60
Auchinleck Estate Ayrshire. *See* Muir Peter
  commercialization of from 1760s. *See* Muir Peter
Ayr Prestwick Airport, 61
Ayrshire, 54
  Ayr, 40
  Ayr - epidemics & poor living conditions, 36
  Ayr engineering companies, 72
  covenanters, 54
  Mauchline, 40, 54
  Robert Bruce, 54
  St Quivox, 54
  Tarbolton, 40
  Tarbolton 1845 ploughing contest, 63
  Tarbolton Mill William Muir owner & Robert burns, 40
Ayrshire farms
  bowing - description of, 62
  description of, 62
  women work like slaves, 65
Ayrshire hiring fairs, 57
Ayrshire Ordinance Survey 1855-1857, 34
Ayrshire Southwest
  & Robert Burns, 40

Baker James, 142
Ballarat Goldfields
   1853-4 township expansion, 104
   anger over Hotham failure to deliver, 116
   Bakery Hill - 100m from Exhibition Mart, 111
   diggers' reps operate as police deputies, 106
   English and Irish conflict, 111
   Eureka lead, 105
   failure of Eureka Lead & Irish desperation from Sept 54, 117
   growing outrage over licence checks, 117
   Irish gangs & local crime 1854, 118
   local government mooted 1853, 104
   Lt Governor Charles Hotham visits Aug '54, 114
   more settled & peaceful than Bendigo, 105
   problem of law & order after Eureka, 127
   storekeepers subjected to constant license checks, 116
   Tipperary Mob, 111
   trade war between diggings & Township, 113
   Victorian Reform League investigation into local crime, 129
   water supply, 148
Ballarat Township
   1853-4 Gov't buildings under construction, 106
   boundaries established, 114
   commencement of public utilities/services & regulations 1853, 110
   existence threatened by mining, 132
   hospital campaign July 1854, 110
   replaces Buninyong as district admin centre Nov '53, 108
   roads gazetted & improved July 1854, 110
Ballarat Voluntary Protection Society
   Robert Muir initiates, 130
Ballarat West
   municipality commences with nothing, 135
   municipality declared Dec 24 1855, 133
   Robert Muir & Market Place controversy, 137
   Robert Muir initiates fire brigade, 140
Bate Weston
   Ballarat historian, 8
Bath Thomas, 144
Bawden Thomas, 186, 192, 199
   & Carr's Creek Sugar Company Grafton, 185
   & Grafton co-operatives, 185
   advice to yeomen farmers on sugar industry, 184
   believer in open-pan sugar production, 185
   does deal with R Muir to make Carr's Creek pay, 187
   Grafton Mayor & businessman, 9

Managing Director Carr's Creek, 189
threatens CSR, 189
Beenleigh Sugar Industry Conference, 231
Belmore Sugar Mill Ulmarra, 185
Bendigo Goldfields
  armed criminal gangs, 99
  Captain Harrison's vision for civic society, 98
Benowa, 239, 248, 257
  100 head dairy, 277
  a beginning for many Gold Coast pioneers, 265
  description of, 181
  establishment 1865, 171
  growing reputation as sugar R & D centre, 206
  horse & cattle stud from 1876, 268
  host of local & Colonial dignitaries, 233
  mixed farming & dairy supplying Southport, 277
  modernized with vacuum plant by 1885, 242
  named by Robert Muir, 253
  new home constructed 1872, 268
  plant modernization 1880s, 268
  ploughing contests, 260
  R Muir's new patent - self acting battery demonstrated, 217
  reputation as sugar R & D centre, 217
  sale of estate by executors 17/10/1887, 295
Black Adam, 258

pledges repeal of 1874 Sugar Act, 227
R Muir candidate for Logan, 227
resigns seat of Logan, 230
touted by R Muir as potential House Speaker, 227
wins Logan, 228
Black George, 210, 272
  friend and associate - assisted R Muir in dummying, 210
Black MLA Hume, 248
Boswell Sir James, son of Lord Auchinleck
  modernisation of Auchinleck estate from 1750s, 51
Brisbane Botanical Gardens
  involvement in early sugar industry, 176
Brisbane Exhibition, 213
  1876 Victor Mill exhibit, 196
  accuses R Muir of cheating, 258
  R Muir demonstrates self-acting battery, 216
Brisbane to Tweed Rail, 240
Brushgrove
  commemoration for R Muir's help to local sugar producers, 1
Bundall Estate
  Benowa neighbour, 277
Burleigh Heads
  1st house erected by Robert Muir, 252
Burnett's of Gadgirth (Stair), 63
Burnley William

acquainted with E G
    Wakefield, 85
fails to accept emancipation,
    85
opposed by Creole/Negro
    population, 84
Trinidad sugar mogul, 83
Burns Robert
    & hiring fairs, 57
    connection to Muir family,
        39
    rage of the tenant farmer, 39
Cairns Adam Rev
    father-in-law to William
        (brother), 71
Cameron Duncan
    Argylshire sheep farmer
        father of Flora, 91, *See*
        Malabar
    father of Flora, 147
Cameron Family
    first met on the 'Malabar', 91
Cameron Flora
    a hasty engagement, 146
    legal action for breach of
        promise, 149, *See* Muir
        Robert engagement
    Robert Muir ends
        engagement, 147
    Robert Muir's Malabar
        'romance', 91
Canada
    a popular destination for
        Scots in 1840s, 75
Cane rust, 197
carbonic clarification, 196
Carr's Creek Sugar Company,
    180, 185, 192
    approaches R Muir 1870,
        187, *See* Thomas Bawden
    prize-winning sugar, 190
Carver Councillor, 145

Chartists, 5
Cities
    avoidance of by Scottish
        farmers, 36
Clark Andrew
    Victorian Suveyor General
        1853, 109
Cobb & Co, 237
Cobden Richard
    free trade, 4
Cockburn John of Ormiston
    teacher of commercial
        methods, 53
Collett Joseph
    develops affordable sugar
        mill with R Muir, 180
Colonial Sugar Refinery, 182,
    See CSR
    sugar monopoly, 1
Commercial Society
    as a social revolution
        implemented by the
        nobility, 27
    colonial potential for full
        expression of, 5
    transition to, 4
Commercialization
    & liberal outcomes of, 4
Coomera Christmas Races
    1882, 273
Corn Laws, 3
    repeal, 35
    repeal as major reason for
        1840s emigration, 38
    repeal of & agricultural panic
        of 1840s, 38
Crocker Harry
    Gold Coast pioneer worked
        at Benowa, 265
Crofthead
    Paterson family home, 57,
        See Paterson family

Crow Dining Rooms
  next to Muir's Exhibition Mart Ballarat, 124
CSR, 186, 190, 199, 205, 267
  attempts at home-grown sugar indust in Grafton 1869, 183
  Chatsworth Mill Grafton, 190
  not impressed with Icery process, 205
  opposition in Grafton & Clarence river, 193
  Southgate mill Grafton, 186
  sugar monopoly, 183
  tenant farming plan for Nth & central Qld, 241
De Keating Jerome, 183
De Lissa, 259
  accuses R Muir of undermining, 204
  attacks R Muir's character, 207
  blind to Icery shortcomings, 204
  engaged by CSR (Grafton) for clarification process, 203, *See* CSR
  irate over R Muir's improvements to Icery process, 207
  monosulphite process unsuccessful in Maryborough, 215
  R Muir proposes a public contest, 208
  R Muir threatens legal action over patent, 209
  takes legal action against R Muir, 209
DeBow's review, 200
Deepwater Point, 275

Dennistoun Brothers
  est Melbourne 1853 by Robert Sellar, 90
  financial difficulty and insolvency of Muir Bros, 151
  international import/export house, 90
  James McCulloch Jr Aust founding partner & Victorian Premier, 90
  Muir & Co Glasgow merchant/creditor, 89
Des Sources
  Trinidadian Editor, 87
Dickson Sir James
  public farewell to Robert Muir, 289
Doughboy Creek Qld
  yeoman farmers form sugar co-operative, 178
Douglas Hon. John
  Qld Premier, 233
Drewe J W
  Pimpama Hotel owner, 272
Duke of Portland. *See* Crofthead
Dumbleton Plantation
  R Muir demonstrates Icery-Muir process, 214
Dummying, 227
  R Muir engages in at Beenleigh, 210
Eagle Farm
  Robert Muir patronage, 272
East Moreton Agricultural Association
  R Muir supporters, 259
East Moreton Mutual Farmers Association

Robert Muir support in
dispute with Brisbane City
Council, 285
Economic crash 1846-1848
railway bust & European
recession, 73
Economic development
ideology of after the
goldrushes, 5
Emigration
to preserve social status, 14
Enlightened self-interest, 4
Ettrick Shepherd
laments loss of talent,
experience & culture to
emigration, 36, *See* James
Hogg
Eureka Rebellion
events leading up to from
Sept '54, 117
Muir Bros in the centre of
the action, 118
Feudalism
Scottish extinguishment of
after defeat of Jacobites,
28
Fitzroy
Benowa prizewinning
racehorse, 273
Floods 1887 South East Qld,
286
Fraser John, 254
Free Church of Scotland, 41
Garrick J F
Qld Minister for Lands, 233
German Vote, 227
Logan, 230
Gibson R, 223
letter on 1874 sugar Act, 223
Glasgow
poor living conditions, 36
Gold Coast

R Muir early pioneer, 7
Goldfields
Act 1853 reforms favourable
to Ballarat, 103
freedom from
social/financial
monopolies, 5
Goldfields Commission, 7
1853 agitation against, 101
removal after Eureka, 125
Government
encouragement of large
capital in Qld, 22
encouragement of local
agriculture in Grafton, 1
yeoman sense of betrayal, 1
Government inquiry into
Goldfields 1853
reported Nov 1853, 103
Grafton
farming co-ops & local
companies, 2
maize cultivation, 2
maize in decline 1860, 160
Grand Hotel (Southport), 236
Great Reform Act of 1832, 3
Griffith Sir Samuel
a hair raising ride with
Robert Muir, 240
Griggs Peter
sugar industry historian, 9
Hall Melmoth
attempts to recruit Clarence
River cane growers 1868,
184
Harper Billy
Benowa Aboriginal, 253
dies crossing Nerang bar,
252
Harris Lord
Trinidad Governor 1840s,
83

young Scottish farmers
recruited to improve
Trinidad cultivation skills,
84
Harris Mr R W
appointed Maryborough
agent for Icery-Muir
process, 215
Harwood Island, 164
Herbert Robert
Qld Colonial Secretary &
Manchester Cotton
investor, 168
Hicks Edward
Benowa overseer,
ploughman, Southport
Mayor, 265
Highland society, 63
Highlands and Agricultural
Society
role in farming innovation,
29
Hill Walter, 227
curator Brisbane Botanical
Gardens, 176
Hogg James
financial cost of farm
establishment in 1830s.
See Ettrick Shepherd
Holland Alfred
purchases Bundall from E H
Price, 173
Holland Julius, 210
troubles 1870s with Robert
Muir & brothers, 210
Home Henry
agric improvement as a
patriotic duty, 26
on agricultural improvement
& commercialization, 26,
See Lord Kames

promotion of Gaelic culture,
27, *See* Lord kames
Hope Hon Louis MLC, 175,
176, 183, 223
disappointing 1st crushing at
Ormiston, 177
employs R Muir to refit &
manage Ormiston Mill,
178
recommendation letter to R
Muir, 187
replaces McDonald with R
Muir at Cleveland, 178
Hume
on land ownership, 33
Humffray J B, 130, 133, 139,
143
establishment of goldfields
civil government, 7
Eureka moderate, 125
Eureka moral force faction,
8
launches initiative for
municipal gov't with
Robert Muir, 129
liberal promotor of regional
development, 126
liberalism, a fair go & self
government, 21
restoring law and order after
the Eureka, 7
threatened by Lalor
followers during Eureka
rebellion, 126
Welsh Chartist, 7
Hutton James
19th century Scottish
agricultural trendsetter, 29
Immigrants British middle
class, 7
Imported Sugar Refiners Act
1874. *See* Nind Phillip

against the best interest of
Qld, 223
Indigenous populations
Stadialism & prevailing
attitudes of British
immigrants to, 14
Ipswich (Steamer)
2 steamers created - SS
Benowa & Scottish
Prince, 275
purchased 1878 from ASN
Co, 275
Jacobites
defeat of & origins of
Muir/Paterson dynasties,
51
Kames Lord
& commercial society, 27
advocate/teacher of
commercial methods, 53
on land ownership, 33
on land utilization &
monopolization, 4, *See*
Henry Home
King Billy
Benowa draft stallion, 273
Kirk D & Sons, 192
engages Robert Muir, 191
Kirkcubbin, 215, *See* Mr R W
Harris
Knox Edward William
CSR, 183
La Rosa sugar Estate Mauritius,
183
Labrador
Deepwater Point, 236
Muir Street - named by
Robert Muir, 236
named by Robert Muir, 236
R Muir land purchases 1881,
236

Robert Street - named by
Robert Muir, 236
Labrador Nova Scotia
inspiration for R Muir's
Labrador Qld, 75
Lalor Peter, 8, 143, 148
his political values, 125
leader of Eureka stockaders,
125
Landlordism
colonies publicised as not
subject to, 50
Lang George
son of J D Lang & possible
aquaintance of Robert
Muir, 157
Lang J D, 175, 266, *See* Sugar
Industry Sydney conference
argeted tenant farmers like
the Muirs, 49
Aust sold as free of social &
political monopolies, 50
book 'Cooksland' an
encyclopaedia of the Qld
& Northern Rivers region,
49
campaigned in Ayrshire
1831, 48
independent farmers
solution to slavery, 162
influence on Robert Muir,
49
lobbies Manchester textile
manuf on Aust cotton,
162
plan for yeoman farmers &
skilled mechanics to
replace convicts, 48
religious reformation of
Aust colonies, 48

[326]

vision of hard-working
Christian yeomen as
civilizers, 2
Law of entail and
primogeniture
the major obstacle to a true
commercial society, 33
Laws of entail and
primogeniture, 53
Leeson's Sugar Mill (Grafton),
192
engages Robert Muir, 191
Lenneberg Theodore, 227, 229,
230
Lennon John
Southport land partnership
with R Muir, 235
Liberalism
& colonial capitalism, 20
colonial & miners'
movement, 21
colonial & protectionism, 21
definitions of, 20
old-fogeyism & Toryism, 21
sugar industry protection
and liberal land laws, 21
License fee (mining)
reduction in Nov 1853, 103
Lieutenant Governor La Trobe
attends Aug '53 meeting in
Melb on miners protest,
102
Logan Electorate
skulduggery & chicanery,
228
Lowlands Clearances
commercialization from
early 1700s, 52
Lukin Gresley
exhibition dispute with
Robert Muir, 259

official & Robert Muir
adversary, 258
Lutwyche Chief Justice, 219
poor man's justice, 219
Mackay
viewed as future of sugar
industry, 241
MacKay Angus
Bendigo miners' leader, 110
MacKay Angus Qld MLA, 230,
231, 248
MacPherson
& Ossian epics, 27
MacPherson Maggie
Benowa housemaid & sister
of bushranger Wild
Scotsman, 265
Maize, 190
Malabar
Muir brothers travel first-
class, 91, *See* Muir Robert
travelling conditions, 90
Manchester Cotton Company,
163, 169, 173, 239
1864 failure, 169
Marx
Karl, 4
Mauchline free church
David Muir (father) a
member 1850s, 41
Mayer's Hotel, 229
McDonald D
controversial letter on
Sutton Pan, 202
fails to produce adequate
sugar at Hope's Cleveland
mil, 177
Hope's controversial
Ormiston manager, 177
loses support of local
growers for Hope's
Cleveland Mill, 178

unsanctioned experiments
with centrifugal machine,
178
McGregor
Tweed River pilot, 252
Mclean Peter
member for Logan, 233
McNee James
owner of Crow tea Rooms
& Mgr Mt Blowhard
Hotel, 124
McNee Margaret, 170
wife of James - marries
David Muir after death of
James, 124
McRobbie Alexander
historian of the Gold Coast,
10
Melbourne-Mackay Sugar
Company, 241
Melmoth Hall, 188, 189, *See*
CSR
struggles to convince
Grafton yeomen, 184, *See*
CSR
Meston Alexander, 161, 170,
214, 266
joins R Muir & Co, 193
R Muir father-in-law, 9
successful Grafton cotton
crop 1864, 163
Meston Archibald, 240, 265
& teenage treks with
Benowa Aboriginals, 253
A bush memory, 251
Aboriginal Protection Act
problems with, 254
Aboriginal Protector, 180
architect of 1st Qld
Aboriginal Protection Act,
17
brother-in-law, 180

R Muir brother-in-law &
protege, 17
urges R Muir to investigate
cane rust, 198
Meston Jane
1st wife d May 1870, 251
marries 1863 daughter of
Alexander Meston, 165
Meston Robert
member for New England,
161
Meston William
Jacobite, 161
Meyer's Ferry, 253
Mill J S, 4
Millar John
& commercial society, 27
Miners Protests
arrival of Captain Brown at
Bendigo & increase in
instability, 98
calls for civic integration,
109
Diggers Congress Dec 1853,
109
intimidation of storekeepers,
100
license fee becomes
unaffordable, 98
Melbourne Protestant Hall
meeting, 102
Muir bros in the centre of
activities, 98
riots against police, 99
Monopolies
Aust colonies promoted by J
D Lang as free of, 50
Monopoly
old British conservative
institutions, 3
Tooth & Cran considered to
be, 223

[328]

Monosulphite clarification
   De Lissa Aust agent for Dr Icery process, 203
Montgomerie Estate, 34
Mossblown farm
   on Auchincruve Estate, 60
Mossblown farm St Quivox
   David Muir leaseholder from 1821, 60
Mount Alexander Road 1853
   description of, 96
Mt Blowhard Hotel, 130, 171
   construction commences March 1857, 123
Mt Tambourine, 237
   R Muir sugar cane project, 235
   Robert Muir land purchase 1883, 239
   Robert Muir sawmill, 239
   St Bernard's estate, 240
Muir & Co
   located at 38 Queen St Glasgow, 89
Muir Alexander (uncle)
   early migrant under Wakefield Scheme to SA, 46
Muir Bros
   Ballarat - huge profit in 1st year, 111
   Ballarat agent for Australian Freehold Association, 142
   Carboni Raffaello friend, neighbour & regular customer, 116
   commences at Ballarat end of 1853, 106
   construction of Exhibition Mart, 112
   decision to commence operations in Ballarat, 104
   Exhibition Mart managed by Matthew Paterson Muir, 125
   Exhibition Mart reduced business activity late 1854, 116
   insolvency & sale of Ballarat properties, 152, *See* Dennistoun Brothers
   Northern Assurance Company (fire and life), 142
   Robert appointed manager of Ballarat operation, 104
Muir Brothers
   Ballarat site selected at intersection of the richest discoveries, 105
   Robert Muir leaves company and dissolves partnership, 150
Muir Brothers & Co
   Fiji cotton, 276
   Fiji cotton wins at Brisbane Exhibition 1873, 276
Muir David & Alexander
   gold prospectors at Bendigo 1853, 96
Muir David (brother), 251
   died Dec 1893 Townsville, 296
   dummies for Robert Muir, 210
   insolvency, 171
   joins Matthew & Robert in Qld 1866, 170
   markets Icery-Muir proces in Grafton district, 212
   utopian land scheme, 47
   wins sugar prize at Brisbane Exhibition, 212
Muir David (father), 54

an early dissenter, 41
b 1786 Corsehill 5th son of John, 56
dissenter - free church member, 41
encourages family to emigrate from 1830s, 35
exhibition ploughing judge, 63
girls appear ignored, 65
horse whisperer, 64
occupation as labourer 1813, 59
occupation 'farmer' 1853, 67
ploughman contractor & bower, 62
skills in high demand, 57

Muir Elizabeth
2nd wife Elizabeth Meston returns to Ulmarra-McLean NSW, 296

Muir family
1841 census & occupations, 61
18th century cottars/farm servants, 52
early adopters of commercialization/high farming, 52
importance of the plough, 54
maintenance of social status, 41
moved to St Quivox around 1821, 60
parents married during an agricultural industry boom, 57
tenant farming dynasty, 51
twins David & Christie b St Quivox 1831, 60
victims of 1846-7 commercial crisis, 35
Weber & protestant ethic, 69

Muir James (brother)
d 1849 Ashford Estate Louisiana, 80

Muir Janet (sister)
emigrates to SA to join relatives at Strathalbyn 1851, 89

Muir John (brother)
1838 married Mary Stirling widow of James Stirling (daughter of uncle William), 67
1849 commences Muir & Co Glasgow shirt & slop manufacturer, 67
apprenticed to James Stirling Ironmonger 1830s, 67
b Mauchline Sept 1813, 59
d July 1874, 68
home at 12 Ure Place Glasgow, 89
religious mentor to his brothers, 71
will, 68

Muir John (Grandfather)
a successful tenant farmer, 54
acquisition of financial/administrative skills, 56
description of Corsehill farm, 55
elevation in social status, 55
long-term resident of Corsehill/Crosshill, 54

Muir Marion (sister)
b 1819 Corsehill (mother living with parents-in-law), 59

  emigration 1838 with relatives to South Aust, 46
  skilled immigrant (dairy maid), 46
  William Rankine (uncle) agent/sponsor, 46
Muir Matthew Paterson (brother)
  1852 travels to Bendigo goldfields with party of relatives & friends, 89
  Benowa mgr while R Muir in Grafton 1870-72, 187
  death at Goodna Assylum 1885, 211
  dispute with brothers over dummying, 210
  dummy 320 ac selection 1865 for brother Robert, 170
  emigrates to SA with sister Janet, 89, *See* Muir Janet
  founding board member Gramzow state School, 211
  helped establish Strathalbyn SA, 96
  joins brothers on Bendigo goldfields, 96
  moves to Grafton 1872, 193
  Patron South East Queensland Agricultural Society, 211
  ploughing contest judge, 262
  takes position as mgr of Logan Sugar Factory, 210
Muir Matthew Paterson (son)
  b Ulmarra Dec 1863, 166
  engineer Bingera Sugar Mill Bundaberg, 295
  engineer Mulgrave Sugar Mill Gordonvale, 295
  trained in sugar production, farming & engineering, 269
  wins Brisbane Exhibtion prize for sugar cane, 269
  wins sugar prize at Brisbane Exhibition, 269
Muir Peter
  ancestor b1753 Stair, 51
  b at Stepends Auchinleck Estate S/W Ayrshire (Boswell Family), 51
Muir Robert. *See* Brisbane Exhibition
  & American sugar innovation/experimentation, 77
  & Ballarat Chamber of Commerce, 142
  & Ballarat Commercial and Agricultural Bank, 142
  & Ballarat Water Supply, 148
  & Sutton Pan, 201
  1846/7 leaves with brother James for America/Canada, 75
  1849 takes position Trinidad and the Orange Grove, 81
  1860s Grafton cotton grower, 157
  1863 exploring new Grafton enterprise, 166
  1869 reputation as a successful independent sugar producer, 184
  1875 controversial Benowa ploughing competition, 260
  1880-4 Brisbane Exhibition working models of sugar production, 268
  1881 hospitalization, 268

1881 invests heavily in horses - draft racing & show, 271
1885 land & estate sale advertising campaign, 278
1st homemade sugar mill, 172
1st sugar samples 1866, 172
a colonial liberal, 291
a hard working teenager, 70
a notorious court case, 149
accused of Exhibition cheating, 258
achieves success for Hope at Cleveland mill, 178
activist for township landowners, 132
Adelaide Street Brisbane timber yard, 276
advocate for storekeepers on diggings, 113
an interest in both camps in Ballarat dispute, 132
an open-ended engagement to Flora Cameron, 93
another controversial ploughing match, 262
anti-CSR monopoly project, 193
antipathy to monopolies, 1
appointed Magistrate for Nerang Creek District, 219
appointed to board on Pests & Diseases, 227
apprentice engineer (fitter), 72
arrives Melbourne March 1853, 95
attempts to bar him from exhibitions, 258
back in black by 1866, 172

Ballarat Agricultural Society foundation, 138
Ballarat Industrial Institute, 143
Beenleigh cattle sale 1878, 275
Benowa estate credited with giving life to the sugar industry, 10
big loser on Clarence Rivermouth project, 167
Brisbane to tweed rail, 234
Brisbane to Tweed rail, 233
burial Beenleigh Cemetery, 288
cane rust inquiry - tours Qld properties, 199
cane variety innovator, 188
challenge for a hat, 224
completes apprenticeship on eve of the railway bust 1846, 75
constructs cottage in Grafton, 159
constructs private road to foot of Mt tambourine, 240
conveyed family in style, 251
dashed hopes of a railway career, 72
death of his mother 1847 & return to Ayr, 79
debunks Thomas Scott sugar theories, 188
declines nomination for Logan, 226
deputised by Govt to investigate cane rust, 198
determination to make yeoman class competitive, 200

District Roads Board founding president, 139
drowns in 1887 floods with son Peter, 288
dummying, 157
duplicitous actions & ultimatums, 136
elected to Ballarat West Municipal Council, 133
emigration to Australia, 6
endorsement & uptake of Icery-Muir process in Grafton district, 213
ends engagement with Flora Cameron, 147
engineering apprenticeship, 68
est piggery and farm at Harwood Island, 160
finalization of Labrador land sales Jan 1887, 286
fond memories of Springbank farm Ayrshire, 66
founding committee member SE Qld Ag Society, 220
from a dynasty of commercial tenant farmers, 6
Grafton Brewery & Hotel, 158
Grafton cotton grower, 161
Grafton local merchant and carrier, 168
Grafton properties leased, 166
Grafton sugar monopoly 1871-2, 189
Harwood Island NSW selector 1860, 156
hay cutting at Stoneyfield near Springbank Ayrshire, 66
his open-pan sugar deemed equal of vacuum pan, 215
horseback trek from Benowa to Grafton, 180
Icery-Muir process endorsed in Sydney, 216
improves monosulphite process, 205
joins brothers John & William in Glasgow 1851, 89
joins Muir & Co & plan for expansion to Victorian Goldfields, 89
judge at 1st Ballarat Ploughing contest, 139
leader of opposition against Phillip Nind, 223
leads crime investigation after Eureka, 129
leads local Ballarat movement to make Gov't accountable after Eureka, 131
leaves for Bendigo with David & Alexander & a large consignment of goods for sale, 95
left Greenock on 'Malabar' Oct 1852, 90
Letter on Sutton Pan, 203
liberal outlook & experience on slave-owning properties, 19
lobbies for roads & bridges in Logan & Albert, 226
makes a big impression on Grafton yeoman farmers, 188

makes strategic land purchases during Eureka unrest, 119
manager appointed to Grafton brewery & hotel, 165
manager Bundall 1864, 169
markets Icery-Muir process in Mackay Maryborough district, 211
marries Elizabeth daughter of Alexander Meston, sister of Jane 12 March 1872 (Adelaide), 296
mentor for younger brothers David & Alexander, 80
mixed feelings about Flora Cameron, 93
more 1876 ploughing contest controversy, 262
Mt Tambourine legal dispute, 279
multiple prize-winner for sugar, 258
nominated for seat of Logan, 225
obituary, 289
of typical yeoman stock, 6
official party for Nerang Bridge opening, 233
open-pan innovator, 200
Oxley ploughing challenge, 260
personality, 197
persuaded by Brother William to stand for Ballarat local gov't, 133
pioneering journey Logan to Casino, 173
potential cost of farm lease in Ayrshire, 33
proud of upbringing by a tenant farmer/ploughman, 24
proud to be a ploughman, 261
proud to be an agriculturalist, 264
publishes sugar A/C sales for 07-08 1879, 215
purchases Icery Monosulphite patent from De Lissa, 209
purchases three cane properties Tweed River, 195
quest for land ownership, 7
religious platitudes & Flora Cameron, 70, *See* Flora Cameron
relocates to Carr's Creek Mill Grafton, 187
relocation to Mt McIvor 1853, 100
removes CSR yolk from yeomen necks, 192
resigns all Ballarat positions, 151
restoration of goldfields law & order & civil government, 7
return to Melbourne Sept 1853, 101
returns to Brisbane Exhibition with multiple wins, 259
returns to Ulmarra 1866, 173
sale of Manchester Cotton farms 1883, 277
seeks opportunities in Canada/America, 75
selects 640 ac on Nerang River April 1865, 170

self-acting battery, 222
slavery and the yeoman
    farmer, 77
succeeds at Carr's Creek
    Sugar Mill, 187
successful 1st cane crushing
    with Collett Mill, 181
successful Bendigo venture
    1853, 97
supporter & associate of
    moral force leader J B
    Humffray, 125
sympathizer with Eureka
    diggers, 125
tales of legendary hospitality,
    264
the poor man's friend, 192
the shooting of Billy Tully,
    256
threatens to leave Qld over
    Polynesian Bill, 248, *See*
    Polynesian Workers
Trinidad experience in fields
    & boiling house, 84
unfounded accusations of
    financial distress, 270
unrecorded birth 1827, 60
voyage to England 1859, 153
will, 294
wins 3rd prize for trotter
    Botheration at National
    exhibition, 270
wins exhibition prize for
    hereford bull, 269
wins sugar prizes in all
    categories at National
    Exhibition, 269
withdraws patronage from
    Brisbane Exhibition, 258
Muir Robert Jr (son)
    farmer at Packer's Camp
        Gordonvale Qld, 295

Muir William (uncle)
    farmer at Campsie
        (Stirlingshire), 67
Muir William Paterson
    (brother)
    a political interest in Ballarat,
        132
    assn with Chalmers
        Presbyterian Church, 141
    Australian Freehold
        Association, 95
    member of Melbourne's
        political & commercial
        elite, 133
    returned from St Kitts to
        join Muir & Co, 89
    son-in-law to Rev. Adam
        Cairns, 71
Muirlands, 239, 278
Municipal Reform Act 1835, 3
Napoleonic Wars
    effects of recession after, 30
Nerang Bridge Opening, 233
Nerang Divisional Roads
    Board
    political interference of by
        land developers, 237
Nerang races 1883, 273
Nerang River, 253
Nicholls C F, 127, 131
Nicholls H R, 127, 131, 132
Nind Phillip, 199, 220, 224,
    226, 257
    introduces controversial
        1874 sugar bill, 221
    owner Yahwulpah plantation
        Beenleigh, 220
    resigns seat and leaves for
        England, 225
    viewed as traitor to
        independent sugar
        producers, 222

Northern Rivers
  R Muir early pioneer, 7
Oddie James, 131, 133, 148
  !st Chaiman of Ballarat West municipality, 125
  supporter of Eureka leader Peter Lalor, 125
Open Pan Sugar, 185
  Delissa claims equality with vacuum pan, 204
  developed to its utmost potential by Robert Muir, 270
  end of an era, 242
  R Muir innovator for yeomen/small capitalist, 200
Ormiston Plantation. *See* Hon Louis Hope MLC
Ormiston Plantation new sugar plant, 176
Owens Dr Bendigo
  leader of miners protests 1853, 102
Owens R
  utopian, 4
Parbury, Lamb and Raff
  Brisbane agent/accountant for R Muir, 270
Parkes Henry MLA, 175, *See* Sugar Industry Sydney conference
Pastoral regime
  eclipse of with the goldrushes, 5
Paterson Alexander (Grandfather)
  Crofthead leaseholder, 58
Paterson Christian (Mother)
  b1793 - at age 19 married to David Muir 1812, 57
Paterson Estate, 34

Paterson family
  bonnet lairds associated with Skeoch, 59
  tenant farmers at Crofthead, 57
  tenant farming dynasty, 51
Paterson Matthew (Father)
  Barskimming Mains leaseholder, 58
Paterson William
  of Ayr, 34
Peterloo massacre 1819, 3
Pimpama Christmas races
  Robert Muir steward, 272
Pinwell's Koorooroo Estate Beenleigh, 196
Plough
  technical innovations, 54
Politicians
  predominance of small capitalists in Govt after the goldrushes, 5
  radicals as anti-monopoly/pastoralist/British capitalist, 3
Polynesian Workers, 243, 257
  & PM Andrew Fisher, 243
  & white labour shortage, 249
  1884 Qld regulations Bill, 245
  conditions at Benowa & Riverside under management of Muirs, 249
  dependence of sugar industry on in 1870-80, 10
  Europeans difficult to recruit, 248
  J. E. Matthew Vincent on denial of legal equality of, 245

Premier Samuel Griffith
  replies to Vincent, 246
Robert Muir & Benowa
  Estate, 244
Robert Muir charged, 244
Robert Muir disproves
  climate argument, 248
Robert Muir leads campaign
  against legislative changes,
  245
Robert Muir negotiates a
  compromise, 249
Presbyterian Church
  & Great Disruption 1843, 40
  free church dissenters, 41
  the problems of population
    growth & urbanisation, 40
Price Edmund Henry, 173, *See*
  Manchester Cotton
  Company
    established Manchester
    Cotton Co in Qld 1863,
    165
Protesant ethic
  Calvinist commercial
    adaptations, 14
Queensland
  1860s cotton industry, 162
Queensland Exhibition, 258
  R Muir accusation of bias,
    258
Queensland Government
  investment in Mackay sugar
    central mills 1885, 277
Queensland National Bank,
  211
Queensland Sugar and Coffee
  Regulations of 1864, 170
R Muir & Co
  establishes mill for Pringle,
    Shankie & Byrne at
    Tweed Heads, 194

Rabbit Island
  1860 camp on Clarence
    River, 156
Raffaello Carboni, 8
  appoints Muir Bros
    distributor of his book on
    Eureka, 116
Railway Brisbane to Southport,
  275
Railways (British)
  a booming industry in early
    1840s, 72
Rankine brothers John and
  William
  co-founders of Strathalbyn
    with other Fairfield
    passengers, 46
Rankine John
  Glasgow Dr & owner of
    Albion Steel works, 46
Rankine Matthew
  cousin, 96
Rankine William
  Barr (Ayrshire) sheep
    farmer, 46
  pioneer & co-founder of
    Strathalbyn SA (uncle), 46
Rede Robert
  Resident Commissioner
    initiates Hospital, 110
Rillieux Norbet
  vacuum-pan sugar
    production, 200
Rix Dawn Hasemann
  Labrador Qld history, 7
Robertson George
  19th century Scottish
    trendsetter/author on
    commercial faming, 29
Robertson Land Acts of 1861,
  1, 156

Robert Muir a Grafton
    selector, 160
Rodier Charles, 142
Royal Highland Agricultural
    Society of Scotland, 64
Sandhurst
    1853/4 beginnings of
        renewed miners activism,
        109
Scotland
    historians of, 26
Scots
    19th century notoriety for
        making money, 16
    1st to coherently articulate
        nature of commercial
        society, 26
    Australian settlement, 266
    significance of union with
        England in 1707, 26
Scott Sir Walter
    influence of Ossian epics of
        McPherson, 27
Scott Thomas, 176
    early sugar industry pioneer,
        175
Scottish Enlightenment, 26
Shaw & Co, 196
Shaw Frederick
    Agent for Cobb & Co, 230
    wins & resigns in Logan, 231
Sloan Family
    Strathalbyn SA & Inglewood
        Vic (in-laws), 96
Small capitalist
    Australian dominance of in
        2nd half of 19th century,
        9
Small John Jr, 213
    1st in Grafton to employ R
        Muir's Sutton Pan/Icery-
        Muir process, 206
    De Lissa makes legal threats,
        209
    ignores De Lissa legal
        threats, 209
    publicizes Sutton Pan/Icery-
        Muir in Grafton, 207
    sugar deemed as good as
        CSR No1 grade, 213
Smith Adam
    & commercial society, 27
    & contradiction of slavery,
        79
    influence of Gaelic culture
        on, 27
    on Gov't regulation, land
        monopolization, 4
Smith Francis Gould
    the Australian Protectionist, 22
Smith J T Mayor of Melb
    & miners protests 1853, 102
Smith W C, 144
Southern Queensland
    Agricultural Society, 230
Southgate mill, 186, *See* CSR
Southport
    a summer resort in 1880,
        235
    Muir Robert land purchase
        1878, 235
    railway station, 236
Southport Races, 274
Springbank Farm (Ayrshire)
    Muir family moves to early
        1830s. *See* Muir family
    Muir home 1830s-1840s on
        Paterson Estate, 34
Springbank Farm (Ballarat)
    managed by David &
        Alexander Muir, 119
    named after Ayrshire home,
        66

new modern house & farm
   buildings constructed, 123
praised as a model for
   successful commercial
   farming, 120
SS Benowa, 279
   created from the Ipswich
      1884, 275
   twice weekly service April
      1885, 276
St Helena penal colony
   affordable sugar mill
      innovation, 179
St Quivox free church
   David Muir (father) member
      1830s, 41
St. Quivox club
   & David Muir (father), 64
Stadialism
   & Aboriginals, 14
   & land use, 255
   commerce & new legal &
      contractual arrangements
      underpinning society, 27
   Gaelic epics & progress, 27
   land use & private property,
      17
   philosphical assumptions, 13
Staiger Karl, 214, 227
   Government chemist, 208
Stair
   parish church parents
      marriage 1812, 57
Stair Parish of
   long association with Muir
      family. *See* Muir &
      Paterson families
Stair village of, 54
Stephens M MLA, Logan, 248
Stephens T B, 230
   R Muir friend & associate,
      231

Stewart James Councillor, 148
Stirling Alexander Muirhead
   son of James Stirling
      (employer) & husband of
      Mary, 67
Stirling James
   Glasgow Ironmonger friend
      of William Muir (uncle),
      67
Stirling James (Alexander's
   son)
   assisting William at Muir
      Bros Melbourne, 102
Sugar Industry
   decline of in Southern Qld,
      242
   early experiments, 176
   Robert Muir convinced of
      Grafton's potential, 158
   Southern Qld decline of, 235
   Sydney conference 1865, 175
Sugar Plantation 1840s
   America
   operation of, 78
Sutton J W, 201
Sutton Pan, 196, 199, 201, 222,
   See J W Sutton
   & sugar refiners, 203
   1879 improvements, 202
   1st demonstrated by R Muir
      at Benowa, 202
   essential for profitable sugar,
      203
Technical innovation
   competitiveness of small
      sugar industry capitalist,
      10
Tenant Farmers
   & effects of farm
      consolidation, 35
   & Scottish literacy, 29

1820s hard times & emigration, 32
a career - no longer a way of life, 53
entrenched culture of improvement, 30
fear of corn law repeal from 1830s, 35
hopes of land ownership in 19th century Scotland, 33
increasing financial pressures in 1840s, 38
innovation essential to survival, 30
lack of investment opportunity & generational legacy, 37
Scottish capitalizers of commercialization, 29
Scottish credited with driving 18 & 19th century agricultural improvement, 29
Scottish existential crisis, 30
security dependant on profit, 53
social consequences of new status, 31
The large capitalist opposition against at Grafton, 1
Tooth & Cran, 199, 222, 223
Trade Unions
& Polynesian workers, 243
Trinidad
a destination for the desperate in 1840s, 83
attempts to entice British workers under Wakefield Scheme, 85
British racial superiority challenged 1840s, 83
Burnley & failed immigration schemes, 85
Burnley & Orange Grove Est under attack, 86
collapse of Eccles Burnley and Company, 83
effects of 1846 Sugar Act, 83
emancipation and Trinidad property price collapse, 83
Lord Harris land reform, 87
only the tough & resilient stay 1840s, 83
past its prime by 1840s, 82
resistance to oppressive labour laws, 86
resistance to taxes imposed by unrepresented Legislative Assembly, 86
Robert Muir finds land ownership unattainable, 88
Scottish emigration to 1840s, 81
social unrest in 1840s & 1850s, 86
William Burnley opposed to progress, 84
Tullaman – Nerang River Talgiburri man, 253
Tully Billy
case of, 256, *See* Muir Robert
Utopian immigration schemes 1840s, 82
Vacuum pan
affordable by mid-1880s, 242
most advanced & expensive technology, 200
near universal with independent producers in 1880s, 267

[340]

out of reach of small 1870s producers, 200
Victor Mill, 196
Victorian Reform League
 formed after Eureka, 126
 Robert Muir a close associate, 127
Vincent J E Matthew
 campaigner for Polynesian legal equality, 245
 free & fair trade & the Victor Mill, 245
 Victor Mill promoter, 197
Wakefield E G, 266
 his Australia Felix utopia in SA, 44
 plan for transplantation of civilization, 2
 social engineering & exportation of capitalist dynamics, 44
 systematic immigration, 43
 systematic migration scheme attractive to the better class of farmers, 46
Watt Alexander
 friend, neighbour, rival and sugar producer, 269
White & Robinson, 202
 winner (open-pan) at Brisbane Exhibition 1877-78 in Muir's absence, 259
White John
 Clarence Rivermouth project contractor, 166
White Labour, 241
White shoe brigade, 237
William Wallace, 54
Wise family
 owners of Ashford Estate Louisiana, 78
Withers W B
 1st Ballarat historian, 8
Yengarie, 221, *See* Tooth & Cran
Yeomen
 & campaign for 'unlocking the lands', 3
 1867 association of independent farmers/sugar growers, 185
 a focus of J D Lang migration schemes 1830s & 40s, 48
 as civilizers, 2
 Brushgrove (Grafton) commemorative dinner for Robert Muir 1872, 192
 expectations of emigration, 2
 Grafton farmers explore sugar industry options, 184
 Grafton growers convinced by Robert Muir's success, 190
 Grafton investment, 1
 Grafton/Clarence farmers seek advice from Robert Muir, 185
 Lang J D & Grafton district, 162
 Lang's ideal immigrant, 267
 Mackay plan for, 241
 private sugar mills praised by media, 191
 Qld opposition to 1874 sugar bill, 221
 R Muir determination to keep them competitive in sugar, 200
 sugar production innovation/experimentation, 196

Young Davie
    Benowa draft stallion, 274
Young Honest Tom
    Benowa prize draft horse, 271

Young Muir Lad
    Benowa draft stallion, 274
Zanelli Angelo
    1st successful Grafton cotton crop, 163

www.ingramcontent.com/pod-product-compliance
Lightning Source LLC
Chambersburg PA
CBHW051534010526
44107CB00064B/2721